INSIGHT GUIDES
Indian WILDLIFE

APA PUBLICATIONS
Part of the Langenscheidt Publishing Group

INSIGHT GUIDE
Indian WILDLIFE

Editorial
Managing Editors
**Richard Carmichael
and Maria Lord**
Editorial Director
Brian Bell

Distribution

UK & Ireland
GeoCenter International Ltd
Meridian House, Churchill Way West,
Basingstoke, Hampshire RG21 6YR
Fax: (44) 1256 817988

United States
Langenscheidt Publishers, Inc.
36–36 33rd Street 4th Floor
Long Island City, NY 11106
Fax: 1 (718) 784 0640

Australia
Universal Publishers
1 Waterloo Road
Macquarie Park, NSW 2113
Fax: (61) 2 9888 9074

New Zealand
Hema Maps New Zealand Ltd (HNZ)
Unit D, 24 Ra ORA Drive
East Tamaki, Auckland
Fax: (64) 9 273 6479

Worldwide
**Apa Publications GmbH & Co.
Verlag KG (Singapore branch)**
38 Joo Koon Road, Singapore 628990
Tel: (65) 6865 1600. Fax: (65) 6861 6438

Printing

Insight Print Services (Pte) Ltd
38 Joo Koon Road, Singapore 628990
Tel: (65) 6865 1600. Fax: (65) 6861 6438

**©2007 Apa Publications GmbH & Co.
Verlag KG (Singapore branch)**
All Rights Reserved
First Edition 1986
Third Edition 2007

CONTACTING THE EDITORS
We would appreciate it if readers
would alert us to errors or out-
dated information by writing to:
**Insight Guides, P.O. Box 7910,
London SE1 1WE, England.
Fax: (44) 20 7403 0290.
insight@apaguide.co.uk**

www.insightguides.com
In North America:
www.insighttravelguides.com

ABOUT THIS BOOK

The first Insight Guide pioneered the use of creative full-colour photography in travel guides in 1970. Since then, we have expanded our range to cater for our readers' need not only for reliable information about their chosen destination but also for a real understanding of the culture and workings of that destination. Now, when the internet can supply inexhaustible (but not always reliable) facts, our books marry text and pictures to provide those much more elusive qualities: knowledge and discernment. To achieve this, they rely heavily on the authority of locally based writers and photographers.

How to use this book

Insight Guide: Indian Wildlife is structured to convey an understanding of the wildlife and ecology of the region as well as to guide readers through its sights and activities.

◆ The **Features** section, indicated by a yellow bar at the top of each page, profiles the region's environment and wildlife in a series of informative essays. It also provides a broad background, the current wildlife situation and prospects for conservation.

◆ The main **Places** section, indicated by a blue bar, is a complete guide to selected Wildlife Reserves and National Parks. Places of special interest are coordinated by number with the maps.

◆ The **Travel Tips** listings section, with an orange bar, provides a handy point of reference for information on travel, accommodation and an eminently practical article on the art and practice of observing wildlife.

Map Legend

▬▬ ▬▬	Regional Boundary
— — —	Province Boundary
—•—	National Park/Reserve
✈ ✈	Airport: International/Regional
🚌	Bus Station
❶	Tourist Information
✉	Post Office
✝ ✝ ✝	Church/Ruins
✝	Monastery
☪	Mosque
✡	Synagogue
🏰 🏰	Castle/Ruins
🏠	Mansion/Stately home
∴	Archaeological Site
∩	Cave
⌶	Statue/Monument
★	Place of Interest

The contributors

This revised edition of *Indian Wildlife* has been completely updated by **Richard Carmichael** and **Maria Lord**, at Insight Guides' London offices and by **Dr Asad Rahamni**, Director of the Bombay Natural History Society.

The book builds on the foundations of previous editors, **Samuel Israel**, **Toby Sinclair**, and **Bikram Grewal**. A range of experts contributed chapters to the original book. The two major parks in Nepal, Chitwan and Bardia, are covered by **K. K. Gurung**, who also wrote the Observing Wildlife article. **Kaushalya Ramdas** provided the chapter on forests and some of the mammal species. **H. S. Panwar**, former Director of the India Wildlife Institute, wrote the chapters on tigers and Kanha National Park. Veteran Indian naturalist and Honorary Secretary of BNHS, **Dr J. C. Daniel**, wrote the chapter on lions, leopards and lesser cats. **Dr D. K. Lahiri Choudhury** wrote the Asian Elephant chapter. **Dr M. K. Ranjitsingh**, wildlife expert and Chairman of the Wildlife Trust of India, contributed the section on deer, antelopes and bovines. **Kunal Verma** covered primates, dogs, hyenas and bears, as well as Kaziranga and Manas national parks. **Rom** and **Zai Whitaker** co-authored the section on reptiles. **Zafar Futehally** one of India's leading ornithologists, provided the Birds chapter.

Other contributors whose work has been retained from earlier editions include: **Arjan Singh** (Dudhwa National Park), **Brijendra Singh** (Corbett National Park), **Gillian Wright** (Keoladeo and Bandhavgarh), **Divyabhanusinh** (Ranthambhore, Sariska and Gir), **Ullas Karanth** (Nagarahole and Bandipur) **Kailash Sankhala**, **Dr E. G. Silas**, **Joanna Van Gruisen**, and **Dr Kamala Seshan**. Thanks also to **Bittu Sahgal**, editor of Sanctuary, producer of wildlife films, wildlife photographer and treasurer of the Bombay Natural History Society.

Ashish Kothari and **Neema Pathak**, members of Kalpavriksh Environmental Action Group, wrote the new chapter on Community Conservation Areas based on the authors' field visits. **Richard Carmichael** revised and rewrote the introductory chapter, "India's Environment". The editors have also compiled a new Travel Tips with a completely updated accommodation listings. A number of the pictures used are by **D.K. Baskar**. This edition was proofread and indexed by **Penny Phenix**.

INSIGHT GUIDE
Indian WILDLIFE

CONTENTS

Maps

Indian Giant Squirrel, Mudumalai

THE ORIGINAL JUNGLE

India, the original "jungle", matches Africa in wilderness and wildlife but is also home to one sixth of humanity

Deep in the jungle gloom a striped predator lurks. Programmed by instincts genetically implanted millions of years ago, the cat waits patiently for a herd of spotted deer to make their way through tall grass towards a nearby water hole. Barely one in 10 attempts to kill will be successful but, with sheer persistence, such odds work in favor of the hunter. Contrary to popular belief, success depends less on speed and power, more on stealth and ambush. In all probability a young, weak or careless deer will fall prey to the tiger. The fascinating drama between predator and prey has gone on uninterrupted for countless years and its savageness is responsible for the beauty in nature that so moves and inspires us.

Africa is universally accepted as the world's greatest haven for wildlife. Few are aware that, of the four greatest cats in the world belonging to the genus *Panthera*, India has three species to the African continent's two, and has three species of wild ox and eight species of deer to Africa's one each. In fact no country in the world, not even Russia, possesses the number of distinct species of cervids that India has. India was also the likely evolutionary cradle of the wolf – and the only place where three distinct lineages can be found. India is the land of the tiger and so much more.

This first section of the guide presents this diversity in broad spectrum: the habitats, wildlife and the major conflicts and conservation issues. The tiger, the Indian elephant and the great one-horned rhinoceros are covered in dedicated chapters, as are the Himalayan, desert and marine habitats. Others are grouped for coverage under headings such as Primates, Birds, Reptiles etc. The section begins with chapters overviewing the state of the Indian environment and the diverse forest flora, and ends with an essay on the traditions of conservation in rural communities – a background for the National Parks and sanctuaries detailed in the second half of this guide. ❏

PRECEDING PAGES: the big cats of India: tiger, Asiatic lion, leopard, and snow leopard.
LEFT: jungle cat, hunting, Bandipur.

THE INDIAN ENVIRONMENT

Beset by government ineptitude, corruption and rampant poaching
India's wildlife is at crisis point and facing widespread extinction

India is one of the 12 megadiversity regions of the world and contains two of the world's 25 biodiversity hotspots – so-called for the extraordinarily high levels of species-richness and endemicity, and threatened status. Unique, still mysterious, and forever fascinating, the natural history of the Indian subcontinent remains largely unstudied and its ecological wealth little appreciated. Geological events that took place millions of years ago created an incomparable diversity of ecosystems. In the north the legendary snow-capped Himalayan ranges house rare and elusive creatures such as snow leopard, musk deer, ibex and pheasants of all descriptions. The Thar, also called the Great Indian Desert, sprawls between India and Pakistan in the northwest and supports a surprising variety of hardy plants and animals, several found nowhere else on earth. Towards the east, bordering Bhutan, Bangladesh and Burma, cloud forests and swamps shelter life forms ranging from tigers, elephants, rhinos and gibbons to the largest moth and some of the rarest orchids in the world. The lower slopes and foothills of the Himalaya, clothed in verdant coniferous forests and grasslands, are the last refuge of several endangered plant and animal species.

The great floodplains of the Indus, Ganga and Brahmaputra rivers, though radically altered by man's agricultural lifestyle, are still among the most fertile areas in the world. The Ganga is home to river dolphin, turtle and crocodile. The Western Ghats, an ancient chain of hills running from north to south, fringing the western coast of India, are perhaps the last hope for some of Asia's densest rainforests. In the scrub and grasslands of the Deccan Plateau, naturalists rediscovered Jer-

don's double-banded courser, a ground bird that was for nearly 80 years presumed extinct. Running all along the peninsula's coastline are some of the world's finest coral formations, sand bars and mangroves. Several species of turtle nest along the coast and seagrass meadows provide food for the gentle dugong.

Eden besieged

For many years, Africa has been regarded as the definitive destination for wildlife spotting, and justifiably so. However, in recent years naturalists, tourists and researchers have recognised that the natural wealth of the Indian subcontinent offers a fascinating complement to that of Africa. Tropical Asia, after all, probably houses the richest diversity of life forms on the face of the earth, and the Indian peninsula might well be considered the cornerstone of this Eden. Unfortunately, with a population now over a billion, this Eden is under siege from a sixth of humanity.

In 1271, a young adventurer departed from

PRECEDING PAGES: 24 elephants were killed in India by speeding trains between 2001 and 2004.
LEFT: forest guards burn seized skins and skulls.
RIGHT: horn chopped from the body of a rhino killed by the poachers near Pobiotora Wildlife sanctuary.

his native Venice on a voyage of discovery. Among the other incredible stories he related in his *Book of Marvels*, he spoke of a wondrous land filled with curious animals, like elephants, rhinos and great striped cats. That land was India. The man was Marco Polo. Incredibly, more than a thousand years before Marco Polo discovered the riches of India, Emperor Ashoka, who then ruled most of this vast region, had realized the value of its natural wealth and passed edicts to protect it. But that was still an age when people had need to "conquer" nature to carve an acceptable niche for themselves in a hostile world. Yet, somehow,

the awe and respect for natural systems, on which the very existence of the Indian people has always been dependent, prevailed. Animals have always played an important role in the daily lives of Indians. Regional mythology, religion and even social mores are entwined with rituals that involve the deification of plants, animals and the elements.

It was only when the British occupied the subcontinent that exploitation first began to take a serious toll. Vast Burmese teak forests were razed to construct ships and homes for the Empire. Countless natural habitats were destroyed to grow valuable cash crops such as tea and cotton. The land was ripe for the taking and

exploitation began in earnest. Those who fervently hoped that India's independence would reverse this pattern of land-use were mistaken. After 1947 the face of the Indian subcontinent began to undergo its most drastic change. The people were poor, and for the most part there was a genuine desire on the part of their leaders to provide the people with a better standard of living. The only freely available commodity was land. No one thought of the disastrous consequences of converting wild grasslands and forests to pastures or industrial dumpyards. India, Pakistan, Bangladesh, Nepal and Sri Lanka are all still reeling under the stress of shortsighted past decisions. And, in spite of knowing better, today's managers often continue to opt for minor political gains, using land as a tragic medium of barter to appease people. The resultant havoc caused by nature's response to bad land-management – floods, droughts and famines – is too well-known to merit further comment.

To understand how blessed the region once was, one needs merely travel to reserves such as Kanha or Bandhavgarh in Madhya Pradesh, Ranthambore in Rajasthan, Manas in Assam, Chitwan in Nepal, and the Sundarbans in West Bengal. At one time the entire subcontinent was as rich and productive as these islands of restraint and tolerance.

In such havens, the sight of thriving ecosystems provides a glimpse into the way things were before the evolution of Man. The profusion of life is truly staggering, as lianas, vines, fungi and animals of every description are seen living out their threatened existences, oblivious of the inexorable press of humanity around them. These isolated green vaults are defended by those with an understanding of the consequences of environmental imbalances. But for vast areas it is already too late. The malaise has taken a firm grip on the land and many once-verdant expanses have forever been reduced to dust.

What is likely to strike most visitors to the many reserves in the region is the stark contrast between the outside and inside of protected places. Almost without exception, the approach roads are barren and, often, a sense

LEFT: Pabitora forest officials examine the body of a pregnant rhino killed by poachers, Assam, 2004.
RIGHT: domestic ivory trading has gone underground.

of apprehension creeps in as you begin to wonder what lies in store. The moment you enter, say, the Periyar Wildlife Sanctuary, however, the apprehension vanishes as you are transported to a primeval peace so familiar to anyone whose soul is stirred by the outdoors.

Stripes and ivory

At one time "tigerland" comprised virtually the whole Indian subcontinent. Fearing no animal, the great cats colonized every imaginable habitat, from the lower slopes of high mountains, to desertified scrub lands, rainforests and swamps. Positioned at the apex of the food

the jungle. Many of the other animals that shared the tiger's domain did the same.

Elephants, perhaps more than any other animal, typify the man-animal conflict in India. Although there is also an ancient history of cooperation, crop-raids and killings on both sides are a recurrent problem.

The large beasts require vast ranges in order to survive. Their daily requirement of green fodder can exceed 200 kg (450 lb) per day. Plantations, hydroelectric projects, roads and jungle clearances have so totally fragmented their habitats that elephants, which once roamed virtually contiguous forests, must now contend with

chain, tigers managed to carve a secure niche for themselves while still allowing adaptable predators such as the leopard and several lesser cats to co-exist. With the arrival of *Homo sapiens* all this changed. Having learned to alter the environment to suit their own convenience, they began to make inroads into virgin jungles, slashing and burning in their frantic haste to convert hostile habitats into hospitable havens.

Over a period of time, having established dominion over the natural world, humans began to hunt for pleasure. Persecuted for their skin and for the illusion of bravery surrounding *shikar* (hunting), and as the number of people began to swell, the tiger retreated deeper into

existence in small pockets, and when they do try to migrate to distant pastures they come into conflict with man, most often with disastrous results for both. The problem of habitat degradation is compounded by man's persistent greed for ivory. Even today, despite stringent laws, elephants regularly fall victim to poachers who often use poison and pit traps to bring down their quarry, wiping out entire families.

Wildlife and tourism

There is no doubt about it. Natural India awaits discovery. Despite the lack of an extensive tourist infrastructure, the heat and humidity, people are drawn back to the forests that

Kipling immortalized. In any event, the secret for visitors lies in knowing what to expect and in understanding that the privilege of stepping into a pure and untouched world is a reward in itself. Actual animal sightings must be viewed as a lucky bonus.

There is a fundamental difference between the wildlife experience of Indian jungle and that found in Africa. To begin with, tropical jungles are dense and most often visibility is fairly restricted. All too often visitors, lured to India by tourist brochures that promise exciting "tiger safaris", are disappointed to see fewer animals than they expected. It's not that the surviving

eastwards to Assam, organized treks, river rafting and wildlife-viewing facilities are emerging, as private and government agencies gear up to meet the new influx of adventure-seekers from all over the world and within India. The Royal Chitwan National Park in Nepal has become a routine stopover for all categories of tourists. Here, visitors are given very basic but well-designed creature comforts and the rest is left to nature.

Excursions into the forest are arranged on elephant back, one of the most satisfying and effective ways to view animals such as the great one-horned rhino and the tiger. Trained guides

jungles are so thinly populated, but that most creatures, which have mastered the art of camouflage and deception over millennia, are virtually impossible to spot unless you know what to look for. With the help of an experienced guide, however, a moving twig becomes a praying mantis, part of a tree stump takes wing to reveal itself as a roosting nightjar, or, with some luck, an almost imperceptible movement in the grass turns out to be none other than a tiger.

Recognizing the tourist potential of wildlife, the governments of India and Nepal have gone out of their way to cater to the basic requirements of nature lovers. From Kashmir and Ladakh, through the Garhwal Himalaya and

and four-wheel drive vehicles are also on hand to help visitors to get a "feel" of the habitat in the shortest possible time. Varying degrees of creature comforts are available in virtually every protected area of India. And, in some of the more remote locations, where comforts fall short, the basic hospitality of locals can be depended upon for a simple meal and a place to bunk down. One has need of little more than mosquito repellents, water purification tablets, a sleeping bag and a basic love for nature.

Today however, conservationists and naturalists ask whether our besieged natural areas can withstand the added trauma of uncontrolled tourism. Relative to other threats such fears can be exaggerated, but are sometimes well founded. Consider the plans that were slated for the exquisite islands of Lakshadweep some 200–400 km (124–249 miles) west of the Kerala coast. Terms such as "tropical island paradise" are wholly inadequate when describing the pristinite nature of such areas. To cater for and exploit the tourist potential of the coral formations, some misguided enthusiasts suggested that a channel be blasted through the ring of corals to admit large ships capable of carrying thousands of tourists. The resultant death of living corals, as unfettered tides pour sand on the reefs, would have caused the ecosystem to be destroyed within a decade – fortunately this plan seems to have been shelved.

Project Tiger in Crisis

A wake-up call for Indian conservation was the forced acceptance in the late 1960s that the tiger was destined for extinction – numbers had dropped to below 2,000. An international appeal followed to save one of the world's most magnificent beasts, often voted top in "favourite animal" polls around the world. The Wildlife Protection Act came into force in 1972, banning the hunting of threatened species and giving legal powers to state governments to protect wildlife habitats. The following year, Project Tiger was launched by then Prime Minister, Indira Gandhi. The first step was to abolish tiger *shikar* (hunting), the second was to save its vanishing home. Choosing habitats as far removed from each other as the Sunderbans in Bengal, Corbett in Uttaranchal, and Periyar in Kerala, the authorities decided that the only long-term way to save the tiger was to save its forest. Many of these tiger reserves were established in the old hunting grounds of the former Indian and British aristocracy. Since 50 percent of the Project's funds were met by the Central Government, the states were able to protect tigers better than ever before. In the process, innumerable other animals gained protection, including the Asian elephant and the great Indian one-horned rhinoceros. Dry deciduous habitats such as Ranthambore and Sariska, in Rajasthan, received a new lease of life. The

hard ground barasingha of Kanha recouped their dwindling numbers. In Manas, Assam, a score and more endangered animals such as the hispid hare and the pygmy hog were retrieved from the brink of extinction. The tiger can recover relatively quickly from low numbers because it is highly reproductive and the number of tigers in Indian jungles recovered substantially. Project Tiger was a success.

However, in the early 1990s tigers disappeared from the Ranthambore Tiger Reserve and 400 kg (880 lbs) of tiger bones were seized in Delhi en route to China for medicinal use. This second crisis – with poaching and habitat

loss claiming one tiger per day at this time – roused the project into action again and tiger numbers once more increased.

The tiger is now in the throes of a third crisis. In 2004 it emerged that tigers had dissapeared from the Sariska Tiger Reserve. Worse yet, this is part of a wider pattern and a dozen tiger reserves are very fragile: many tigers have again been lost from Ranthambore, and from Panna in MP, Buxa in West Bengal, Kela Devi Sanctuary and Sawai Man Singh Sanctuary in Rajasthan, and the Rani Durgawati and Palpur Kuno sanctuaries in Madhya Pradesh. There has been a decade of management failures, denials and cover-ups. Census numbers were

---

LEFT: pressure from excessive, poorly-managed tourism is over-burdening some habitats.
RIGHT: an estimated 100,000 turtles have washed ashore on the Orissa coast in the last decade.

inflated by officials seeking to protect their jobs and obtain grants. It consistently falls to NGOs to raise the alarm and wildlife researchers have even been harassed by government officials for talking about poaching. The true figure for the tiger population at present is uncertain but may be little over 1,000, with the largest population being in Sundarbans.

In April 2005, in response to a national outcry over Sariska, a Tiger Task Force (TTF) was set up by Prime Minister Manmohan Singh to determine how to save the tiger. Much of the decline is due to poaching to satisfy demand for tiger parts from East Asia: between 1999

The Tiger Fund, some Tibetans have burnt tiger-skin robes in public and prices are falling.

With the support of the Beijing-based World Federation of Chinese Medicine Societies and the American College of Traditional Chinese Medicine, the CATT is also preparing a global petition to end the use of tiger-bone in medicines for all time. Worryingly, China has proposed a lifting of the ban on the trade in tiger parts. The skins of both tiger and leopard are still in high demand in China, and European MPs have called on China, Nepal and India to increase their efforts. So far, India is failing to protect the few remaining tigers and the shelv-

and 2004, 20 seizures across India and a further nine in Nepal and China recovered 80 tiger skins, 20,000 tiger claws and 1,200 leopard skins (Environmental Investigation Agency, EAI). An investigation by the EIA and the Wildlife Protection Society of India (WPSI) revealed an estimated 46 shops in Tibet trading in tiger, leopard and otter skins. This may be the world's largest wildlife blackmarket and supplies a strong demand for the traditional Tibetan *chuba* robe bedecked with tiger skin. Investigators saw hundreds worn at festivals in Tibet. The Dalai Lama has spoken out against this tradition and, six months into the Campaign Against Tiger Trafficking (CATT) by Save

ing of the Wildlife (Protection) Act Amendment Bill, 2005 is very disappointing. Unless concerted action is taken to combat this threat – and this means funds and commitment from central and state governments – the tiger will soon be extinct in India. Efforts like the Wildlife Conservation Society's "Tigers Forever Initiative" may offer the tiger a final chance.

Saving the land

The twin causes of wildlife loss are poaching and habitat destruction. Despite increased awareness, the rate at which the overall forest acreage is dwindling is nothing short of alarming. Domestic and industrial wood consumption far exceeds the regeneration capacity of existing forests. At the beginning of the 20th Century a full 40 percent of the subcontinent was under natural cover. Satellite pictures indicate we are now down to less than seven or eight percent. Roughly 5 percent is designated as protected.

But forest reserves are not being protected from poachers, extraction industries or encroachments. Mining of coal and ores, quarrying, industrial plants and logging are conducted within protected areas both legally and illegally. Dams, canals, roads and railways further destroy and dissect habitats, cutting off migration corridors and separating populations thereby causing further genetic decline. These activities all bring workers into the forest in their thousands who then take their food and firewood needs from the forest. Transport routes are a hazard to wildlife crossing them, make more forest accessible, and products transportable to distant cities.

Environment Impact Assessment reports are often erroneous and skirt around important ecological issues in order to expeditiously gain clearance for the project proponent. The public hearings are conducted in a routine and cursory manner, or worse, and the proceedings have little or no consequence on the environmental clearance subsequently accorded to the project.

In Madhya Pradesh for instance, even in the face of continued opposition from local and international bodies, the Narmada dam projects inundated vast areas of land, much of which supported viable populations of endangered species. In the process of siphoning power for distant industries, thousands of tribal people (Adivasis) and local villagers were displaced. The promised "resettlement and rehabilitation" to displaced people has been inadequate or non-exsistent. The height of the Namarda dams has been raised several times and countless other dams projects replicate its effects.

The Ganges drainage area is one of the most densely populated in the world, being home to roughly one tenth of the world's human population. More than 50 dam and irrigation bar-

rages, along with municipal and industrial pollution, have severely affected the flow, sediment load and water quality of this mighty river. In the last century thousands of Gangetic dolphin rolled and jumped in the sacred waters. This revered animal is also plagued by fishing and, along with 11 species of turtle and two species of crocodile, is struggling to survive. The Ganga Action Plan to clean the river was launched in 1986 but little has been achieved.

The marine coastal environment is also under seige from prawn, shrimp and trout farming "barons". On the east coast at Orissa, thousands of endangered olive ridley turtles drown in fish-

ing nets due to illegal trawling. Most alarming perhaps is the proposed Sethusamudram ship canal which, if it goes ahead, will carve up the shallow sea beds of the Gulf of Mannar and Palk Bay between India and Sri Lanka. These closed marine systems have been categorised as a Biosphere Reserve of global significance and are the most important habitat in the Indian Ocean for the endangered dugong (or "sea cow"). The spoil, silt and noise from dredging and blasting will kill seagrass meadows and coral reefs, drive away marine life and destroy the fishing industry.

Fortunately, there is opposition to environmentally ill-advised plans – two classic exam-

LEFT: dead tigers from the King Emperor's Indian Coronation Durbar of 1911–12. The king is George V.
RIGHT: millions of Adivasi people have been displaced by dam projects like those in the Narmada valley.

ples being the saving of Silent Valley's rainforest in Kerala from the jaws of a hydroelectric project (though a smaller hydro project is now being proposed), and the famous "Chipko" movement, where women in the Garhwal Himalaya prevented contractors from exploiting already degraded forestlands. With increasing frequency, enlightened public figures – such as writer Arundhati Roy – have also begun making their views on the degradation of the environment known.

The law allows the authorities to come down hard on known traders, poachers and exploiters but enforcement has been sporadic

diversity has economic value and needs to be protected from bio-piracy. Recently, India passed a law protecting its bio-resources and traditional knowledge from foreign biotechnology companies but although loss through extinctions of such valuable genetic resources underscore the conservation message, the legislation is unlikely to benefit either conservation or rural communities.

The protection of the forest reserves requires bold action with a sense of urgency: a protection force engaging local people with well-trained khaki-clad forest guards to deter poachers. But there is a clear lack of political

and still lags far behind intention and rhetoric. In booming India, industrialisation and development are king and corruption favours "development" projects profiting well-connected individuals and companies.

Agriculture, too, is destroying forests in the form of pesticide use and plantations – monocultures of teak, eucalyptus and palm utterly destroy biodiversity. There is active connivance of officials with rich, large-scale encroachers. The rural poor are not provided for and tensions rise, invarably to the cost of wildlife.

If another reason were needed now to save forests, there is a growing awareness among biodiverse developing countries that their bio-

will to respect The Wildlife (Protection) Act of 1972 and the Forest (Conservation) Act 1980. The burning question is why the implementation of environmental laws has been left to the Courts whilst the ineffective functioning of Government Ministries continues.

Local Pressure

With no other resources, villagers turn to forests to meet their daily requirements of fuel and fodder. To win elections, politicians often make unrealistic promises to their electorate, thus creating friction between park managers and local people. Another major problem, of course, is that of human-animal conflicts. In Assam, tea estate owners still occasionally shoot elephants to protect their cash crops. In Gir, the last 340 lions are constantly under threat from Maldharis who poison them in retaliation for cattle lifting. Cattle-lifting, crop destruction and occasional man-killing incidents are genuine and very serious problems, but incidents are often blown out of all proportion and a frenzy is whipped up to pressure the authorities into giving in to the demands of the local people.

Conservationists have come to the conclusion that the way to reduce such hostility on the periphery of protected places is to improve the socio-economic standards of people who fringe forests. This, however, is easier said than done. Attempts to introduce stall feeding of cattle, or improve their bloodstock, and plans for the large-scale use of new, smokeless *chulas* (ovens), which can reduce a household's fuel consumption by over 30 percent, did not work because of a lack of investment. Meanwhile, rural women each walk more than 1,600 km (1,000 miles) each year in search of firewood.

After over 50 years of independence, India has still not hammered out a national fuel wood policy. Consequently, 50 percent of the domestic fires in some of the country's largest cities are fed by wood. Even as sporadic social forestry efforts meet with success, natural forests are literally being transported to the cities to vanish in smoke. And the pressure on the land is growing. The population of 1.1 billion is twice that of when Project Tiger began.

What is now angering local communities is that small-time livelihood encroachers are being evicted in apparent enforcement of the "forest case" orders, whilst nothing is being done about a pattern of powerful encroachments by "big-timers" throughout India's forest states.

The recently revised Scheduled Tribes (Recognition of Forest Rights) Bill, 2005, has focussed attention on the marginalised forest-dwelling people who have been subject to forced evictions. The bill would grant them land rights and transfer powers to implement the new law from the forest department to local communities. Although these beleaguered people undoubtably deserve respect and protection,

critics argue the bill also grants land rights to encroachers and will result in a license to plunder and the hounding of tribals by timber and land sharks. The bill – drafted by the Ministry of Tribal Affairs, with little consultation or consideration for wildlife – needs proper debating and redrafting.

What is needed is a bill to protect the rights of the forest, wildlife and forest-dwellers. "In a land where people are dying", say some, "they want to save forests and animals!". Saving the land is saving the people. And we cannot save wild habitats without helping the people who live alongside. Once this reality is accepted,

everything else will follow. Indeed, there are strong traditions of conservation of wildlife and trees in many areas, where sacred sites and species have long enjoyed protection by rural communities. The Tribal Bill could, perhaps, provide legal protection for such traditions and community conserved areas (CCAs).

Vanishing Vultures

In recent years another extinction crisis within Indian Wildlife has unfolded with alarming speed. The vulture has long been a prominent cast-member in the tableaux of natural India. In the last 15 years their population of 85 million has dropped by around 98 percent. This

LEFT: a man points towards his now submerged farmland – for which he was paid only about $68.
RIGHT: the Tribal Bill will affect forests, forest-dwellers and wildlife.

decline may be the fastest extinction ever seen in the biological world.

Three griffon vulture species have been affected and are now classed as critically endangered by the IUCN: the Slender-billed Vulture, the Oriental White-backed Vulture and the Indian Vulture. Vultures play an obvious and critical link in the food chain by disposing of carrion. It is through feeding on the remains of livestock that they have been exposed to Diclofenac – an anti-inflammatory drug banned in most parts of the world but used widely in India and Pakistan. Even a single ingestion can cause kidney failure and

the relevant authorities. Two captive breeding centres have been set up by the Bombay Natural History Society (BNHS) and the UK's RSPB But reversing this decline will be a long and difficult process. Raptor experts warn that it may be too late for these birds, who do not breed until five years old and produce only one chick a year.

Projections

India is probably the last hope of survival for the one-horned rhino, the great Indian bustard, the gharial (a fish-eating crocodile), the Malabar large spotted civet, the Namdapha flying

death in the birds. The scale of their former numbers suggests the impact of their absence. India has the largest livestock population in the world – around 300 million cattle and buffalo – of which around 10–20 million die annually. These now lie and rot in the sun or are preyed upon by a growing number of dogs and crows who become vectors of disease threatening human health.

Faced with irresponsible drugs companies who have failed to switch to the alternative drug Meloxicam, government intervention has again been slow and the ban on the manufacture, sale and use of Diclofenac which came finally in March 2005 has yet to be acted on by

squirrel, the pygmy hog, the lion-tailed macaque, the giant squirrel, the slender loris and a host of other highly endangered species, many endemic to the subcontinent. Unfortunately, the situation for these and other species and their habitats is precarious. The failures of Project Tiger are part of a much wider pattern.

Project Elephant was created in 1992 by the government of India to conserve and protect populations of Asian Elephant, whose numbers are a fraction of that of the African Elephant. Progress has been painfully slow and 77 elephant deaths were recently reported in the Nagarahole Sanctuary. Project Rhino has had success in the past but poaching (for its horn) eradicated the rhino from three Assamese reserves (Manas, Laokhowa and Burhachpori) while the population in Orang has declined by more than half. The "Indian Rhino Vision 2020" scheme will fund protection and relocations.

The endangered tiger, elephant and rhino are often regarded as "keystone" or "cornerstone" species – that is, their survival depends on a complex web of other species across a wide habitat range. Saving them acts as an umbrella for other, less charismatic species and should be the basis for biodiversity conservation.

A third Indian "umbrella species" is the Snow Leopard. Also endangered, the estimated population is between 3,500 to 7,000 in the world, of which India has about 500 in Jammu and Kashmir, Himachal Pradesh, Uttaranchal, Sikkim and Arunchal Pradesh. Poaching for skin and body parts, retaliatory killings for livestock depredations and the decline in wild prey populations casued by hunting, are the main threats. In 2006 Project Snow Leopard was constituted. Hopefully this will be a success but on the basis of the tiger, elephant, projections are not good.

A glimmer of hope has come in the form of a clutch of significant wildlife enforcement results in recent years. The well-known timber smuggler and outlaw, Veerappan, was killed by the authorities in 2004. In 2005, Sansar Chand, India's most nortorious wildlife criminal, known to have been active in Sariska, was finally snared and a Bollywood star, Salman Kahn, was sentenced to five years for hunting endangered black buck and chinkara. Also in 2005, the Rajasthan State Government arrested the Chief Wildlife Warden of Sariska and seven of his staff and this year saw the capture of Jagdish Lodha, king-pin of a tiger and leopard poaching and dealing network across Nepal and India. Hopefully enforcement will be bolstered by the newly-formed National Wildlife Crime Prevention and Control Bureau formed with the support of wildife crime experts from the UK. Also encouraging is that India has announced it will become a member of the US-led Coalition Against Wildlife Trafficking (CAWT).

LEFT: as vulture species face extinction, the feral dog population has exploded.

RIGHT: after a lengthy trial, Bollywood star Salman Khan was convicted in 2006 for poaching.

Wildlife and Climate Change

But Indian wildlife is dependent not just on activities in India, or even South Asia, but also on environmental policies around the globe. A recent study published in *Nature* indicates that climate change is the most significant new threat for mass extinctions. It predicts that by 2050 climate change will cause the extinction of one third of the world's wildlife and almost as many plant species. A joint DEFRA-MOEF study found that climate change in India is likely to cause changes in habitats and migration patterns, including forest die-back and loss of biodiversity.

This indicates an urgent need for two things. Firstly, greenhouse gas (GHG) emissions need to be drastically reduced. With 39 percent of the world's population between them, the route taken by the fast-growing economies of India and China will be pivotal to future climate change. Secondly, wildlife conservation policies need to be informed by climate change effects: strategies must focus upon establishing and strictly protecting large and connected networks of conservation areas. This would offer the best chance of affording protected habitats not only for current seasonal migrations (taking animals into unprotected areas) but also future migrations driven by immanent changes in climate and ecosystems. ❏

FORESTS AND FLORA

With rainforest, alpine forest, grassland, desert and mangrove swamp,
the Indian subcontinent has a matchless variety of forests and flora

Today, forest development has, like many other matters of ecological significance, become a focal point of activity. Forests were greatly valued in ancient India. Everyday life was closely connected with nature; kings protected forests and ascetics retired to them for peaceful meditation in their quest for salvation *(moksha)*. Emperor Chandragupta Maurya, as early as the 3rd century BC, had forests classified as those used for religious purposes and others to be exploited commercially. He also allotted some forest areas for hunting. Forest offences and careless deforestation were punishable by death. During Emperor Ashoka's reign (3rd century BC), several species of trees were identified for protection. The abundant evidence of natural forms in the Indian art of this period reflects a great affinity with nature.

Alexander is said to have used Indian timber for building ships in the 4th century BC. For many centuries Indian wood was exported to Persia and Arabia, but this commercial activity was on a very small scale compared to the immensity of India's then forest resources and had no noticeable effect on the extent of forest cover. Hundreds of years later, in Mughal times, there was a great deal of hunting in the forests of North India.

Nevertheless, although the Mughals had no positive interest in conserving forests, they did not harm or denude them. At the turn of the 19th century, however, the British developed a keen interest in the valuable woods of the Indian jungle. Some of the ships in Nelson's fleet at Trafalgar had been built by the famous Bombay shipbuilders, the Wadias, teak replacing the English oak. Trees yielding prized wood like sandalwood, rosewood, satinwood and ebony were felled for commercial purposes, doing great damage to India's forest wealth.

Despite steps taken by the British in the early 19th century to regenerate forests, in the long run they encouraged agriculture at the expense of

forests rather than as complementary to them. This short-sighted policy did immense damage.

Since Independence, the Indian Government's New Action Plan for Forestry has declared 33.3 percent of the whole land area of the country (60 percent on the hills and 20 percent in the plains) as reserved for forests. However, this has

not prevented further extensive encroachments on India's forest cover (now less than seven or eight percent in India) and unless firm and effective action is taken soon, the future does seem grim indeed. The situation in Nepal is equally serious. Destruction of forests there has resulted in frequent landslides and bare hillsides.

An immense variety of flora is found in South Asia. In fact, due to climatic diversity in the subcontinent, it covers a whole range of types of vegetation regions from swamp and thorn forests to alpine forests. The amount of rainfall and average temperature, the topography, soil conditions and altitude are the major factors that affect the vegetation of a region. Clean-cut lines

PRECEDING PAGES: tropical rainforest canopy.
LEFT: Sal tree at sunset.
RIGHT: looking across Silent Valley.

demarcating each type are naturally impossible, and there are many areas where a mixture of vegetation is seen. The overlapping of types occurs both on the mountains and in the plains. Nevertheless, India can be divided into broad phytogeographical zones.

The Deccan

This region, otherwise known as the Deccan Plateau, comprises Tamil Nadu, Andhra Pradesh, a large part of Karnataka, Madhya Pradesh, Orissa, and parts of Maharashtra and Gujarat. Even within this peninsular area, the differences in annual rainfall cause variations

in the natural vegetation.

In the southern portions, consisting of hilly terrain, the annual rainfall is 86–100 cm (34–40 in) whereas in the northern parts of the Deccan the rainfall increases to 142 cm (56 in). Dry deciduous forests rich in teak *(Tectona grandis)*, known for its excellent timber, is the dominant variety.

Other large trees like mahogany *(Swietenia)*, Indian rosewood *(Dalbergia)*, Terminalia and Chikrassia also grow here. These trees have abundant foliage and are of majestic dimensions, often growing to great heights and spreading wide. The sandalwood tree *(Santalum)*, with its fragrant wood, is particularly

common in Karnataka. This tree is slender, with small leaves and tiny fruit. The wood in the living tree has no scent, yet the dry wood has a strong fragrance.

Intermittent patches of colour break the monotony of vast expanses of forestland. The flame of the forest *(Butea frondosa)* is a burst of pale orange when in bloom, while Bauhinias and Lagerstroemias are laden with delicate white, pink and mauve blossoms in the flowering season. Cassia fistula with its shower of pale yellow flowers and Cassia nodosa, which has pink inflorescences, are exotic flowering trees that dot these forests.

Many forests have a mixture of Acacia, Dillenia, red sandalwood, Odina, Grewia, Buchanani, etc. Many epiphytic orchids adorn the trees in some areas – using the host tree for support and to gain access to sunshine, not living off the tree as parasites do.

In the northern stretches of the Deccan, sal *(Shorea robusta)* forests extend from Madhya Pradesh to Orissa, and present a totally different picture. Sal trees are straight, compact and tall, with rounded leaves, and grow close together, forming stretches of homogeneous forests in continuous belts for many miles.

In those areas of the Deccan where rainfall is lower, the vegetation changes to scrub forests. The hardy trees here are, to a large extent, thorny and well adapted to dry climate conditions. The mixed population of trees consists of Zizyphus, Acacia, Capparis, Balanites, Euphorbia, Flacourtia, Prosopis and others, forming thinly wooded forests.

Coastal areas

These form a striking contrast to the forested areas although lying in close proximity to them. Here, there are long stretches of coastline with symmetrical coconut palms that bear a rich yield of coconut. Further inland in the coastal plain jackfruit and mango trees are plentiful along with tamarind. In some pockets of the Deccan coast, near the river estuaries, mangroves, typical of wet marshy areas, are common.

The west coast region comprises the Western Ghats and extends from Gujarat in the north to Kerala in the south. It has, in places, an annual rainfall of over 250 cm (100 in). Its natural ex-

LEFT: flame of the forest in a blaze of colour.
RIGHT: sal forest, central India.

uberance is apparent in its rich forests and lush tropical vegetation. The tropical evergreen forests are remarkable for their luxuriant growth of trees, both tall and medium-sized, which do not as a rule shed their leaves annually. To add to the prolific vegetation, many shrubs, climbers, epiphytes, bamboo and ferns grow in abundance. These thick-set jungles have been utilized by man in several ways. Hevea and Ficus elastica yield rubber, while ebony *(Diospyros)* and toon *(Cedrela)* are good timber sources. The species common here are Dipterocarpus, Artocarpus, sandalwood *(Santalum)*, red sandalwood *(Pterocarpus)*, nutmeg *(Myristica)*,

which grows in dense clumps. The bamboo here is very long and has a large girth. It is used in house-building and furniture-making.

In the higher ranges of this region, tucked away in comparatively smaller areas, are temperate evergreen forests with Michelia, Eugenia, Ternstroemia, etc.

Dry Lands

In sharp contrast to the green West Coast Region is the Indus Plain. This phytogeographical region covers parts of Indian Punjab, Rajasthan, and most of Pakistan. Annual rainfall varies from a low 25–50 cm (10–20 in) in

Alexandrian laurel *(Calophyllum)*, Michelia, Ternstroemia, Hopea and Sterculia. Coconut palms *(Cocos)*, mimusops, talipot palms, thick shrubbery and climbers complete the scene of tropical splendour.

In most areas of the west coast region where rainfall is relatively low (150–200 cm/60–80 in), vegetation is sparse and consists mainly of deciduous trees. These shed their leaves annually and remain bare after leaf-fall. Mountain ebony *(Bauhinia)*, teak, Dalbergia, Adina, Lagerstroemia, Terminalia and Grewia form an assortment of trees of many sizes, some with beautiful flowers and others with high-quality wood. Characteristic of this area is bamboo *(Bambusa)*,

Rajasthan to 64–76 cm (25–30 in) in the Punjab. The area suffers from extremes of temperature and low humidity. Winter can be harsh and summer equally unpleasant, with blistering heat and hot winds. The soil has a high percentage of salts and is sandy. A large part of Rajasthan is covered by the Thar Desert, and shifting sand-dunes cause desertification. On the fringes of the desert the vegetation is typically xerophytic, adapted to dry surroundings – with long roots penetrating deep below the earth's surface and enabling the plants to utilize the subsoil's moisture. Such vegetation requires very little water and can survive in extreme climates and tolerate harsh soil conditions. In order to prevent evaporation the leaves are small, the stems greatly reduced, and the pores on the leaf-surfaces few in number.

Along the riverbanks there is abundant sub-soil moisture although the soil is sandy. Where there is black saline soil there is no vegetation at all. The desert thorn forests of this area consist mainly of Prosopis, Salvadora oleoides and Capparis. These grow in isolated clumps. Acacia, Tamarix, Albizzia lebbek, Morus alba and flame of the forest are the mixed varieties that constitute such forests. Arabian grass, saltwort and seablite grow where there are salt tracts. The undergrowth consists of thorny shrubs.

Gangetic plain

The vegetation of the Gangetic Plain slowly changes from that of the Indus Plain since the rainfall increases gradually as one moves eastwards. This region can be divided into three parts. The upper, dry sub-region extends from Punjab to Allahabad in Uttar Pradesh. It receives 50–100 cm (20–40 in) of rainfall annually. Peganum, Acacia, Moringa, Prosopis, Tecoma, Rhus, along with some palms, are found in this sub-region. The vegetation is still quite sparse in the area and, where the soil is alkaline, Salvadora is common. This region also has grasslands or savannahs interspersed occasionally

Dune scrub, which differs from the forest vegetation, also resists desert conditions and is characterized by stunted trees and bushes with adaptive thorns. This vegetation is found in southern Punjab and Rajasthan. The only tree found here is Acacia jacquemontia. Sandy alluvial deposits are found on the banks of the rivers of this region. Dominant here are forests consisting mainly of species like Acacia catechu and Dalbergia sissoo. Poplars *(Populus)* and Tamarix occur here and there.

On the whole, the Indus region consists of hardy plants that can protect themselves against trying weather conditions.

with Bombax, Butea, Zizyphus and Randia.

In the lower Gangetic Plain, which stretches from Allahabad to West Bengal, the rainfall is 190–250 cm (76–100 in). Mangifera, Artocarpus, Ficus, Areca, Borassus, Phoenix, Lagerstroemia, Pterospermum, Bombax, Polyalthia and Casuarina grow commonly in the area. The vegetation grows more prolifically and many different aroids begin to occur. Aquatic plants, several types of grasses and sedges abound in the vicinity of lakes and small reservoirs.

The third part of the Gangetic Plain is an unusual area forming the vast Sunderbans around the delta of the Ganga. Characteristic of this region are interconnected waterways and marshy swamps. The tidal swamp forests of the delta region cover an area of 15,500 sq km (6,000 sq miles), the largest stretch of swamp forest in the world, most of it lying in Bangladesh. The area is thick with evergreen trees and shrubs typical of mangrove or littoral forests, which thrive in the saline water washed in with the tide. Typical mangrove trees like Rhizophora, Ceriops, Kandelia and Bruguiera are prolific in the area. Of the 36 species of mangrove trees found in the Sunderbans, Avicennia officinalis is the largest. Mangroves protect from coastal erosion and extreme waves. The little swampy islands found here and there are covered with savannah grass. Palms like Nipa fruticans, Phoenix paludosa, coconut palms and cane *(Calamus)* occur extensively. Elephant grass and screwpine grow near streams, ponds, swamps and canals. The vegetation is thick and many species bind the mud and prevent it from being washed away. Ferns and orchids are also found here. The flora of the Sunderbans is of infinite variety and uncommon growth conditions, making it exceedingly attractive for botanical study. The forests of this area give economic support to the people – firewood and timber being the most important products.

Assam region

The northeastern region of India is exceedingly wet and humid. Annual rainfall varies from 280 cm (110 in) in the Garo hills to 1300 cm (510 in) at Cherra Punji. On the whole it averages at a high 80 inches (200 cm). The region does not experience large fluctuations of climate. The temperature is mild and ranges between 68°F and 86°F (20°C and 30°C). The hills, however, are much colder. Humidity is between 80 and 90 percent. The torrential Brahmaputra river flows right through the Assam Valley, spreading its rich alluvial deposits on the banks. The soil is extremely fertile and all these favourable conditions together result in extraordinarily rich and lush vegetation, making some pockets of Assam the world's richest in flora. Hills and plains have an abundant supply of water and are covered with uninterrupted forests.

The tropical evergreen or rainforests extend from northeast Arunachal Pradesh to Darrang district in Assam. They also occur in Nowgong,

and Cachar districts in Assam and most of the Khasi hills in Meghalaya. The peculiarity of these forests is their three-tier structure. The top tier looms over the rest and consists of isolated, tall, evergreen or deciduous trees, which grow to a height of around 46 metres (150 ft). The most common species among them are Dipterocarpus macrocarpus, Artocarpus, chaplasha, Tetrameles and Terminalia, each growing tall and handsome, with spreading branches and abundant foliage. The middle tier consists of several medium-sized trees growing up to a height of about 25 metres (80 ft). Calophyllum, Mesua, Amoora, Cinnamomum, Phoebe, Machilus and

Duabanga form the mixed middle layer. Ficus elastica, Michelia, Magnolia and Schima are also found. The ground tier consists of shrubs and climbers, orchids, aroids and ferns that cover every inch of land.

The pine forests of the Khasi hills, however, are devoid of the brush that gives the forest elsewhere its dense cover. Other trees present here mixed with pine are oak *(Quercus)*, Pieris, chestnut *(Castanopsis)* and birch *(Betula)*. In other areas, yew *(Taxus)*, spruce *(Picea)*, silver fir *(Abies)*, deodar or cedar *(Cedrus)*, Tsuga, cypress *(Cupressus)* and juniper *(Juniperus)* occur. Pines, yews and Tsuga are the few varieties that survive at very high altitudes.

LEFT: sal forests and hills in Bandhavgarh National Park.
RIGHT: mangroves, Andaman Islands.

In the lower Assam Valley, in the Garo hills and North Cachar hills, there are sal forests that are mainly of the deciduous type. Scrub forests also occur here and are dotted with colourful trees like Lagerstroemia, Cassia fistula, Bombax, Sterculia and others like Schima wallichii, Careya arborea, Dillenia, Kydia, Albizzia, Gmelia, Alstonia, Walnut, Terminalia and Dalbergia.

In certain parts of this belt, the forests are strikingly different, as they are pure sal forests, consisting of a variety peculiar to the region *(Shorea assamica)*, which grows to a height of 30 metres (100 ft). These unmixed sal forests present a beautiful and eye-catching picture.

In the dry regions of Cachar, forests are heterogeneous, consisting of Dipterocarpus, Adina, Bombax, Stephegyne, Ficus and Cassia nodosa. Bamboo and several grasses are common. Colourful flowering shrubs provide an attractive ground cover – white Coffea bengalensis, blue Strobilanthes, white and yellow Mussaenda and scarlet-red Holmskioldia.

Assam is unique and is unparalleled in the variety and richness of its forest wealth. In the swampy regions of the Assam valley, aquatic and semi-aquatic grasses and aquatic ferns of many varieties are prominent. The flowering plants that occur commonly are Euryale, Alpinia, water lilies *(Nymphaea)*, and lotus *(Nelumbo)*.

Among the trees, Barringtonia, Cephalanthus, and some Ficus species are seen here.

Another variation in the vegetation of Assam occurs in the low-lying areas that have very little rainfall. Along the riverbanks are exceptionally tall grasses, whereas the dry lands have short and sturdy varieties.

In the foothills of the Bhutan range, extending from Goalpara district to Darrang district, are the riparian forests that grow along large streams and are composed mainly of two tree varieties, Acacia catechu and Dalbergia sissoo. The few others are mostly of Duabanga, Bombax, Trewia, Barringtonia, Salix, Anthocephalus.

In the northeast region, there are more interesting species of flora – carnivorous plants and parasites abound. Over four hundred species of orchid and innumerable varieties of fern, and even fern trees, are special to this region.

Himalayan Flora

The vast area covered by the magnificent Himalaya mountain range lies to the extreme north of India and includes Bhutan, Nepal and parts of Pakistan. On the basis of climatic conditions, the Himalaya can be divided into three fairly distinct regions: the eastern Himalayan region, extending from the Arun Valley in East Nepal to the Mishmi hills of Arunachal Pradesh, has an average precipitation of 300 cm (120 in) a year. The next division, namely the central Himalayan region, is demarcated by a sharp decrease in rainfall, and comprises chiefly Nepal and Eastern Uttar Pradesh in India. The third division, the western Himalayan region, originates in Peshawar in Pakistan, where the annual precipitation is 50 cm (20 in) and extends in a southeasterly direction towards the Kumaon hills in Uttar Pradesh, with the precipitation increasing gradually to approximately 100 cm (40 in) in Kumaon.

However, the most important factor contributing to regional variations in the Himalayan flora is the altitude determining the temperature. The three divisions mentioned, can, in turn, be split up into zones according to altitude running in a northwest to southeast direction across the whole expanse of the Himalaya. These divisions and zones, however, often do not have well-defined boundaries and vegetation types overlap.

LEFT: lotus flower, Rajasthan.
RIGHT: wild iris in the Himalayas

The tropical zone, with rainfall of 100–150 cm (40–60 in), lies south and east of the Himalayan foothills, and is known locally as the terai region. The thick forests of the terai can be divided into two types: areas having an annual rainfall of over 250 cm (100 in) support evergreen forests, whereas deciduous forests are found in regions where the rainfall is sparse.

The temperate zone with rainfall 150–350 cm (60–140 in) is otherwise called the coniferous zone due to the predominance of conifers. This region has abundant flora and exhibits a decrease in vegetation with an increase in altitude.

here are several species of rhododendron adorned with flamboyant blossoms. Berberis, Impatiens, Saxifraga, and Himalayan poppies are a few examples of the numerous flowering plants of this region. Adding to the lush vegetation are orchids, bamboos, palms, epiphytes and creepers.

The common conifers are found in many varieties of pine and juniper. *Pinus longifolia, P. excelsa* and *P. gerardiana* are the predominant varieties of pine, while *Juniperus communis* and *J. recurva* are the common junipers. The mixed species found in this region are Abies pindrow, cypress *(Cupressus torulosa)*, deodar

North of the coniferous zone lies the alpine zone where the harsh temperature and low rainfall 350–450 cm (140–180 in) conditions support only a meager plant cover. This region stretches from above the tree line to the permanent snow line.

The eastern Himalaya is populated with varied and profuse flora. Over 4,000 species of flowering plants and a few hundred varieties of ferns make it a richly vegetated area. Amongst the conifers, the predominant species are many varieties of pine *(Pinus khasiya, P. excelsa, P. longifolia)*. Himalayan silver fir, junipers, Podocarpus and Picia are also common varieties. Growing abundantly

(Cedrus deodara), Picea morinda, etc. The exuberant growth in the east formed by rich flowering plants, orchids, palms and bamboo is far from being equalled in the western region. The variation in the two regions is apparent in the fact that the epiphytes and creepers that form an important part of the eastern forests are in quite insignificant numbers here, whereas grasses and leguminous plants are comparatively common due to the drier climatic conditions. Although rhododendrons are found here, the number of species is considerably less than in the eastern Himalaya. Rubus, Rosa, Prunus, Pyrus, and Ranunculus are among the vegetation of the upper reaches. ❏

TIGER

The charismatic giant of the cat family is the jewel in India's wildlife crown
but is envied by poachers and failed by the authorities

The tiger, unlike the lion, is a predator that relies on cover for success in hunting. Again, unlike the lion, it leads a solitary life. The only associations that occur are between male and female during the short courtship period and, of course, the long association between a mother and her cubs, till the latter grow and they can fend for themselves. Young siblings, on parting company with their mother, may sometimes stay together in an area for a few months, but soon tensions develop among them that break up the company. Socialization is extremely rare and is generally limited to a young adult occasionally visiting its mother, who is now caring for her next litter. Such a gathering may take place at a kill, but is invariably shortlived – a day or two at the most.

The parental care and upbringing of the young is the responsibility of the mother alone. This solitary way of life and the stalking or ambushing strategy of hunting is the only way food can be secured by a large predator in a forest environment or one with plenty of other forms of cover, such as the tall, dense reeds of the terai grasslands. Communal hunting by a large predator, as in the case of lions, depends upon fair visibility and lack of obstructions, a situation not available in a closed forest environment. It is for this reason that the tiger and lion are mutually exclusive in their distribution, the two having adapted themselves to forest and savannah environments respectively. The past and the present distributions of the tiger and lion in the Indian subcontinent, where alone both the species occur, bear testimony to this.

Habitat and population

Having originated in Siberia, as suggested by fossil evidence, the tiger found its best home in the Indian subcontinent. It is a truly Asian animal and science recognizes nine subspecies, three of which are already extinct in the wild

(the Balinese, the Caspian and the Javan). The other six are – in descending order of populations – the Bengal or Royal Bengal, Indo-Chinese, Malayan, Sumatran, Siberian and South China. The Bengal tiger is found in India, Bangladesh, Nepal and Bhutan. The Indo-Chinese tiger has ranges in Cambodia, China,

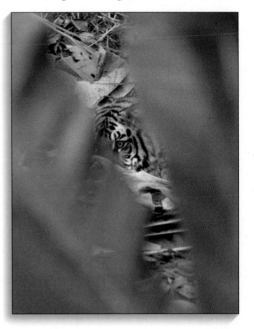

Laos, Myanmar, Thailand and Vietnam, while the other sub-species are restricted to one range state. The total world tiger population is estimated at less than 6,000 animals. Body-size diminishes as the distribution advances from the cold Siberian scrub thickets to the multi-tiered evergreen forests of Java and Sumatra.

On the Indian subcontinent, the Royal Bengal tiger *(Panthera tigris tigris)* is at home in a variety of environmental situations, from the high-altitude, cold, coniferous Himalayan forests to the steaming mangroves of the Sunderbans delta, from the swampy reedlands of the terai to the rugged, scorched hills of the Indian peninsula, and from the lush, wet evergreen forests of the

---

PRECEDING PAGES: young macaque and mother.
LEFT: a Royal Bengal tiger relaxing in the shade.
RIGHT: tiger, as often observed, Nagarahole.

northeast and the south to the scrub-thorn arid forests of Rajasthan. The average male Bengal tiger is approximately 2.9 m (9.5 ft) in length and weighs about 220 kg (490 lb). The average female Bengal tiger is approximately 2.5 m (8 ft) in length and weighs about 140 kg (300 lb). Like most big cats, tigers are solitary animals.

An estimate placed the population of tiger in India at the turn of the 19th century at 40,000. While this could be an exaggeration, the present plight of the tiger became evident when, in 1972, an all-India tiger

FELID CANINES

Since the sabretooth's demise, tigers have the longest canine teeth of any living felid, (10cm/ 4 in), but the clouded leopard has the longest relative to body size.

over 4,000 in 1986. Census figures were inflated or invented to protect jobs and funding. Present-day estimates put the population at below 1,200 – largely due poaching; poisoning, trapping and shooting are the most common methods used. The largest population is in Sundarbans.

The hunters of yesteryear regarded the tiger as the symbol of India's wilderness. Its savage beauty and might and its ability to melt into the forest like a phantom not only whetted the hunter's spirit of adventure but also provided the base for countless hair-raising *shikar* stories. But, more importantly, the tiger is a barometer of the health of the country's wilderness. The tiger is the ultimate consumer in the complex food web in many of the forest ecosystems of India. The soil fertility in these ecosystems rests on the micro-organisms that decompose the plant and animal residues to form humus. The diverse vegetation so supported is the food of a thriving community of herbivorous insects, birds and mammals and also helps to conserve the soil and enhance water flow.

Among the terminal carnivorous users of this productivity, the tiger stands at the head. Conservation of the tiger in its natural environment can be achieved only by total conservation of the wilderness based on an ecosystem approach, as was established by India's Project Tiger. Truly, therefore, the status of the tiger in India is the index of success for the conservation of its wilderness as a whole.

census reported that a population of only 1,800 had survived. The history of the decline of the tiger is the pathetic story of the shrinkage and ravaging of the Indian wilderness, pressed forward by the onslaught of demographic pressures.

Fortunately, under Project Tiger, India did embark on a massive conservation effort covering over 550 national parks and sanctuaries accounting for over 4 percent of the country's total area under forests. A number of these protected areas still harbour the tiger. India is the only country that undertakes an annual census of its tigers, but in the past the figures reported have sometimes borne no relation to the actual numbers of tigers, which supposedly reached

Cunning predator

Even in areas of prey abundance, the tiger has to work hard for its food since all its prey species have highly evolved systems of self-preservation that the tiger must beat. The ungulates, the hoofed herbivores, which constitute the main food of the tiger, have a highly developed sense of smell and reasonably keen senses of sight and sound. Whether living singly (as the sambar do) or in herds (like the chital, nilgai and gaur), they are constantly vigilant as they move, forage or rest. Herd security and leadership is provided by the matriarchs who keep a close watch while the herd is foraging or resting. They constantly shift their muzzle to face the breeze in order to catch scents and funnel their ears in different directions to catch sounds. On apprehension of danger, the first alarm is signalled by stamping a forefoot. If, on further assessment, the danger seems real and imminent, a vocal alarm is sounded. Finally, the matriarch provides the lead and the herd drifts, scampers or bolts. Different species of deer have their distinctive alarm calls, which are heeded by all the prey species. Langur and monkeys, from their strategic position in trees, also constantly observe and notify the presence and movements of predators by calling out in alarm. In order to beat their vigilance, the tiger takes to stalking behind cover, treading silently. It approaches its quarry against the direction of the breeze so as to avoid detection by smell.

A young tigress was once observed sitting on a high rock in a clearing in a sal forest for over half an hour. Hearing the mating call of a chital stag, it became alert and sensed the direction of the call by funnelling its ears, but did not move. When the call was repeated after a couple of minutes, it gently got down from the rock and moved very slowly towards the chital, which were about 100 metres (100 yards) away. Her movements could be discerned only from a slight quivering of the bush. The stag kept calling intermittently. The tigress took 35 minutes to come within 20 metres (20 yards) of the small chital herd. Then, in a split second, in a couple of lightning leaps, she pounced on the stag, killed it instantly and dragged it further into the bush.

On another occasion a limping tigress was offered a tethered buffalo calf to help her survive the temporary disability. The buffalo was walked to within 75 metres (75 yards) of the tigress. It was then tethered to a bush in full view of the tigress. The buffalo, however, remained ignorant of the tiger's presence. As soon as the elephants and the park staff moved away, the tigress who was already on sharp alert, moved in an out-flanking stalk, taking cover of shrubs and grass clumps. Her movements were observed from elephant back. Stretching her body in a low posture her advance was in the slowest possible slow motion, carefully taken silent measured strides, zig-zagging so as to remain in cover. She took more than 20 minutes to cover those 60 metres (60 yards), and when she came to within about 15 metres (15 yards), she waited for almost two minutes behind a grass

clump, the buffalo still oblivious of the tigress's presence. Then in a lightning outburst she was on the buffalo's neck, burying her sharp long canines into it. The buffalo could not even emit a shriek and fell to the ground under the weight of the tigress. She clung to the quarry for well over two minutes, until all movement ceased and the buffalo died of suffocation. The tigress herself was exhausted. She sat panting beside the kill for half an hour, went to take a drink of water and began to feed only an hour later.

A tiger usually takes its quarry from behind, laying its chest on the back of the animal, grabbing the neck in its canines, sometimes

bracing a forearm on the forelimb of the quarry and trying to pull it down by their combined weight. As the prey falters, the tiger usually gives an upward jerk to the neck and is sometimes able to break the spinal cord, killing the prey instantly. Alternatively a common method is to keep the prey pressed under its weight and hold onto its trachea, preventing breathing. Even experienced *shikaris*, having often seen tigers in this posture, believe the tiger to be sucking the blood of its victim. This cannot be true because its long canines and short lips do not allow the tiger, and most other feline and canine predators, to create a vacuum in their mouth to enable them to suck. It is for this reason that all

LEFT: tiger with langur kill, Ranthambhore, Rajasthan.
RIGHT: scratching tree to sharpen claws.

cats and dogs have to lick and lap up water.

The tiger's formidable and sharp retractile claws play a significant role in capturing and holding on to its quarry. A mighty swipe of the huge forearm is sometimes used to stop a fleeing animal or to kill small prey like monkey or pea-fowl. The tiger starts feeding from the rump and hind legs and, as the stomach cavity of its kill is opened, by a neat surgical operation, the tiger removes the intestines and the stomach and then feeds on the fleshy organs in the cavity. It does not feed on the rumen and the viscera. Its rasping tongue enables it to remove flesh from the large bones and proves useful in clean and com-

grove habitat of the Sunderbans, where they feed a lot on fish, sea-turtles and water monitors, in addition to chital and wild pig.

Occasionally the tiger gets a windfall. Once in Kanha, a massive gaur bull easily more than a ton in weight became sedentary, lounging around a water pool in a dry stream bed, foraging on the grass growing there. Its movements were seemingly constrained by old age, as there were no visible signs of disease or injury. For over a fortnight the bull was observed at the pool, its ambit progressively shrinking. Every day, the pugmarks of a young tigress resident in the area were seen in the vicinity. One day,

plete utilization of the food. Depending on the size of its kill, the tiger may feed on it for four to five days, without taking note of the stink of the putrefying meat. By the end, it may have fed on all the flesh, small bones, skin and hair: the hair acts as roughage and helps in digestion.

The tiger's choice of quarry is not chosen by species. It is, rather, by size – the bigger the better. With very large prey, such as the gaur or the buffalo, the tiger goes for the subadults. When a tigress is training her cubs many monkeys and langur are killed – the only form of communal hunting seen among tigers.

Tigers are powerful swimmers and are in full command in the difficult tidal-swamp and man-

from these marks, it was evident that the tigress had even stalked and approached the bull. It was apparent, however, that the tigress was not able to muster up the courage to attack the huge gaur, which might have snorted and scared her away with his formidable horns.

Finally, one evening, the bull became stationary at the edge of the pool and did not move at all even at the passage of vehicles on the road barely five metres (16 ft) from the pool. Early next morning the bull was gone, dragged by the young tigress some 50 metres (50 yards) away into bamboo thickets, up above the two-metre (7 ft) high bank. From the marks on the carcass it was evident that the helpless bull was brought down by hamstringing and was probably dragged up the bank even before it died. After a week, when the kill was abandoned by the tigress and her two six-month-old cubs, there was still plenty of food left for the scavengers. The amazing side of the episode is the evidence it provides of the enormous strength of the tigress – she probably weighed no more than 150 kg (330 lbs) whereas the bull must have weighed over a ton.

A tiger may feed on an average size kill (like chital) for a day or two and then may not hunt for two or three days. It usually hides its kill under cover and tries to remain nearby to protect it from scavengers, particularly vultures who, once they detect it may descend in hordes and polish off the kill in half an hour if the tiger is not around.

Typically, a tiger may kill up to three average-size prey every two weeks or about 80 every year. Depending upon the quality of habitat, a tiger would need a base population of 300 chital-sized animals to sustain itself .

Devoted mothers

Tiger cubs are tiny, blind and helpless when they are born. But a tigress is a loving mother and brings up her cubs with great care and effort. Despite this, usually only two make it to adulthood from a normal litter of six. Until they are about three months old, the cubs are not allowed to trail the mother and food is brought to them. Their lair has to be frequently shifted, because if detected, they may be killed by other predators and scavengers, and even by rival male tigers. They are trained and disciplined to be quiet while the mother is away on hunting errands. A carefully worked-out scheme of vocalization further guides the cubs to lie low or to respond and come out to meet the mother.

The cubs' first lessons in hunting consist of learning to pounce on their mother's tail, which she shifts to dodge them, and playing hide and seek with her. They learn to stalk by searching for mother who hides under cover, and practice by stalking each other. Training hunts take place in bushy cover during daytime, pursuing deer fawns, langurs or monkeys foraging on the ground. The cubs are taught to keep clear of man, the most crafty of all predators.

LEFT: tigers often cool themselves in water and mud.
RIGHT: pugmarks are used for censuses.

A tracker employed in a park once went surveying for water holes during the dry season. As he peered over a pool from a nullah bank, he was charged by a young tiger. The height of the bank allowed him just enough time to scramble up a slanting tree on the bank. From there he could see the young tiger's mother with two more cubs, lying in another pool nearby. The cubs were about a year old and too grown up for the tracker's comfort. The young tiger repeatedly came charging up the thick slanting stem, but could not reach the man. The mother beckoned the cub by calling, and when he did not give up, she got up

and moved towards the cub. Thereupon the young tiger thought it prudent to obey and joined his mother. All four then disappeared into the bush and the man safely walked back to the park headquarters to recount the tale, which was verified from clear pugmarks on the ground and claw marks on the tree stem.

Territory

Social organization among tigers varies with the quality of habitat in a given area, the determinant of quality being the relative abundance of prey and optimum hunting cover. In a high prey-density area, the territorial definition of land tenures is prominent. In such an area, the dominant males occupy very extensive territories, as large as 50–100 sq km (20–40 sq miles). Up to three or even five females may occupy mutually exclusive sub-territories within a large male territory. The females in such an organization are assured of food supply for themselves and their progeny and, in return, owe allegiance to the territorial male. This also affords protection to their cubs from rival males as the territorial male meticulously demarcates and jealously guards his territory against rivals. Such a high prey-density area in a region thus serves as the main natal area with most of the breeding taking place there.

Moving radially away from the natal area, as the prey-density declines, the territorial definition also becomes less rigid.

The young cubs stay under the care of the mother for anything from 1½ to 2½ years, whereafter they are compelled to leave the natal area. But a young tiger is seldom able to find a place in the adjacent medium-prey-density areas because of their firm occupation by either the past-prime adults recently thrown out from the natal area, or the pre-prime adults preparing to find a foothold there.

Thus a young tiger dispersing from the natal area may be required to travel far and may, in fact, remain transient in the low-prey-density peripheral area for a long time. If contiguous tiger habitats are available, such a dispersing sub-adult may never return to its natal area and may in fact join another nearby population, thus ensuring the exchange of genes so essential to the viability of the population of a long-ranging, major predator like the tiger.

Males demarcate their territory by spraying scent with their urine on prominent trees on their territorial boundaries. They also often deposit their scent on the underside of the drooping branches of low bushes. This way the scent lasts longer, preserved from excessive evaporation or from being washed away by rain. Another and simultaneous way of marking territory is to make scrapes on the ground and tree trunks with the paws and then to deposit a foul-smelling secretion from the anal gland. These markings are intelligible to the other tigers and are recognized. Territorial integrity is further maintained by frequent patrolling.

The females also mark their territories in the same manner, but not as frequently or meticulously. The intensity of scent markings by a female becomes very high when she is in oestrus and ready to have a mate. Her physiological condition is advertised by this scent and helps attract the males. The courtship period usually spreads over a week or 10 days, but the actual mating period may be only two to three days, during which copulation is frequent. Such prolonged association of the courting pair is necessary among cats in whom ovulation is promoted by frequent copulation.

The gestation period in the case of the tiger is short, being about 105 days. Because the tigress, even during the terminal days of her pregnancy, has to hunt for herself, nature has ensured that her pregnancy does not disable her from doing so. It is for this reason that the gestation period is so short, the fetal size at birth small, and the stage of development of the cubs, when they are born, rather low. In order to provide against likely losses in rearing from this low developmental stage at birth, the litter size tends to be large – sometimes up to six cubs.

Both the males and the females occupying the natal area are prime members of a population. This ensures that only the best animals of both

LEFT: unlike many cats, tigers are not averse to water and are good swimmers.
RIGHT: a family outing in Ranthambore.

sexes are able to breed. Expectedly, therefore, confrontations take place among dominant tigers, particularly males, in order to establish supremacy and possess a territory. Such confrontations may range from a skirmish to a serious fight, depending upon the match between the contenders. All-out fights are by no means uncommon and very serious and deep wounds may be sustained. Such grievous wounds may not heal and may eventually cause death after a few days or even weeks.

However, tigers are generally able to heal all their wounds by licking them. Where direct licking is not possible, they manage to reach the conventional method. No canine marks were seen on the neck or the nape of the carcass. It appeared that the smaller male had intruded into the territory of the larger male in the belief that the latter was away from the intruded segment of its territory. Nevertheless, the presence of the smaller male was probably advertised to the territorial male by the alarm calls of langur or the deer and this alerted the territorial male and brought him out in search of the intruder. Suddenly confronted with the territorial male, the intruder may have offered submission, which the territorial master was not magnanimous enough to accept. He probably took the intruder

spots and apply saliva by first depositing it on one of the limbs, usually a forearm, and then wiping the injury with the limb. It is those injuries on which saliva cannot be applied and those that are too deep and grievous, that prove fatal. Usually, in the natal area a wounded tiger may be helped by another tiger, a mate by its mate and a mother by her young.

In one case, a huge territorial male was observed over the carcass of an only slightly smaller male he had killed in an encounter. The former cannibalized and persisted on the kill for four days, in much the same manner as he might persist over a herbivore kill. The intriguing aspect was that the killing was not made by the by surprise by holding his head between his powerful forearms and twisting his neck with a vicious jerk, snapping the spinal cord.

Even subadult males are not tolerated and there have been numerous other recorded instances of half-grown cubs having been killed and partly eaten by the territorial male. Tigers are also known to kill and eat leopards. However, such internecine fights should not be regarded as being in quest of food, even though the killed animals may have been eaten. It should also not cause excessive worry in terms of loss of a member of a rare and endangered species. In nature, this is the only means of auto-regulation of the population of a supreme predator.

Cattle-lifters and man-eaters

Tigers are often maligned for their aberrant behavior, reflected in their lifting cattle and sometimes killing and eating people. Though such behavior cannot be tolerated, invariably it is disturbance or damage to the tiger or its habitat that induces or compels it to act in such a manner. As already mentioned, the tiger, by training and instinct learns to avoid man. However, when a wildlife habitat is degraded, causing a reduction in the population of natural prey, tigers are driven to occasionally taking cattle. This may lead to conflict between humans and tiger and there may be situations when, while

being chased away from a livestock kill, a hungry tiger launches an attack on people to prevent such deprivation. A few such instances may embolden a tiger to take to man-killing and man-eating. Also, there are sometimes attempts by people to avenge livestock killing by shooting at tigers. Often such attempts only end in wounding or injuring a tiger who, partly out of vengeance, and partly because of its inability to kill free-ranging wild prey because of the injury, instead goes for cattle or even humans.

The Government of India has permitted destruction of proven man-eaters, while providing compensation to owners of the cattle killed – although this is so badly administered that WWF

have set up their own livestock compensation schemes. At the same time, attempts are underway to rehabilitate habitats for the tiger both in the protected as well as in other forest areas.

Identification

Each tiger has a pattern of stripes and facial markings unique to itself and individuals can thus be identified. While such identifications by visual or photographic confirmation are usually employed in long-term behavioral studies in a given area to great advantage, counting tigers by this method is not practicable in large areas. The tiger's partiality to cover, its nocturnal habits, unpredictable movements and generally secretive behaviour do not allow repeated sightings or photography, especially of all individuals in an area. The standard and practical method of counting tigers is to identify individuals by their pugmarks .

Features in a pugmark – the shape and relative size of the right, left or bottom lobe of the pad, the top edge of the pad, the relative sizes and placings of the toes with respect to the pad and several other features vary – from tiger to tiger. An individual can be identified from a study of a combination of these features unique to itself, ascertained replicably, from frequent tracings of pugmarks recorded in the field.

Important statutory, regulatory and restorative measures have benefited a host of species and their habitats in a number of tiger reserves, national parks and sanctuaries. Some of the best places to see the tiger are Kanha and Bandhavgarh in Madhya Pradesh and Corbett and Dudhwa in Uttar Pradesh. Other unique tiger habitats with a fair chance of encountering one on excursion are Manas and Kaziranga in Assam and Nagarahole and Bandipur in Karnataka.

Nepal's Royal Chitwan National Park is a fine example of tiger conservation in action, but during recent years of conflict between Maoist insurgents and government troops Bardia National Park lost many of its tigers and rhinos.

Family meal

An account of a night-long observation, in the light of a full moon, of a tigress caring for her young would be an apt epilogue to this essay on the tiger. A well-hidden sambar kill by a tigress

LEFT: the eye of the tiger.
RIGHT: resting after a meal.

was located along a nullah in Kanha. A makeshift, thatch hideout was erected across the nullah, about 50 metres (50 yards) from the bush where the sambar carcass was lying hidden. Nothing remarkable happened until two hours after dark, when the copious chital alarm calls signified the approach of a predator. The tigress appeared in the nullah bed some 15 minutes later, leading towards the kill. After inspecting her kill, she sat alongside the bush for another 15 minutes – a picture of beauty, moonlight glinting in her bright eyes – apparently assessing the security environment for her cubs. She then rose and disappeared into the forest. An hour and a

nudging her to take them to the kill. The tigress then went inside the bush and dragged the kill out and took a few bites, not so much as to feed but to expose fresh tender flesh for the cubs to eat. The cubs fed on the carcass for about 15 minutes whereafter the tigress again helped them, by opening up fresh meat. After a little while, the cubs having satiated themselves came to the mother. She licked them as if demonstrating to them how to clean themselves.

The cubs then indulged in a bit of cleaning by themselves. Later they became very playful and the three engaged in a mutual display of affection by licking and rubbing each other's

half later, sambar and barking deer alarms were heard in the distance. The tigress reappeared on the scene in another half an hour and patrolled the nullah bed up and down for about 15 minutes. Then, standing near the bush where the sambar carcass lay, she gave two short, low calls. Presently came an equally short and muted response, apparently from the cubs. The tigress then again went into the forest and reappeared at the edge 10 minutes later. Having reassured herself after a brief survey of the scene she beckoned the cubs by a barely audible call.

Two very young cubs, the size of a large domestic cat, came out and skirted around the mother, rubbing themselves on her flanks, as if

bodies. The mother would beat her tail from one point to the other and the cubs would pounce on it and try to grab it. Occasionally the cubs would come up on the low branches of the trees on the bank and then jump down into the sand below. Such play went on for most of the night. In the early hours, the tigress herself fed on the carcass for over an hour and intermittently the cubs joined her. At least an hour before sunrise, the tigress disappeared into the jungle with the cubs, and until sunrise there was nothing more to it. As the morning sun peeped over the tree line, the moist sand in the nullah provided evidence in its markings of the love of a devoted mother for her offspring. ❑

LIONS, LEOPARDS AND WILD CATS

*Besides the tiger, India is home to the Asiatic lion, the snow leopard
and over a dozen other large and lesser cats*

The Indian or **Asiatic Lion** (*Panthera leo persica*) is the lion that has figured in history, distributed as it was within historic times from Southern Greece in the northwest to Palamau, Bihar, in India in the east. Separated from the African lion and the extinct Barbary lion by the breadth of the Sahara, the Indian, West Asian or the Persian lion (the common name depending on its area of occurrence) disappeared by the beginning of the 20th century from all areas of its distribution except the Gir Forest in Saurashtra, Gujarat. The disappearance of open grass and scrub forestlands under the plough, the increase in pastoralism, better arms for the hunter and the subsidence of political turbulence and settlement of human communities throughout its erstwhile range of distribution were the main causes of its wide-ranging extinction.

The Asiatic lion is a shaggier creature than the more well-known African lion and a distinct belly fold is invariably present. The coat and the belly fringe are denser, and the elbow and tail tuft longer. Typically, males weigh 150–225 kg. In size, the average measurements compare favourably with that of the African lion. The record Indian lion measured, nose to tail-tip, 2.92 metres (9 ft 7 in) as against the 3.23 metres (10 ft 7 in) for the African lion. However, the Indian lions measured are from a tiny fraction of territory when compared with the extensive range of the African lion.

Though in general habits and behaviour the Indian lion differs little from the African, there is one significant difference that is perhaps the key to the survival of the small population presently living in the Gir Forest. This vital behavior pattern is the tolerance of humans by the Indian lion. During the several decades that lions and people have lived together in the forests of the Gir there have been remarkably few willful instances of aggression by the lion. Although they avoid inhabited areas during the day they are remarkably fearless of humans and

will permit their near approach before moving off with dignity. Living with the lions in the Gir are the Maldhari and Rabbari herders of cattle and buffaloes whose *ness* or settlements bear a close resemblance to African settlements, with their thorn bomas to keep lions out. Lions live largely on the cattle of these forest villag-

es rather than the wild ungulates such as the sambar, chital, nilgai and wild pig. They also take whatever they can kill including goats and camels. The Gir lion is a gregarious creature and prides often hunt in concert to separate and drive the selected prey to other members of the pride lying in ambush.

Males often live in pairs, the association usually one of long standing; instances are known of such pairs being seen together for several years. The Indian lion has not been sufficiently studied to understand the territorial system occuring among the prides. During the day, the lions lie in cover near a water hole or stream or in the shade of spreading banyan trees or within the dense

---

LEFT: the elusive snow leopard.
RIGHT: lion family at pool.

cover provided by the evergreen Carissa, which stand out in summer as islands of green in the starkly desolate forest of bare and gaunt trees. They come out to hunt at dusk, skulking near the outskirts of the villages as the cattle are driven home, to try and pick a stray cow or buffalo. Often the male spends much of the night roaring. The females are much more circumspect. Lions, however, are noisy animals, especially when mating. October and November are the main mating months and the cubs are born in January and February.

THE NATIONAL ANIMAL

The lion was once the national animal of India and still continues to be a national animal from its presence on the nation's crest, the Lions of Ashoka.

lions to the verge of extinction and it was believed that not more than 20 existed.

The Nawab's government then placed a strict ban on shooting, which was enforced rigidly. At a much later date a limited quota of never more than three in a year were permitted to be shot at the discretion of the Nawab. The protection measures were wonderfully successful and the number of lions increased to a remarkable extent. A census held recently indicate that Gir holds a population of approximately 350 lions. However,

The Gir is the last home of the Asiatic lion and is itself a relict, being the only patch of extensive forest in the Saurashtra Peninsula. As the only forest of any extent in Saurashtra, it is of considerable importance not only as the home of the lion but also for its effects on the climate and water table of the surrounding districts.

By the beginning of the 20th century the Indian lion had already been driven to the Gir Forest, situated in the princely state of Junagadh before India became independent. Without any doubt the continued survival of lions is due to the protection given to them by the Nawabs of Junagadh. At the end of the 19th century, poaching and uncontrolled shooting had brought the

having the entire population in a single, now overcrowed, location leaves them vulnerable to inbreeding and disease outbreaks. A proposal to relocate a small number to Kuno wildlife park in Madhya Pradesh has been resisted by the Gujarat government's proprietory politics. A new lion sanctuary at Jesar hills in the Bhavnagar-Amreli forests looks set to go ahead however.

The Leopard

The **leopard or panther** *(Panthera pardus)* is probably the most successful model of a predator. The known distribution within recent times was enormous, covering the whole of Asia from Asia Minor to the Caucasus to Manchuria and Amurland and reaching south to the islands of Indonesia and almost the whole of Africa south of the Sahara. That it is still not uncommon over a substantial portion of this range is a testimonial to the survival capability of the leopard. It is thought to have evolved earlier than the lion and the tiger and, like them, moved into India from the north. Fossil remains have been recovered from central and southern Europe. It obviously entered India well before the tiger and before Sri Lanka separated from the mainland as it occurs there too.

In size, leopards are considerably smaller than the lion and the tiger, the largest male hardly exceeding 2.36 m (7 ft 9 in) in total length with a

black ear. The pattern of the coat consists of solid black spots on the head and upper neck, outer side of the limbs and belly. Elsewhere rosettes of varying size occur. In some areas, notably in the high-rainfall areas of the Western Ghats and eastern India, black (melanistic) leopards are not uncommon. Cubs of the normal and 'black' form may occur in the same litter. White leopards also occur although they are very rare.

Although the habitats differ, the habits of the leopard throughout its range are more or less the same. The most successful and adaptive of the larger cats, the leopard lives in all types of habitats from open country with rocky outcrops

maximum weight of about 80 kg (179 lbs). The female is much smaller in length and weight, 30 cm (12 in) less in total length and about 34 kg (75 lbs) less in weight. The wide distribution and the ability to adapt to different environments has resulted in several races of the leopard being described from different habitats. Among these are six sub-species from the Indian subcontinent.

The coat and colour of the leopard are distinctive. The ground colour is of varying shades of greyish or whitish buff, the underside of the body white, with a white patch on the otherwise

LEFT: lioness on the prowl.
ABOVE: the more widespread leopard, Ranthambore

to thick forests. The environs of villages and even the environs of large cities such as Mumbai (if it has a forest nearby) hold leopards. They have adapted to people's habits and, though they live on their domestic stock, remain invisible to the untrained and searching eye.

Catholic in diet, they eat anything they can kill, from crabs to cattle, and can be a pest in the neighbourhood of villages and towns, living on domestic stock and being particularly fond of dogs. Monkeys are another favourite food and are often killed as they panic and seek safety on the ground. For its size, the leopard is quite powerful and often carries its prey up a tree to store, probably to prevent other stronger predators from appropriating the kill. Apart from humans, the leopard's natural enemies are other carnivores such as the tiger, wild dog and hyena. There are instances of leopards being killed and eaten by python and the mugger crocodile. Leopards are a deadlier menace than the tiger when they become man-eaters, particularly from their greater boldness and knowledge of the habits of people.

The call of the leopard heard, more often during the breeding season, is distinctive, being three or four short bark-like roars very like the sound that a saw makes on wood. Leopards breed right through the year. The pairs stay together up to and after the cubs (two to four in number) are

small ones as it can neither roar nor purr. An exclusively high-altitude cat, it rarely descends below 2,130 metres (7,000 ft) in winter and in summer frequents the fringes of the snow line, the pasture area of its normal prey: the wild goats and sheep of the Himalaya. It is smaller in size than the leopard of the plains, hardly exceeding 2 metres (6 ft 8 in) in total length but has perhaps the most beautiful coat among the cats. It is gray above with a buff or cream tint, and has grey-centred black rosettes on the body and spots on the head. In winter the coat is dense and the tail bushy. The male's head is usually much squarer and wider than the female's and

born. The gestation period is slightly over three months. The Indian leopard (*Panthera pardus fusca*) is now a protected species in India, largely to protect it from the commercial exploitation of its skin by the fur trade.

Other Cats

The **snow leopard** (*Uncia uncia*), the grey ghost of the snows, occurs along the length of the Himalaya from Kashmir to Arunachal Pradesh. Previously classified in the genus *Panthera* with several of the other largest felids, it was recently placed in its own genus, *Uncia*. Along with the Snow Leopard, it represents an intermediate between so-called big cats and

the high position of the eyes on the head permits it to peep over a rock without exposing itself to its alert natural prey of bharal and ibex. Its habits are little known.

The breeding season is in spring and two to four cubs form a litter. The pelt of the snow leopard is in high demand and poaching, prey-species hunting and retaliatory killings for livestock predation have made the species endangered.

The **clouded leopard** (*Neofelis nebulosa*) is a wide-ranging species being distributed from Nepal in the west to south China and south and east to Borneo. However, it is still a rare and little-known species. A dark grey or ochre-coloured cat, it is marked with bold-black or dark-grey blotched patches giving a clouded pattern and hence the popular name. The face has the cheek stripes seen among many of the smaller cats. It is equal in size to a small leopard, measuring up to 2 metres (6 ft 8 in) in total length and weighs up to 20.5 kg (45 lbs). A feature peculiar to the clouded leopard is the proportionately enormous development of the upper canines, which present the nearest approach among the living cats to the massive teeth of the extinct sabre-toothed tiger. An inhabitant of dense forests, it is supposed to live on prey up to the size of the smaller deer. Nothing has been recorded of its breeding habits in the wild but it has been bred in captivity.

The **marbled cat** *(Felis marmorata)* is widely -distributed but elusive and little-known cat of eastern India, ranging in distribution from Nepal to Borneo. The marbled cat, as its name implies, has a marbled coat pattern made up of dark blotches more or less lined with black. The face has the usual cheek stripes. The general body colour varies from gray to earthy or yellowish-brown of varying intensity; white or tawny below. It is slightly larger than a domestic cat, being about 1 metre (3 ft) in total length, half of which is the tail. The marbled cat is a forest animal, at home in trees, and feeds on small mammals and birds.

The **golden cat** *(Felis temmincki)* has a peculiar distribution, one species occurring in the west and central African forests, and another from the forests of Nepal to South China, Sumatra and Java. The colour of the coat varies from dark brown to red to nearly gray with a distinct stripe pattern on the cheeks. About 1.22 metres (4 ft) in total length, including a comparatively short tail, it is next in size to the clouded leopard. It is a forest and hill-area cat of eastern India capable of killing animals up to the size of small deer. Not often spotted, little is known of its habits.

LEFT: clouded leopard in a tree.
ABOVE: the rare leopard cat, Dachigam, Kashmir.

The **lynx** *(Felix lynx)* is primarily a cat of the palaearctic zoogeographic region, the fringes of which extend into India in Kashmir and the Western Himalaya. The Himalayan race, also occurs in Outer Mongolia, North China and the Russian Pamirs. Other sub-species occur in the tundra and boreal zones of Europe and North America. The lynx is a medium-sized cat with a very short tail and powerfully developed legs. The Himalayan sub-species is pale *isabelline* in colour, lacks a pattern of spots and, unlike in other races, the pads of its feet are not covered by hair in winter. The ears are pointed and tufted as in the caracal and the lower cheek has a fringe of long hairs. The body length is about 85 cm (34 in) and it stands about 50 cm (20 in) at the shoulder. It weighs about 16 kg (35 lbs). An uncommon animal, the Himalayan lynx is a resourceful hunter and feeds on a variety of prey ranging from young ibex to voles. It has an unusual habit for a cat: hiding or burying for future use portions of the prey it cannot eat at a sitting. The young are born in late spring or early summer, the gestation period being about two months. The litter size varies from two to four.

The **fishing cat** *(Prionailurus viverrina)* is a stocky, medium-sized cat with a tail shorter than its head and body length – 80 cm (31 in) body plus 30 cm (12 in) tail. The general body colour

The **leopard cat** *(Prionailurus bengalensis)* is more widely distributed than the three small cats described above, occurring as it does throughout the whole of Southeast Asia, from Baluchistan in the west to Manchuria and Korea in the north to Borneo and the Philippines in the south. The leopard cat looks like a miniature replica of its namesake; spots of black replacing the rosettes. The ground colour varies from whitish, creamish-white buff, ochre-buff to ashy grey. It is about the size of a domestic cat, being just under 60 cm (2 ft) in total length, more than half of which is the tail. A forest cat, it is not uncommon. It feeds largely on birds and small mammals, and in

varies from dark olivaceous-tawny with gray flanks to nearly ashy-grey. The stripes on the nape and head, and the spots on the body and base of the tail, and the bands on the tail, are black. Widely distributed in Southeast Asia, it prefers marshy habitats and its distribution is therefore patchy. In the Indian subcontinent it occurs in the Indus Delta, Keoladeo National Park at Bharatpur, Rajasthan, coastal backwaters, estuaries and swamps of the southern maritime states and of West Bengal. It is very adept at fishing and is also powerful enough to kill sheep, calves, dogs and large snakes. The litter is usually of two kittens. The cat apparently does not have a fixed breeding season.

the vicinity of forest villages is an inveterate poultry-stealer. The young, three to four in a litter, are born in the first half of the year. Its beautiful coat is a coveted item for the illegal fur trade.

The **rusty-spotted cat** *(Felis rubiginosa)* is closely related to the leopard cat but is smaller in size and has no markings on the tail. The spots on the body are ferruginous and the ground-colour is fawn-grey. This cat was thought to be peculiar to south peninsular India with a subspecies in Sri Lanka. Recently is has been reported from Kashmir. It frequents fairly open country as well as forests. An excellent climber, it feeds on birds and small mammals and is known to take poultry. A litter consists of two or three kittens born in the hollow of a tree or in a cave or burrow among rocks.

The **desert cat** *(Felis silvestris ornata)* is believed to be one of the progenitors of domestic cats. Slightly larger in size than the domestic cat, the average size is about 50 cm (20 in) in body length with a 25-cm (10-in) tail, and it is about 30 cm (12 in) in height at the shoulder. The general body colour is yellowish with distinct black spots; the tail is banded with black distally. The desert cat is a sub-species of African wild cat that is widely distributed in Africa, and southwestern and Central Asia to North India. In India it occurs in the deserts of Ladakh and Rajasthan and the drier areas of Kathiawar. It has been reported as far south as Puné.

Adapted to life in desert conditions, it is nocturnal and spends the day in burrows it has dug, emerging at dusk to hunt. It lives largely on rodents, but when necessary can subsist on insects and reptiles. The gestation period is about six weeks and a litter is of two to three kittens. The female alone cares and fends for the young.

The **jungle cat** *(Felis chaus)* differs from the cats so far described in being longer in the leg, and with a short tail. It is widely distributed, ranging from the Caucasus to the Middle East and Mediterranean, North Africa through Iran to the Indian subcontinent and Sri Lanka, and through Myanmar to Indo-China. There is a distinct spinal crest of hairs and a small pencil or tuft of hairs on the ears. The general body-colour is gray to tawny to deep brown. Ear tips may be black. The two stripes on the foreleg are distinctive.

Three races have been described from India. In size they range up to 75 cm (2 ft 6 in) in body length with a tail half the length. The maximum weight recorded is 9 kg (19.8 lbs). It is most adaptable and occurs in habitats ranging from the vicinity of human dwellings to the densest forest. It often hunts during the day and is a swift and powerful predator, being exceedingly strong for its size. Though catholic in diet, it lives largely on small mammals and birds. It breeds during the early months of the year. Three to four kittens form a litter and the coats of these young ones are faintly spotted.

The **caracal** *(Felis caracal)* is a handsome, lithe, graceful, medium-sized cat occurring throughout Africa, except in forested areas, and

from the Middle East to northern India. The colour varies from pale sandy-fawn to reddish brown or dark gray. The pointed ears are black above, frosted with white, white on the inside, and with pencils or tufts of black and gray hairs. Its tail is short, about 22 cm (9 in), its body length is about 74 cm (29 in) and its shoulder-height is about 40–45 cm (16–18 in). It weighs up to 18 kg (40 lbs). Incredibly agile, it is able to knock over several birds from a flock of pigeons that it has charged and is capable of killing animals up to the size of gazelles. The caracal breeds once a year but has no fixed breeding season. Litter sizes vary from two to six. Caracals

when taken young are easily tamed and they used to be trained for hunting in the past.

Pallas cat or **Manul** *(Felis manul)* is a small one, about the size of the domestic cat, and is peculiar to the arid high altitudes of Ladakh in India. Elsewhere it occurs in Pakistan and Central Asia. Its appearance is distinctive, the head being flat with widely spaced ears. The fur is dense and soft with a grizzled appearance and the tail black-tipped and banded. The face is strikingly marked as if wearing a bandit's mask of black and white. Little is known of the habits of this high-altitude desert cat. It is said to live on the mouse-hare, rodents and ground-dwelling birds and its call to resemble the yelping bark of a small dog. ❑

LEFT: the fishing cat is rarely seen.
RIGHT: jungle cats are found throughout India.

THE ASIAN ELEPHANT

*The king of the forest, the Asian elephant is the
most intelligent and also the most dangerous of Indian wildlife*

Zoologists put the elephant in the order Proboscidea, the natural group of animals with a proboscis or trunk as their distinguishing physical feature. Delving back into Earth's history, scientists have identified 352 members of this order that now survive in two genera, each represented by a single species, the African elephant *(Loxodonta africana)* and the Asian or Indian elephant *(Elephas maximus)*.

While the African elephant has at least one recognized subspecies, there is no unanimity among specialists on the question of subspecies of the Asian elephant. According to one taxonomic classification, the forma typica for the Asian animal is the Sri Lankan species; and there are three subspecies of the animal, one found in Sri Lanka, one on the Asian mainland extending to Myanmar and adjoining territories, and one in Sumatra. Some would find a fourth subspecies in West Malaysia. However, scientists working in the field in Sri Lanka did not find any significant morphological difference between the Sri Lankan and the mainland elephants. Recent gene study found that elephants in Southern India evolved into two genetically distinct groups thousands of years ago.

The Asian elephant is smaller than its African relatives, and is most easily distinguished from them by its smaller ears and more arched back. Asian elephants have one semi-prehensile 'finger' at the tip of their trunk as opposed to two, plus four nails on each hind foot instead of three, and 19 pairs of ribs instead of 21. Female Asian elephants, unlike their African counterparts, lack tusks. Some males may also lack tusks and are known as *makhnas*. The forehead has two hemispherical bulges unlike the flat front of the African.

To most people, particularly from the West, the elephant and India are inseparable. For an Indian, the elephant is a part of history, tradition, myth and culture and, in many outlying areas, very much a part of the way of life. In northern Bihar and eastern Uttar Pradesh it is still the most coveted status symbol among the landed gentry; in South India there is no temple of any importance without its elephant; for some peoples in Arunachal Pradesh in northeast India, it is just another domesticated ani-

mal, which lives as a part of the household, serving its owner in many capacities, including that of a plough-animal.

It is difficult to say exactly when the art of capturing and training the wild elephant was mastered in India. Elephants have been in the service of humans in India For at least 3,000 years yet most of these animals have been taken from the wild and subsequently tamed and trained to serve people. They have seldom been bred for the purpose of developing a domestic strain. This is where the elephant is unique and different from all other domesticated varieties of animals and birds. A certain number of calves are born to domesticated cow

LEFT: up close with a young elephant.
RIGHT: a large bull elephant is an impressive sight.

animals living in forest conditions, usually but not exclusively sired by wild bulls; but their number is insignificant, at least in India, compared to the number captured from the wild. In fact, in India, animals taken from the wild are preferred to those born in captivity, as the former have a better temper and are more amenable to training.

There is enough evidence to suggest that, historically, the elephant had a very wide distribution in India. During the Indus Valley civilization (3rd to 2nd millennium BC) when, as available evidence suggests, the western part of the subcontinent had not yet been desertified, el-

Central India (in Orissa, Bihar and the adjoining southern part of West Bengal); North India (in the sub-Himalayan tracts of Uttar Pradesh); and northeast India (in Arunachal Pradesh, Assam, Meghalaya, Mizoram, Nagaland, Tripura and the northern part of West Bengal; a few come into Manipur from Myanmar seasonally).

Apart from India, Nepal and Sri Lanka, wild elephants are found in Bangladesh, Burma, China, Indonesia, Cambodia, Laos, Malaysia (including Sabah), Thailand and Vietnam. In Nepal, the few elephants that survive keep to the sub-Himalayan belt of forests. In Sri Lanka

ephants were probably very common all over the land, barring the higher reaches of the Himalaya and the coastal salt-water mangrove swamps. Even in the Himalaya, evidence of casual visits by elephants has been noticed at a height of 3,200 metres (10,500 ft) in recent times.

Today, the Asian elephant is considered an endangered species. The distribution of wild elephant in India is limited to four widely separate geographical zones: South India (in Kerala, Karnataka and Tamil Nadu; recently a small group has found its way into Andhra Pradesh, much to the amazement and understandable consternation of the local people who had never seen a wild elephant before);

they are confined mostly to the forests of the eastern and northern provinces.

This fragmentation of the once-compact geographical range of the elephant in the subcontinent (Pakistan has no elephants) is a direct result of drastic shrinkage of habitat. Elephants make large demands on their environment, an adult animal of average size consuming something like 200 kg (450 lbs) of green fodder a day, and probably wasting an equal amount in the process. A degraded habitat, therefore, cannot sustain elephant.

ABOVE: a herd of elephants, Periyar.
RIGHT: inquistitive youngsters.

Indicators of ecological health

The elephant has few natural enemies. Calves are jealously guarded by their mothers and tigers seldom have the opportunity to take them. Even more rare, but not unknown, are instances of adult animals being attacked and killed by tiger. But these cases are noteworthy only because of their rarity. Lesser predators like the leopard, do not, of course, count in the context of the elephant. By and large, therefore, the elephant is truly an apex species, indicators of the health of their habitat, mostly tropical forests, but also some limited areas of subtropical forests.

ings is about four years. On the other hand, it is a long-living animal. The first calf is generally born to a female elephant around the age of 14 or 15 years. Instances of much younger cows calving are not unknown. And they can go on calving till the age of 60 or more. The longevity of the elephant in the wild is largely a matter of conjecture. The average life-expectancy of a healthy animal is assumed to be around 70 to 80 years.

The long reproductive period of the female of the species is a cushion against temporary setbacks suffered by a population due to natural calamities like extreme drought con-

A habitat that is good for the elephant is also good for its associate species, the sambar deer *(Cervus unicolor)*, the spotted deer *(Axis axis Erxleben)*, the barking deer *(Muntiacus muntjak)*, and so on, which in their turn keep predators like the tiger or the leopard happy. When the forest is good for these animals, the ecosystem is thriving, which means the water-regime is right, and so also is the condition of the soil; it is, therefore, also good for the environment in general.

The elephant is a slow-growing species: the gestation period is between 19–21 months. Given the best living conditions, it has been estimated that the interval between two calv-

ditions (not a common happening in those Indian forests where the elephant now survives),
or epidemic diseases like anthrax. This long life-expectancy combined with the fact that elephants are extremely adaptable in their preference of habitat – they thrive in all kinds of tropical forests except in dry scrubland and desert (which do not put off the African elephant), and salt-water mangrove – helps to explain why they have managed to survive despite a massive destruction of their habitat. The latest estimate of their number in the wild for the whole of India is between 10,000–14,000, which shows some reduction

on previous estimates. Sri Lanka has an estimated wild elephant population of 2,500, and Nepal of about 50.

The elephant's is a matriarchal society. The leader of a group is a female, usually the oldest, the largest, and the wisest of the lot. This is also called the family group, which consists of a nucleus of two or three mature cows, subadult animals still moving with their mothers, and calves. The basic unit consists of a cow with its unweaned calf. The size of such a family group can vary from three to 10 or more in number.

Sometimes, in some particular season, especially when elephant are on the march,

the African elephant than previously, thanks to the research of Iain Douglas-Hamilton and others since the 1960s. We still lack such quantified research data for the Asian species. It seems, however, that the same group-behaviour pattern prevails for both the African and the Asian species. As with the African animal, the adult male of the Asian species seems to lead a free, unattached existence, sometimes forming loose 'bachelor parties' of their own, called *maljuria* in northeast India. An adult male goes into a herd when a cow comes into oestrus, and leaves the group when the period of mating, which can last from a week to 15 days or more, is over.

moving from one area of forest to another, several family groups come together to form what can be termed a "herd". They usually split up into smaller units once they settle down in any particular area for foraging. One such famous elephant herd in Manas Tiger Reserve in Assam numbers more than 140 animals. Subadult male animals, when they approach adulthood, are expelled from the group. This is taken to be nature's protection against inbreeding.

The nature of the relationship of mature old bulls of reproductive age to these family groups is a matter that has caused controversy. We now know a lot more about the social behavior of

Ivory, through the ages, has been coveted by humans. This has made the species peculiarly vulnerable in our era of modern firearms. Fortunately, the female of the Asian species, unlike its African counterpart, does not carry ivory, and a good percentage of the male elephants in northeast India are tuskless (called *makna* locally) and hence do not attract ivory-poachers. This is not true of the forests of the south, where poachers have killed a considerable number of elephants for their ivory. Incidences of poaching and ivory seizures have increased noticeably since 2002, when the CITES-member governments reopened the international ivory trade of stockpiled ivory from Botswana, Namibia and South Africa.

How big do they come? There is no currently accepted standard of judging the size of an elephant except by its height. The traditional method of measuring the height of an elephant, following the practice with horses, is at the withers. The average height of an African male elephant is around 3.20 metres (10 ft 6 in) at the withers, the very tall reaching 3.65 metres (12 ft) or even slightly more. An exceptionally large Asian male animal may be as tall as 3 metres (10 ft). The average height of the adult Asian female elephant is 2.43–2.59 metres (8 ft–8 ft 6 in).

> **CAPTIVE ANIMAL**
>
> Of the estimated 40,000 Asian elephants in the world, approximately 13,500 are tame elephants in Asia; Europe and North America also have 700 each.

Elephants "Never Forget"

How intelligent is the animal? Many tantalizing stories circulate about the alleged sagacity of the beast, and extravagant claims are sometimes made regarding its intelligence. Most experienced naturalists dismiss these claims. However, of all animals in the service of man, this is the only one that continues to be taken from the wild. Its ability to learn quickly is proverbial. A really well-trained animal can respond to about 40 command words. Tool-use is supposed to indicate intelligence. That elephants scratch themselves with sticks which help them to reach inaccessible areas of their body is well-known. Recently it was observed that elephants were breaking down electric fences with branches of trees, often collected from some distance away, seemingly specifically for the purpose.

The elephant's long memory is probably not just a tall yarn. There is an authentic account of a tusker running away to the forest, and then returning to its stall four years later, not having forgotten in the meanwhile a single one of the 40-odd command words it had been taught in its years of domestication.

Which is the most dangerous animal in the Indian forests? Barring such aberrant and unusual creatures as the man-eating tiger or leopard, undoubtedly it is the elephant. Docile zoo animals or circus animals performing tricks can give a very false impression of the animal in its natural state. Unquestionably, it is the King of the Forest, before whom all animals,

including humans, must give way. Not surprisingly, Kipling made Hathi (elephant) the keeper of the law of the jungle at a time of exceptional stress, a terrible drought, and made Sher Khan the tiger slink away from its wrath after attempting some petty transgressions. There is nothing more magnificent (and more dangerous) in the forests of India, nothing that will give a greater thrill, than an encounter on foot with a lone 3-metre (10-foot) tusker in full musth (an elephant with its temporal glands secreting,

when the male elephant tends to become psychologically unbalanced and, sometimes, aggressive).

A good photograph of an elephant in the wild is worth the time and patience (and caution) it demands: the Asian elephant is largely a forest-dwelling animal and one has to be lucky to see it in the open in good photographic light. In July–September in Lahugala, one can see as many as 100 elephants or more grazing out in the open. In India, wild elephants can be seen in Manas *(Assam)*, Dalma and Palamau *(Bihar)*, Bandipur and Nagarahole *(Karnataka)*, Periyar *(Kerala)*, Mudumalai *(Tamil Nadu)* and Corbett *(Uttar Pradesh)*. ❑

LEFT: a herd of elephants playing in water, Bandipur Wildlife Sanctuary.
RIGHT: elephant calf.

THE INDIAN RHINO

The rhino family's origins stretch back 60 million years,
but the last century has brought the Asian rhino to near-extinction

One misty morning in Chitwan National Park, southern Nepal, a magnificent male rhinoceros feeds nonchalantly in a lake. Occasionally, he submerges almost completely as he grazes on aquatic plants on the lake bottom. Suddenly, he pricks up his ears, perhaps on hearing the human intruder. He rushes out of the water grunting angrily, and disappears into the tall grass. Such a sight can now be seen in only a few other places on the Indian subcontinent, mainly in Kaziranga in the eastern Indian state of Assam. Small numbers of rhino still survive in some other areas.

Only a few hundred years ago the Indian Rhinoceros or Great One-horned Rhinoceros *(Rhinoceros unicornis)* ranged over all of the grassy floodplains of the Indus, Ganga and Brahmaputra rivers. The Mongol invader Timur, during his conquest of Delhi in 1398, and later, Babur, the founder of the Mughal empire in India in 1526, hunted rhino in northern India. But the rhino's habitat was also suitable for human settlement, and was gradually turned into farmland.

By the beginning of the 20th century the Indian rhino was fast heading towards extinction. Because of excessive hunting for sport and poaching, by 1908 such prime rhino habitats as Kaziranga in Assam had only a dozen or so rhino left. It was only when hunting was stopped and immediate protection afforded to the area that the rhino showed signs of recovery. Kaziranga was declared a game sanctuary in 1926 and renamed a wildlife sanctuary in the late 1940s. In 1950 Chitwan in Nepal had the largest concentration of this animal anywhere, with 800 to 1,000. But, again, as a result of indiscriminate deforestation and poaching during the next 20 years their numbers fell to about 100 at the close of the 1960s.

Chitwan was declared a Rhinoceros Sanctuary in 1962 and gazetted a National Park in 1973, but the killing of the rhinos in the park stopped only in 1976, when a contingent of the Nepalese Army was entrusted with the task of combating poaching. The rhino has since staged a comeback, and there are now about 1,700 in Kaziranga and 400 in Chitwan, with about 100 in Pabitora Wildlife Sanctuary in Assam.

Appearance

With its deeply folded thick skin, studded with rivet-like tubercles on the shoulders, flanks and hindquarters, the Indian rhino appears armour-plated, which even sparked off myths that it was bullet-proof. Its massive build, its peculiar hide, its short stumpy legs, its huge head and the horn (actually a mass of densely matted hair) on the top of its snout, gives one the impression of a truly prehistoric beast. Which is not far from the truth as the rhinoceros has changed little in the last million years.

The Indian rhino averages about 1.6 metres (5 ft 6 in) at the shoulder and weighs 1,820 kg

LEFT: the Indian rhinoceros is now confined to a few parks in Assam, West Bengal.
RIGHT: the Indian rhino is most active at night, in early morning and late afternoon.

(4,000 lbs). Grey in colour, although they look jet black when wet, their skin may also appear whitish, or the colour of the wallow, once the mud dries on their skin. Adult males may be differentiated from the females by their larger size, their more pronounced skin folds on the neck, their genitals being visible from behind, and by horns that are usually thicker at the base and often broken or split at the tip (the horn of the female is usually slender and unbroken). The horn averages 20 cm (8 inches) in length, although it may be longer. Adult females may also be recognized by the presence of their accompanying calves.

Both the Sumatran and Javan rhinos roamed eastern India until the end of the 19th century, but have since disappeared.

Habitat

Floodplain grassland interspersed with marsh, swamp and lake, and the adjoining riverine forest, are the favoured habitat of the Indian rhino. They prefer to feed on short grasses and seek shelter in thick stands of tall grass, sometimes 6–8 high (20–25 ft).

Although largely grazers, Indian rhinos will also browse leaves from shrubs and trees and, when near farms, will supplement their diet

To a casual observer, all rhinos look alike, but to a naturalist, a nick in the ear, a scar on the flank, a notch in the fold or a split in the horn is a definite mark of each individual.

Other rhinos

There are five species of rhinos: two in Africa and three in Asia. African rhinos, both the black *(Diceros bicornis)* and the white *(Ceratotherium simum)* have two long horns, set one behind the other. The Sumatran rhino *(Didermocerus sumatrensis)* has two smaller horns, often thick stubs. The Javan rhino *(Rhinoceros sondaicus)*, like the Indian species, has a single horn, usually less than 15 cm (6 inches) long.

with crops, which they habitually raid at night. They are fond of water and will spend hours wallowing. Besides cooling their huge bodies, the swamps and lakes also provide them with nourishing food in the form of aquatic plants.

Behavior

Rhinos occasionally feed and wallow in scattered groups of up to 10 or so, but they are solitary by nature and normally confine their movements to a small area of 0.75–5 sq km (0.3–2 sq miles). This, therefore, is their home range, which meets most of their requirements of food, water, and shelter. Males may have to wander further for mates. When two rhinos meet, ritualized behaviour, a series of displays and postures involving the curling of lips and baring of sharp tushes, accompanied by snarls and grunts, usually decides who is dominant and violence is avoided. But at times only physical battle will settle the dispute. These fights are noisy and sometimes lengthy affairs, and can lead to serious injury; in rare instances, losers are mortally wounded. The horn is not the rhino's chief instrument of attack; their razor sharp tusks are, which can cut an opponent's hide without difficulty. Male rhinos become sexually mature at about 10 years old, females a few years ear-

together for three to four years. Meanwhile, the mother will probably have mated again and be ready to produce another young. Rhinos live for up to 50 years.

Rhinos usually avoid humans, but anyone straying too close to one, cornering one, or threatening a mother with calf, should be wary. It will usually warn an intruder with an angry snort, but sometimes it will charge, occasionally without any provocation. Human casualties from rhino attack are not uncommon. Most charges are displays of threat, stopping short of the target, but a rhino will, on occasion, press home its attack.

lier. During courtship, violent encounters between the male and the female usually ensue and after much noisy chasing of the female by the male, mating finally takes place. Mating takes up to an hour or more, the female sometimes dragging the male about while still mounted.

After a gestation period of around 16 months, a calf (exceptionally two) is born. At birth they are pink and weigh about 60 kg (130 lbs). The mother and the calf will stay

LEFT: rhinos feed on 183 species of plants.
RIGHT: the rhinoceros calf is dependent on its mother for protection against the tiger.

Signs

Rhinos leave distinct three-toed spoor on the ground, squarish in shape and not quite as large as those of the elephant. From constant use a large network of rhino trails is formed in the grassland, often forming 'tunnels' through the thick grass. They also have favourite rubbing posts: a low overhanging branch, a sloping tree trunk or a stump. From regular rubbing, a distinct smooth patch is left, often coated in mud.

In rhino country, large piles of dung, known as middens, are common. These are accumulations from months, even years of use. The dung pile probably serves to inform other rhinos about an individual using a particular area.

Poachers have taken advantage of this habit of the rhino to hunt them. They would either dig and conceal a pit on the approach path to the dung pile, or they would lie in wait for them in a nearby tree.

Myth, medicine, masculinity

Rhinos have long been regarded as magical beasts surrounded by strange myths, and early Europeans have confused them with the fabled unicorn. In fact, for hundreds of years, until the late 18th century, rhino horn was imported into Europe as unicorn horn and used as a drug. In medieval Asia cups were carved out of rhino

Asian rhino horn can be sold for more than twice its weight in gold. After processing, it has been known to reach $30,000 per kg in Bangkok or Mandalay. Although the primary poachers get only a small percentage of this, they still make more than if they were to toil on the land for up to three years. Because of poverty, lack of education and unemployment, the poacher finds it worthwhile to take risks.

In India and Nepal, every part of a rhino is used: skin, horn, hooves, flesh, bone, penis, the internal organs and even blood, urine and dung. They are believed to cure diseases, ward off evil spirits, reduce labour pains, bring good luck,

horn – often with exquisite designs on them – in the belief that the liquid in such a cup would froth, or that the cup itself would split in two, if the liquid contained a poison, thus warning and saving the life of the intending drinker.

In East Asia, rhino horn is believed to have medicinal value, notably as a fever-depressant. The Chinese do not use rhino horn as an aphrodisiac, although some Indians do. In Nepal it has no medicinal significance but a bowl made of rhino horn (or hide) is used to offer libations during the Hindu memorial ceremony of shraddha. And were it not for the incredible value placed upon this protuberance, the rhino's future would perhaps have been more secure.

ensure good harvest, improve health and, above all, one's sex life. When a dead rhino is found, its horn (if there), hooves and skin are taken into government custody and the local people rush to buy parts of the carcass. To those who do not understand the concerns of conservationists, a rhino is of more value dead than alive. Apart from satisfying their medicinal and ritual beliefs when dead, live rhinos are a menace to their farms and a threat to their lives and livelihoods.

The future

There has been excellent progress throughout the last century towards securing a future for the Indian rhino. In terms of increasing rhino numbers, Kaziranga and Chitwan may be viewed as a success. Project Rhino has had success in the past but political disturbances in Assam slackened park vigilance in Kaziranga for some years and over a 100 rhinos were poached in the first half of the 1980s. Amid civil disorder in Assam in the 1990s, poachers wiped out the rhino populations in Manas National Park and at Laokhowa and Burhachpori, while the population in Orang has been reduced by more than half and poaching still continues here. Chitwan, in Nepal, where rhino numbers had increased from 50 in 1950 to 650 in 2000, has lost 250 of its rhinos in the last five years.

Reserve in Assam already exceed the carrying capacity. Numbers must be reduced to protect the habitat and to mitigate the increasing rhino-human conflicts when rhinos venture onto agricultural land. Already crop damage by rhinos is considerable in some areas.

To alleviate the situation, the Government of Assam, International Rhino Foundation (IRF), WWF and other NGOs have developed a protection and relocation initiative called "Indian Rhino Vision 2020". This programme aims to increase rhino numbers to more viable levels overall but keep them in balance with the habitat. This will involve moving rhino from Kaziranga and

It is still a matter of anxiety that this rare and endangered creature should be confined to a few habitats: 85 percent of India's rhinos (75 percent of the worldwide population of Indian Rhino) is in Kaziranga. Having so many rhinos in a single protected area exposes the species to risks of calamities such as epidemics, floods and massive poaching attempts. At Kaziranga rhinos are already being lost to flooding and in collisions with vehicles on a major road.

Further, the 100 rhinos in Pabitora Wildlife

Pabitora to other areas. This will provide more security against the catastrophe that can occur when most of the rhino are in one location.

Three new secure protected areas will be established capable of supporting at least 100 rhinos each. These will be secured by constructing new anti-poaching camps and involving the local communities in protection, as eco-guards and through economic incentives such as ecotourism. Manas National Park will be the first to receive rhinos translocated from Kaziranga and Pabitora. A captive breeding programme also hopes to improve gene diversity through exchanges of animals between zoos in India and the US. ❏

LEFT: rhinos can swim: water or mud is important for thermoregulation and the elimination of parasites.
RIGHT: rhino with egret, Kaziranga.

DEER, ANTELOPE AND BOVINES

From the tiny mouse deer to the great sambar,
India has more species of cervids than any other region

The largest and the most widely spread of the Indian deer, the **sambar** *(Cervus unicolour)*, has the widest distribution of all deer in the world, extending from Saurashtra to Taiwan and the Philippines, and from the Himalaya to Laos and Borneo, Sumatra and Sri Lanka. Yet nowhere does the species reach the same proportions in body and antlers as it does in India. The largest antlers, including the record specimen of 127 cm (50 ins), come from the Vindhya and Satpura ranges of Central India. A large stag may stand 150 cm (59 ins) at the shoulder and weight 300 kg (660 lbs).

Essentially not gregarious in behaviour and mainly nocturnal and wary in the major portion of its area of distribution, the sambar has become common, confiding and diurnal in parks and sanctuaries where it has been adequately protected, and Sariska and Ranthambhore National Parks in Rajasthan are among the best places in the world to see and photograph them by daylight. The Betla Tiger Reserve in Bihar, the Melghat and Tadoba National Parks in Maharashtra, Bandhavgarh and Satpura National Parks in Madhya Pradesh, Nagarahole National Park in Karnataka and Periyar National Park in Kerala are other excellent places to see sambar. They also occur in the Gir forest, in Corbett and Dudhwa, Manas and Kaziranga and in fact in most forested parts of India, except the mangrove, and extend up to 3,000 metres (9,800 ft) in the Himalaya.

The larger stags are usually solitary, except during the rutting season, which extends from November to January. The antlers are shed from March to May and the animal moults, often assuming a very ragged pelage. New antlers begin to grow soon after shedding, but during this period the stags are secretive and rarely seen. The most often seen sambar group is one or more hinds with their progeny of different years.

LEFT: hangul or the Kashmir stag is found only in a few areas of Kashmir.
RIGHT: sambar stag, Ranthambore.

They are a preferred prey species of the tiger and are widely preyed upon by the wild dog *(Cuon alpinus)*. However, the greatest threat to their survival, apart from the common factor of habitat destruction, is their susceptibility to bovine diseases, contagion contracted from India's ubiquitous livestock. The sambar popula-

tion of Sariska was severely ravaged some years ago by an epidemic disease.

At the other extreme of the scale – in rarity as well as in the restricted area of occurrence – is the **Manipur brow-antlered deer** *(Cervus eldi eldi)*. The smallest in both body and antler development of the three subspecies of this deer (the other two being the Burmese thamin and the Thailand subspecies), the Manipur deer, locally called the sangai, was from historical times confined to the vale of Manipur.

Standing a little over 1 metre (3 ft) at the shoulder and weighing about 100 kg (200 lbs), the stag sangai is much larger than the hind.

They are a very handsome deer, turning dark chocolate-brown in the rutting season from their ochre-fawn pelage during the molt. Their most notable physical feature is the unique formation of their antlers, which form a continuous arc from the highly developed brow-tines to the main beam of the antler, without the angular junction over the pedicle characteristic of all other deer antler formations. Hence the name brow-antlered deer.

Adapted to the grassland-forest mosaics, the most productive ecological entities of Asia, the sangai were driven to extinction by man in their preferred habitats. Until World

War II, however, they were still not uncommon in the swamps where the survivors had sought refuge. They had adapted to their semi-aquatic existence by developing elongated hooves and hard and hairless posterns, which assisted them in their movements in the morass and floating islands.

The intrusion of the Japanese army into Manipur in the war – their westernmost advance – followed by Indian independence, augured unsettled times for the sangai and an end of the princely patronage that had previously protected it. Being in close proximity to human settlements, the sangai were doomed, and by 1951 they were believed to

be extinct. However, E.P. Gee, a pioneer of the conservation movement in India, located a small, surviving population of the deer in a remote swamp at the southern end of the Logtak lake. A unique ecosystem, consisting of a contiguous floating mass of dead and living grass, the 28 sq km (11 sq mile) area of the Keibul Lamjao was estimated by Gee to hold about 100 sangai.

The nature of the swamp, where the floating morass supported the weight of the deer with their long hooves and specially adapted gait of small hops (earning them the nickname from Gee of "dancing deer") – but on which humans sink to their waist every few steps, made a true ground survey of their numbers almost impossible. In 1972, a gross estimate, based on a sample survey, placed the sangai population at 50. It was only when, for the first time, a helicopter survey was carried out in 1975 that the grim position became evident. There were only 14 Manipur brow-antlered deer left in the wild – five stags, six hinds and three fawns. In 1978, 23 animals were counted; in 1984 the tally had increased to 51. A census conducted in 2000 in the park showed that there were 162 deer (54 stags, 76 hinds and 32 fawns). A small number of sangai, whose main home is the Keibul Lamjao National Park in the Loktak lake, were shifted to the Irioshembba area recently. The total population of the sangai in the state is now reported to be around 150 animals. Poaching is rampant in the 40 sq km (15½ sq mile) sanctuary, with offenders including a minister and police personnel.

But still there are far more sangai in captivity than there are in the wild and searches have not revealed any area really suited to their rehabilitation in a second home in the wild. Thus, the survival of the wild sangai is as yet irrevocably linked with the fate of the miniscule Keibul Lamjao National Park. Almost the only chance that a visitor has of seeing this most graceful deer in its natural environs is to quietly punt a dugout canoe with a pole over a specially cleared water channel to the Pabot Hill, a feature within the park, and from the elevation of this lookout point observe the animal.

LEFT: a brow-antlered deer of Manipur.
RIGHT: the multi-tined antlers of the swamp deer lent it the Hindi name barasingha ("twelve horns").

Costly specialization

The **barasingha** or **swamp deer** *(Cervus duvauceli)* is another deer that has paid the price of its specialized adaptation to alluvial and riparian grasslands so coveted for agriculture by humans. Gregarious, and living in favorable habitats, the barasingha in the past attained great density of population in the Ganga-Brahmaputra and Central Indian grasslands. No deer species in India has suffered such a drastic decline of habitat as the barasingha. It survives today only in fragmented herds, frequently wide apart and often small. There was a period in the 1960s when there was despair about the future

National Park, Kishanpur Sanctuary and the Pilibhit forests of Uttar Pradesh, with a relict population close to Hastinapur near Meerut and a sizable herd in Sukla-phanta Wildlife Sanctuary in Nepal, now listed as vulnerable. The eastern race *C.d. ranjitsinhi*, now confined to Assam, and there almost only to Manas and Kaziranga, is critically endangered. The southern or Central Indian race, *C.d. branderi* (upland barasingha), in Kanha and Indravati National Parks in Madhya Pradesh, is classified as endangered, with a total world population of 4–5,000. In Kanha, their numbers have increased from 66 in 1968 to approximately

of this elegant deer, especially the southern race in Central India. Protection has been sporadic, with populations recovering only to decline again, and fluctuating numbers are still cause for serious concern. Threats include destruction or modification of habitat for wetland reclamation, grass and timber cutting and poaching for meat and antlers. Poaching has gone largely unchecked despite the knock-on effects this has for tigers. Declining prey species forces tigers into livestock lifting, for which they are poisoned by farmers.

Barasingha are divided into three subspecies. *C.d. duvauceli* (wetland barasingha), the nominate race occurring today mainly in Dudhwa

500 animals and this park is the best place to both view and photograph them. Dudhwa and Kaziranga are two other excellent areas to watch this deer.

In Assam and Uttar Pradesh the barasingha continues to remain almost exclusively partial to its grassland habitat, remaining in the open meadows even in the noonday summer sun. In Central India they move into the sal forests, especially in early autumn. They are almost exclusively grazers, another manifestation of their grassland adaptation, but fortunately they are not prone to crop-raiding, which has been the downfall of many herbivores. They frequently wade into water to eat the sedge-grasses, sometimes even immersing their heads.

With the approach of winter the barasingha emerge from their khaki-saffron coat to their rutting pelage of dark brown. The stags, standing about 127 cm (50 ins) at the shoulder and weighing approximately 180 kg (400 lbs), lose the velvet from their antlers, develop a swollen neck and a ruff, characteristic of many deer species in the same situation. The antlers, 12- or-more-pointed in an adult (hence the name, bara = "twelve"; singha = "horns") – are usually more polished and hence lighter coloured in the northern and eastern races than in the southern ones. Grass is thrashed and a deliber-

ate attempt is made to carry grass tussocks on the antler rack to give it more impressive proportions. Wallowing in mud and "bugling" are other manifestations of the rut, the call being a hoarse braying not dissimilar to that of a donkey. The stags are not territorial and the male hierarchy and dominance of the master stag is achieved more by display than actual combat.

Spotted beauty

The **chital** or spotted deer *(Axis axis)* is among the most widely distributed and common of the larger wild mammals of the Indian subcontinent. Indeed, it is also one of the most ornamental, and unlike many other spec-

tacular ungulates both sexes sport an exquisite pelage throughout the year.

Its watchful and alert behaviour, seeking safety in numbers, coupled with a high rate of reproduction and ecologic adaptability, has enabled it to attain its current safe status. In the Andaman Islands, where it was introduced around the beginning of the 20th century, it had assumed pest proportions. It is found from the Gir forest in the west to Manas in the east, and from the Himalayan foothills to Point Calimere Sanctuary in the south. Chital, of all the south Asian deer, also has the greatest tolerance to human proximity. In many national parks and sanctuaries they seek the safety of human habitations at night – often moving amongst the tourist huts – as a precaution against predator attack.

Being both a browser and a grazer, chital prefer grassland-forest borders. In the vast grassland chaurs of Corbett and maidans of Kanha national parks, both favoured habitats, they congregate in great number. In early July when the chital rut is at its peak, about 4,000 chital have been seen milling around in an area of barely 10 sq km(4 sq miles). Their numbers in Kanha increased from about 8,500 in 1973 to 14,500 in 1985. Bandipur in Karnataka, Tadoba in Maharashtra, Palamau in Bihar, Barnawapara in Madhya Pradesh, Chila in Uttar Pradesh, and Sariska and Ranthambhore in Rajasthan are other protected areas notable for their chital concentrations.

A daily drink or two is essential for chital and they are never found too far away from water. But of the larger species of Indian deer, chital is the one that does not wallow when in rut. The rutting period of the chital is also less defined and there are always some stags in hard antlers throughout the year, a factor contributing to its prolific propensity. The rutting stags thrash saplings, strut and emit harsh, bellowing calls.

The chital has a symbiotic relationship with the common langur *(Presbytus entellus)*, congregating beneath the feeding monkeys for pickings falling to the ground. Primates have been seen riding the back of a chital. The chital and the langur are the most frequent and first

LEFT: the musk deer is recognisable by its distinctive jumping movement and long upper canines.
RIGHT: the mouse deer, the region's smallest.

notifiers of the presence of predators, the shrill, musical whistle-calls of the deer often interspersed with the harsh, staccato barks of langur marking the march of the tiger.

Though preyed upon by both the tiger and the leopard, in many parts of its habitat it is the wild dog that is the chital's main predator.

Closely related to chital is the **para** or **hog-deer** *(Axis porcinus)*, a squat, rotund deer adapted once again to riverine grasslands. The stags carry a three-point antler formation, like those of the chital and the sambar, but with the inner, top tine curved characteristically downwards.

sporadically in the Jumna and Ganga highgrass khadars, along the terai and dooar grasslands from Uttar Pradesh to Arunachal Pradesh, in suitable high grasslands and lowland grassland-forests on both banks of the Brahmaputra, and in Manipur.

High floods take a heavy toll of the hog-deer in Kaziranga. But the numbers recover fast and this park is the best place to see and photograph the animal in India, Corbett being the other. Dudhwa in Uttar Pradesh, Jaldapara in West Bengal, and Manas and Orang in Assam are other protected areas where hog-deer are prominent.

The rutting of the hog-deer occurs in autumn, earlier than that of most other deer of the plains. Consequently, the antlers are also shed earlier in early spring, the deer then assuming a lighter- coloured coat on which the spots are visible more distinctly. When disturbed, a hog-deer dashes off with a characteristic lumbering lope, head slung low and stretched out, the long tail raised to reveal the white underside as a danger-flag.

Once found from the grassbeds of the Indus in Sind to Assam, and beyond to Indo-China in the east, it was later restricted to the Indo-Gangetic and Brahmaputra valleys in the Indian subcontinent. Today in India it occurs

Shy tush-bearers

An earlier-evolving member of the Cervidae family, the **barking deer** *(Muntiacus muntjak)* represents the transition phase of the deer family, from oversized canines or tushes as weapons of offense and defense, to antlers that serve the same purpose. While the musk deer and some other species elsewhere have tushes, the barking deer carries both tushes and a unique pair of antlers. These grow from a pair of elongated skin-covered pedicles, which themselves appear as an extension of two elevated ribs or ridges that so prominently mark the forehead of the deer. The antlers have a short brow-tine, but the main beam is then not bifurcated in its journey upwards and then inwards. Both these are used as weapons in combat but the tushes are used more effectively and frequently.

Solitary, shy and secretive, restricted in their movements and often confined to small home ranges, barking deer are seen in ones and twos, often for mere fleeting glimpses. The best and frequently the only method of photographing them is to watch over a water hole or salt lick. Their alarm call is barely distinguishable from the barking of a village dog; their mode of escape not dissimilar to that of the hog-deer. They are easily startled by any movement and their alarm call, unless end-

Closely related to the hornless, tush-bearing deer is the **chevrotain** or **mouse deer** *(Tragulus meminna)*. A diminutive, speckled-grey creature, barely a 30 cm (1 ft) high, whose male members have small dagger-like tushes, the mouse deer is not a true deer, having only three compartments to its stomach and belonging to the family Tragulidae. Its present range extends from the heavily forested regions of the Western Ghats, through eastern Madhya Pradesh, to the sal forest belt of southern Bihar and Orissa. Even smaller, more solitary, evasive and cryptic than the barking deer, the mouse deer is rarely seen except with the aid of a powerful light at night.

lessly repeated, is not taken as an indication of the presence of a predator.

Found in heavily forested regions from the Himalayan pines and firs to the southern tip of the Western Ghats near Kanyakumari and from the Satpura Hills in Western Central India to Arunachal Pradesh and Nagaland and beyond, barking deer can be seen in most of the protected areas in this vast region. Yet none is an easy place to view them. In Nagarahole and Bandipur in Karnataka, Nagzira and Melghat in Maharashtra, Satpura and Bandhavgarh in Madhya Pradesh, Rajaji and Dudhwa in Uttar Pradesh, Manas in Assam, and Simlipal in Orissa, to name a few, the chances are better than in other places.

Elegant antelope

Africa is the continent for antelopes, with a multitude of species from the magnificent greater kudu to the tiny dik dik. But with the exception of the sable, there is no antelope that can really match the male **blackbuck** *(Antilope cervicapra)* for its colour combination and elegance, the matching proportions of its horn shape and length to its body size. There are few animals that one can truthfully describe as exquisite. The male blackbuck in his chocolate-black rutting pelage, strutting stiff-legged, with face upraised and horns swept back, is one such. It is also an animal truly representative of

India, having evolved in this subcontinent and having become extinct in the wild except in India and on the India-Nepal border. It is one of the swiftest animals in the world and a herd traveling at 80 km (50 miles) per hour for a distance of over a kilometer (¾ mile) has been clocked.

Dominant herd males are intolerant of the presence of other mature males and male blackbuck maintain territories, often very small and in close juxtaposition to each other. Aggression is mostly confined to strutting displays, but sparring, jousting and chasing are not infrequent. There is, however, rarely any

Pure white blackbuck are not uncommon, though this occasional lack of pigmentation appears to be more common in Saurashtra.

Blackbuck were perhaps the commonest wild animal in India prior to independence. Being in close proximity to human habitations, living in open, easily approachable habitats and raiding croplands as they did, no animal in the subcontinent has suffered such a steep decline in numbers, and reduction in areas of occurrence, as has the blackbuck. There were hardly any parks or sanctuaries that held blackbuck populations prior to the 1970s. They survived in isolated pockets, particularly in Rajasthan,

serious injury, evolution having provided in the convoluted horn-shape of the bucks, as it has provided in the branching antler-tines of stags, a locking mechanism that prevents an animal from making a fatal thrust. The preorbital glands exude a strong-smelling musky secretion that is rubbed on grass stems or tree holes if they are available. Horns are thrashed on vegetation and if none is available, as is sometimes the case in blackbuck country, on the bare ground.

LEFT: a magnificent display of blackbuck, Velavadar, Gurjarat.
ABOVE: chinkara, Desert National Park, Rajasthan.

Madhya Pradesh, Andhra Pradesh, Maharashtra and Gujarat, almost entirely due to the religious sentiments of the local people, notably the Bishnois and the Valas. According to one estimate there were once some 4 million blackbuck on the subcontinent.

Today, the estimated number is around 25,000. The foremost places to view the blackbuck are the Velavadar National Park in Gujarat with a population of about 2,000; Talchapar, Gajner, Doli and other Bishnoi areas in Rajasthan; Bagdara and Noradehi in Madhya Pradesh, the last having a small herd in a unique habitat; Vetnoi in Orissa; Point Calimere in Tamil Nadu and Rane Bennur in Karnataka.

Frisky gazelles

Even more independent of water and moisture content in food plants than the blackbuck, the **chinkara gazelle** *(Gazella gazella)* has a wider range of distribution than the blackbuck in the arid lands. They are also at home in rolling hills and scrub forest, and being less prone to raid crops and living less in agricultural areas in the proximity of man, the rout suffered by the gazelle, though drastic, has not been as much as that of the blackbuck. The decline of the chinkara and the blackbuck in the past two centuries has been a major contributory factor in the

Blue 'Cow'

The **nilgai** *(Boselaphus tragocamelus)*, the largest of all Asiatic antelopes, has been fortunate. Firstly, it possesses an insignificant pair of horns, which is no real trophy for the hunter. But what is more important, its somewhat physical resemblance to cattle has earned it the name blue cow and the religious sanction that goes with it. Despite its serious crop depredation propensities it has been left unmolested in areas of Hindu predominance, and Muslims have been hired on occasions to get rid of them. Its flesh is still taboo to the Hindus.

decline and final extinction of the Asiatic cheetah *(Acinonyx jubatus venaticus)* in the subcontinent around 1947. Asiatic cheetahs are critically endangered, with just a few hundred remaining in Iran.

Less gregarious than the blackbuck (groups of over a dozen are rare), chinkara tend to keep within definite home ranges. They are in a constant state of animation, black tail wagging, ears twitching, heads frisking one way and the other. Chinkara are presently found in good concentrations in the Desert National Park and the Bishnoi areas of Rajasthan, and Kunu Sanctuary and Panna National Park in Madhya Pradesh.

Occurring in small groups from Jammu and the Punjab to Karnataka and Saurashtra to Bihar, the nilgai prefers open forests and scrubland, though where persecuted they have moved into heavier cover. Living mainly in areas where the tiger is absent, and the leopard rarely being able to tackle them, man has been their main predator in the present and recent past.

Sariska and Ranthambhore in Rajasthan, Panna and Shivpuri National Parks in Madhya Pradesh, Paneli in Gujarat, and the more open-forested protected areas of Maharashtra and Andhra Pradesh are the best places to view the nilgai.

Unique antelope

The only wild animal in the world to possess four horns, the **four-horned antelope** *(Tetraceros quadricornis)* is the smallest antelope in Asia, being about 60 cm (2 ft) high and weighing about 16 kg (35 lbs).

Exclusive again to the Indian subcontinent, the animal possesses a pair of short anterior horns with a pair of sharp-pointed longer posterior horns that can be used as rapiers.

Preferring patches of grassland amid forests and open forests with a grassy understory, the **chausingha**, as the four-horned antelope is commonly called, is home-range oriented, living singly or in pairs. Its range extends from the terai forests and Jammu to Mudumalai Sanctuary in Tamil Nadu, though in the past it was reported even in the Palni Hills. It occurs in the Barda and Gir forests of Gujarat, extending eastwards to Bihar. It is another very difficult animal to photograph in the wild.

It is interesting to note that the only other known ruminant to have possessed four horns, the Sivatherium, whose fossils are found in the Siwalik hills, also occurred in India and was the largest known ruminant.

Wild oxen

The tallest, sleekest and, colourwise, one of the most striking of the 11 species of the subfamily Bovinae or wild oxen that survive in the world today, the **gaur** *(Bos gaurus)* is also, next to the **wild yak** *(Bos grunniens)*, the best adapted to hilly terrain. It is also currently the least endangered of the Asiatic wild bovines.

Preferring dense forests away from human habitations and livestock, quite content to confine itself to its beloved bamboo thickets and even to steep slopes, and not raiding agricultural crops even if they are close at hand, the gaur has avoided, as it were, the pitfalls suffered by the wild buffalo, which in the historical past had a far greater distribution and numbers.

Extending from the Agasthyamalai hills at the southern tip of the Western Ghats to Satara and Kolhapur in Maharashtra and up to the central segments of the Narmada river in Madhya Pradesh, the gaur distribution sweeps eastwards and northwards past the Amarkantak massif, where the Narmada and Sone have their sources, into the Chota Nagpur tracts of Bihar, Orissa and West Bengal, and then on to the northeastern regions of the subcontinent.

The animal attains its most impressive proportions in the moist, semi-deciduous and evergreen forests of southern India. The glistening black bulls, bulging muscles rippling under the skin, heavy-

> **BISONS**
>
> Though the gaur is sometimes called the Indian Bison this is a misnomer, as the only two true bisons that survive today are the European and American.

horned and with a pronounced dewlap and hump on the withers, white stockinged feet in contrast to the dark pelage of the body, are some of the finest sights of the parks and sanctuaries of the South – Nagarahole, Bandipur and Bhadra in Karnataka, Mudumalai and Annamalai in Tamil Nadu, Parambikulam and Periyar in Kerala. Mollem in Goa, Tarboa in Maharashtra, Pench, Kanha, Achanakmar off Satpura in Madhya Pradesh, Belta in Bihar and Simlipal in Orissa are some of the other places where the gaur can be readily seen.

The older bulls are frequently found alone or in pairs. Male dominance is mainly achieved by lateral displays in slow, measured

---

LEFT: chital stags fighting, Sariska.

RIGHT: Asia's largest antelope – the nilgai, or blue bull, Bharatpur.

steps wherein the masculine attributes of the bulls, the dorsal ridge, the dewlap and fore-shoulders, are displayed to best advantage. There is rarely any actual combat. The gaur is very susceptible to bovine diseases: rinder-pest and anthrax have decimated their herds in the past in Bandipur, Mudumalai, Periyar and Kanha, in the first two more than once. They have yet to recover their previous numerical strength in these areas. Until they attain an age of about two years, gaur calves are preyed upon by the tiger, and it is this that prevents the small herd of gaur in Bandhav-garh from increasing in numbers.

istence in the river basin. In the more recent historical past, the range of the animal extended over the riverine and forest grasslands in the Ganga, Brahmaputra, Narmada and Godavari river systems. Today it is found mainly in the surviving Brahmaputra valley grasslands – Kaziranga, Dibru, and Manas.

A small herd survives in Kosi Tappu in Nepal. The peninsular Indian wild buffalo population, perhaps the purest genetically, survives in small scattered populations in Udanti in Raipur dis-trict, Bhairamgarh, Indravati and Pamed in Bas-tar district of Madhya Pradesh, and perhaps a small herd in the Koraput district of Orissa. The

Fearless buffalo

Were it not for the similar appearance of the ubiquitous domestic buffalo, the **Asiatic wild buffalo** *(Bubalus bubalis)* would surely have ranked as one of the most impressive and mag-nificently built animals in the world today. It is the most powerful and heaviest but yet most pro-portionate of all the South Asian wild bovines, and in the record specimens it carries the largest horns of any surviving animal in the world today. The females carry even longer though more slen-der horns than the bulls. A large buffalo bull can weigh nearly over 900 kg (2,000 lbs).

Seals of the Harappan Culture (2,500 BC) de-picting the wild buffalo testify to its then ex-

total population in the subcontinent is in all probability less than 2,000.

Its preference for alluvial grasslands most coveted by man for agriculture is the main rea-son for the wild buffalo's loss of habitat. Its fear-less, even truculent behaviour has also not helped. But what has perhaps been a most vital factor, both direct and insidious, contributing to the numerical and physical decline of the wild buffalo, is the propensity of the bulls to com-

ABOVE: gaur, largest of the world's wild oxen, in Nagarahole, Karnataka.
RIGHT: only small pockets of pure wild buffalo survive in Assam, Madhya Pradesh and southeast Nepal.

mandeer domestic buffalo cows for mating. The deprived owners of the livestock take pot-shots at the offending bull if one is around, as it can cause the loss of access to milk and often the loss of the impregnated domestic buffalo cow who cannot safely deliver the oversize calf.

Not infrequently, the wild bull prevents the return home of the domestics, which not only means the permanent loss of the livestock to the owner but also the creation of feral buffalo populations that are not of the same proportions and grandeur as their wild sires. This genetic 'swamping' is very evident amongst the wild buffalo populations that come in con-

though uncommon are not unknown.

The major part of the day is spent in grazing or resting, with a midday dip, an almost unvarying routine, especially in the hot season. The necessity of water in adequate quantity is, therefore, a restrictive factor in the wild buffalo's movements and habitat selections.

In an economy-conscious world where even a living being has to have a price-tag attached to it to be of value to a decision-maker, the wild buffalo's close affinity with the most important domestic animal in Southern Asia should make it genetically one of the most important wild animals in the world today. Yet man has

tact with the domestic animals, as in Kaziranga and southern Manas.

Though calves are occasionally killed by tigers, the willingness of the wild buffalo to stand its ground and drive off and even attack a tiger, helps in keeping away all but the largest and most determined tigers. They form a phalanx and face their adversary, the youngsters in between.

The threat display involves a direct frontal approach, the muzzle slightly depressed to show the vast sweep of their massive horns to their best advantage. Snorting and foot-stamping are other manifestations. Horned combats, resulting in injury to one or both participants,

allowed the wild buffalo to become one of the most threatened animals in India, and to be almost wiped out elsewhere. Extensive hunting, habitat loss, diseases and parasites transmitted by domestic livestock, and interbreeding with domestic stock have all reduced their numbers. Estimates in 2004 put the total world population at less than 4,000, 90 percent of which is in Assam, but very few of these are purebred wild Asian buffalo. Delhi's Wildlife Trust of India (WTI) has now initiated a three-year plan for conservation and revival of its present small population. Studies to identify threats and conservation strategies will look at populations, habitats and the degree of hybridisation. ❏

PRIMATES

Both revered and hunted, the primates of India include

bold macaques, elegant langurs, nocturnal lorises and a rare lesser ape

Classified in the same Natural Order as human, non-human primates have always excited people's interest. Hindus in the region will hardly ever assault monkeys as they are held to be sacred, and their protection is further strengthened by the Hindu legend that the monkey god Hanuman, with his monkey army, helped the divine prince Rama recapture his bride Sita.

Primates include apes, monkeys, lemurs and tree shrews. They evolved from arboreal ancestors, developing the prehensile hands and feet distinctive to them.

There are two suborders of primates: the earlier-evolving Prosimii and the later Simiae. Prosimii include tree shrews and lorises whose brains are not as highly developed as those of the Simiae. More widespread than the Prosimii, the Simiae include the many types of monkeys and one species of lesser apes found in the Indian subcontinent. They are mainly diurnal and arboreal, though some species spend a considerable amount of time on the ground.

Most primates are essentially vegetarian. Some are exclusively so, while others add animal food, such as insects, crabs, mollusks, birds, birds' eggs and even mammals, to their diet. A macaque, which can be distinguished from a langur by its sturdy, squat and solid build, has cheek pouches to store food that cannot be consumed immediately. The langur, by contrast, is tall, slim and stately, and has a special pouch in its stomach that serves the same purpose. Apes, tree shrews and lemurs eat whenever food is available.

While most Simiae primates are social animals living in troops of up to 100 individuals and found throughout almost the whole subcontinent, thriving in tropical conditions, tree shrews and lorises are found only south of the

LEFT: the rare lion-tailed macaque found in the South Indian hills.
RIGHT: the golden langur is confined to a pocket on the Assam-Bhutan border.

Ganga and in eastern India. Of the 21 species of primates found in the subcontinent, including Sri Lanka and the Andaman and Nicobar Islands in the Bay of Bengal, there are three types of tree shrew and two species of loris. The former, previously classified as insectivores, are the smallest of all primates and though in

appearance tree shrews resemble squirrels, they display little squirrel-like behavior.

Tree-shrews

The **Madras tree shrew** (*Anathana ellioti*) is a small, rat-sized, squirrel-like animal that has prehensile hands and feet. Reddish-brown to grey-brown in colour, it has a bushy tail and a pale oblique shoulder stripe. Well-distributed south of the Ganga, it lives on trees in tropical rainforests and in thorny jungles. It is diurnal and catches insects on the ground, but it also feeds on fruit and often takes to the trees as a means of escape. It is easily tamed and is commonly kept as a pet in southern India.

In the northeast, the **common tree shrew** *(Tupaia glis)* ranges in Sikkim, Assam and Manipur. Similar to the Madras tree shrew, it has short ears and a bushy tail. Its dorsal parts and tail are brown to reddish-brown, speckled or grizzled. The ventral parts are buff to brown, and there is a pale stripe just in front of the shoulders. Two subspecies are found in India, one in thick rainforest and mountain jungle, the other in bamboo bushes and trees near human dwellings.

Though expert climbers, common tree shrews do not leap from tree to tree as squirrels do, nor do they jerk their tails or cling

Lorises

Two subspecies of Loris are the only primate species in this part of the world that are nocturnal. The **slendor loris** *(Loris tardigradus)* is found in Sri Lanka and southern India, while the **slow loris** *(Nycticebus coucang)* prefers the densest parts of tropical rainforests in eastern India.

The slender loris is a small, thin and lanky creature with long thin limbs. Its body is well-furred, with a dark-grey, reddish-brown back. It has a white muzzle and huge, round eyes enclosed in a black or dark-brown circle. Though it has the same secretive and nocturnal habits as the slow loris, it is not confined to dense jungles

head-downwards on tree trunks. Instead, they spend a considerable amount of time nosing for food among fallen leaves and in rock crevices. They eat fruit, seeds and leaves and also insects, small mammals and birds. Found in pairs, they are more sociable than their peninsular cousins, and as many as five tree shrews have been observed together. Of the third species, the **Nicobar tree shrew** *(Tupaia nicobarica)*, very little is know. It has a long tail, and its ventral parts are a pale brown, the dorsal part is brownish-black while the head and limbs are brown. Two different subspecies are found, in the Great and the Little Nicobar Islands.

and is found both in tropical rainforest and in more open woodland and swampy coastal forest. Usually found alone or in pairs, it sleeps through the day in shady, inaccessible places – in the hollow of a tree or at the leafy extremity of a branch, rolled up in a tight ball, with its head between its legs and grasping its perch with its arms.

The slow loris also sleeps through the day, rolled up in a ball, but during hot weather it stretches out on a branch. Its diet includes shoots, fruit, insects, reptiles and birds – in fact anything it can lay its hands on. True to its name, the slow loris is very deliberate in its movements. When hunting insects it never springs, but catches them with a sudden lunge, never letting go of the branch on which it maintains a tenacious grip. Unlike the solitary slender loris, the slow loris is found in small family groups. In appearance it is less lanky, with a brown streak on its crown and dark markings on its pale brown face.

Macaques

Few people, if any, would need an introduction to either the macaque or the langur. While some of the species are commonly seen around temples, bazaars, villages and even railway stations, others live in isolated pockets in some of the most inaccessible areas.

Of the three types of monkeys found in the region, the macaques are the largest family, being represented by eight species. Northeast India is the home of some of the rarest macaque species, such as the **stump-tailed macaque** *(Macaca arctoides)*, which is found in the hilly forests of Assam, Arunachal Pradesh and Nagaland. Its fur is dark chestnut and shaggy. Its forehead is bald with only crown hairs radiating from the center, short in front, longer at the back and on the sides. Its face is pinkish; its buttocks and genitalia reddish. As among all other macaques, the sexes are alike, though the male is sometimes heavier and bigger.

The stump-tailed macaque is fairly terrestrial but does spend a lot of time in trees as well. Just before daybreak, troops of up to 30 individuals head for their feeding grounds, and if there are any ficus trees with ripe fruit, they will almost certainly be found there. They rarely stray far from their feeding trees. During the afternoons, they rest or groom themselves, before feeding again and returning to their resting trees. Though extremely noisy while feeding, they have been known to raid village fields in absolute silence. They are relatively unafraid of humans. In fact, Naga Adivasis are said to be afraid of them, for they can be terribly pugnacious when it comes to giving up a field they are feeding on. They use their hands to carry food to their mouth, and after filling their cheek pouches, again use the flat of the hand to press their cheeks to bring food back into the mouth.

LEFT: the nocturnal slender loris.
RIGHT: the rhesus macaque, common throughout North India.

The **pig-tailed macaque** *(Macaca nemestrina)* inhabits the same forests as its stump-tailed relative, but it is more arboreal and keeps strictly to dense evergreen forests. It is one of the largest of the genus, with long legs and an elongated muzzle. Its face is bare, light brown, and its crown hairs are short, radiating from a central whorl and forming a thick cover of erect hairs. The body colour varies; the dorsal parts are greyish-olive to russet (with a buff to yellow tinge in places), while the forehead and crown are darker; the ventral parts are mostly greyish while the lower abdomen is slightly reddish. The face and hindquarters are pinkish-brown

and the tail is short, dark reddish-brown on top and carried half-erect like a pig's tail.

The pig-tailed macaque is one of the few monkey species found in the subcontinent that faces a threat from human poachers. Its meat is sought after by certain Naga groups and it is also in great demand in Southeast Asia for coconut picking – the monkey is sent up the tall palms to pick the fruit. Shy of people, it abandons the trees and tries to flee from any threat by running on the ground. Because of its wariness, attempts to obtain reliable estimates of its declining population have been unsuccessful.

The **Assamese macaque** *(Macaca assamensis)* gets its name from Assam, but its habitat is not confined to the northeast. Its range starts from as far west as Mussoorie in Uttranchal and moves eastwards to the hill ranges of Assam and the forests of the Sunderbans in the Ganga delta. It is relatively large, with a pendulous well-haired tail, which is anywhere from a third to a half of the head and body length. The face is pale and flesh-coloured with four or five deep diagonal wrinkles. The body fur is felted, and the crown hair is brushed back. The Assamese macaque, like the pig-tailed variety, is also hunted for its meat, but to a lesser extent.

Large troops of this macaque are not uncom-

The ubiquitous rhesus

Perhaps the best known macaque in India is the **rhesus macaque** *(Macaca mulatta)*, which lives in a variety of habitats, including cities, villages, farms, forests and mountains. It inhabits the semi-desert forests of Rajasthan, the swamps and mangroves of the Sunderbans, and extends across to Burma in the east.

It is at home in trees or on the ground, and equally at ease sitting on a temple roof or a tin shed in a railway depot. Devoid of fear of humans, it often grabs food from unwary pilgrims. The origin of its commensalism is not clear and it is also not known if commensal groups differ

mon, often seeking strength in numbers, and sometimes large troops gang up to raid crops. They are particularly abundant in the valleys around Darjeeling and a troop can sometimes consist of over 100 individuals, moving around in the forests like a ghost army. They prefer hilly areas and dense jungles, and by and large prefer to keep their distance from humans; and like most macaques, they display an amazing indifference to humans unless molested.

The **long-tailed macaque** *(Macaca fascicularis)* is really a Burmese monkey and, but for its existence in the Nicobar Islands, it can hardly be described as an Indian animal. Very little is known about the Nicobar subspecies.

from wild populations morphologically.

The rhesus has the usual squat, thickset build of a macaque. The hairs on its crown radiate backwards from the forehead without the neat centre-parting that marks its relative, the macaque of southern India. Its body is olive-brown, with orange-red fur on its loins and rump that distinguishes it from all other Indian monkeys. Almost throughout its range, the rhesus is free from human molestation, but its capture for scientific research has affected its status. In the 1960s, the demand stripped India's rhesus population from an estimated ten million monkeys down to an estimated 200,000 in 1978 when India banned export of the animals. Rhesus macaques are still captured from the wild for use in Indian research laboratories.

Rhesus macaques live in highly organized troops, the largest of which are found in the plains where over a hundred individuals coexist under the leadership of a dominant male. In very large troops, smaller subgroups are formed, each under a male, and a clear-cut social order exists within the troop.

The relationship between adult males ranges from peaceful and even cooperative to highly antagonistic, while females are quite tolerant of each other. Grooming forms a major part of

affected. Solutions to the problem should include banning all trappings of monkeys from forests; increasing the abundance of wild fruiting trees and waterholes in the remaining natural habitat for these primates; and the capture and relocation to the wild of monkeys within human habitations. Attention needs to be paid to the management of commensal species as well as wild populations.

Southern cousins

Almost as if a line had been drawn across the subcontinent by some unseen hand, the rhesus macaque of northern India is replaced by

their daily activities, but it is the relationships of juveniles that is most fascinating. Little play-groups of three to four young individuals display a natural exuberance rarely seen in other animals.

The rhesus is the most aggressive of the macaques and a rising population living around human habitations is leading to increasing conflict and a growing health issue from attacks on humans. Urban areas, where people are ignorant of rhesus behaviour, are worst

ABOVE: rhesus macaques, mother showing threat display, Sariska.
RIGHT: a toque macaque peers from the canopy.

another pale-faced monkey commonly seen with itinerant entertainers in southern India.

The **bonnet macaque** *(Macaca radiata)* is similar to its cousin, the rhesus, except for the reddish rump and long dark hairs that radiate in all directions from a whorl on its crown. Found near villages and in jungles, it is particularly fond of ficus trees, and where there are two or more banyan trees and water, the chances of finding a troop of 20 to 30 animals are quite high.

Found more or less throughout southern India, troops of bonnet macaques living in the jungles are quite shy, but those that are quartered near human settlements lose all fear of people. The troops are controlled by a central core of highly dominant males who collaborate when necessary. In a highly defined social set-up, the fluctuations of a male's status depends on various factors. In an instance where a dominant male once broke a canine, he kept his mouth shut as long as he could, but once the secret was out, the other males set upon him and considerably reduced his status.

In the south, there is yet another macaque: the **lion-tailed macaque** *(Macaca silenus)*, which can be distinguished from other macaques by its long, gray or brownish mane around its face and its striking black body. It has a tail almost

covery of a large population in the rainforests of Karnataka has tripled the estimate of its numbers. Information on this macaque is still relatively sparse, but it is known to share its habitat with three other primates. While the bonnet macaque avoids a confrontation, there have been reports of ferocious battles being fought with the only other black coloured primate – the Nilgiri langur (see below) – with both sides suffering severe casualties. The lion-tailed macaque are very deliberate in their movements, and when crossing from tree to tree, they avoid jumping, but descend to the ground and walk across in single file. A troop usually con-

two-thirds the length of its head and body, with a small tuft at the end that is very pronounced in the case of adult males and from which the macaque gets its common name.

It is perhaps the most arboreal of all macaques, normally remaining at the top of the forest canopy. Because of its shy nature, black colour, and its habit of living in dense, dimly lit, lonely forests, it is rarely seen. Found in the thick forests of peninsular India, it is most common in the Western Ghats, the Nilgiri, Anaimalai and Cardamom Hills and also in the vicinity of Periyar Lake in Kerala.

Until recently, the lion-tailed macaque was considered to be highly endangered, but the dis-

sists of 10 to 20 individuals, and the females usually outnumber the males.

Langurs

Every morning, at dawn, the rainforests of Periyar Tiger Reserve echo to the deep booming of the **Nilgiri langur** *(Presbytis johnii)*, which is among the five langur species recorded in India and Sri Lanka. It has a glossy black body and the back of its head is yellowish-brown with a brown crown. Females differ from males slightly in that they have a white patch on the insides of their thighs. It generally inhabits the sholas (woods of the plateau – strips of forest surrounded by grassland, usually with a stream running through) of the Western Ghats south of Coorg, and the Nilgiri, Anaimalai, Brahmagiri and Palni Hills. Though essentially arboreal in the Nilgiri, it can often be seen crossing the grassland, from one shola to another. Destruction of its habitat has threatened the very existence of the Nilgiri langur. Troops are sometimes quite large, with as many as 30 animals. They travel over a well-worn route, each individual stepping in exactly the same spot as the leader. Though shy of humans, they sometimes raid plantations but, by and large, they are fairly elusive.

The range of the **Hanuman langur** *(Presbytis entellus)* stretches north and then east to

In the wild the Hanuman langur's keen eyesight makes it an effective part of an early warning system against the tiger and the leopard, both of which it hates without reservation. Consequently, it has developed an effective relationship with deer, and chital can often be seen feeding under a tree inhabited by langurs.

Both species react to each other's alarm calls, and nine times out of 10, langur and chital alarm calls lead to a tiger or leopard sighting. The langur live in large troops and their diet includes some of the (for many creatures) most poisonous leaves, which are avoided even by insects. They can also be seen sitting on the

encompass almost the entire subcontinent. Represented by 16 subspecies, it can be found above the snow line in Kashmir, in Sri Lanka in the south, Rajasthan in the west and right across to Burma in the east. It is a large, black-faced, grey-bodied langur with long limbs and a tail that is longer than its head and body. Indifferent to man if left alone, it will retreat quickly if threatened, but, on the other hand, Hanuman langurs living near temples are know to mob pilgrims, panicking them into parting with their food.

LEFT: common langur grooming.
ABOVE: the common, grey or Hanuman langur

ground, eating mud from which they get their required salt intake. They are territorial, but rarely does a group fight to defend its ground.

In 1907, reports of a cream-coloured langur came in from the east bank of the Sankosh river, near the India-Bhutan border, but it was only in 1953 that the tea planter-naturalist, E.P. Gee, came forward with any real evidence of the **golden langur** *(Presbytis geei)* as it was subsequently named. It has a cream back that looks golden in good light, darker sides and a black face with no sign of any hair. It has a long tail with a tassel at the end. In winter the langur looks a lot more golden than it does in summer when its coat looks almost white or creamish.

The golden langur is highly arboreal, descending to the ground only during the early hours of the morning or late in the evening to drink from a river or a stream. It lives in dense, tropical deciduous forests, and is exclusively vegetarian. Its range extends over south-central Bhutan and northwestern Assam. Easily seen on the Bhutan side of the Manas river, it is a shy animal that leaps from tree to tree at the approach of humans. A troop can number as many as 40, their movements controlled by a dominant male who moves fast, followed by the rest. Juveniles make a shrill, nervous, whistling sound before jumping, but otherwise they move and feed in relative silence.

season do they leave the sanctuary of the trees to drink. They are extremely shy, either taking flight through the trees or sitting absolutely still when approached. Left alone, they are noisy animals, and very often it's the whoosh of a branch bending under their weight as they leap that gives them away.

Yet another species of langur, the **silver leaf monkey** *(Presbytis cristatus)*, is found mainly in southern Burma, but may also extend its range into Tripura and Bangladesh. However, no record of it has been made in the subcontinent in recent years, but the possibility of its existence here cannot be dismissed.

The range of the **capped langur** *(Presbytis pileatus)* extends further east from Manas, covering northern Assam, Arunachal Pradesh and parts of Bangladesh. A large, colourful monkey, it has a black face and head with sharply contrasting paler cheeks suffused with red. The dorsal colour is grey to blackish-grey and the distal half of the tail too is black. The ventral parts are a brownish-yellow or orange, while the insides of the thighs and the hindquarters are tinged with light cobalt-blue, this tinge being more prominent in adult males.

Little is known of the habits of the capped langur, but they prefer dry tropical forests and dense evergreen jungles. Only during the dry

Lesser apes

Finally among the Indian primates are the lesser apes, though represented by only one species, the **Hoolock gibbon** *(Hylobates hoolock)*, which is found in the rainforests of Arunachal Pradesh, Assam and parts of Nagaland. The Namdapha Tiger Reserve in Arunachal Pradesh is probably one of the best areas in which to look for gibbons.

When standing erect, they reach a size of approximately 90 cm (3 ft) and weigh up to 9 kg (20 lbs). The genders are about the same size, but they differ considerably in colouration: males are black coloured with remarkable white brows, while females have a grey-brown fur, which is darker at the chest and neck. It has small legs on which it runs, sometimes along the boughs of trees, but usually it prefers swinging from branch to branch, using its grotesquely long arms. Young hoolocks are born after a seven month gestation, with a milky white fur. After about six months their fur turns black. At eight to nine years they are fully mature and their fur reaches its final colouration. Their life expectancy is about 25 years.

The Hoolock gibbon's habits in the wild are relatively unknown. Each group is usually a fam-

ALL IN THE WRIST

One unique aspect of gibbon physiology is a ball and socket joint in the wrist, allowing for biaxial movement with less effort and stress on the shoulder joint.

cial protection, similar to the projects for tigers and elephants that are already in place.

In general, primates in the region have so far been lucky, living under the protection of a religious umbrella, as it were. Nevertheless, as traditional protection afforded by religious belief in their sacredness wanes, the future, not only of the Hoolock gibbon, the langurs and the macaques, but also that of the lesser primates, will be increasingly threatened.

In addition to the bio-medical research labo-

ily, with each adult male having a single female consort. It feeds on fruit, leaves, young shoots and birds, and is known to have a special liking for spiders. Their loud whooping early in the morning carries a considerable distance and is one of the most evocative sounds of the jungle.

But the gibbon, like many apes throughout the world, is also facing a stiff challenge to its survival, as pressure for land and timber mounts. As India's only ape it must merit spe-

LEFT: the capped langur, forest-dwellers in northeastern India.

ABOVE: the Hoolock gibbon is the only ape found in India.

ratories mentioned above, primates are taken form the wild in India for a number of other reasons. They are captured for zoos or private collections, to be trained for street performances, and, commonly, to be used as pets. They are also killed for their pelts (for example, the Capped langur is commonly used for making the scabbard of swords locally known as *dhow* in Arunachal) and for their meat (poached using guns, or arrows tipped with plant poison). Even tribes who do not eat meat use primate body parts in traditional medicine, especially in the northeast. Body parts are also valued in some tribes as auspicious charms, amulets to increase courage, or ornaments to ward off evil spirits. ❏

DOGS, HYENAS AND BEARS

More versatile, social and widespread than the cats, the region's
dogs, hyenas and bears are highly successful predators and scavengers

Stories like *Little Red Riding Hood* featuring the misdeeds and cunning of the wolf are widespread. Told to us at a tender age, they inevitably plant the seeds of fear of the wolf into our young minds. It is easy for us to picture the wolf of the story – the large ears, the big fangs and everything else that builds up this rather misleading picture. Not surprising then, most women in Bihar even today keep the children at home with stories of the wolf, for even the tiger does not command the respect most Canidae do.

The dog family

In India, the Canidae (as the dog family is known) are among the most widely distributed of all beasts of prey. A near relative, the striped hyena, is mainly a scavenger by habit, but will on occasion attack an animal if it can be overcome easily. Unlike the cat family, the paws are tipped with nails that are non-retractile, and this is one of the characteristics which points to a relationship between dogs and bears. To find any further resemblance, one would have to go back to the fossil remains of primitive animal forms which suggest a common ancestral stock.

The different modes of life adopted by their forebears led to differences in structure and habits which are now so apparent in the two families. While the progenitors of the wolves, jackals, foxes and dogs became hunters who took their prey by swift and enduring chase, the ancient bears probably lived as they live now – feeding on grasses, roots, herbs, fruits and insects. Yet the bears still retain the ability to kill for food, and a bear will eat meat whenever an opportunity is offered.

The Canidae – with the exception of the jackal, which lives mainly off carrion – are among the most efficient predators in the world and their physical evolution has built them into efficient killing machines.

LEFT: sloth bear, Ranthambore.
RIGHT: Indian peninsula wolf, one of three wolf lineages found in India.

A long pointed muzzle with large erect ears, a well-shaped head, deep-chested muscular body and a bushy tail enable them to secure prey by swift and open chase. The feet are equipped with five toes, including the dew-claws, and the toes, resting on deep, well-cushioned pads, are held close together by elastic-rimmed webs. Canidae

do not rely on their feet for striking at their prey, or even gripping it – their feet are designed solely with one specific purpose – to follow prey over hard ground.

Besides the ability to outlast their prey over a large distance, for which their lungs are well developed, the main weapon for attack is the powerful set of teeth set in equally powerful jaws, which allows for a tenacity of hold that is their mainstay in attack. With a few exceptions, most dogs have a great array of 42 teeth and a powerful set of cheek muscles gives them a vice-like grip. Interlocking canines and incisors form formidable weapons for seizing or lacerating live prey, and the latter are well adapted for biting, gnawing, or stripping the skin from flesh. Further, their cheek teeth also help adapt them to a vegetable diet for, meat-eaters as a rule, Canidae also live on grass, herbs and fruit.

The dog family is among the most diversely distributed species throughout the world. The animals found in the subcontinent do not differ in essential habits from their cousins in other parts of the globe, the marked difference being only in size and local colouration.

DHOLE CALLS

The dhole has a range of vocal calls – it can make high-pitched screams, mew, hiss, yelp, chatter and cluck like a chicken, though is best known for its strange whistle.

have an advanced communication system; dholes, as wild dogs are known in India, communicate with each other by whistling, and the pack will usually set a perfect ambush, meeting with a higher rate of success than some of the better-known carnivores. For foxes and other animals that do not live in packs, the prey is usually rodents and small animals. For them, their speed is more a method of escape, though in the case of jackals, wolves and even hyenas, 'playing dead' is yet another method of escape.

Food habits also depend largely on local conditions, as do the number of animals living in a pack. It is a well recorded fact that a pack of wild dogs living in a certain area will sometimes swell, then decline again, leaving a more or less constant population. Food relationships within the pack are a complex business, and any undue increase or decline in the number of any one species affects the lives of many others.

A highly developed sense of smell and keen eyesight are two of the most prized assets of the dog family. All are nocturnal, though most kills are made either in the late afternoon or at dusk, leaving people to argue about their nocturnal habits. Within their own packs, they

The dogged hunter

The **dhole**, or the **Indian wild dog** (*Cuon alpinus*), is perhaps the most widely distributed of all species. Three races are known to us, a trans-Himalayan race that are paler, the deeper red species of the Himalaya and the tawnier peninsular form. Their range in India starts from Ladakh where they are said to hunt wild sheep and goats. In the lower reaches they inhabit forested area. Like wolves, they too hunt in packs that are usually family groups, the social life originating from a prolonged association between parents and their young, well-looked-after offspring. There is very little aggressiveness or bullying between pack members and there is group care of young. Like domestic dogs, they wag their tails.

They prefer hunting by day, though on rare occasions they will also hunt at night. Once on the trail of the unfortunate victim, their prey is followed by scent in silence, though in heavy cover the yaps of the leader indicate the line of approach. Once the animal is in visual contact, the pack often breaks out into excited whimpering and yapping, panicking the herd ahead to stampede. In the chaos that follows, an individual is guided away from the main body and then brought down ruthlessly. Large packs of up to 40 are known to have taken on

would often be told. But of late, dholes have often been observed close to a potential prey-species, both seemingly unconcerned by the other's presence. On the other hand a herd of over 300 chital has been observed to run blindly through a human habitation when wild dogs appeared. Perhaps both the hunter and the hunted know when the former is on the lookout for food.

Wolf Evolution

The **Indian wolf** *(Canis lupus pallipes)*, unlike the dhole, is not often seen, as its habitat has suffered adversely at the hands of humans.

animals like the gaur and the buffalo, and records of tigers being killed by dholes also exist. The tiger is not hunted by dholes, a battle usually taking place more out of a chance encounter than anything else.

Until a decade ago, accused of killing more than they could eat, wild dogs were considered vermin and many state governments offered cash incentives to hunters to wipe them out. Shikaris of yesteryear often talked of an absolute "stillness" that would set in when dholes appeared – "you might as well go home", one

LEFT: Indian wild dogs, or dholes, with chital kill.
ABOVE: jackal, Desert National Park.

Found more in the bare and open regions, its range extends from Ladakh and Kashmir into the desert zone and the dry open plains of peninsular India. The wolf has often come into conflict with humans for attacking livestock and for rare attacks on children, when prey species are low and livestock protected, which has lead to heavy hunting. There are an estimated 2,000–3,000 Indian wolves remaining in India.

Its size, large skull and teeth distinguish the wolf from the rest of the family. Animals from the plains of India have sandy fawn coats stippled with black. The wolves from Ladakh, in contrast, have predominantly blackish coats in the summer, and their winter coats are variegated with long, black and white or black and buff underwool.

Eastern Kashmir, Himachal Pradesh, parts of Tibet and Eastern Nepal is home to the **Himalayan wolf** *(Canus lupus chanco –* Himalayan Lineage), separated from the Indian wolf by the Himalayan foothills and the Terai – a band of lush wet tropical grasslands. Recent research has found that the Himalayan wolf and the peninsular Indian wolf populations are genetically unique within themselves, different from all other wolf and dog populations recorded worldwide (the wolf-dog clade) and represent the most ancient wolf lineages. Both

are physically and genetically different enough to be considered distinct species of wolf. This, together with the presence of the wolf-dog clade *(Canus lupus chanco* – Wolf-Dog Lineage) in the northwestern Himalaya, makes India the likely cradle of modern wolf evolution.

Camp Followers: The long-drawn, eerie howling of the **jackal** *(Canis aureus)* at dusk or just before dawn is perhaps more familiar to most people than the animal itself. Three races occur, and it is found throughout India and Sri Lanka. Its closest relative is the wolf, but it is much smaller in build, and lacks the arching brows and elevated forehead that give the wolf a noble look. The Himalayan jackal has a slightly

darker coat, but by and large they are pale and tawny with a bit of white and black around the shoulders, ears and legs. Perhaps the most nocturnal of all Canidae, jackels usually come out as dusk creeps across the subcontinent. On a cloudy day, they will sometimes come out earlier, and in very hot weather, they may make a daytime trip to a water hole.

Kalighati watchtower in Rajasthan's Sariska Tiger Reserve is an excellent place to observe these animals, of which very little is known. In jungle terms they are referred to as "camp followers" and tales of the jackal following meekly in the wake of the largest predator of the Indian jungle, the tiger, are common to Indian folklore. Jackals play an important role in clearing carcasses and offal, but they sometimes gang up into a pack and attack deer fawns or antelope in a manner similar to that of dhole. They also feed on fruit and some vegetables, and prefer to live around towns and villages, contributing in a large way to village sanitation.

Wily elegance

The richly coloured **red fox** *(Vulpes vulpes)* is the most widely distributed terrestrial carnivore in the world. Its long silky fur and superb bushy tail, with the black of its back continuing to the upper half of its ears, and the white tip to its tail, distinguish it from the Indian fox of the plains. Red is the dominant colour of its lovely coat, though local variations from grey to yellow occur. Three races are recognized in India: the hill fox of the Himalaya, which ranges from Ladakh and Kashmir to Sikkim; a northern desert subspecies, and the western desert whitefooted fox, which ranges from Rajasthan to Kutch.

Red foxes are said to pair for life and they occupy the same den year after year. They live in thorn bushes and willows fringing the edges of streams and are sometimes found in cultivated areas. They occasionally venture out during the day, but usually hunt at night, generally alone or at the most with a mate. They prey chiefly on rodents, which include squirrels, and they also take a toll on ground birds, like the chukor, partridge and pheasant. In winter, driven by hunger, they will sometimes raid human habitations for food, picking up offal and other tidbits of food.

The **Indian fox** *(Vulpes bengalensis)* is the common fox of the Indian plains, smaller and more slender than the red fox. Its tail has a black tip and its ears are not black like those of the red fox. Its coat, too, is never as luxuriant, and the dominant colour is grey. It ranges through the entire country, from the foothills of the Himalaya to Kanyakumari. It will sometimes attack poultry, and feed off rodents and insects, shrubs and berries. It will gobble up emerging termites as they take to the wing, and by its constant destruction of rats and other pests, it is of great value to the farmer. It rarely enters forested areas, preferring the cultivated areas near a canal, using a bund to live in. Its main defence is its speed and nimble turning ability – it will also double back on its own tracks to throw trackers off balance.

smell, its sight and hearing being almost defunct. It too is a camp follower, but gets to the kill after the vultures and jackals have had their fill, feeding mainly on bones and coarse remains – its powerful jaws being perfectly adapted for bone crushing.

In the subcontinent, the **striped hyena** *(Hyaena hyaena)* extends its range through forested districts, open country and ravines. Often a hyena will enlarge a porcupine burrow where it lies through the day, foraging for food almost exclusively by night.

When searching for food, a hyena will tramp along with its awkward, ambling gait and once it

Ungainly scavenger

The build of a hyena and its dog-like appearance would suggest it to be part of the Canidae. Its legs and feet are similar to those of a dog but the structure of the skull, the teeth and other points in the anatomy of the animal would place it in the cat family.

A sort of a link between the two orders, the hyena at first sight looks like an ungainly dog. A scavenger by nature, it seeks food entirely by

LEFT: the Kashmir Fox, *Vulpes vulpes griffithi*, found in Jammu and Kashmir.
ABOVE: the Indian or Bengal fox, known as *lomri* in Hindi and *kulla naree* in Tamil.

has located a kill, it will stand its ground to hold it against even the rightful owner. Although it is no match for the tiger, it is known to have often taken on leopard successfully. It is otherwise a shy animal, avoiding a confrontation with domestic dogs and it often resorts to "playing dead" until its persecutors lose interest in a seemingly lifeless body. It is famous for its laughing chatter, and though some photographs and notes have been taken of its denning behavior, little else is known about these animals. Supposedly common, they are rarely seen, mainly because of their nocturnal habits, and they too have been reported to indulge in man-eating, snatching babies occasionally from the doorways of houses.

Bears

It comes as a surprise to many that bears and dogs come from the same ancestral stock. Neither their appearance, nor their habits, show any close affinity. Yet fossilized remains reveal a close relationship. The explanation for the subsequent differentiation could lie in the fact that dogs became hunters and therefore developed the necessary lines and limbs to help swift movement, whereas bears probably lived, as they do now, on insects, termites, roots, fruits and honey, and therefore developed heavy bodies and strong paws to facilitate digging and climbing of rocks, cliffs and trees.

Bears find much of their food on the ground or just below the surface. Their long, curving claws, longer in the forefeet, are well-adapted for digging. Their mobile, protruding lips are used to suck up termites from their deep galleries. Their padded feet and inward-turned forepaws are suitable for climbing. The belief that bears are vegetarian is mistaken; they eat a varied diet, occasionally including animal flesh. Another popular misconception is that bears kill by hugging their victims. Actually, they usually swat the enemy with a swinging arm blow, like a boxer's "hook" and, digging claws deep, they scalp the victim.

In general, bears have large heads unusually small eyes and round ears. Their large bodies and heavy limbs are covered by a shaggy coat. They have very short tails. Their prime sense is that of smell. Their senses of touch, sight and hearing not being well developed, bears can very often be taken by surprise. In such situations their reactions are unpredictable and bears are often known to attack even when approached gently.

Bears lumber along with a shuffling gait and walk miles every day in search of food. When frightened or alarmed, they can gallop at a fast though clumsy pace. All bears are good swimmers.

Some types of bear hibernate during winter to avoid the cold, but more often it is a means of surviving a period of extreme shortage of food. The heart action is reduced almost to a standstill and all body functions are suspended. No energy is expended and, therefore, no food is required. With the coming of spring, bears emerge from hibernation in good health.

The **sloth bear** (*Melursus ursinus*) has inhabited India from very early times. Bear fossils have been found here. Originally confused with the sloth, scientists have now classified it under a separate genus in view of differences in skull structure and the fact that the two middle incisors are missing in the upper jaw of the sloth bear. Estimated to number between 6,000 and 11,000 individuals, this bear remains widely distributed in India, and is found in most areas where large patches of forest exist. However, the population is fragmented into several relatively large but disconnected units. Habitat loss is the greatest threat

Sloth bears grow 1.5–1.8 metres (5–6 ft) long, standing 60–90 cm (2–3 ft) at the shoulder, and weigh between 54 kg (120 lbs) for lighter females and 140 kg (310 lbs) for heavier males. With its shaggy, dusty-looking black fur, it looks somewhat uncouth. It has a V- or Y-shaped patch of white on its chest,

lar, a sloth bear has great power and vitality packed into its huge body.

Preferred habitat for sloth bears is tropical deciduous forest – ideally dry deciduous, though they are also found in moist deciduous forest and, to a lesser degree, in wet evergreen forest and dry scrub forest. Most of India's deciduous forest is either degraded or unprotected however. It prefers areas with cover and rocky outcrops to shelter in, and it usually emerges at dusk to spend most of the night rummaging for food. It can smell buried food and can be seen digging furiously to get at even one tasty grub. It is very intelligent and remembers the seasons and places

which is a distinguishing feature. To add to its untidy appearance, it has a mangy-looking face, round eyes with hairless lids, and a long, dull-grey snout with protruding, pendulous lips. Its bowed forelegs with inward-turned forefeet make it a specially good climber. For no apparent reason, the tall Terminalia arjuna is its favourite tree. Claw marks on trunks and branches are proof of this. The long, 10 cm (4 inch) ivory-white claws on its forefeet are perfect digging implements. Large and muscu-

where its favourite food is found. Wild fig, jambul, ber, bael, mohwa, amaltas and ebony fruit are all well-liked. Sloth bears living around human settlements seem to delight in raiding maize crops and sugarcane. Where date palms are tapped, they climb trees to attack the toddy.

Small groups of sloth bear have been seen seemingly drunk on the heady fermented juice of mohwa flowers. It has a very clever way of grabbing honeycombs. In the darkness, it climbs a tree on which honeycombs hang and knocks down a single comb with a firm swipe of the paw, probably realizing that it cannot manage more than one at a time. The bees, confused in the darkness, buzz around the

LEFT: hyenas have highly acidic digestive fluids capable of digesting their entire prey, bones and all.
ABOVE: the sloth bear or 'honey bear'.

branch or settle on other combs, while the bear happily sucks the honey and eats the grubs in the comb that has fallen to the ground. During the monsoon a sloth relies heavily on an insect diet, and to see it attacking a termite mound with the accompanying sound effects is a sight one can rarely forget.

Termite-hunting is a bear's major occupation. Using its powerful paws to tear down the mound, the bear reaches the termites at the bottom. It puffs and blows away the dust and sucks up the termites with great skill. Its overhanging upper lip is pressed back against the nostrils, protecting the animal from inhaling

two or three years old. Male bears move away from the group and lead a solitary existence. Usually quick to run away when threatened, a female with cubs is a dangerous proposition for she gets extremely hostile and savage. Indeed, when angry, the sloth bear is one of the most dangerous animals on the subcontinent.

Sloth bears are hunted for their fur and their gall bladder, which is believed by some to have medicinal properties. They are also captured and trained to perform. Sadly, the sloth bear is also the common performing bear used by itinerant entertainers for roadside shows. It was only in the early-20th century that people took

dust. As if designed for the purpose of clearing a passage for suction, there is an empty space at the point where one would expect the two middle teeth of the upper jaw to be. A concave palate facilitates the process.

The sloth bear grunts and squeals loudly while turning over stones in a stream, eating grubs and insects with its blubberous mouth. It grunts very differently when angry.

The sloth bear mates in the hot weather. Two cubs are born in the winter, after a gestation period of seven months. Born in an underground den, they stay there for several months, after which the mother carries the cubs on her back and looks after them till they are

to hunting the sloth bear. Before that they were to be seen in immense numbers.

The **Himalayan brown bear** *(Ursus arctos)* is seen in different sizes but all are of a heavy build. An average male can measure 170 cm (5 ft 8 ins) in length. The coat varies from a rich dark-brown in summer to a tawny, worn-out brown in old animals. It has a heavy underwool during winter and its white-tipped fur sometimes gives it a silvery sheen. This bear lives in the cold north temperate zone in the higher reaches of the northwestern and central Himalaya, among the bare peaks above the tree line. It hibernates in winter and in spring lives on new grass shoots, insects, voles and marmots, which it digs out of burrows. Since food is scarce in its habitat it also attacks sheep, goats, ponies and livestock. Shortage of food at these altitudes drives it to eat carrion, and in Zanskar a brown bear was once seen fighting off Tibetan ravens while it fed on an ibex that had died earlier of natural causes.

The brown bear rarely climbs and usually picks its food off the ground and digs in search of tubers and roots. Berries, wild fruit, peaches, apricots, apples, mulberries and walnuts offer a welcome change of diet. The mating season is in summer. Cubs are born in December and remain with the mother for four or five years.

brown bear. It has a smooth black coat, black claws and a brown muzzle with a white or buff lower jaw. A prominent V-shaped patch of white or yellow is seen on the breast. Found in Kashmir, the Himalaya and Assam, this bear lives below the tree line, around 3,660 metres (12,000 ft), and sleeps in rocky nests and hollows of trees. The black bear found in Assam is marginally smaller. In winter it comes down to 1,525 metres (5,000 ft). It is nocturnal, but is surprisingly active by day in Kashmir's Dachigam National Park.

It is a good climber and gets most of its food off fruit trees. Pears, apricots, berries,

Brown bears have never been known to attack humans, but it can be disastrous if one of them gets into a sheep pen. Reports of the yeti in the Himalaya have been attributed to sightings of the brown bear. A "yeti scalp" in one of the monasteries of Nepal proved to be that of a brown bear. The Tibetan blue bear is also reported in the same area, but this animal is an almost unknown species.

Finally, the **Himalayan black bear** (*Selenarctos thibetanus*) is smaller than the

LEFT: two brown bears playing in the snow.
ABOVE: Himalayan black bear occasionally feed on carrion.

honey, corn, insects, termites and larvae of beetles, make up its varied diet, but sheep, goats and even cattle are attacked and eaten. It attacks and mauls even human beings in self defence or if surprised. These bears are able to climb trees with great ease, and have a strange technique of climbing down – carefully making their descent until a few feet are left, then landing with a thump as they seem to lose interest.

These bears are solitary, with a mating season is in late autumn. Two cubs are produced in spring. They remain with the mother for a year or two. Bears are sometimes seen with four cubs but these must belong to two successive litters. ❏

OTHER MAMMALS

Red panda, mongooses, pangolin and flying foxes,
Indian wildlife is more than big cats and deer

In additon to the large animals of the preceding chapters, India has a huge variety of other mammals – amphibious, subterranean and even flying. Though mostly smaller, lesser-known, or less charismatic, they include the fearsome boar, the mongoose (of Rikki-tikki-tavi Jungle Book fame), and the fascinating pangolin,

Pandas

Although pandas resemble bears in many ways – round heads, heavy bodies, short legs and a bear-like gait, they are classified under the Family Procyonidae, which includes the racoon, the North-American carnivore.

The **red panda**, also known as the lesser panda or red cat bear *(Ailurus fulgens)* looks a little like a racoon, with a very long tail. It has a round head, upright pointed ears and a short muzzle. The soles of its feet are matted and hairy, as in the case of the polar bear. It is rich brown in colour, with alternate brown and white rings on its bushy tail. Its face and lower lip are white and a prominent red stripe from the eyes to the nape of the neck is its distinguishing feature.

Found in Nepal, Sikkim and the Eastern Himalaya, the red panda lives at altitudes above 1,525 metres (5,000 ft). Adept at climbing, it is arboreal and gets a good grip on branches with its well-formed toes and semi-retractable claws. Large molars, with many pointed edges for grinding food, are assets for its almost totally vegeterian diet – roots, grasses, leaves and fruit. On rare occasions it will also eat eggs, grubs and insects as supplements to its normal diet.

A fine sense of smell, far better than its sight and hearing, is its main guide. When excited, a strong odor is ejected by the anal gland. A scent trail is left on trees and other surfaces to enable one panda to find another, an activity most probably linked with the mating season. Not much is known of the red panda's breeding habits or its period of gestation. Two young are normally

LEFT: the handsome red panda is distributed throughout the eastern HImalaya.
RIGHT: common palm civet.

seen in spring. The mother, or sometimes both parents, look after the young for a year.

Pigs

Pigs, South American peccaries, and hippo-potamuses form an order called Artiodactyla. In India only two subspecies of pig are now

found – the wild boar and the pygmy hog.

The **Wild Boar** *(Sus scrofa cristatus)* is a large, heavily built animal, the male on average growing to 90–95 cm (36–38 ins) in height and 90–225 kg (200–500 lbs) in weight.

The typical feature of a pig is its elongated, suddenly truncated, movable snout, ending in a flat disk-like surface supporting the nostrils. The upper canines grow upwards and outwards. These are dangerous appendages used to great advantage by the boar. The most distinct difference between the Indian boar and its European counterpart is its greyish-black coat ,which is very sparsely covered with hair. However, it has a fuller crest or mane of black bristles rising from the nape of its neck and running to its hind quarters. When it scents danger, this crest stands up as an impressive ridge of angry bristles.

An immense area covering India, Myanmar, Thailand, Sri Lanka and West Malaysia is the home of the boar. Scanty bush jungles, forests with clearings and grassy areas are its favourite haunts. It always lives in the proximity of water and enjoys wallowing in shallow pools but not in slush like the buffalo. It is a noisy animal and grunts loudly when it fights, and when it sharpens its tusks against tree trunks and other hard surfaces the squeak and clatter can be heard from quite a distance away.

showing a rare tenacity and a grim determination to survive. During the day, the boar is not as self-confident as it is at night. Surprised in broad daylight, it prefers to bolt.

The boar's high intelligence becomes evident when it moves to new grounds cautiously following deep *nullas* (water-courses) to avoid detection or camouflaging itself under lone palms or clumps of bushes.

Pigs do not seem to have any fixed breeding cycle. A sow bears four to six young in a litter, after a gestation period of four months. Before the birth, she builds a comfortable shelter. With tall grass or bamboo, she lays out a circular pat-

The omnivorous pig eats a variety of food – roots, tubers, insects, mollusks, offal, carrion, small mammals, and even the remains of a tiger-kill. It is also a determined crop-raider and attacks cultivated areas near the forest edge. A field of peanut could be uprooted by a group, or sounder, in a night.

The sharpest sense in a boar is that of smell; its sight and hearing are mediocre. It is noted for its courage and determination, its self-possession, and its daring. It is one of the few animals that can stand up to a tiger. Many cases are known of tigers, despite their agility and strength, being gored to death by a ferocious boar. Bleeding and torn boars are known to have kept up the fight,

tern with the heavier ends on the outer edge. She then burrows below the material she has laid down, thus making a chamber under a protective roof. In this snug room she has her young and shelters them.

Wild boar were once abundant in Indian forests. Poaching and killing for crop protection have reduced their numbers. The wild pig is popular prey for humans, tigers, leopards and crocodiles. Destruction of its habitat is another factor that has affected its numbers. However, in parts of Madhya Pradesh such as Bandhavgarh, sounders of up to 70 are again being seen.

Dunbar Brander has described how in Central India he saw, during the spring rut, a congregation of about 170 animals that formed a circle in a forest clearing. In the arena were two master boars locked in combat, two others seemed to have just finished. In all there were 11 master-males competing quite obviously for the best sow. A notable feature of the fight was that it seemed a contest governed by rules.

The **pygmy hog** *(Sus salvanius)*, only 25 cm (10 inch) high, is the smallest of all pigs. Short-tailed, with small ears, a short snout and upper tusks, it has a coarse, blackish-brown, scanty-haired coat. By and large, its ways are similar to those of a wild boar. It has nocturnal habits and feeds on roots, bulbs, insects and lizards. Typi-

Human settlements, ruthlessly infringing on the pygmy hog's natural habitat, have endangered the species. Rediscovered in 1971 in the dooar grasslands, it was later reported in southeast Bhutan, parts of Bangladesh and the Kamrup, Goalpara and Darrang districts of northern Assam. Although not seen there for many decades it may still occur in the terai forests of Nepal, Uttar Pradesh and Bihar.

Mongooses

These were originally classified under the civet family. However, since various distinctive features have been observed, they have now been

cally, a litter of four young appears in April–May.

First classified by Hodgson in 1847, it lives in the tall grasslands of the Assam terai. The only known population exists in the Manas Tiger Reserve, with possibility of its existence in Sunai-Rupai Wildlife Sanctuary. A conservation breeding programme has been started near Guwahati, where nearly 80 pygmy hogs are presently found. The Assam government is planning to reintroduce the species in a few selected grasslands after improving the habitat and protection level.

LEFT: long thought to be extinct, the pygmy hog was rediscovered in 1971.
ABOVE: wild boar feeding on a hangul carcass.

grouped in a family by themselves, the Herpestidae. A long body, short limbs, a long, bushy tail, and bright beady eyes are characteristic of the mongoose. Its ears are small and form neat semi-circles close to the head. Its ear is admirably structured and consists of many folds, which tightly close the opening of the ear. This is probably a natural protection against the dust that is raised when the mongoose burrows into the earth.

Its strong predatory instincts make the mongoose a good hunter. It preys on hares, rats, mice, snakes, frogs, lizards, crabs and grasshoppers and is partial to birds' eggs. Roots and berries also form part of its varied diet, though it shows a strong preference for meat. Its sharp-edged, blade-like teeth are made for meat-tearing and cutting. The prey is bitten, crushed and then eaten. Sometimes, the mongoose drinks the blood of its victims. It often sucks eggs after piercing a hole in the shell.

Unlike cats, which stealthily surprise their prey, the mongoose attacks openly and directly, pouncing relentlessly on its victim. It follows its quarry by its scent and tracks it down to its burrow and digs it out. Its body seems built for the purpose, with strong forefeet and well-developed digging claws. Though it is a low-strung animal, it gains height for a quick look around by standing on its hind legs.

against the immense good they do by keeping the numbers of rats, mice, snakes, insects and scorpions under control.

The **common mongoose** *(Herpestes edwardsi)* is yellowish-grey in colour. It has a grizzled coat and tail, with a white or yellowish-red tip. Common all over India, Nepal and Sri Lanka, it is found on open land and in scrub jungle, where it lives in thickets. It is diurnal and can be seen scurrying along even at the hottest time of the day. It breeds thrice times a year, three to four young being born after a gestation period of two months. The mother is often seen moving with the young in a family group.

The mongoose has a reputation as a killer of snakes, including the deadly cobra. It is its agility that enables it to avoid the snake's bite. Also, when excited, its hair bristles and this makes it seem larger than it really is, thus baffling the enemy. Cautiously, the mongoose waits for an opportunity to overpower the snake. In that split second when the snake lowers its head after an attempt strike, the mongoose snaps on to the back of the snake's head and crunches it to death.

When the opportunity offers, a mongoose will kill more than it can consume – out of sheer excitement. Domestic poultry are often their victims, which somewhat strains their relations with humans, but this has to be weighed

The **ruddy mongoose** *(Herpestes smithi)*, recognisable by the black tip on its tail, is about the same size as the common mongoose. It is not seen very often as it lives in forested areas.

The **stripe-necked mongoose** *(Herpestes vitticollis)* is the largest of the Asiatic mongooses. It is distinguished by a black stripe that runs along its neck from ear to shoulder. Its coat is a rich, grey colour highlighted with red tips. It is found in clearings of swampy areas, near running water, or in open scrub country, from where it sometimes enters forests. It has a keen preference for a meat diet and hunts chital fawns, mouse deer, hares, field rats, bandicoots, frogs, fishes and crabs, but it also eats fruit and roots.

The **crab-eating mongoose** *(Herpestes urva)* is almost as long but heavier than the common mongoose. It has an untidy, rough coat of a dark-grey colour. It occurs in Nepal and Assam and can be seen there near small streams, on the banks of which it hunts for crabs, deftly cracking the shell of its victim by knocking it against a rock. When attacked, it protects itself by squirting out a fetid fluid from its anal glands on its attacker.

Otters, martens and weasels

Otters belong to a large family known as Mustelids, which also includes stoats, weasels,

fact have rudimentary claws.

The otter is a beautifully streamlined animal. It has short legs, a thick neck and a long and powerful tail, which is its most striking feature, accounting for almost half its length. The tail is furry like the rest of its body and its main use is in swimming. When otters stand on their hind legs, the tail is used to keep balance.

While otters feed primarily on fish, they kill any prey they can handle and, indeed, range over several miles of land in their quest for food. It has also been observed that certain Indian otters often fish as a cooperative, forming a semicircle to drive fish towards the shallows.

minks, martens and badgers. Otters are found all over the world, with the exception of Australia, New Zealand and the polar regions. As can be expected of a group of animals that has such a varied distribution, otters vary considerably in size, ranging from the 1-metre (3-ft) long, clawless otter of the East Indies to the 2½-meter (8-ft) long Brazilian otter. However, all of them have a number of common features. All are largely amphibious; all have five digits on their feet and non-retractable claws. The two otters generally called clawless do in

Three species are found in the Indian subcontinent: the **common otter** *(Lutra lutra)*, the smooth **Indian otter** *(Lutra perspicillata)*, and the **clawless otter** *(Aonyx cinerea)*. The common otter, which is distinguished from the other races by its fuller and rougher coat, is found in Kashmir, the Himalayan ranges and Assam. In South India a subspecies is found. Basically a creature of hills, rivers and streams, it has been recorded at altitudes exceeding 3,660 metres (12,000 ft). Their upward migration has probably a lot to do with the migration of fish. Hunting mainly at night, they move over land from one stream to another. A characteristic often observed is that they kill more fish than they require. This is

LEFT: a pair of ruddy mongooses.
ABOVE: a common mongoose.

attributed to the excitement of the hunt. Little is known of their breeding habits. The young are born in conveniently located hideouts, usually beside a stream, with at least one underwater entrance. The mothers care for the young till they are nearly fully grown.

The smooth Indian otter is about the same size as the common otter but has a sleek smooth coat, which varies in colour from blackish to sandy-brown. Essentially a plains otter, it has adapted itself to life even in the arid regions of northwestern India. Like other otters, it prefers living next to water, but during the dry season it can adapt itself to living

They prefer an arboreal existence, hunting their prey in trees. They have long snouts, large ears and a long tail that helps them maintain their balance while leaping from one branch to another. In India, two types are found: the **beech** or **stone marten** (*Martes foina*) and the **yellow-throated marten** (*Martes flavigula*). The stone marten is found in the alpine and temperate zones of Kashmir and the Himalaya, as far east as Sikkim. They are rarely found below 1,524 metres (5,000 ft). They inhabit both the forest and the barren areas above the tree line. Martens in the higher regions live primarily on rodents and mouse hares. The jungle dwellers have a

off the jungle. These otters are often trained to act as decoys for capturing river dolphins.

The clawless otter is so called because its claws are very rudimentary and do not project beyond the toe pads. This is the smallest of the Indian species and is dark brown in colour (the South Indian subspecies is distinctly darker). It is found in the lower Himalaya extending up to Assam. The South Indian species is confined to Coorg and the Nilgiri ranges. Its habits and ways are similar to those of the other Indian otters, except for its preference for crabs and some other aquatic creatures over fish.

Martens are purely land animals and their feet are adapted for running and climbing trees.

more varied diet of birds, honey and fruit.

The yellow-throated marten gets its name from the yellow band that runs down its neck. It is larger than the stone marten and is found in the Himalayan and the Assam ranges. It lives in the plains and hunts in the trees, where its extreme agility makes it a menace to the other inhabitants. It also hunts snakes and rodents on the ground and has been known to attack young deer. The South Indian subspecies, the **Nilgiri marten** (*Martes gwatkinsi*), is confined to the Nilgiri and Coorg ranges.

These are several types of weasel in India, the most common being the Himalayan weasel (*Mustela sibirica*), of which there are three subspecies. Another Himalayan weasel is the ermine *(Mustela erminea)*, which is found in Kashmir. The pale weasel is found in the upper reaches of the Himalaya. Besides these, two other types are found in India, the **striped-back weasel** *(Mustela strigidorsa)* and the **yellow-bellied weasel** *(Mustela kathiah)*.

Though weasels can climb trees, they usually spend their time on the ground and often chase their prey into underground burrows, where rats and mice live. Their slim bodies are specially adapted for such activities.

True badgers are not found in India, though two types akin to it do exist. They are the ferret badger and the hog badger. The first gets it name from its being a mixture of a ferret and a badger. It has a long protruding snout, which it uses for probing for food. It uses its non-retractable claws for digging. It is also known for its ability to climb trees. The **Indian race** *(Melagale millsi)* is confined to Assam and Nepal, where it is reported to be encouraged by the local population to enter their houses to eat cockroaches and other pests. The **hog badger** *(Arctonyx collaris)* looks like a bear with its short stumpy legs and long powerful claws. It has a long mobile snout like that of a pig, which ends in a disk containing the nostrils. Its coat is blackish-grey with a pale throat and a dark stripe on the cheek. Nocturnal and omnivorous, it lives in the tropical forests and prefers rocky areas, with a range extending from Northeastern India to Southeast Asia. It is seclusive and rarely seen, when attacked it discharges a stink from its glands.

The **honey badger** or **ratel** *(Mellivora capensis)* is again bear-like with a squat body, short legs and stumpy tail, sharp teeth, strong claws and stink glands. It is tawny-white above and black on the sides and below. The underpart of the face and tail are also black. Found all over India, from the Himalaya to Kanyakumari, it lives both in deserts and deciduous forests. Ratels live where they can burrow easily. They prey on mammals, birds, poultry, reptiles, insects, and, like bears, even eat fruit and honey. Ratels feed on carrion and are known to dig up graves. They are fearless and even attack humans in self-defence. They live in pairs and two young are produced in a litter.

LEFT: the fearless honey badger or ratel.
RIGHT: smooth Indian otters.

Insectivores

Included under this order is a group of animals with varied lifestyles like tree shrews, hedgehogs, moles and ground shrews. Small and active, these animals, with the exception of the tree shrew, are usually nocturnal. The common features that lead to their being grouped together, other than the fact that they are insectivorous, are their tapering snout, which protrudes far beyond the jaw-bone, their short limbs with five toes each, their distinctive gait, and teeth especially suited to insect eating, all the teeth being more or less similar.

The **tree shrew** *(Anathana ellioti)* belongs to

the family Tupaia, which in Malay means squirrel – a suitable name because, though it has the tapering snout of a shrew, it resembles the squirrel in appearance in many ways. Rounded ears, a long tail, feet well-adapted for climbing, naked soles that grip better, long toes and sharp claws are all squirrel-like characteristics. It is a rusty grey-brown on top and its underparts are near white. It is found in the deciduous forests south of the Ganga. In the eastern Himalaya and Burma, from the plains to 1,830 metres (6,000 ft), a close relative, the **Malaya** or **common tree shrew** *(Tupaia glis)* is found. Although it is arboreal and retreats to the security of trees when attacked, it feeds on the ground, looking for its insect-food under rocks, in cracks and crannies and under heaped leaves. Active and alert, it never leaps from branch to branch like a squirrel, nor does it jerk its tail and move with its head pointing downwards. Not much is known of its breeding habits and it is seen with only one young at a time. A family of tree shrews establishes territorial rights over an area and chases out all intruders.

Hedgehogs: The pig-like flattened snout of this animal gives it its name. Two species are seen in India: the **long-eared hedgehog** *(Hemiechinus auritus collaris)*, which has deep blackish-brown fur on its head and underparts

of their holes, which are dug under thorny bushes. They cover long distances in search of food: insects, worms, rats, mice, birds' eggs and lizards.

Moles: Cylindrical bodies, very short necks, and very strong shoulders and forelegs used for digging, are perfect equipment for these diminutive animals that live mainly underground. Their bodies narrow gradually to a short tail. Moles have minute eyes and their fur is so thick and soft that mud does not stick to it while they are burrowing.

The Indian **short-tailed mole** *(Talpa micrura micrura)* is found in the central and eastern Himalaya and in Assam up to heights of 2,440

and the **pale hedgehog** *(Paraechinus micropus)*, which is light-coloured and has parted spines on its head.

Hedgehogs are small and can fit into the palm of one's hand. They have an odd-shaped, rounded body, stubby legs with claws used for digging, and well-formed eyes and ears. Their back and flanks are covered with closely-set spines. A remarkable facility in hedgehogs is their ability to stretch their loose, spiny skin with a muscular action to cover their head and limbs. Rolled up into spiky balls, hedgehogs manage to protect themselves.

Desert areas and the plains abound with these species. They are nocturnal and at dusk move out

metres (8,000 ft). It rummages for insects in black vegetable mould and eats larvae, grubs and earthworms. It lives in burrows under the shelter of trees. Another variety, the **white-tailed mole** *(Talpa micrura leucura)* has a longer tail, thick at the end, covered with white hair. It occurs in the Khasi and Naga hills.

Ground shrews: Pointed snouts reaching far beyond the lower lips, round ears, small eyes, small bodies covered with soft fur, comparatively bare tails, feet adapted for climbing and digging, and two curved front teeth are the distinguishing features of ground shrews.

The **grey musk shrew** *(Suncus murinus)* is common in India. The male has a musk gland on either side of the body and gives out a strong smell of musk, especially during the mating season. It enters human dwellings and is of help to them since it cannot tolerate rats. It also destroys insects. This shrew breeds before it is fully adult, two or three young being born at a time. They can be seen with the mother, each holding the tail of the one in front, thus forming a chain.

Rodents

More than a thousand species, each found in enormous hordes, are classified under the order Rodentia. They are to be found on land, in water and even in the air. Squirrels, marmots, rats, mice and porcupines are all common rodents. They are all small and share an important feature – their teeth are specially structured and they all eat their food in a similar manner. Otherwise they present a great variety of characteristics.

A rodent's front teeth are deeply rooted and are like sharp chisels – designed for cutting. The four incisors, two each in the upper and lower jaws, are covered with a very special layer of hard, yellow enamel that does not wear out in spite of the heavy use to which they are put. Rodents have no canine teeth. At the rear end of the mouth are six pairs of molars with sharp cusps that grind the food into a paste. The gap between the front and rear teeth serves an interesting purpose. The animal's cheeks, which are hairy on the inner surface, can be drawn into the gap to form two chambers in the mouth. The inner hair acts as a mesh between the two chambers preventing coarse particles from passing to the rear chamber but letting more finely chewed food pass into it for grinding by the molars. All rodents break up their food by gnawing then grinding with strong molars that have transverse grooves.

Easily adaptable, rodents are found all over the world and can survive climatic conditions up to heights of 5,500 metres (18,000 ft). Changes in colour are therefore common. Some rodents, like marmot, are known to hibernate during the winter, some migrate, while still others remain active even in severe conditions. Their burgeoning numbers are kept in check by predators, parasites, diseases and natural disasters.

Flying squirrels: These are arboreal and conspicuous. They have a slim build and a long bushy tail. A translucent membrane connects their limbs, forming a parachute. Although known as flying squirrels, they cannot truly fly and can only glide through the air, covering wide gaps. Before alighting, they rise upwards in order to make a smooth landing. When not in flight, the elastic parachute is tucked close to the body and can barely be noticed. Flying squirrels are nocturnal forest animals and roost in tree-holes or build large, leaf nests. They live on fruit, nuts, bark, gum, resin, larvae and buds. Their monotonous call can be heard at night. Their breeding habits are not known. Young squirrels do not have fully developed parachutes.

Of the larger flying squirrels that are about 105 cm (3 ft 6 in) in length, many varieties are found in India. The Kashmir **woolly flying squirrel** (*Eupetaurus cinereus*) is found in northern Kashmir and Sikkim above the tree line and lives on rocks and cliffs. The common **giant flying squirrel** (*Petaurista petaurista*), light brown on top with a yellow-brown tail, and the **large brown flying squirrel** (*P. petaurista philippensis*) are found in peninsular forests, south of the Ganga. The **red flying squirrel** (*P. petaurista albiventer*), rich brown in colour, with pinkish-buff underparts, occurs in the western Himalaya, north of the Ganga. A maroon-coloured squirrel, with a yellow line

LEFT: a long-eared hedgehog.
RIGHT: giant malabar squirrel.

in the middle, black-tipped tail and reddish underparts, Hodgson's flying squirrel, is found in Assam and the eastern Himalaya.

Among the smaller flying squirrels, the small **Travancore flying squirrel** (*Petinomys fusco-capillus*) is the only variety found in the south. The blackish-buff **Kashmir flying squirrel** (*Hylopetes fimbriatus*) lives in the western Himalaya, near the tree line. The **particoloured flying squirrel** (*Hylopetes alboniger*), blackish with white underparts occurs in the eastern Himalaya and Assam, together with the **hairy-footed flying squirrel** (*Belomys pearsoni*) recognized by clumps of brown hair near its ears.

Its back and tail are brownish-grey in colour. The **Malayan giant squirrel** (*Ratufa bicolour*) has a black-brown coat, buff underneath. It is found in Nepal, Sikkim, Bhutan, Assam, Burma and Malaysia.

Himalayan squirrels: The **orange-bellied Himalayan squirrel** (*Dremomys lokriah*) is dark reddish-brown, touched with yellow. The fur on its back is greyish-brown, the longer hairs forming a single yellow ring. The lower parts are orange. This species has a pointed snout and lives in forested areas above 1,525 metres (5,000 ft). Though arboreal, it finds its food on the ground, a favourite being fallen fruit.

Giant squirrels: These live only on the tops of very tall trees and rarely come to the ground. They are very agile and active and can be seen stretched across high branches or leaping from tree to tree across gaps up to 6 metres (20 ft) wide. They have loud rattling calls and raise an alarm when any alien creature is sighted. Alone or in pairs, they build their nests on very slim branches, safe from predators. When the trees lose their leaves, these nests can be clearly seen.

The **Indian giant squirrel** (*Ratufa indica*) is found in both deciduous and evergreen forests. It occurs mainly in peninsular India, south of the Ganga. The **grizzled giant squirrel** (*Ratufa macroura*) occurs in South India and Sri Lanka.

The **hoary-bellied Himalayan squirrel** (*Callosciurus pygerythrus*) is grey for the most part, with a reddish belly, the longer hairs forming two light rings. It lives in dense forests in Nepal, Sikkim, Bhutan and Assam and makes a grass nest high up in the trees and raids orange groves.

Striped squirrels: The **five-striped palm squirrel** (*Funambulus pennanti*) is a small species with three dark longitudinal stripes on its back and two pale ones on the flanks. It is found all over the subcontinent, south of the Himalaya, and often lives around human habitations. It is

ABOVE: three-striped palm squirrel.
RIGHT: the Indian Porcupine.

active and scampers up and down all the time.

The **three-striped palm squirrel** *(Funambulus palmarum)* has three stripes on its back and occurs commonly in peninsular India in two segments: Madhya Pradesh, Bihar and Parucha district of West Bengal in the north, and Andhra Pradesh, Karnataka, Tamil Nadu and Kerala in the south. Like the five-striped squirrel, it is an animal of forests and urban areas with large gardens and orchards, where its shrill call can be heard repeatedly.

The **dusky-striped squirrel** *(Funambulus sublineatus)* has a speckled greenish-grey coat and four stripes down its back. Small and shy, it is

Marmots are found in the Himalaya, in Nepal, Sikkim, Kashmir, Ladakh and Garhwal at an altitude of 4,300 metres (14,000 ft). They live on roots, leaves, grass and seeds. They are often seen sitting on their haunches, calling out with a loud whistling scream. The young are born in spring and are three to four in number.

Gerbils: Gerbils belong to the rat family. They can be identified by their tails, which end in tassels. Their unusually long hind feet seem to prompt them to leap from place to place. The **Indian gerbil** *(Tatera indica)* is reddish-brown in colour, with pale streaks on either side of the tail. It is found all over the peninsula. The **Indian**

found in the dense forests of southern India.

The **Himalayan-striped squirrel** *(Callosciurus macclellandi)* is small and has a greyish-brown coat with black, brown and buff lines. It is found in Assam and Myanamar around heights of 1,525 metres (5,000 ft).

Marmots: Marmots belong to the squirrel family. They live in underground burrows are stoutly built and have short tails and very small ears. The **Himalayan Marmot** *(Marmota bobak)* has a pale, tawny colour. Its face and the end of its tail are dark brown. The **long-tailed marmot** *(Marmota caudata)* is of a handsome rich, reddish-brown colour with a black back and a very long tail.

desert gerbil *(Meriones hurrianae)* is smaller, sandy-yellow coloured and occurs in the desert or semi-desert areas of northwest and central India.

Gerbils live on the plains near cultivated fields and eat grain, roots, leaves and grass. The desert variety eat seeds, tubers and nuts. They appear in large numbers and are crop-pests. As many as 19 young are born after a one month gestation.

Voles: These, the Microtinae, form yet another division in the order Rodentia. They are somewhat different from rats in appearance with their short muzzles, round heads, small ears, short tails, and rounded bodies designed for burrowing. Their teeth have special features. The grinders are flat with triangular cuts on the surface, making them specially good for crushing coarse grass and roots. They live in the higher areas of the Himalaya in Kashmir and Ladakh. **Royle's vole** *(Alticola roylei)* is common at a height of 3,000 metres (10,000 ft). They live in rocky areas that abound in coarse grass. They are reddish-brown in colour, with pale sides and under-parts and a dark tail, and they have protruding ears.

The **Sikkim vole** *(Pitymys siki-mensis)* is a forest animal occur-ing at heights around 3,700 metres (12,000 ft). Dark brown in colour, males measure 10–17 cm

NATURAL ARMOUR

Pangolin scales are said to be bulletproof and a unique scale coat and helmet made from gilded pangolin scales was presented to King George III in 1820.

Southeast Asia. Hill peoples eat its meat. There is no information regarding its breeding habits.

Porcupines: Very different from the other fam-ilies of Rodentia, porcupines belong to the fam-ily of Hystricidae. Hair modified to form long spines is their dis-tinguishing feature. They live in rocky areas, open land, forests, tall grass or near cultivation. Nocturnal in their habits, their sense of smell is very good. They are very intelligent and cannot easily be trapped or poisoned. Vegetables, grass and roots form their chief food, and they

(4–6½ in) plus tail (4 cm/2 in). Old tree stumps and roots are its favourite haunts. It is a forest animal and makes a grass nest.

Bamboo rats: These form a separate family of rodents, the Rhizomyidae. They look like moles but have rodent-like projecting incisors. Digging with their teeth, they live in burrows in open grassy ground. They feed on grass, roots and leaves. When attacked they expose their teeth in anger and bite fiercely. The **bay bamboo rat** *(Cannomys badius)* is a small chestnut-brown rat that occurs in the lower Himalaya in Nepal, Sikkim, Bhutan and Assam. The **hoary bamboo rat** *(Rhizomys pruinosus)* has a flecked, grizzled, dark-brown coat. It is found in Assam, China and

can destroy gardens by burrowing. To balance their diet with a regular intake of calcium they gnaw and scrape bones and horns, which can be seen strewn around burrow entrances.

15–30 cm (6–12-inch) bristles grow from the neck and shoulders of the porcupine. Its back is closely covered with long, backward-slanting quills, ringed with black and white. There is an inner layer of shorter quills. However, the strong, short, white quills at the back are its most dan-gerous weapons. It is mistakenly believed that porcupines shoot their quills.

When attacked or irritated they puff themselves up by erecting their spines, they fume and grunt and rattle their hollow white quills near the tail.

They turn their rear to their adversaries and suddenly lunge backwards, leaving their enemies looking like pin-cushions. These quills enter the bodies of the animals attacked, and sometimes fatally damage the organs of even large animals like tigers and leopards.

The **Indian porcupine** *(Hystrix indica)* is found all over India from the Himalaya to Cape Comorin and in Sri Lanka. In the hill ranges of South India, the colour varies to a rich reddish-brown and there the animal is known as the red porcupine. **Hodgson's porcupine** *(Hystrix hodgsoni)*, which occurs in Assam and Bengal at heights of 1,525 metres (5,000 ft) has a very

replaced individually. The underparts are covered with coarse bristle-like hair.

Living on an exclusive diet of ants and termites, the pangolin has no teeth but its long tongue is glutinous, attracting ants that stick on to it. Its tongue is linked to the stomach and is controlled by muscles attached to the pelvis. With quick movements, the tongue protrudes up to 25 cm (10 ins) and is suddenly drawn back, covered with insects. Rhythmic movements of the throat sieve the debris, acting as a filter.

The pangolin's body is designed to meet specific needs and the legs are perfectly built for digging. They are curved; the forefeet are

small crest. Another variety, the **brush-tailed porcupine** *(Atherurus macrourus)*, is said to dwell in lower Bengal, Assam and further east up to Malaysia. It has a long tail with a tuft of bristles and is rather rare.

Pangolin

This scaly anteater is a quaint old-world animal, a survivor from past ages. A series of strong overlapping, brownish-grey scales, a form of modified hair, cover the upper part and sides of the body and the long tail. The scales are shed and

LEFT: pangolins are found south of the Himalaya.
ABOVE: the black-naped hare.

longer and have blunt claws. The pangolin lives in deep burrows under the ground.

A strong sense of smell guides the animal and its sight and hearing are poor. The strong prehensile tail helps to make the pangolin a good climber and is also used in self defence. When moving, the back is arched and the tail held above the ground. Often, the animal stands on its hind feet to get a better view of the surroundings. When attacked, the animal rolls itself into a tight ball showing great muscular power and is almost impregnable. The only sound it emits is a strong hiss, when alarmed or disturbed. Usually one young is produced at a time and the baby is carried by the mother on her back and tail.

Two species are found in India, the **Chinese pangolin** *(Manis pentadactyla)*, which occurs in the northeast, and the **Indian pangolin** *(Manis crassicaudata)* found in peninsular India. It is hunted for its flesh and for its scales, which are said to have medicinal and magical powers.

Hares and mouse hares

Hares and rabbits of the family Leporidae, and mouse hares of the Ochotonidae family are distinguished from rodents by the fact that they have four incisors in the upper jaw, unlike the rodents which have only two. Hares have long ears, long hind legs and are born with closed eyes and

almost hairless skin. Both hares and rabbits have short tails. Mouse hares are small and have no tails. They have rounded ears and short front legs.

Hares live in bush, jungle and near cultivated land on the outskirts of villages. They are nocturnal and can be seen singly scampering across roads and fields at night. Grass and vegetable matter are their main diet. One or two young are produced during the colder months. Leopards, jackals, wild dogs, mongooses, owls and crested hawks prey on them. People hunt them for their meat and fur.

There are three important varieties of Indian hare. The **black-naped hare** *(Lepus nigricollis nigricollis)* is a large, heavy variety, with a dark,

blackish-brown patch on the back of its neck, up to the shoulder. The upper part of its tail is also black. It is found in most parts of the peninsula.

In the **rufous-tailed hare** *(Lepus nigricollis ruficaudatus)* the nape-patch is grey, while the body and tail are a rich reddish-brown. Black patches are found on the back and face. The underparts are white. This variety occurs from the south of the Himalaya to the river Godavari.

The **desert hare** *(Lepus nigricollis dayanus)* is sandy-yellow in colour and has no nape-patch. The upper part of its tail is a blackish-brown. It is found around the desert in Sind (Pakistan), Punjab, Rajasthan and Kutch.

The **Himalayan mouse hare** *(Ochotona roylei)* looks like a guinea pig, is small and has a round head, round ears, short muzzle and no tail. Reddish-brown in colour, it has a band on the upper neck of its shining coat of short hair. It is found right across the Himalaya, commonly seen in rocky areas above the tree line, among coarse grass or under trees. Both timid and inquisitive, its behavior is interesting, racing across the ground playing hide and seek with any intruder. It lives in burrows but not much is known of its breeding habits or whether it hibernates.

The true rabbit does not exist in India. The nearest to it is the Assam rabbit or the **hispid hare** *(Caprolagus hispidus)*, which is the same size as a hare but has a shorter, dark-brown tail. Its coarse fur of bristles is also dark-brown becoming paler below. The outer side of the ears is brown, the eyes small, the hind legs short and stout, the claws long and the teeth large. Bark and roots are its main food. Seen in the terai, dooars and Himalayan foothills, it is very elusive and therefore very little is known about it.

Bats

There is no mammal that can fly in the real sense of the term except the family of bats, Chiroptera (the so-called flying squirrel really only leaps and glides). The very name, chiroptera, derived from Greek, means hand-wing. Bat's wings are attached to their forearms. From the wings, membranes extend to the feet and spread between the legs, enclosing the tail. An additional membrane joins the neck to the forearms. Thus, an unbroken, complete parachute is formed. Bats have strong hearts and lungs. Powerful flying muscles

LEFT: flying-fox eating wild figs.
RIGHT: short-nosed fruit bat.

make them strong fliers. The tail, which curves towards the belly, acts as a brake. In cold weather they hibernate. Bats can be divided into two distinct categories: the larger, fruit-eating bats *(Megachiroptera)* and the insectivorous bats *(Microchiroptera)*, which are generally smaller.

Fruit bats have excellent grinding teeth. The molars are oblong and have smooth crowns divided by a long deep groove. The food is ground to a pulp and the juice goes directly into the gullet through their grooves. Fruit bats feed in the early evening and have good eyesight.

Insectivorous bats have teeth that serve a different purpose. They have molars with sharp, pointed cusps in the crown, forming a W shape. These are perfect for holding and piercing. Insectivorous bats feed at night and manage to fly with the help of a highly developed echoapparatus, similar to a sonar system. They have very strong voice-boxes and muscles and can produce shrill signals at a rate of 50 pulses per second. When these sound waves strike an object, they bounce back and are picked up by the bat. This helps bats to avoid colliding with objects.

The **flying fox** *(Pteropus giganteus)* is the largest Indian bat. Its wings spread across 120 cm (4 ft). It has a reddish brown head with a black snout and black wings. Its neck, shoulders, chin and flanks are varied hues of brown. It is seen all over the subcontinent except in arid areas like West Rajasthan and the higher reaches of the hills. Flying foxes roost together on trees in noisy groups and fly to far-off orchards in search of fruit. They breed once a year, with a gestation period of five months.

The **fulvous fruit-bat** *(Rousettus leschenaulti)* is medium sized and light-brown in colour. It has a strong smell of fermented fruit juice. Common in the Indian peninsula, large colonies roost in caves and in ruins and fly out looking for fruit at dusk. They breed twice a year. The young are carried by the mother for two months.

The **short-nosed fruit-bat** *(Cynopterus sphinx)* is large and brown and is recognized by its divergent nostrils and white-margined ears. Found in peninsular India, it roosts among palm leaves and aerial roots of the banyan and eats fruit and sips honey from flowers. Its breeding habits are not exactly known, although young are seen carried by their mother in September.

The medium-size sandy-grey, **bearded sheath-tailed bat** *(Taphozous melanopogon)* has a beard that is drenched during the rainy season

with a thick fluid produced by the chin glands. Colonies of over 4,000 are found in ruins and cave temples, clinging to walls. They fly out before dusk and feed on insects. Found in peninsular India, the young are born in April–May and separate from the mother after a month.

Another species, the **Indian false vampire** *(Megaderma lyra)* is dark grey in colour with body length of 65–95 mm (2½–3¾ in). Groups of around 30 live together in wells or caves and feed on large insects, spiders and small vertebrates such as bats, birds, rodents and fish. The young are born in April and are carried by the mother till almost full-grown.

The **great eastern horseshoe bat** *(Rhinolophus luctus)* has long, woolly, curly fur that is jet black with ashy-grey tips. It has large ears and a horseshoe-shaped nose-leaf covering the upper lip and cut in the middle. Found in the Himalaya, Western Ghats and Sri Lanka, it occurs in pairs, but is seldom seen. Little is known of its breeding habits.

The **Indian pipistrelle** *(Pipistrellus coromandra)* is small in size, with dark fur above and pale hair underneath, and dense fur between its eyes. A fast flier, it is busy all through the night. It lives in the eaves of houses and enters them while seeking out insects. Its breeding habits are not yet known. Two young are observed in May. ❑

BIRDS

There are four times as many bird species in the region as there are
mammal species – including parakeets and peacocks, herons and hornbills

The distribution of birds over the globe is a fascinating subject, and the reason why some species are so widespread and others so restricted is largely a matter of speculation. The changing physical pattern of the world over geological periods has much to do with the presence or absence of birds in various parts of the globe. A striking example of discontinuous distribution, as a result of geological changes, is provided by the existence of laughing thrushes and spider hunters in northeastern India in the Himalaya, and then again, after a gap of 3,200 km (2,000 miles), in the Western Ghats in southwest India. It is presumed that at one time there was a continuous Satpura range of mountains joining these two areas and these species then were presumably linked. With the disappearance of the mountains under geological forces acting through the Deccan Plateau, only a relict population of these species remain in two distant parts of the country.

But ornithologists wonder how some land birds manage to colonize areas across the oceans, far away from their original home, like some on Tristan Da Cunha 3,200 km (2,000 miles) away from land, while some, which have proliferated all over the United States, have been unable to reach even the West Indies. The same is the case with Sri Lanka. Though most Indian species have no difficulty in crossing the short sea barrier (even poor fliers and essentially land birds like the paradise flycatcher go over), it is a curious fact that no vulture has crossed the negligible sea barrier and, consequently, there are none beyond the southern tip of India. Only one or two scavenger vultures *(Neophron percnopterus)* have been seen in Sri Lanka, and the fact that these birds are strong fliers, seen everywhere in South India, makes their absence across the Palk Strait inexplicable.

At the other end of India, Nepal, an exceptionally beautiful country, has a splendid assortment of colourful birds, some like the Himalayan snow-cock *(Tetraogallus himalayensis)* and many birds of prey are found even above the tree line. In fact an eastern steppe eagle *(Aquila nipalensis)* was found on the South Col of Everest. From its jagged peaks in the north with arctic conditions, to moist lowland forests in the south, there are as many as 800 species of birds as compared to the 1,225 of India. Many species are of course common to both countries, and because of its geographical position the birds of Nepal have strong affinities with those of the palaearctic region. But it has only one truly endemic species, the spiny babbler *(Turdoides nipalensis)* as against the 55 in India.

As a result of the drastic changes in India's environment in the course of the past six decades – particularly as a result of the cutting down of forests and extending the range of grasslands and

---

PRECEDING PAGES: demoiselle cranes.
LEFT: immature open-billed storks, Bharatpur.
RIGHT: purple moorhen.

agricultural areas, there has been a corresponding change in the pattern of the avifauna throughout the country. Woodpeckers, for example, have been drastically reduced and seed-eating birds, finches and larks have multiplied.

Zoogeographically speaking, the world is divided into the Palaearctic, Nearctic, Neotropical, Ethiopian, Asian and Australian regions. India's avifauna has strong links with the African as well as with the birds of the Indo-Chinese region. Only a few have palaearctic affinities. But there are several species that are endemic to India, that is, they are not found anywhere else in the world, and a few of these

Scott bred these birds in captivity in Slimbridge in the United Kingdom and some have been reintroduced in Assam.

Not all endemic species in India are rare or extinct. The Indian robin *(Saxicoloides fulicata)* for example, slightly larger than a sparrow, a black bird with white on the shoulder, and a rusty red patch under the tail is found in dry open lightly wooded country throughout India. The rufousbellied babbler *(Dumetia hyperythra)* and the blackheaded babbler *(Rhopocichla atriceps)* are also common birds, the range of the former extending from the Himalaya to South India and the latter to the

might be mentioned. The chir pheasant *(Catreus wallichii)*, larger than a village hen and reminiscent of an English hen pheasant, is found in West Himalayan conifer and deciduous forests; the pinkheaded duck *(Rhodonessa caryophyllacea)*, a rare species even in the 19th century, was last seen in Bihar in 1935 and is probably extinct. Another bird that is feared to have become extinct is the Himalayan mountain quail *(Ophrysia superciliosa)*, last recorded in Nainital in Uttar Pradesh in 1876.

The white-winged wood duck *(Cairina scutulata)*, a resident of the swamp forests of Assam, though not endemic, is on the danger list because of habitat destruction. Sir Peter

evergreen biotops of the Western Ghats.

One of the most exciting events of the 20th century for bird conservation was the rediscovery of Jerdons Courser *(Cursorius bitorquatus)* on 14 January, 1986, in Cuddapah in Andhra Pradesh. An attractive bird, it is about the size of a partridge but with longer legs and pinkish-brown with two white bands across the breast. This courser, whose nearest relatives are in faraway Africa, was last seen in 1900, and had eluded the keenest observers because it is nocturnal in its habits and was only rediscovered at night. A sanctuary has been established by the Andhra Pradesh Government in the area where some birds of this species still exist.

Ecologically, India is a rich country, with few vacant niches where exotic species can get a foothold. The Java sparrow *(Padda oryzivora)* is perhaps the only foreign species that has acquired a breeding status in India; but the fact that it is not spreading significantly is fortunate because the problems caused by exotics – their displacement of the local avifauna for example – are well known.

Out of the 9,650 species in the world India has as many as 1,225, and so on a land surface of only 4 percent it has 16 percent of the total number on the earth. If subspecies are included there are 2,061 forms in all, and out of these 1,750 are residents and the rest are migrants. If vagrants and pelagic species like shearwaters, petrels and boobies are included, the total may go up to 2,346. Ornithologists have classified birds into 27 Orders and 155 Families and India's status in ornithological terms can be judged from the fact that it has representatives from 20 Orders and 77 Families.

Easy access

In spite of urbanization there are places very near India's busy cities that have a wealth of birds. Any visitor to Mumbai with an interest in birds will find Sanjay Gandhi National Park, on the outskirts of the city, very rewarding, particularly during the migratory season from September to April. In a small stretch of country between the hills and the lake, you might well see a wide spectrum of both forest-dwelling as well as aquatic species – racket-tailed drongos, tree pies, jungle owlets, minivets, ioras, golden orioles, magpie robins, three species of bulbuls and of sunbirds, hornbills, woodpeckers and the dazzling peacock, India's national bird. With luck, you might even spot the gorgeous paradise flycatcher. On the damp meadows encircling the lakes, there will be bee-eaters, kingfishers, drongos, mynas, pipits and larks, while swallows and swifts hunt in the sky. In the water there can be gulls and duck of many species, with plovers, egrets, herons and maybe even an osprey plunging into the water to catch fish with its talons. Altogether, the Sanjay Gandhi National Park is a splendid place to see a multitude of species living cheek by jowl, yet in their separate micro-habitats.

LEFT: purple heron waiting for prey.
RIGHT: the tree pie is usually found in noisy pairs.

An even more glamorous place than the Sanjay Gandhi National Park is the world-famous Keoladeo National Park, just 50 km (30 miles) from Agra. It is one example of people's tampering with the natural ecosystem, resulting in a spectacular increase in its birdlife. It is the artificially maintained water levels within this comparatively small (29 sq km/11 sq mile) park that sustains its wealth of birdlife.

Bharatpur is considered to be unique in the total number of bird species as well as the quantity of birdlife that it harbours. It has an impressive assortment of land and arboreal birds, but the grand spectacle is provided by

the aquatic species. For example there are four species of cormorants, eight species of egrets, three ibises, 17 species of duck and geese, and two species of crane, of which one, the Siberian crane *(Grus leucogeranus)* is one of the rarest species in the world, and Bharatpur is its only known wintering ground in India. These cranes have not been seen here for several years, possibly due to poaching on their migration routes.

Protection

As in most countries, there is both national and international protection for birds. Under the Wildlife Protection Act of 1972 no birds except certain specified vermin like crows can be trapped and killed without a permit from the appropriate wildlife authority. Permits are granted only for game birds that are not endangered. But a most timely measure to check commercial exploitation by poachers is CITES, the Convention on International Trade in Endangered Species of Flora and Fauna, which came into force in 1975. This Convention has three schedules, and in Schedule I are listed those species that are totally protected. Some of the

LIGHT AS A FEATHER

Many of the shimmering, iridescent colours of the peacock plumage are due to optical interference effects caused by nanostructures in the feathers.

rarer protected bird species in India include the chir pheasant to which we have already referred, the Himalayan monal *(Lophophorus impejanus)*, Sclater's monal *(Lophophorus sclateri)*; Blyth's and western tragopan, the Siberian and the black-necked crane; the great Indian and Houbara bustard, the Bengal florican and the Nicobar pigeon. With the stopping of imports by Western countries and the consequent ending of the high prices fetched by the sale of these birds, the main incentive for poaching is removed.

In an agricultural country birds play a very important role in the cross-pollination of flowers, the dispersal of seeds, and keeping insect pests under control. In his Azad Memorial Lecture, Dr Salim Ali said "over 50,000 species of insects have been described from the Indian subcontinent, doubtless with many more still to come. Many of them, such as locusts, beetles, moths, caterpillars and termites, are extremely harmful pests of agriculture and forestry upon which our national economy leans heavily". He went on to say that a single pair of Colorado beetles *(Leptinotarsa decemlineata)* "would without checks – in which birds play an important part – increase to 60 million in a year".

It is not realized what a significant role birds of prey play in keeping down rodent population. An owl, for example, is reputed to kill as many rats as 30 cats, and rodents destroy a substantial portion of India's food-grain production. Another way in which birds add to the health of the ecosystem is through guano, the droppings of fish-eating water birds, which is considered to be the finest nitrogenous fertilizer in the world. The famous Guano Islands off the coast of Peru are a major economic asset of that country. At least in one water-bird sanctuary in India, Vedanthangal near Chennai, the agriculturists surrounding the sanctuary area protect the birds because they recognize the value of guano as a fertilizer with matchless properties.

While, on the one hand, a conservation consciousness is growing in the country, and birds are not being wantonly destroyed, the rampant use of pesticides in agriculture and for public health has led to the death of birds, particularly birds of prey, which are at the top of the food chain. Grain-eating birds eat insects killed or contaminated with synthetic poisons. The toxic preparations are ingested into their systems and when they in turn are devoured by predatory birds, the predators either die or lay sterile eggs. It is to be hoped that biological control methods will soon replace the organo-chlorine and organo-phosphorus compounds which do such widespread damage to the environment.

The use by livestock-owners of a drug called Diclofenac has had the most calamatous effect of all. In 15 years it has wiped out 98 percent of three of India's griffon vulture species. India relied on its 85 million vultures for the disposal of carrion and carcasses on a massive scale. Their disappearance leaves in its wake worsening problems with the millions of carcasses left rotting across the land and the increased risk to human health from zoonotic diseases. Explosions in the population of crows, rats and feral dogs have been reported in some areas. The disappearance of the vultures also looks set to end the Parsi tradition of placing their dead atop Towers of Silence to be consumed by vultures.

Bird watchers in India lament that the skies are virtually empty. The king vulture is hardly ever seen, and even birds like the white-eyed

gion and are, therefore, most likely to be seen by the visitor. The keener naturalist can add many more birds to their list by visiting bird sanctuaries such as the Keoladeo in Bharatpur (Rajasthan), Vedanthangal (Tamil Nadu) and Nal Sarovar (Gujarat) for the winter migrants, and any of the many wildlife sanctuaries for resident species.

A sample of Indian birds

For the purpose of this guide it has seemed appropriate to list the birds not in taxonomical order, but according to the frequency with which they are likely to be encountered. For reasons of

buzzard, which was so common in the past, are now rarities.

Birds are reputed to be good indicators of the health of our environment because their fast metabolism gives us an advance warning of environmental hazards to come. Humans must protect them even if only to protect themselves – for the early warning system they provide.

The notes on birds that follow cover only a small and inevitably arbitrary sampling, but they attempt to include those species that are most common over the greater part of the re-

LEFT: spotted owl in tree burrow.
ABOVE: peacock courtship dance.

space the description has to be limited to size, main colouring (omitted for the commonest species) and the most noticeable characteristics.

Crows (Family *Corvidae*) – House Crow (*Corvus splendens)*: In spite of the fact that this is the commonest bird in every locality that has a sizable human population, little is know about its life history. The nesting season, during which they make loose, ungainly nests from all available material, is from April to June.

Jungle Crow *(Corvus macrorhynchos)*: This bird is heavier than the house crow and is black all over, without a grey patch on the neck. It has recently begun to encroach on the territory of its smaller cousin, even invading highly populated areas, functioning side by side with the house crow. Although not as quick and bright as the house crow, it is physically stronger, and is responsible for destroying a large number of our smaller birds. Like the house crow, the jungle crow is also a victim of the koel's 'parasitism' during the nesting season.

Mynas (Family *Sturnidae*): This family is widely distributed on the subcontinent and Sri Lanka. The common myna (*Acridotheres tristis*; 3.5 inches/9 cm) is perhaps the most characteristic of the birds of the subcontinent. It is thoroughly at home among humans. One size smaller than a dove, the common myna has a dark brown back

It is omnivorous, not averse to human society, and builds even inside human dwellings.

Bank Myna *(Acridotheris ginginianus)*: Common in north and northeastern India, this myna has a bare red patch around the eye. It is at home among people, and saunters along confidently on railway platforms, in and out of passengers' feet. It nests in tunnels excavated along embankments and large groups build together in colonies.

There are two migrants in the Sturnidae family, the Rosy Pastor *(Sturnus roseus)* and the Starling *(Sturnus vulgaris)*. The rosy pastor renders enormous service by devouring locusts and

with bright yellow legs and beak as well as a bare yellow patch on the face, and white patches on the wings, which show up conspicuously in flight. It does not depend on the discarded food of humans, because it is omnivorous and eats fruit, earthworms and insects.

The nesting season is long-drawn (April–August). Mynas enjoy argument, and quite often small flocks can be seen screaming, fluttering and attacking one another on the ground. No casualties result.

Brahminy or Blackheaded Myna *(Sturnus pagodaram)*: A rather dressy creature; slightly smaller than the common myna, its glossy black crown contributes to its handsome looks.

keeping their numbers under control in their breeding grounds in Central Asia.

Hill Myna *(Gracula religiosa)*: Well-known for its talking and mimicking skills, this bird was trapped in large numbers for export, and was a valuable foreign-exchange earner. It is found mainly in the Himalayan foothills and in the Western Ghats.

Bulbuls (Family *Pycnonotidae*): The 120 species now placed in this family are found only in the Old World, 19 in India, nine in Nepal and about six in Sri Lanka. Bulbuls are sober-coloured but elegant birds. Most are olive green, yellow or brown, while one species is black.

Red-vented Bulbul *(Pycnonotus cafer)*: This, the commonest of the bulbuls, is very characteristically Indian. Bigger than a sparrow, slim and elegant, with a longish tail, it is mainly brown with a prominent black crest and a red patch under the tail. It is common throughout India, and can adapt itself to busy cities, although being arboreal it is less visible than the House Sparrow and Common Myna. A liquid call from within a leafy shrub or tree is likely to be the first indication of its presence.

Red-whiskered Bulbul *(Pycnonotus jocosus)*: Equally common, with its black recumbent crest and crimson cheek-patch, in addition to the red vent, this is a very attractive species. Its extremely pleasant call has resulted in its being known as 'the Indian Nightingale' (there are no nightingales in India). The quiet beauty of its voice and looks, and its trusting disposition, have given it a special place in Urdu poetry.

White-cheeked Bulbul *(Pycnonotus leucogenys)*: Though modestly wearing only a sulfur-yellow patch at the root of the tail, this bulbul has the liveliness of the family. It is distributed south of the Himalaya down to Bombay, and eastwards up to Central India.

Sunbirds (Family *Nectariniidae*): Purplerumped Sunbird *(Nectarinia zeylonica)*: Because of its general looks and habit of 'hovering' in front of a flower, this is sometimes mistakenly called a hummingbird (there are no hummingbirds in India). Two sizes smaller than a sparrow, with a stumpy tail and a long thin curved beak, the male glistens in crimson, green and purple and its pale-yellow front is just the foil required to set off its brilliant upper plumage. Male and female are a devoted couple, always together, and are usually present wherever there are large bright flowers.

They breed throughout the year, nesting in the most exposed situations, but by a wonderful feat of camouflage, the nest is often mistaken for rubbish by friend and foe alike.

Purple Sunbird *(Nectarinia asiatica)*: This is purple only during its breeding season; at other times, the male assumes the sober light-yellow and brown appearance of the female. Nesting is mainly between March and May. The species is more widely distributed than the purple-rumped, and can be found throughout the country.

Even in this sparkling group the Yellow backed Sunbird *(Aethopyga siparaja)* with its distinctive yellow rump, is outstanding, and makes an arresting sight in evergreen forests.

Drongos *(Family Dicruridae)*: These are solitary, insectivorous and arboreal birds, mostly black and with a long forked tail. Of the 20 species in the east, nine are found in India. The commonest is the Black Drongo *(Dicrurus Macrocercus)*, a slim, elegant all-black bird, easily recognizable by its two long, forked tail feathers. A white dot at the base of the bill is the

hallmark of this species. Although smaller than a myna, the drongo is a tough character, and can often be seen chasing away crows from its territory. On the other hand, it does not raid the nests or eggs of smaller birds, and several species find safety in building nests close to a drongo's. It is this watchdog activity that has earned it the Hindi name of *Kotwal* ("policeman").

Parakeets *(Family Psittacidae)*: There are no parrots in India, and what the visitor may be tempted to call a parrot will turn out to be, in fact, a parakeet. The shape is that of a parrot and the basic colour is parrot-green; and over this the male Rose-ringed Parakeet *(Psittacula krameri)* has a dark pink stripe around its neck.

LEFT: cliff swallow.
RIGHT: the hoopoe's "oop-oop-oop" song gives it its English and scientific names.

The rose-ringed parakeet makes itself conspicuous when noisy flocks streak across the sky to settle on a tree with ripening fruit. The early mornings and evenings are their working time, and owners of fruit trees have to continuously look for new ways of keeping them away.

Uninhibited in whatever they do, the parakeets have a prolonged courtship display in which the beak plays an important role. There are some handsome birds in this family. In Northern India the Alexandrine or Large Indian Parakeet *(Psittacula supatria)*, which is as large as a pigeon, can be identified by the maroon patch on the shoulder.

The Blossom-headed parakeet *(Psittacula cyanocephala)*, apart from its red head, also has maroon shoulder patches, but prefers the countryside to the city.

Barbets (Family *Capitonidae*): Crimson-breasted Barbet or Coppersmith *(Megalaima haemacephala)*: A bird that is heard by everybody but seen by few. Its loud repetitive tapping sound has been called "the most monotonous sound of the Indian countryside". If you do manage to follow the sound to its originator, you will see a dumpy bright-green bird (bigger than a sparrow) with a bright-red chest, yellow throat and heavy whiskers. It is widely distributed in India and is equally at home in an uninhabited forest and busy city.

Large Green Barbet *(Megalaima zeylanica)*: Another barbet more often heard than seen. It is larger than the myna – grass-green overall with a brown head. The colours merge completely with the foliage, and to add to the problems of the birdwatcher its "kutroo, kutroo, kutroo" calls have a ventriloquistic quality, leaving one wondering from which direction the sound comes.

Flycatchers (Family *Muscicapidae*): Literally catchers of flies, they can twist and turn with incredible dexterity while chasing their prey. Of the 378 known species, India has 38. Many of these reside in the Himalaya and the Western Ghats, but some are at home in the plains.

Paradise Flycatcher *(Terpsiphone paradisi)*: Undoubtedly the most gorgeous, it is about the size of a bulbul, silvery white with a glistening black crest and long pliant tail feathers. The female is chocolate-brown and lacks the ribbon-like tail, but is most engaging nonetheless.

White Spotted Fantail Flycatcher *(Rhipidura albicollis)*: Another lovely creature – smoky-brown, about the size of a sparrow, with a distinctive white eyebrow and white-spotted front. It will waltz about on a branch with its fan-like tail spread out.

Tickell's Blue Flycatcher *(Muscicapa tickelliae)*: Is mainly blue with a pale-orange breast. Sparrow-sized, like all members of the family, it is hardly ever at rest, and it has a pleasant jingling song that is usually the first sign of its presence.

Oriental Magpie Robin *(Copsychus saularis)*: A black and white version of the christmas card robin formerly in the thrush family Turdidae, but more often now treated as part of the Old World flycatchers. Avoiding both city and jungle life, it patronizes gardens and groves. During the breeding season, just before the rains, it becomes both audible and visible, for its coat takes on a smart sheen, and it positions itself on a pillar, or top of a tree and sings loudly and unselfconsciously. It is said to be the most beautiful songster in the country. But in this respect its close cousin, the Shama *(Copsychus malabaricus)*, a denizen of forests, has an even more melodious and attractive song. The shama has a chestnut belly and a long drooping black and white tail.

The magpie robin is a good example of a songbird that sings to establish territorial rights over its breeding area. Rival males are driven off by aggressive singing and posturing. In the event that a male is unable to establish its sway over a territory, it refuses to raise a family and leads a bachelor existence.

Doves and Pigeons *(family Columbidae)*: These two names are to a certain extent interchangeable. The characteristic quality of these birds is that they can drink like horses by immersing their bills in the water and sucking it up. Most birds have to raise their heads to that the water can trickle down from the bills.

Blue Rock Pigeon *(Columba livia)*: Of the 20 species of pigeon in the subcontinent, this is

fruit and berries, they are much sought-after.

There are nine species of doves in India, of which four are fairly common, and their English names give a hint about their general appearance. All of them are a little larger than the myna.

Collared Dove *(Streptopelia decaocto)*: This has a prominent black hind collar on its soft brown neck, and is found in the drier portions of India.

Spotted Dove *(Streptopelia chinensis)*: This is the most widely distributed dove and can be identified by the white spots against a dark background on the back and sides of the neck.

the most common. Although there are wild populations, they are also partial to the most congested localities, and are disliked for the mess they make in godowns, warehouses and other storage areas. Their throaty cooing and the bullying courtship display of the male, which the female tries to escape, is a familiar sight.

Yellow-legged Green Pigeon *(Treron Phoenicoptera)*: These are found in the hills and in wooded areas. They are modestly but attractively coloured, in shades of green, purple and yellow. Because of their tasty flesh, built on a diet of

It is a curious fact that in its "kruk kru kroo kroo" calls the final "kroo" is never repeated more than six times. Usually the effort ends with the third or fourth utterance.

Little Brown Dove *(Streptopelia senegalensis)*: Like the collared dove, a bird of the drier regions.

Babblers *(Family Muscicapidae)*: This is an Old-World group of insect-eaters. They have short rounded wings and are poor fliers, but they have strong beaks and legs and spend much of their time turning over fallen leaves looking for worms and insects. They 'babble' a great deal, hence their name. There are about 45 species of babblers in India.

LEFT: a drongo, or *kotwal* - the "policeman"
ABOVE: rose ringed parakeet.

Jungle Babbler *(Turdoides striatus)*: Smaller than the myna; a grey-brown bird with a yellow bill and legs and an untidy look about it. Known as the 'Seven Sisters' because they move around in groups of about that number, they have strong family attachments and the young are sometimes fed not just by the parents, but also by members of the community. They are found in wooded areas and gardens where there is a reasonable quantity of leaf litter.

Common Babbler *(Turdoides caudatus)*: Similarly coloured as the jungle variety, but a slightly smaller bird that prefers drier areas.

Spotted Babbler *(Pellorneum ruficeps)*:

more gregarious than the spotted species.

Kingfishers (Family *Alcedinidae*): White-breasted Kingfisher *(Halcyon smyrnensis)*: Perhaps the most widely distributed kingfisher, it is easily visible because of its penchant for sitting and calling from exposed locations. It is smaller than a pigeon, but its electric-blue wings, thick red beak, and white front catch the eye. Even a small patch of water, like a garden pool, may offer it a meal. Indeed, it is not dependent on water for its food and manages to survive in the dry places on a varied diet.

Common Kingfisher *(Alcedo atthis)*: Of bulbul size, with a white throat, orange breast,

Among the many species of babblers inhabiting forested areas, this one needs to be mentioned for its exceptionally beautiful voice. It is about the size of a bulbul, with a white breast prominently spotted with brown. A group of birds calling together from the edges of an evergreen or deciduous jungle provides a joyful and melodious outpouring that is seldom excelled even in the bird world. Less attractive is the monotonous call of solitary birds rendered as "he'll beat you", repeated endlessly.

Quaker Babbler *(Alcippe poioicephala)*: Somewhat similar in appearance to the spotted babbler and found in the same locality, this one also has a pretty voice. It is largely arboreal and

black bill and cobalt-blue wings and head, this is a well-distributed species in the old world. Since it is dependent on fish and aquatic insects, it is found by the coast, along river banks, estuaries and around inland lakes and marshes. It nests between March and June in tunnels excavated in embankments.

Pied Kingfisher *(Ceryle rudis)*: A rather arresting bird, especially while it is hunting. It is black and white, larger than the myna. It flutters over water in a vertical position and plunges bill first to land on its prey.

Orioles (Family *Oriolidae*) – Golden Oriole *(Oriolus oriolus)*: In a competition to select the handsomest bird in India, this bird would certainly be short-listed. It is slightly larger than a myna, golden yellow all over, with black wings and a pink bill. The black streak through the eye seems to say that no detail of its make-up has been overlooked and then its glorious long-drawn whistle compels the watcher to try to locate it. Orioles are completely arboreal.

Black-headed Oriole *(Oriolus xanthornus)*: Lives only in well-wooded areas, and is therefore not as common as the golden. It is distinguished by its black head and throat. A harsh nasal "waak" usually reveals its presence.

Wagtails (Family *Motacillidae*): All species of wagtail share certain mannerisms – the tail wagging, the short spurts of running, and undulating flight.

Large Pied Wagtail *(Motacilla maderaspatensis)*: The only resident species of wagtail; about the size of a bulbul. During the breeding season (March–September), the male produces a pleasant song.

Grey Wagtail *(Motacilla cinerea)*: In India breeds only in the Himalaya, and is the commonest of all wagtails. As ringing data show, it has a remarkable tendency to return to the same spot year after year during its migrations.

White Wagtail *(Motacilla alba)*: Has a black head and a white face. Breeds in Kashmir and spreads out widely over the subcontinent in winter, sometimes reaching Sri Lanka.

Munias (Family *Ploceidae*): Smaller than sparrows, munias are not true weavers as their untidy globular nests reveal. Of the seven species in India, the Spotted Munia *(Lonchura punctulata)*, the White-throated *(L. malabarica)* and the White-backed *(L. striata)* are the commonest.

The English names give an indication of the colour patterns of these birds, which are mainly brown and white. A rather elegant species, popular as a cage bird, is the Red Munia or Avadavat *(Estrilda amandava)*. Munias are very sociable birds, and unless preoccupied with feeding or preening, they stay closely huddled together. The stiff-legged courtship dance of the males, consisting of a leap upwards, returning to the same spot each time, is a comic but entertaining performance.

Egrets (Family *Ardeidae*) – Cattle Egret

(Bubulcus ibis): An all-white heron with a yellow bill and black legs. The yellow bill, in contrast to the black bills of its cousins, is an easy identification mark. In the breeding season, during the rains, it acquires an orange-buff plumage on the head, neck and back. The birds often stand around grazing animals to snap up insects raised by their feet.

Little Egret *(Egretta garzetta)*: This bird has a black bill and legs and yellow feet. It was hunted in the old days for its ornamental, pure white feathers, which appear in the breeding season, and which were once in great demand for gracing women's hats.

Other Birds – Koel *(Eudynamys scolopacea)*: The male is all black, about the same size but slimmer than the crow. The colour of the male and the crimson eyes make identification easy. The female is brown, profusely spotted and barred with white. The male's loud, monotonous calls of "kuo kuo kuo" are a feature of the Indian summer, and are supposed to herald the monsoon. The female has a metallic clicking call that carries a long way.

The koel is the only bird that seems to outmaneuver the crow. The female manages to lay its egg in the crow's nest and the young koel often pushes the fledgling crows overboard.

House Sparrow *(Passer domesticus*; 6 cm/

LEFT: black winged stilt.
RIGHT: collared dove.

2½ ins): The busy twittering flocks of house sparrow are at home in the most congested localities. Indeed, the sparrow is a true commensal of people and breeds away from human environments only in exceptional circumstances.

Tailor Bird *(Orthotomus sutorius)*: This bird is so trusting that it even nests in bungalow verandahs. Two sizes smaller than a sparrow, it is olive-green with a chestnut cap and a long thin upright tail. Its "towit-towit-towit" calls go on for minutes on end. The Hindi name *durzee*, also pays tribute to its skill as a tailor. It sews itself a tidy little nest by stitching togeth-

er, with twigs, the leaves of suitable plants and providing a professional inner lining.

Ashy Wren Warbler or Ashy Prinia *(Prinia socialis)*: Frequenting small shrubs, this cousin of the tailor bird is about the same size and shape. It is dark grey above and creamy below, with a loose dangling tail. The nest, which it constructs in low bushes, is a poor imitation of the tailor bird's. Like the latter, it calls vigorously for long periods from the tops of small trees.

Indian Roller *(Coracias benghalensis)*: This pigeon-sized bird with a startling dark-blue plumage, brings the only touch of brilliant colour to bare brown fields in the dry season. It is usually perched on electric wires adjoining agricultural lands, and from this vantage point it swoops down on insects, frogs or lizards on the ground.

Common Iora *(Aegithina tiphia)*: Like many arboreal birds, it is likely to be heard before it is observed. Smaller than a sparrow, it is usually well camouflaged. During the non-breeding season, it is clothed in shades of mustard green. However, during the breeding season, the rich yellow and black colouring of the male catches the eye, particularly when it performs its courtship display by flying up and fluttering down in a manner obviously designed to display its brilliant colours. It has several beautiful calls, one of which spans a full octave.

Water Birds

There are some water birds that are generally found together, whether along the coast or in and around an inland water body. While some fly back and forth, plunging into the water when prey is sighted, others walk in the squelch within close reach of their food. Each species has its own specialized food.

Red-wattled Lapwing *(Vanellus indicus)*: This is a ground bird in the sense that it feeds and nests on the ground, but it is energetic in the air and often seen in rapid wheeling flight, calling stridently all the while. It is about the size of a partridge, but with long legs and its well-known call sounds like the plaintive question, "Oh…did he do it?" and leaves no doubt about its identity. The red-wattled lapwing has a crimson wattle by the side of the eye while the Yellow-wattled lapwing *(Vanellus malabaricus)*, a bird of drier regions, has a yellow lappet in the same place.

Pond Heron or Paddy Bird *(Ardeola grayii)*: A little smaller than the cattle egret, this is a very widely dispersed species, found wherever there is water, whether fresh or brackish – on the coast or around the meanest pond. It has phenomenal patience and will wait frozen for long periods in the hope that a frog, fish or crab will blunder within striking distance of its powerful bill. When at rest, it is all brown, but in flight the white wings and rump show up prominently. Like all herons, it is capable only of a harsh croak when communication is necessary.

LEFT: the diminutive common kingfisher.
RIGHT: red-wattled lapwings.

Night Heron *(Nycticorax nycticorax)*: The heron that city dwellers are likely to come across, it is a little larger than the pond heron, grey-black above and white below. It is gregarious and often roosts in colonies, departing after sunset to its favourite marsh for feeding. During this flight its loud "kwaark kwaark" is invariably heard.

Gulbilled tern *(Gelochelidon nilotica)*: Easy to identify because of its silver-white feathers and, in contrast to other terns, by its black bill and legs.

Brown-headed Gull *(Larus brunnicephalus)* and Black-headed Gull *(Larus ridibundus)*:

entiating it from the commoner cousin.

Common Greenshank *(Tringa nebularia)* and Redshank *(Tringa totanus)*: Both are large sandpipers, about the size of a partridge, but with long legs. Common Greenshanks often give themselves away by their rather melodious "tew tew" calls, and they seem to have strong social bonds.

Blackwinged Stilt *(Himantopus himantopus)*: Always stand out in waterside congregations, conspicuous by their long red legs. They have weak flight, in which the legs trail behind the tail, but they are competent swimmers.

Little Ringed Plover *(Charadrius dubius)*: In

Seen usually in large congregations, these are the commonest of the gulls in India. In flight the former can be identified by a white circle on its black primary feathers.

Common Sandpiper *(Tringa hypoleucos)*: Lives up to its name by being invariably present wherever there is a little stretch of water. It is brown above and white below and a streak of white extending upwards through the shoulder reveals its identity.

Spotted Sandpiper *(Tringa glareola)*: Shows up the spots on its back when it is lit up by the slanting rays of the sun in the morning or evening. The lack of the white intrusion on the brown shoulder is a useful clue for differ-

a gathering of water birds it is easy to spot this plover. It is about the size of a quail, with yellow legs and a black band around the neck. Like many other plovers, it employs the 'broken-wing technique' to protect its nest from predators. It will pretend to have broken its wing, trailing it to the ground, and thus induces the pursuer to follow hopefully. Then it flies off suddenly when the predator, human or beast, is some distance from the nest. The nest is merely a scrape in the ground, and the bird relies on the obliterative colouring of the eggs, and of its own body, for camouflage.

Golden Plover *(Pluvialis dominica)* and Grey Plover *(Pluvialis squatarola)*: Two attractive water birds, about the size of a francolin, which migrate to India. The former species, brown above, decorated with gold, favours moist pasture land while the Grey Plovers without the gold colouring are usually found along the coast. They take a few swift steps, stop erect for a moment, dip down quickly, pick up a morsel, and move along again.

Bird-watchers are sometimes treated to an exhibition of a flock of small birds turning and twisting in flight in perfect unison, and are left wondering whether there is a leader directing operations. They are likely to be stints, mainly Little *(Calidris minuta)* and Temminck's

brown. It flies with rapid wing beats and is among the most expert of hunters.

Harriers: In open country, during the migratory season in winter, harriers are an exciting feature of the environment. The Pale Harrier *(Circus macrourus)* is a little smaller than the pariah kite, ashy-grey with a black tip to its long pointed wings. In the words of one writer, it knows how to overcome the laws of gravitation as it sails close to the ground. A close cousin is the Marsh Harrier *(Circus aeruginosus),* of which the adult male is reddish-brown and the female and young are like a slender pariah kite with rounded tail and buff cap.

(Calidris temminckii) stints. Both are winter migrants and seen in huge numbers on mudflats and coasts. They are smaller than quails, grey-brown above, white below and appear to be incredibly active.

Birds of Prey

There are about 60 species of birds of prey in India, 12 in the family Falconidae and 48 in Acciptridae. The pariah kite and the brahminy kite have already been mentioned.

Shikra *(Accipiter badius)*: Found everywhere, in open country, as well as in city gardens. It is the size of a pigeon, grey above and white below, closely cross-barred with

Blackwinged Kite *(Elanus caeruleus)*: A bird with a specialized hunting style. About the size of a jungle crow, it hovers in the air to take aim at a morsel on the ground and then parachutes down with wings held up at an angle to land on its prey. It is distributed patchily throughout the region.

Kestrel *(Falco tinnunculus)*: This is another bird of prey that hovers competently. A migrant from the Himalaya and beyond, though there is one resident race in South India. Pigeon-sized, it is brick-red above, with a grey head.

Red Headed Merlin *(Falco chiquera)*: Has a grey back and a red head. Pairs hunt in concert, leaving the quarry little chance to escape.

Pariah Kite (*Milvus migrans*; 24 cm/9½ ins): The commonest bird of prey in Indian skies. Despite its unflattering name ('pariah' means scavenger), it is a rather beautiful bird. With the general look of an eagle, it is reddish brown all over, and a good identification mark is its forked tail. In spite of its apparently leisurely flying habits, it can swoop swiftly and accurately in crowded city streets, and make off with some item in a dustbin or a sandwich in a child's hand. It perches and nests in high trees. Like many birds of prey it nests after the monsoon.

Brahminy Kite *(Haliastur indus)*: Can be

waste. The King Vulture *(Sarcogyps calvus)* is about as large as a peacock, minus the tail, and its high status amongst vultures can be seen from the respect it receives from the other species when the birds are gorging themselves on the flesh of an animal.

A disaster has befallen the vultures of India in recent years. Populations of three of India's griffon vultures have declined by 98 percent in little over a decade. The Indian vulture *(Gyps indicus)* plus the once very common slender-billed vulture *(Gyps tenuirostris)* and oriental white-backed vulture *(Gyps bengalensis)* are now on the critically endangered

distinguished from the pariah kite by its white head and underparts and rounded not forked tail. Both are likely to operate in the same areas, but the brahminy kite has a preference for picking rubbish off water surfaces, while the pariah is more terrestrial.

Vultures: Though classified with birds of prey, vultures are not hunters of live prey. They live on the carcasses of dead animals, offal, and some, like the Scavenger Vulture *(Neophron percnopterus)* even on human

list and facing probable extinction. Widespread use on livestock of the drug Diclofenac is fatal to the birds when they feed on the carcasses.

Initially the reason for the dramatic decline in the population was not understood, but parmaceutical companies and the government have been very slow to react despite an alternative drug being available for some time. The manufacture, sale and use of Diclofenac was banned in 2006 but despite this and a captive breeding programme set up by Bombay Natural History Society (BNHS) and the UK's RSPB, it may be too late to save these slow-breeding species from extinction. ❏

LEFT: the Indian robin is longer-tailed than its European relative.
ABOVE: long billed vulture, Sariska.

REPTILES

India has the largest reptile in the world and the largest venomous snake
but also a host of harmless lizards and turtles

Reptiles are a well-represented and diverse group of animals in this region, with over 400 species of snakes, lizards, turtles and crocodilians in India alone. Contrary to popular belief, it is not only in forested areas that one comes across reptiles; most of the larger, rodent-eating snakes and lizards are prevalent in open, cultivated areas, which have an abundance of rats and fresh water. In fact this is probably the only animal group that has benefited somewhat from the large-scale conversion of forestland to farmland over the past 60 years. Thus, travelling along country roads bordered by fields, one often sees a monitor lizard *(Varanus bengalensis)* running across the road or a large rat snake *(Ptyas mucosus)* hunting along a bund between fields.

Reptiles play a significant role in Hindu religion and mythology and several of the major deities are associated with snakes. But while people worship snakes, they also fear them, and snakes are usually killed on sight; even the harmless species are not spared, as all snakes are generally considered venomous.

Consumer exploitation has been high in this animal group. Before it was banned in 1976, the skin trade tanned 10 million snake skins a year, and several species such as the rock python *(Python molurus)* became locally extinct in many areas. The illegal skin market nevertheless continuous to flourish.

Snakes

There are 275 species of snakes in India, ranging from the giant reticulated python *(Python reticulatus)*, which grows to 10 metres (30 ft), to the tiny worm snake *(Ramphotyphlus braminus)*, which achieves just over 10 cm (4 ins), and is often mistaken for a worm. Snakes inhabit a wide range of environments, from paddy fields and open sandy areas to thick rainforests, mangrove swamps, moun-

tains up to 4,500 metres (15,000 ft), and even the open sea. Their food varies considerably, depending on the size of the snake and prey availability. Frogs and rodents are perhaps the most generally acceptable items for the open-country species, but there are interesting exceptions. The king cobra *(Ophiophagus*

hannah), the largest venomous snake in the world, which grows to 5 metres (16 ft) in India, are 'ophiophagus'; that is, they eat only snakes, mostly the ubiquitous rat snake. Sea snakes eat fish, and small burrowers like the fascinating group of shield-tails or uropeltids eat insect larvae and worms.

Some snakes lay eggs; other have living young. Several species of egg layers such as pythons, cobras *(Naja naja)* and water snakes have been found to stay with the eggs until hatching. The king cobra is the only snake in the world that builds a nest: the female, incredibly, scrapes leaves and humus into a 46-cm (18-inch) high mound in which she lays her eggs.

PRECEDING PAGES: gharial.
LEFT: Indian king cobra, alert position.
RIGHT: the garden lizard can change colour.

Right from the egg stage through to adulthood, most snakes have a variety of natural enemies. Many have startling defence stances, the most well known of which is the dramatic hood display of the cobra, which inflates its body and expands its rib cage to spread a 'hood' to intimidate enemies. Others exhale breath forcefully, and "hiss". The saw-scaled viper *(Echis carinatus)* produces this sound by rubbing its rough scales together.

Venomous snakes: Although there are more than 50 species of venomous snakes in this region, the majority, for various reasons, pose no threat to humans. The king cobra, for exam-

Together, they cause 10,000 snakebite deaths every year in India alone. It is important to learn to recognize these four, and to remember that antivenom serum, available at large hospitals, is the only cure for their bite. Each of these snakes is fairly easily distinguishable, though it is easy to confuse them with other harmless species. The cobra varies in colour from cream to black; generally, it is brown. The hood may not have the typical speckled or monocle marking. Russel's vipers are heavy-bodied snakes with narrow necks, triangular heads and a regular chain-like pattern on the back. The scales are very rough and the overall colour is yellow-

ple, lives in dense evergreen forests, into which people do not usually venture; nor is the king cobra given to unprovoked attacks as is commonly believed. The 20 species of sea snakes that inhabit the coastal waters are timid, shy animals that won't bite unless restrained or injured, and the same is true of the banded krait. Other species such as the pit viper usually have only a mild venom, which is adequate to kill small prey like frogs and lizards, but which causes only pain and swelling in larger animals like adult humans.

The Big Four to watch out for are the cobra, krait *(Bungarus caeruleus)*, Russel's viper *(Daboia rusellii)* and the saw-scaled viper.

ish and brown. Kraits are blue-black and shiny with transverse thin white cross bands, which may be very faint or even absent. The saw-scaled viper is the smallest of the Big Four, growing to just 30 cm (1 ft) in South India; it is brownish with white markings and has the triangular head typical of the vipers. In some areas, this viper is amazingly abundant, such as in Ratnagiri District in Maharashtra.

Harmless snakes: There are several species of non-venomous 'garden snakes' common throughout the region. The large rat snake is often mistaken for a cobra, but has a more pointed head, large eyes and of course does not spread a hood. The bright green vine snake *(Ahaetulla* *nasuta)*, with its pointed head and elliptical eye pupils is the target of many derogatory myths. In Tamil Nadu it is known as the *kunn kuthi pambu*, eye-pecking snake. The bronze-back tree snake *(Dendrelaphis tristis)* is very fast, thin and chocolate-brown with a light-bronze stripe down its back. It, too, is widely feared and stories abound about its evil characteristics. Other groups of harmless snakes include the kukri snakes *(Oligodon)*, wolf snakes *(Lycodon)*, trinkets *(Elaphe)*, racers, cat snakes *(Boiga)* and freshwater snakes. There are several interesting burrowers, like the stubby sand boas *(Eryx)*, the worm snake and the shield-tail.

The most productive places to see the common species of snakes are in agricultural areas and bordering bushes and thickets. Just before sun-down is a good time, since this is when cobras, rat snakes and others hunt for rats and frogs. But the excellent camouflage of these reptiles plus the heavy hunting pressure for skins, which has made them wary and timid, makes it difficult to spot them. As opposed to temperate areas where snakes are often diurnal and live in accessible places, here most species tend to be nocturnal and live in secure rat holes, termite mounds and other cool refuges.

In some parts of the region there are specialized groups of people who hunt snakes (traditionally for the skin trade) and they are the best guides. The Irulas of Tamil Nadu are probably the best snake hunters in the world and the Irula Cooperative in Chennai can be contacted for a day's snake hunt around Chennai. From a faint, barely visible scrape on the ground, an Irula can tell the species and size of the snake, which way it went and how long ago.

Places of interest: Unlike mammals, there are few places where one can be sure of seeing a particular snake. One exception seems to be the Keoladeo National Park, where in the winter months one can almost always see big rock pythons basking on low branches or in front of the burrows where they live. The tourist's first encounter with a snake in India is usually through the snake charmer, who travels around the country with his sick, de-fanged cobras and makes them 'dance' to his flute. In truth, snakes hear practically no airborne sounds and the cobra's swaying dance is a defensive movement with which the snake warily watches the flute and the 'charmer', potential enemies of which it is terrified.

The Irula Cooperative is a venom-production centre where tourists can see the Big Four venomous snakes and the extraction of venom. It is run by the Irula hunter-gatherer Adivasis. Members catch and supply the Big Four snakes to the Cooperative, where they are kept for three weeks and the venom extracted three times. The snakes are then released back into the wild. There are snakes on display at the Chennai Snake Park, Kolkata Snake Park, Pune Serpentarium and Sundervan in Ahmadabad.

There are several festivals and ceremonies associated with snakes. The most dramatic is the August *nag panchmi* harvest festival of Battis Shirala near Sangli, Maharashtra. Wild cobras are caught by the local farmers and labourers and worshipped for the few days of the festival. Then they are released into the fields, unharmed. In the evenings during the festival, one can see large numbers of cobras lined up, hoods spread, in front of the temporary snake charmers, as women step up to propitiate them with flowers, ghee and kum kum powder. In West Bengal, the Jhampan festival, which takes place in July–August, is conducted by Jhampanias, priests who are the gurus of

LEFT: python, Bharatpur.
RIGHT: the green vine snake can display black and white interscale colours when threatened.

snake charmers. They arrive at the ceremony in colourfully decorated carriages *(jhampans)* with baskets containing king cobras, cobras, vipers, kraits, rat snakes and other species. Snake charming, traditional singing and other festivities take place.

Lizards

There are over 150 species of lizard in the sub-continent. The majority are forest dwellers and consequently difficult to sight. The most commonly seen are a few species of geckos *(Hemidactylus)*, which quickly colonize houses, darting about on the ceiling in the

breeding colour is an impressive creature, with his handsome, sharp crest, orange head and colourful dewlap or throat flap, which is expanded during territorial displays. The Fan-throated lizard *(Sitana ponticeriana)* is a 10 cm (4 in) long colourful agamid with a bright blue throat fan. It is capable of great bursts of speed, sometimes streaking along on its hind legs like the South American basilisk. Skinks, the smooth, crestless lizards, often mistaken for snakes, are another widely distributed group, and range in length from 8–30 cm (3–12 ins). The young of several of these skinks have brilliant, almost electric tails, usually bright blue or orange.

evening, seeking out cockroaches, mosquitoes and other prey. In spite of this free pest-control service, geckos are unpopular animals over-all; people mistakenly believe they are poisonous, and that a gecko falling into food can cause fatal poisoning.

The social behaviour of geckos is fascinating, with a very definite pecking order and ferocious territorialism between males. Their main predators are 'house snakes' like the wolf snake and cat snake, as well as false vampire bats.

Another widely distributed group of lizards is the agamids, and of these the garden lizard *(Calotes versicolor)*, unfortunately called the bloodsucker, is the most common. The male in

There is one species of chameleon *(Chameleo zeylanicus)* found throughout India. Their ability to change colour makes them difficult to spot but is also an expression of the physical and physiological condition of the lizard. They are deaf but their large, independently-moving eyes help them to avoid enemies and find their insect prey. The long, flexible tongue, almost 30 cm (1 ft) long, is shot out with amazing speed to catch a passing butterfly or termite.

The largest, most conspicuous lizards of this region are the varanids or monitors, of which there are four species. The water monitor *(Varanus salvator)* grows to over 2 metres

(6½ ft) and is the most colourful, with black and yellow markings. Where unmolested they become very tame; on the outskirts of Colombo, they can be seen scavenging around rubbish dumps or hanging about markets in expectation of scraps. In India they are found in the Andaman and Nicobar Islands, the Sunderbans delta in West Bengal and at Bhitar Kanika in Orissa, the only places that still have mangrove forests. The Bengal monitor, a uniform or speckled brown, is a 91-cm (3-ft) long lizard common throughout India, Sri Lanka and Nepal that frequents open cultivated areas as well as wooded and forested tracts. The

such as those of the Western Ghats. Of these several are known only from a few museum specimens and the natural history of most is largely unstudied. One of the most dramatic looking of the endemic lizards is the dragon-like creature, *Lyriocephalus*, of the Sinharaja forest in southern Sri Lanka, with its strange knob on the head and startling colours. Another, *Cophotes*, is one of the viviparous lizards in the region.

Turtles and tortoises

According to creation myths of ancient India, the creator of the world took the form of a turtle in order to hold up the land. In Hindu lore,

yellow monitor *(Varanus flavescens)* is a brightly marked monitor, smaller than the Bengal monitor and with a stubby head. It is found only in parts of the north such as the states of Bihar, Uttar Pradesh and West Bengal. A similar looking lizard, the desert or Agra monitor *(Varanus griseus)* is confined to the northwest, notably the Rajasthan desert.

Lizards of this region are unique in many ways. Over 75 species of Indian lizards are endemic, that is, they are found in very limited geographical ranges, many in evergreen forests

LEFT: Tucktoo gecko, common in northeastern India.
ABOVE: monitor lizard.

the world rests on the backs of four elephants standing on the carapace of a giant turtle. They are some of the world's oldest species. Generally, turtles live, feed and breed mostly in water, and tortoises mainly on land; but, as is often the case, there are notable exceptions. There are 26 species of freshwater turtles and tortoises in India, and five species of marine turtles, which feed in coastal waters and lay their eggs on suitable beaches.

Of the freshwater turtles, the most abundant are the flap-shell turtle *(Lissemys punctata)* and the black pond turtle *(Melanochelys trijuga)*, both of which are widely eaten. In West Bengal especially, thousands are slaughtered every week, in spite of protective legislation. Among the tortoises, the most widespread is the star tortoise *(Geochelone elegans),* conspicuous by its black and yellow markings. Its typical habitat is open scrub forest in the dry southeast and northwestern parts of the country. Large numbers are killed in the south for the shell, which is made into souvenirs for the tourist trade.

Of the five species of marine turtles in this region, four nest on Indian beaches and during the two-month nesting season it is possible to witness the whole egg-laying sequence, since once the female begins her task of procreation she is oblivious to the close presence of

129,000 turtles have died over the past 13 years, suffocated in the nets of fishing boats not using mandatory turtle-excluder devices. Federal government money given for buying patrol speedboats and equipment has not been used.

The state of Gujarat on the west coast of India is believed to harbour four species of sea turtles, including the olive ridley, green turtle *(Chelonia mydas),* leatherback turtle *(Dermochelys coriacea)* and hawksbill turtle *(Eretmochelys imbricata).* though only the olive ridley and green turtles breed here. The leatherback has nesting sites in the Andaman-Nicobar Islands which can be reached by air from Chennai,

humans. In Tamil Nadu, the olive ridley *(Lepidochelys olivacea)* nests from November to February and the World Wildlife Fund office in Chennai conducts regular "turtle walks" at night to see this phenomenon and to collect nests for safe incubation; otherwise they usually end up at the local market. But the real turtle-nesting extravaganza takes place in February–March on the Orissa coast – the largest nesting site of olive ridley turtles in the world. At the mouths of the Rushikulya and Devi rivers and at the Bhitar Kanika Sanctuary on Nasi islands in Gahirmatha, over 200,000 ridleys come to nest in the space of three to six nights. The bad news is that an estimated

Delhi, Bhubaneswar and Kolkotta or by ship from Kolkotta, Chennai and Vishakhapatnam.

Places of interest: The Crocodile Bank just outside Chennai has a freshwater turtle breeding programme and several species can be seen there. Turtles are kept and fed, in some cases during rituals, at several shrines in India, such as at Dakor, 56 km (35 miles) from Ahmadabad (Gujarat).

Crocodilians

Perhaps the most unusual of the world's crocodilians, the long-snouted, fish-eating gharial *(Gavialis gangeticus),* is found in India and Nepal and inhabits the large, fast-flowing rivers

(Ganga, Mahanadi, Brahmaputra and their tributaries). By the mid-1970s, the gharial had been rendered almost extinct due to heavy hunting pressure for its valuable skin and from loss of habitat due to the damming of rivers. But thanks to timely conservation efforts – wild-egg collection and captive rearing – there are now over 2,000 gharial in captivity and over 1,200 have been released into the wild. Gharial are very unusual-looking creatures with big bulging eyes, long narrow jaws studded with razor-

> **"SALTIES"**
>
> The largest of all existing reptiles, the saltwater crocodile can attain 7 metres (23 ft) in length and is able to cover 10m from a standing start faster than a race horse.

areas along rivers in Sri Lanka where villagers construct safe, fenced-in bathing areas to protect themselves from the whims of the "salty". In India, salties are found in the Andaman and Nicobar Islands, Bhitar Kanika in Orissa and the Sunderbans in West Bengal. Mugger are extremely adaptable and live in any freshwater (sometimes even brackish water) habitats, from large reservoirs to small streams. During extreme dry months or drought they make deep tunnels or even trek miles overland throughout India but, again

sharp teeth and a big pot-like growth at the end of the snout, which the adult male sports. They feed almost exclusively on fish.

The other two species of crocodiles in this region are the mugger or marsh crocodile *(Crocodylus palustris)* and the saltwater crocodile *(Crocodylus porosus)*. Both are found in India and Sri Lanka; the mugger, like the gharial, is found in Nepal as well. The saltwater crocodile has earned an unenviable reputation because some of the big ones occasionally take cattle, goats or even a human to vary its diet; there are

because of hunting pressure, are now confined to a few protected reservoirs and rivers. Mugger breed well in captivity and the Government Crocodile Project has over 5,000.

Places of interest: The three Indian species, plus others such as Siamese crocodiles and African dwarf crocodiles, can be seen at the Chennai Crocodile Bank which has over 2,000 crocodilians. In the wild, gharial can be seen at the Chitwan National Park in Nepal, and the Corbett National Park in Uttar Pradesh; saltwater crocodile at Bhitar Kanika, Orissa; and mugger at Hiran Lake, Gir Sanctuary (Gujarat), and Ranthambhore National Park (Rajasthan), where they can often be seen basking on the banks. ❑

LEFT: star tortoise.
ABOVE: mugger, Ranthambore.

MARINE LIFE

India's remarkable mangrove coasts and marine life – dugong,
whale shark and the world's largest sea turtle colonies – are also under threat

A rich and varied marine life is present in the Indian seas, which are also characterized by a diversity of habitats – the barrier reefs and atolls of the Lakshadweep Islands, the fringing reefs of the Andaman and Nicobar Islands, the Gulf of Mannar and the Gulf of Kutch, the mangrove and coastal lagoons, lakes, backwaters, estuaries and mud-flats, and the rocky and sandy shores, harbouring myriad animal and plant species.

Human impact

The greatest impact people have on marine life is in the coastal waters and estuaries. Using diverse types of fishing craft and gear, India alone fishes about 1.6 million tonnes of marine fish annually, with sardines, mackerel, Bombay duck (bummalo) and prawns forming the major catches. Thirutai or grey mullet *(Mugil cephalus)*, kanumbu *(Mugil macrolepis)*, Indian salmon *(Polynemus indicus)* and bhekti *(Lates calcarifer)* in the hauls are not uncommon.

Marine penaeid prawns breed in the sea and the larvae of some species, such as the tiger prawn *(Penaeus monodon)* and the white prawn *(P. indicus)*, emigrate to the Cochin backwaters. With the tidal waters they are allowed to enter the paddy fields through sluices, and are netted every few days as the water is allowed to ebb with the tide.

Kovalam: this picturesque palm-fringed beach, 16 km (10 miles) south of Trivandrum, is also a place where you find abundant marine life, the most desired being the spiny lobster *(Panulirus hormarus)* and the brown mussel *(Perna indicus)*.

Lakshadweep: Ten of the islands of the Lakshadweep archipelago are inhabited. The lagoons in these islands are relatively shallow and the largest is in Bitra. Luxuriant growth of branching and massive corals such as species of Acropora,

Montipora, Pocillopora and Porites, along with associated fish and invertebrates occur in the reefs. The one item most sought after in the lagoons is bait fish, some 60 or so species used for attracting the skipjack and young yellowfin tuna. The reefs also support spiny lobsters and a good many species of fish. A few kilometres to

the north of Kavaratti Island lies Pitti Island, which is among the very few rookeries for sea birds in India. Both the sooty tern and the noddy tern breed on this tiny island of about 1.2 hectares (3 acres). A number of other species of sea birds also congregate here.

The green turtles *(Chelonia mydas)* nest on all islands, Suhuli being the largest nesting ground. It is on this island that *mas* – a cured smoked and dried product – is made from the tuna meat. The once ornate sail fishing boats of Minicoy known as *odams* are now almost a thing of the past, having been replaced by mechanized boats fitted with a bait well for carrying live bait fish for rod and line fishing for tuna.

PRECEDING PAGES: lakshadweep coral reefs.
LEFT: dugong or sea cow with pilot fishes.
RIGHT: aerial prop roots and drop roots anchor the mangrove tree in loose and muddy soil.

Mannar: Krusadai Island in the Gulf of Mannar is an important centre for students of marine biology from all over the country. The island now comes within the delineated area of the National Marine Park in the Gulf of Mannar, covering a chain of 21 islands from Rameswaram to Tuticorin. The park has been established with a view to conserving the fringing coral reef and sea grass ecosystems from further human interference and giving adequate protection to the dugong, or sea cow *(Dugong dugon)*, sea turtles and other vul-

RELATIVE EEZ

India has exploitation rights off its coast within an Exclusive Economic Zone covering 1.6 m sq km (618,000 sq miles). The USA and France each have EEZs of 11 million sq km.

Mangrove: Mangroves occupy a very large area in Sundarbans, West Bengal, followed by the Andaman and Nicobar Islands and the Gulf of Kachchh in Gujarat, but large areas have already been denuded for conversion to aquaculture. Shrimp farming has eaten away more than half of the world's mangroves, and in India, mangrove cover has been reduced to less than a third of its original extent. Between 1963 and 1977 alone, India destroyed nearly 50 percent of its mangroves and local communities were

nerable and endangered species, including the unique enteropneustan, or acorn worm *(Ptycodera flava)* occurring in Krusadai.

South of this, off Tuticorin, are the pearl banks of parrs and conch beds. Prior to the mid-1960s, a number of pearl fisheries were conducted from time to time in the Gulf of Mannar, the pearl oyster being Pinctada fucata. A falling number of oysters in the parrs has resulted in the failure of this fishery since the 1960s. The conch *(Xancus pyrum)* is also known as the sacred conch on account of its use in religious ceremonies. Skin divers collect conch in depths up to 20 metres (65 ft) from November to mid-May in the Gulf of Mannar and June to October in Palk Bay.

forcibly evicted.

This is an important issue, as mangrove swamps protect coastal regions from large waves, weathering the impact of cyclones and also serving as a nursery for 75 percent of the commercial fish species that spend part of their life cycle in the swamps. On a global level, mangroves absorb more carbon dioxide per unit area than ocean phytoplankton, a critical factor in global warming. A less damaging aquaculture possibility which is now being promoted is that of seaweed harvesting. The Mandapam-Rameswaram coasts are rich in seaweeds – Agrophytes and Alignophytes – but the natural beds are being rapidly depleted to meet industrial demands.

Dugong and whales

The dugong is the most endangered of India's marine animals. The residual population of this herbivore in the Gulf of Mannar and Palk Bay is very vulnerable. Excessive and unregulated fishing with mechanized boats and canoes, resulting in incidental capture, injuries due to boat hits and various methods of illegal take, have drastically depleted the population. At the turn of the 20th century they were so abundant in the area that there used to be regular organized herding and spear fishing for them. They are closely associated with the sea grass ecosystem in the shallow sub-littoral and intertidal

clinging to the dugong's head probably gave rise to the legends about mermaids.

Not far from here, in the Sri Lankan waters off Trincomalee, is where the blue whale *(Balaenoptera musculus)* has been observed to calve. The stranding of baleen whales *(B. musculus, B. borealis)* and young and adult sperm whales *(Physeter macrocephalus)* in the gulf, Palk Bay and along the Chennai coast indicate the proximity of the breeding grounds of these species, an area promising for whale watching.

The Gulf of Mannar on India's southeastern tip is one of the richest coastal regions in Asia, known for its coral reefs, sea grass meadows

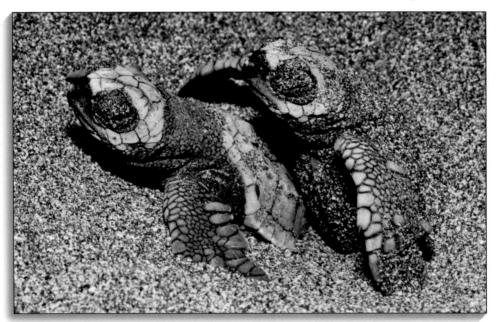

areas where beds of *Halophila ovalis, Zostera sp.* and *Cymodacea spp.* occur.

It is today a rare event to see a dugong in the foraging grounds or in the open water around the islands. They move individually or in small groups, with the calf riding on the cow while submerged. Every three or four minutes they come up to the surface to breathe, normally in a horizontal position, but when curious about a floating object or an approaching boat, or when there is wave action, they break the surface more vertically. The uprooted floating sea grass

LEFT: a Neptune crab.

RIGHT: Olive ridley turtle hatchlings.

and seaweeds and supporting 3,600 species of plants and animals, including 117 hard coral species. The region is home to about 600 varieties of fish, including 200 that are commercially important. Dugongs, dolphins and whales are frequent visitors to the gulf, as are sharks and sea turtles. The Sethusamudram ship canal project announced in 2005 proposes to dredge a deep channel between the Gulf of Mannar and Palk Bay to shorten shipping routes around Sri Lanka, but will cause irreversible environmental damage. These undisturbed shallow waters are sensitive closed marine systems, akin to large lagoons; the spoil, silt, pollution and noise from dredging and blasting, and the temperature changes and shipping traffic in the new channel will kill the flora and drive away the animal life, including the remaining dugong.

Turtles

The world's largest aggregation, or arribada of sea turtles takes place along the Gahirmata coast of Orissa where, in January or early February, over 200,000 olive ridley *(Lepidochelys olivaceus)* females emerge for nesting along a 10-km (6-mile) stretch of the beach within five to seven days. Access to this nesting beach, which forms the eastern fringe of Bitarkanya

where, due to heavy egg predation by man and wild animals, freshly laid clutches of eggs of the olive ridley are transplanted to hatcheries and the hatchlings released on the same beach.

All five species of sea turtles are on the endangered list. Several stretches of the beaches along the mainland coast and Andaman and Nicobar and Lakshadweep have been identified as nesting sites of the green turtle *(Chelonia mydas)*, the hawksbill *(Eretmochelys imbricata)*, the leatherback turtle *(Dermochelys coreacea)* and the olive ridley, with very little known about the loggerhead *(Caretta caretta)*. (*See also Reptiles, page 145–6*)

Sanctuary, is difficult. A second arribada of the same magnitude takes place at Gahirmata in March or early April, although in recent years the nesting has been far less predictable.

The hatchlings, in their millions, emerge after an incubation period of about 45 to 58 days, depending on the time of the arribada and the prevalent temperatures. A recent significant discovery is that turtle eggs developing above a pivotal temperature all turn out to be females and those below, males.

A headstarting programme of olive ridley can be seen at Kovalam (Covalong) 35 km (22 miles) south of Chennai (not to be confused with the place of the same name in Kerala),

Sharks

Large fish, often very spectacular, which have been widely hunted for their flesh also occur in Indian waters. Important species incude: tuna, seerfish, wahoo, marlin, swordfish, sailfish, barracuda, dolphin-fish, rainbow runner, telang queenfish, pelagic shark and many others. They can be observed in most areas along the west coast of India (Ratnagiri, Goa, Karwar, Cochin), in the Gulf of Mannar (Tuticorin, Mandapam), the Lakshadweep sea and the Andaman and Nicobar Islands.

The largest of all sharks, and all fishes, the passive **whale shark** *(Rhincodon typus)*, grows to a length of 15 metres (50 ft) and weight of

8–10 tons, and is a visitor to the Indian coastal waters. It breeds in the tropical Indian Ocean during March–May and then migrate south to Australia, South Africa and Mexico. This gentle, slow-moving creature has tiny teeth and feeds only on plankton.

In 2001 the government declared it a protected species under Schedule 1 of the Wildlife Protection Act 1972, but poaching has continued. It is harpooned or caught in gill nets for its liver oil and fins, the carcass being discarded. The whale sharks are not killed for local consumption, but for exporting to other countries ,especially the far east where shark fin soups

Algal blooms & noxious animals

A major feature along the west coast of India is the very large-scale blooms of the nitrogen-fixing blue-green algae *(Trichodesmium erythreum)* from February to May. No harmful effects are noticed. On the other hand, 'red tides' caused by the dinoflagellate *(Noctiluca miliaris)* results in fish mortality. Still more dangerous are blooms of *Hornellia marina*, another highly toxic dino-flagellate, which are seen at the onset of the monsoon along the Kerala coast, causing mortality of fish, crustaceans and other invertebrates.

In the lagoons of the Lakshadweep one has to be careful not to step on the spines of the well-

are consumed as a delicacy. The Wildlife Trust of India and a local industrial partner have conducted a successful campaign to raise awareness among local community members and fisherfolk. The prospects for whale shark ecotourism are being assessed.

The wholesale slaughter, often in a most barbaric fashion, of sharks of all descriptions along the Indian coast is causing great alarm among conservationists.

LEFT: the docile whale shark, the largest fish, can reach 15 metres (50 ft) in length.
RIGHT: the mudskipper, an amphibious fish, is found in mangrove swamps.

camouflaged stone fish or to handle the beautiful scorpion fish, the spines of which are venomous and injury from which could be excruciatingly painful.

Among the coelenterates, the sting of the nematocysts of *Physalia physalis*, commonly known as the Portuguese Man-o'-War, could even be fatal. *Physalia* occurs along the east coast with the commencement of the northeast monsoon. *Porpita porpita* and *Vellela vellela*, two chondrophorans that immobilize prey organisms with their stinging cells, are closely associated as commensals with young fish. Among corals, the sting from the polyps of Millipora is said to be very painful. ❑

WILDLIFE OF THE HIMALAYA

*The "roof of the world" has biodiversity that rivals the Amazon
but its ecology is surprisingly fragile*

A Sanskrit proverb holds that, "A hundred divine epochs would not suffice to describe all the marvels of the Himalaya" – so long to describe, how much longer to understand. Modern scientific study of Himalayan ecology has but touched a tiny tip of the knowledge to be learnt. But even that tip inexorably leads to the grimmest conclusions. Human onslaught has rendered the Himalaya amongst the most endangered environments in the world. In the subcontinent, the Himalaya rank as the region most in need of conservation, both because of the deterioration in environment and in view of our relative ignorance of the biology and ecology of high-altitude communities. Slowly, this begins to change, but the task is immense. The Himalaya contain more endangered species of mammal than any other area of India and are remarkable in possessing almost a third of the world's mammalian species that could be called true mountain animals. M.K. Ranjitsinh has noted that, "the outlook for wildlife in most parts of the Himalaya is grim, in some places even desperate", and G.B. Schaller warned that just as we are becoming more aware of the splendor of past and present wildlife of the Himalaya we are denying it a future. He describes mountains without wildlife as "stones of silence", an evocative and thought-provoking phrase.

Rich variety

What would we be losing? The youngest, largest and highest chain of mountains in the world, the Himalayan range must lay claim to being one of the most fascinating and spectacular natural wonders of our earth. To speak of the Himalaya may give a false impression of biological homogeneity when in fact it covers a wide and varied mosaic of different biotypes – east–west, north–south and altitudinally.

PRECEDING PAGES: the rare black-necked crane, confined to the Tibetan plateau and Himalayan valleys.
LEFT: Himalayan tahr, Sagarmatha National Park.
RIGHT: grey langurs.

Geologically divided into the three regions of trans-Himalaya, middle Himalaya, and outer Himalaya and Siwaliks, the vegetation ranges from the lush subtropical forests of the foothills to the bitterly cold high-altitude deserts of Ladakh and the Tibetan plateau. Thrown up 60–70 million years ago, with activity still con-

tinuing, the Himalaya have acted both as a bridge and a barrier. The asymmetrical collision of the continental plates resulted in an inflow of oriental fauna through the northeast before the Afro-Mediterranean elements that followed through the northwest.

The present flora and fauna species of the east and west regions reflect this – the former showing a close relationship with the western-Chinese pattern and the latter having Euro-Mediterranean affinities. Besides these, many species have evolved from the previously present Central Asian or palaearctic fauna and given rise to high endemism with strong generic links to Tibet and Central Asia.

Elusive cat

No animal better epitomizes the character and concerns of the mountain environment than the snow leopard *(Panthera uncia)*, that beautiful and elusive cat of the high altitudes of Central Asia. A survivor of the icy rigours of the Pleistocene era, its range is immense, covering the entire Himalaya between altitudes as low as 1,850 metres (6,000 ft) in winter to 5,550 metres (18,000 ft) in summer. Being a shy inhabitant of remote habitats, it has seldom been seen by any but those humans sharing its mountainous home. Only recently have some facts emerged about the ecology of this high-altitude predator.

Somewhat smaller than the leopard *(Panthera pardus)*, but with a relatively longer tail, the snow leopard has a thick and beautiful spotted coat of soft grey, paling to pure white on the underside. This has certainly contributed to its rarity, for although strictly protected, many still fall to poachers' bullets and traps – in the world of fashion there remain those ignorant, selfish and rich enough to make taking such risks worthwhile. The snow leopard covers large areas in order to obtain enough sustenance. In winter months, it sometimes ventures near villages to lift domestic livestock, but its main prey are the wild sheep and goats that share with it these stark and snowy wastes.

Mountain sheep

The Himalaya contain more species of sheep than any other mountain range in the world. Pride of place must go to the Marco Polo sheep *(Ovis ammon polii)*, whose ratio of horn-length to body-weight exceeds that of any animal in the world. These horns form open graceful spirals, with the tips arching up, out and then down again. A northern subspecies of the argali *(Ovis ammon)*, Marco Polo sheep may still be fairly common in the Russian Pamirs and Wakhan corridor of Afghanistan, but within the subcontinent it is a rare animal existing only in northern Hunza, where its magnificent head has long attracted hunters. In its spartan, near-desert landscape home, particularly severe winters also take their toll on this grand creature.

Another race of the argali is the nayan or great Tibetan sheep *(Ovis ammon hodgsoni)*. This is the largest of all wild sheep. Long in the leg and graceful, it inhabits the trans-Himalaya plateau, an area of desolate plains and low undulating hills that experiences extreme temperatures, from scorching summers to freezing winters. Nayan are migratory, wandering wherever food and water may be found, and are natural prey of the Himalayan wolf, which is the chief predator of the trans-Himalayan uplands and plateaux.

The urial, or shapu *(Ovis orientalis)* is the smallest of the wild sheep and is distributed through the western Himalaya, where several different races are distinguished. While horn shapes and colours differ, the adult rams all wear a great ruff growing from either side of the chin and extending down the throat. Adapted to differing environments, from the barren stony ranges of Sind and Baluchistan to steep grass hillslopes in Ladakh, this progenitor of domestic sheep has also attracted hunters' bullets and many populations have been decimated to rarity.

Another Himalayan mammal, originally classified as a sheep, is the bharal *(Pseudois nayaur)*. Its physical characteristics are so intermediate between sheep and goats that taxonomists have had trouble classifying it. Expressing thoughts on their evolution in his book, *Mountain Monarchs*, G.B. Schaller writes that, "in general the behavioural evidence confirms the morphological evidence that bharal are basically goats. Many of

LEFT: the tahr ranges from Pakistan to Arunchal Pradesh.
RIGHT: Siberian Ibexes.

the sheep-like traits of the bharal can be ascribed to convergent evolution, the results of the species having settled in a habitat which is usually occupied by sheep". For bharal, like sheep, graze on open slopes, whereas goats prefer more precipitous cliff habitats. It is an animal of the Himalaya and trans-Himalaya zones and is still common in places as far apart as Eastern Ladakh and Bhutan.

Mountain goats

The Himalaya house three species of true goat – the ibex *(Capra ibex)*, occupying the highest altitudes, with the markhor *(Capra falconeri)* and wild goat *(Capra hircus)* inhabiting cliffs gener-

Panjal to Sikkim and Bhutan in several vegetation zones between 2,500–4,500 metres (8,000–15,000 ft) though rarely going far above the tree line. A beautiful and robust creature, the male Himalayan tahr has a conspicuous coppery brown ruff and mantle of flowing hair draping from the neck and shoulders to its knees and from its back and rump to its flanks and thighs.

Serow *(Capricornis sumatraensis)* and goral *(Nemorhaedus goral)*, two of a group known as goat-antelopes, are also found in both western and eastern areas. The movements of serow and goral in their selected

ally below 3,700 metres (12,000 ft). The ibex, found in the Himalaya west of the Satluj gorge, leads a tenuous existence in spite of its adaptability, as the balance between death and malnutrition in its austere habitat is delicate indeed. The spectacular markhor found in the Pir Panjal range and west to the Hindu Kush and Karakoram, lacks the underwool of the ibex and prefers to remain below the snow line. The markhor's horns are uniquely spiraling whereas the wild goat has scimitar horns similar to those of the ibex.

The Himalayan tahr *(Hemitragus jemlahicus)* differs from true goats in having short curved horns rather than long sweeping ones. This tahr is found throughout the Himalaya from the Pir

habitats are very restricted. The serow, solitary and reclusive by nature, occupies small cliffs and thickly forested ravines, whereas the goral prefers grassy slopes with broken ground, usually at lower altitudes in the southern Himalaya.

The third member of this group, the takin *(Budorcas taxicolor)*, a large heavily built relative of the musk-ox, is found only in restricted numbers in the eastern Himalaya. The Royal Government of Bhutan has declared it the national animal and set up special reserves for its protection. Gregarious by nature, the takin partakes of long seasonal migrations and is at home in general as well as rhododendron forest.

Ruminants

Evolutionally, the earliest known ruminants are the antelope and gazelle group of the family *Bovidae*. In the Himalaya they are represented by the Tibetan antelope or chiru *(Pantholops hodgsoni)*, and the Tibetan gazelle *(Procapra picticaudata)*. The chiru is another creature of the high Tibetan plateau and may also be found seasonally in northern and eastern Ladakh. With a special breathing system and the finest underwool to protect it from the extreme cold, the chiru is well adapted for the high altitude desert areas that constitute its home. Tibetan gazelle have all but disappeared in Ladakh,

region the sambar and barking deer, though found at high altitudes in the southern Himalaya, are not truly mountain species. However, two species of red deer are endemic to the area and both are highly endangered. Indeed, the status of the shou – so-called Sikkim stag *(cervus elaphus wallichi)* though it was never found in Sikkim – is so uncertain that it may well already be extinct. The position of the hangul or Kashmir stag *(cervus elaphus hanglu)*, is a little better, with a population of around 250 living protected in the Dachigam National Park in Kashmir.

In contrast to the restricted ranges of these

though they may be found in Pakistan and Bhutan as well as in the Tibetan plateau.

Other animals that occasionally cross the main Himalayan divide in small numbers from the trans-Himalayan ranges are the wild yak *(Bos grunniens)* and kiang, the Tibetan wild ass *(Equus hemionus kiang)*. The yak is the largest animal of the mountains; massively built and heavily coated, it inhabits the coldest, wildest and most desolate areas and is one of the highest-dwelling animals in the world. The kiang, whose close relative runs in the Rann of Kutch in Gujarat, is another creature of the Tibetan plateau and plains of northern Ladakh.

Of the other ungulates of the Himalayan

red deer, the musk deer *(Moschus moschiferus)* may be found over a wide area of central and northeastern Asia. In spite of this, their status is hardly less endangered for the male carries the musk pod which, commanding exorbitant prices, has made the musk deer the chief target of every poacher in the Himalaya. Though protected by the most stringent laws, unscrupulous perfume manufacturers still encourage the decimation of this delightful creature. Threatened thus throughout its range, the best chances for viewing it are within preserved areas such as the Kedarnath Musk Deer Sanctuary in Uttranchal and the Sagarmartha National Park in Nepal.

Bears

The ungulates described here constitute the largest group of mammals in the Himalaya and many are the main prey species of the larger predators. Though the snow leopard may be the most spectacular of these, the largest carnivore of the mountain species is the brown bear *(Ursus arctos isabellinus)*. Once abundant in the Himalaya, in some parts of its range the brown bear is now even more seriously threatened than the snow leopard. As an inhabitant of higher altitudes, where vegetation is less rich, the brown bear is more of a predator than its lower-living relative, the Himalayan black bear *(Selenarctos thibetanus)* whose food ration of fruits to flesh is higher. But the black bear is also omnivorous and a great meat lover, scavenging carcasses as well as occasionally bringing down sick or young prey of its own. The black bear has the largest range of all the Himalayan mammals, extending over the full mountain range and into Southeast Asia. Safer from human attack than most of the large Himalayan species, it nevertheless comes into conflict with people due to its prospensity for crop raiding. Being especially fond of maize, many injuries and deaths on both sides occur during the harvesting season. A third member of the bear family to be listed among Himalayan fauna is the Tibetan blue bear, but it is so rare that almost nothing is known of it.

CLIMATE CHANGE

Changes in glacial melting are causing flooding and water supply problems. Increasing population and dams are causing rapid deforestation and biodiversity loss.

Wild dogs and cats

Distant evolutionary relatives of the bear family are the dogs. In the Himalayan region of eastern Kashmir, Himachal Pradesh, parts of Tibet and Eastern Nepal, the Himalayan or Tibetan wolf *(Canis lupus chanco* – Himalayan Lineage) exists in small numbers. It is larger than the Indian wolf, with a longer muzzle and longer, thicker coat, and feeds on hares and marmots as well as the larger goats and sheep. With a lineage that departed from all other wolves 800,000 years ago, it is the oldest of all wolves. Although little is known of its status, it may well be one of the most endangered canids in the

world and should be a conservation priority.

The northwestern Himalayan region of Kashmir is home to a third Indian wolf *(Canis lupus chanco* – Wolf-Dog Lineage) – the only one genetically related to the wolf-dog clade to which all the other wolves and dogs of the world are related.

Of this family, the hill fox *(Vulpes vulpes montana)* is the most widespread and common in many habitats, but fox pelts also command a good price and it is not ignored by the ubiquitous poacher. Another member of this family is

the wild dog or dhole *(Cuon alpinus)*, which can be found in the Himalaya and trans-Himalaya, but its rarity in the more accessible areas makes its status uncertain and little information concerning this canine is available.

Several members of the cat family may be included in the Himalayan fauna in that their ranges, including those of the tiger and leopard, extend deep into the Himalaya and at high altitudes. Some lesser cats, like the jungle cat, are recognized as having a separate Himalayan race. However, there are two, other than the snow leopard, which are specifically mountain species – the Himalayan lynx *(Felis lynx isabellina)*, and Pallas's cat *(Felis manul)*. The latter is a

LEFT: kiang, or Tibetan wild ass.
RIGHT: Nanda Devi peak, seen from Rudranath, Uttaranchal.

Central-Asian species and though found in Ladakh, is rare and apparently restricted to the lower Indus Valley. The lynx, which occurs in the upper Indus valley, Gilgit, Ladakh and Tibet, is a race of the lynx of northern Europe and Asia. Similarly rare, both Pallas' cat and the lynx are threatened by trapping and shooting.

Smaller species

Besides these larger animals, there is a diversity of smaller species – hares, mouse hares, bats, weasels and martens – with varying degrees of rarity, range and reports. It is impossible to describe all here, but mention must be

made of the two races of marmot, the Himalayan marmot *(Marmota bobak)*, and the long-tailed marmot *(Marmota caudata)*, both endearing and common creatures of the higher Himalaya. The red panda *(Ailurus fulgens)*, a small animal which extends east from the Nepal Himalaya, is another well-known lesser mammal of the range. Colourful, it is largely arboreal and nocturnal so is seldom seen in the wild.

Birds

The avifauna of the Himalaya similarly present a fascinating and varied range of species, mainly a conglomerate of palaearctic and Indo-Chinese elements, the former predominating in the west-

ern section and the latter richly represented in the eastern areas. Several bird families are endemic to the Himalaya, including broadbills and parrotbills. The chir pheasant and mountain quail are endemic and some 14 other palaearctic species, including the Himalayan pied woodpecker, blackthroated jay and beautiful nuthatch, are considered by Ripley (*The Ripley Guide*) to give strong evidence of relict forms.

Innumerable and diverse, the colourful species of birds that colonize the Himalayan region defy generalization, and the several volumes covering various regions should be consulted by interested visitors. Yet some species must be mentioned here. If for no other reason than their impressive size, two birds of prey of this region are noteworthy. The golden eagle *(Aquila chrysaetos)*, a powerful hunter a metre (3 ft 6 in) from beak to tail, is capable even of taking large mammals such as musk deer fawns and the newborn young of mountain sheep; the lammergeier or bearded vulture *(Gypaetus barbatu)* is best known for its habit of dropping bones from a height to splinter them on the rocks below, thus releasing the marrow and creating bone fragments on which it feeds.

The Himalayan pheasants include such spectacular and gloriously plumed members as the tragopan, with resplendent crimson colour, and the monal, with its glistening rainbow plumage. The blood pheasant, so called for the blotches of crimson that streak its feathers, is distributed only in the eastern Himalaya and graphically exemplifies the Chinese influence in the avifauna there. Most common and abundant is the generally lower-altitude kaleej pheasant, of which five or six races are recognized. The dapper grey, black and chestnut koklas pheasant is found more or less on the entire length of the Himalayan system. The eared pheasant and peacock pheasant should perhaps be mentioned among the Himalayan *phasianidae*, though their distribution only touches on the far northeastern section. Others in this family are the partridges and snow cocks – the Himalayan snow cock and the Tibetan snow cock.

Migration: The Himalaya are important in the context of Indian bird migration. Of the 2,100-odd species and subspecies of birds that

LEFT: chukor are often seen in small coveys on bare, arid hillsides in the western Himalaya.
RIGHT: the monal, national bird of Nepal.

comprise the subcontinent's avifauna, nearly 300 are winter visitors from the palaearctic region north of the Himalayan barrier. One of the most endangered migratory birds of the subcontinent, which nests around the high-altitude lakes of Eastern Ladakh, is the black-necked crane *(Grus nigricollis)*. Thanks to the protection by the local people and the Indian Army, about 55–60 black-necked cranes inhabit the high altitude wetlands of Ladakh, but a much larger population of about 4,000 survive in China.

Many of the geese and ducks to be seen in the north Indian wetlands in winter return to

doyen of Indian ornithologists, that even small birds of starling size are able to withstand the cold and rarefield atmospheres at heights of 6,000–6,700 metres (20,000–22,000 ft) and some of the larger ducks, geese, eagles and other birds. have been observed at heights calculated to be even greater than this.

Forests

Areas of the western region below the tree line contain forests that have a close resemblance to those of Europe and a greater representation of conifers. Among them the aptly named deodar, "tree of the gods", must rank as the most

these high-altitude lakes for nesting between May and October. Apart from the host of long-distance trans-Himalaya migrants and those that descend to lower levels and the northern plains in winter, there are also species which partake of local seasonal migration within the Himalaya itself. One delightful though not too common example is the crimson-winged wall creeper, fascinating with its distinctly butterfly-like flight.

Until recently it was thought that the mountains formed an insuperable barrier so that migrating birds had to take circuitous routes following the courses of river valleys. However in 1981 it was established by Salim Ali,

magnificent. Its massive height and girth make it much prized for its timber, and some of the finest stands have fallen to the axe.

The colourful flowering of rhododendrons in their masses is an unforgettable Himalayan experience. The deep crimsons, reds, pinks and creamy yellows of the blooms have no better setting than their natural environment and backdrop of snowy peaks. The majority of the 80 varieties are found in the eastern Himalaya, which is also very rich in orchids, presenting a profusion of delicate shapes and colours. This eastern zone is at a lower altitude and has higher precipitation with a higher snow line, thus adding to its distinctive botanical identity. ❑

WILDLIFE OF THE DESERT

Far from being devoid of life, the Thar is a fragile gene pool
of hardy species and a lesson in frugal living

A desert environment is one where two basic needs of life – water and shelter, are at a premium and, therefore, it is not a biome in which any life form is likely to have originated. The story of life here is one of the heroic struggle of the survivors who adopted a strategy to withstand the harsh physical conditions – extreme paucity or total absence of free water, inhibitive high temperatures reaching over 55°C (130°F), and desiccation augmented by hot winds. At the other extreme, low temperatures, below zero, accentuated by bitter cold Himalayan winds are another challenging factor in certain deserts. Since the desert landforms of the world are far more recent (about 7 million years old) than the rainforests, the adaptations are often not in physical form but in behavioural pattern – an example of marvellous ecological adjustment.

The strenuous life activities of desert wildlife are concerned mainly with getting water, conserving this important resource, avoiding overheating, getting enough food, and avoiding and escaping from enemies while exposed in the coverless landscape.

The Great Indian Desert, also known as the Thar Desert, is situated between 22° and 32° north latitude in the states of Rajasthan and Gujarat, and lies across India's western frontier with Pakistan. It extends over 700,000 sq km (270,200 sq miles). Landforms such as shifting and fixed sand dunes, interdunal lands, rocky outcrops, flat pavements and salt flats of ephemeral lakes are some of the habitat types of the Thar. These are inhabited by a rich variety of plant and animal life.

Base of life

The Thar Desert is distinct in vegetative biomass, especially the sewan grass that covers extensive areas called pali. Typical shrubs are

PRECEDING PAGES: chital or spotted deer, drinking with peafowl, Rajasthan.
LEFT: wild asses in the Little Rann of Kutch, Gujarat.
RIGHT: chinkara buck, Desert National Park.

phog *(Calligonum polygonoides)*, growing on sand dunes, khair *(Capparis decidua)*, a leafless shrub growing to a middle-sized tree, aak *(Calotropis procera)* and thor *(Euphorbia caduca)*, representing the juicy shrubs. Jal *(Salvadora procera)*, khejra *(Prosopis cineraria)* and rohida *(Tecoma undulata)* are the main

trees scattered very thinly over the desert. There are no cacti and there is no carpet of annual flowers. But khair, rohira and aak, when in flower in March, add colour to the landscape and are the centre of activity for insects and birds.

Most of the major insect orders are found in the Thar Desert. There are 17 species of termites. The colourful members are the butterflies of the group Lepidoptera. The dung beetle (order *Coleoptera*), which rolls dung balls larger than itself, has flight wings neatly placed under a hard cover which slide out, as if under electronic automation, for take off. The hot sandy areas are ideal for swarms of locusts and grasshoppers, many of which are brightly coloured. The velvet mite, which has disappeared from many areas due to chemical sprays, is still to be seen in the desert. Moisture is the governing factor of all insect activity and insects spring to life with the first monsoon shower. They constitute an important source of protein for insectivorous birds and reptiles and even mammals, and being 60–85 percent water, a source of water too. They are thus an important ecological link as first-stage consumers and act as producers for the second-stage consumers – reptiles and birds.

Though a snake called pivana *(breath sucker)* has been identified as the Sind krait *(Bungarus caevuleus)*, myths about the breath-sucking power of the viper continue to circulate all over the desert. It is the snake of the desert's core area.

The deadly saw-scaled viper *(Echis caenatus)*, another poisonous snake, does not leave a serpentine mark on the sand. Its almost parallel lines created by its looping movement leave no clue of its direction of movement. The colour of the Russel's viper *(Vipera russelli)* matches that of the sand so well that only by scanning the ground minutely can one discover the serpen-

Reptiles

Forty-three reptile species inhabit the Indian desert today. The spiny-tail lizard *(Uromastix hardwickii)* lives in underground colonies in flat calcareous interdunal areas and kankar (limestone) pans. Its L-shaped burrow is 15–20 cm (6–8 ins) deep. Its design helps in withstanding sudden changes of weather conditions. The burrow is held exclusively by the owner. With a few drops of rain falling, one can observe the process of closing the hole. With moisture in the air, the calcareous nature of the soil helps to seal the opening. The excavated earth heaped around the hole acts as a check-dam against the rain water.

tine spring ready to uncoil and attack.

Desert monitors *(Varanus griseus* and *Varanus bengalensis)* are miniature dragons with dinosaurian looks. They raid nests, and feed on rodents and insects. The toad agama or horned toad, curiously named since it is no toad and has no horn, is actually a lizard. The blue, green, yellow, crimson, red and black spots in contrast to its sand-coloured body, make it colourful. It buries itself into loose sand, to 'swim' under it to escape predators.

The sandfish *(Ophiomorus tridactylus)* is another lizard that swims under sand. The colour-changing chameleons are commonly seen on the bushes and trees looking for insects.

Wings of the desert

The avifauna of the desert is rich in both species and in population – numbers sometimes swelling to 2,000–4,000 birds at a single spot. No niche of the Thar is devoid of birds. Even in the face of challenging terrain, temperature and repeated deadly droughts, many species of birds have decided to be resident here.

Outstanding among the birds is the great Indian bustard *(Ardeotis nigricaps)*. It weighs 8–14 kg (18–30 lbs) and stands 40 cm (16 in) high on strong legs designed for walking. This tall, heavy bird can be seen walking with confidence and grace in the desert. It holds its head at an angle; its body feathers form a pattern of black bars and dots; its head looks like a crown; its white neck makes it conspicuous in the landscape. While changing its feeding grounds or to escape danger, the bird reluctantly takes to the wing. The bustard feeds on a varied diet – cereals, grasshoppers, locusts, dung beetles, lizards, snakes, berries and small, sparrow-size birds. It lives in family flocks of four to six but at times over 40 birds assemble on a feeding or breeding ground. A polygamous male every now and then inflates its neck air-sac and fluffs its feathers to display its size to court females.

Overhunting, since it provided substantial meat, trampling of its eggs (only one and very rarely two) by cattle, and loss and disturbance in its habitat, had not long ago reduced its numbers to near extinction. Thanks to public awareness and conservation efforts, including the establishment of the Desert National Park, the bustard population recovered to some extent in the 1980s but now it has again declined sharply due to human disturbance and poaching. There could be less than 400 bustards left in the whole Thar desert.

The morning silence of the desert is broken by a sudden twitter in the sky and one spots the flight of a distant pair. A few more definite and louder twitters are heard in the same direction. These are the Indian sandgrouse *(Pterocles exustus)* flying for their morning drink. At a water hole they wheel and turn to land, first at some distance from the free water and later directly on the water hole. Soon they crowd in hundreds for the day's sip and take off, to return

LEFT: grey partridges.
RIGHT: conservation measures have helped the great Indian bustard make a comeback.

the next day – the same place, the same time. They live in small flocks of 10–15. They are distinguished by the male's chestnut band on his chest, spots on the body and a tapering long pintail. Similar is the watering behavior of painted and spotted sandgrouse. They feed on grass and grains and pick up grit to grind the grain between their powerful gizzard muscles.

The grey francolin *(Francolinus pondicerinus)* is known for its morning call and its elegant walk. It is the only species of the Francolinus genus that dares to live in the harsh desert. Its secret is its comparatively low dependence on drinking water. It lives in family

coveys of 8–10 birds, but separates in pairs for breeding in spring.

The bush quail *(Perdicula asiatica)* and the common quail *(Coturnix coturnix)* only inhabit the favourable fringes of the desert; they do not reach the core. The peafowl *(Pavo cristatus)* and roseringed parakeet *(Psittacula krameri)* live only close to human settlements where water is available, and can hardly be called desert birds in the true sense. Ring doves *(Streptopelia decaocto)* are common and congregate at watering places in their hundreds. Spotted doves and red turtle doves are seldom seen.

The avifauna is greatly enriched by insectivorous birds such as the bee-eater *(Merops superciliosus)*, blue tailed bee-eater *(Merops philippinus)*, common bee-eater *(Merops orientalis)*, Indian roller *(Coracias bengalensis)*, larks, shrikes, orioles, drongos, babblers, fly-catchers and warblers. Among bulbuls, the white-eared bulbul *(Pycnonotus leucogenys)* is commonly seen on khair bushes.

Sparrows, including the house-sparrow *(Passer domesticus indicus)* and Spanish sparrow *(Passer hispaniolensis)* fly in gliding movements and congregate on khair bushes near waterholes in incredible numbers. They are in constant motion, diving into the leafless bush every time a predatory bird makes a swoop.

Whitethroated munia *(Lonchura malabarica)* gather in small flocks and perch on dry bushes.

Winter visitors: The desert even attracts many visitors. Its rich food supply, clear, storm-less weather, warm, sunny days and clear comfortable nights, attract birds of the temperate region. Hundreds of thousands of common crane *(Grus grus)* and demoiselle crane *(Anthropoides virgo)* pass through the desert during October on their to and fro winter migration. The cranes live in grassy depressions and along salt flats like Tal Chhapar, Kanodia Tal, the flood flanks of the Luni river and shallow drying lakes and open agricultural fields in the Saurashtra region of Gujarat. The graceful

greater flamingo *(Phoenicopterus roseus)* and the colourful lesser flamingo *(Phoenicopterus minor)* visit the shallow saline lakes all over the desert, including Sultanpur near Delhi. Their assemblies of over 1,000 birds are seen in several places. In May and June, at Nal Sarovar (Gujarat) over 100,000 of these birds congregate. They probably assemble every summer to locate sites for their nesting somewhere in the Greater Rann of Kutch.

The saline points in the process of drying, if they happen to hold enough water till winter, attract rosy and grey pelicans *(Pelecanus onocrotalus* and *P. philippensis philippensis)* and migratory waterfowl – barheaded geese *(Anser indicus)*, whistling teal *(Dendrocygna javanica)*, ruddy shelduck *(Tadorna ferruginea)*, pintail *(Anas acuta)*, shoveler *(Anas crecca)*, coot *(Fulica atra)* and waders, including curlew, sandpiper *(Calidris testaceus)* and snipe *(Gallinago sop)*.

A significant event in Indian ornithology was the establishment of the fact that the desert courser *(Cursorius coromandelicus)* nests in the Indian desert. This bird is cream-coloured and arrives in November to feed on termites and insects. The Kashmir roller *(Coracias garrulus)* arrives by October and stays till March. In contrast, orioles *(Oriolus oriolus)* visit the desert in hot summer and delight listeners with their melodious note. Migration of rosy pastors *(Sturnus roseus)* and starlings *(Sturnus vulgaris)* in swarms across the desert is seen in October and on their return flight in February–March.

The houbara *(Chlamydolis undulata macqueenii)* hit world headlines in the late 1970s when some oil-rich Arabs managed to persuade the Indian Government to permit them to hunt the birds with falcons. This 'sport' created a problem since the size of the bag became a status symbol with the sheiks. The hunts played havoc with the population of this lesser bustard. In 1978, as a result of countrywide protest, this sport was ended once and for all.

The sandgrouse, identified by its black lower-half belly and wing tips, is a gregarious bird. Large flocks of them visit waterholes for a morning drink. They come in their thousands and the only sound is the soft, whistling wing beats of the flying birds wheeling, landing and taking off.

The large pintail sandgrouse *(Pterocles alchata)* flies into the area in large flocks during winter, but not as large as reported by Alan Octavian Hume in the late 19th Century as "tens of thousands – like a thin cloud – darkening the air".

Antelope territory

The core of the desert ecosystem is the prime habitat of the true antelope, the blackbuck *(Antilope cervicapra)*. It inhabits the open plains, short grasslands and saline depressions called chapper or rann. It depends for its survival on its keen sight and high speed (60 km/40 miles per hour) with occasional leaps. It lives in large herds of 40 to 60 animals, mostly fawns and fawn-coloured females and a few jet black, dominant, co-dominant, and light-coloured,

ly brackish water is acceptable to them.

The buck was once the dominant mammal of the desert region but, as a result of merciless persecution over 50 years, it is now confined only to certain pockets. It is estimated that there are 15,000 in the Jodhpur District in areas that have been notified for strict protection, but the most impressive of them are to be seen in the Velavadar National Park in Gujarat, where more than 2,500 of them live in a short-grassland area of less than 36 sq km (14 sq miles).

Striding across clumps of grass, the gazelle, or chinkara as it is also called, stops only on the crest of a sand dune. One wonders why this

recessive bucks. The does are hornless, whereas the bucks have a pair of spiraled horns ending in a rapier-sharp tip, which lends the buck masculine magnificence.

Ferocious combats of territorial blackbuck are common. Rival bucks are chased away and the 20–30 doe harem is regrouped with an impressive display of speed and determination. They are short-grassland animals. They are water-dependent, and, therefore, do not venture into the desert's waterless regions. However, even high-

animal, having pointed hooves unsuited to walking on loose sand, has chosen to live in the desert. In fact, sand dunes form less than 10 percent of the Great Indian Desert, the other 90 percent consisting of craggy rocks, pavements, and compacted salt-lake bottoms, interdunal areas and fixed dunes, for which the gazelle is well equipped to fly over at high speed. The gazelle is the only species of the Indian antelope of which the female have horns, vestigial though they be. The horns of males are over 23 cm (9 in) long and are pointed at the tip, well adapted for a fight to the finish. The chinkara buck is able to stand up to desert predators, including large eagles and foxes.

LEFT: an Indian sandgrouse family.
ABOVE: adult male black bucks fighting at the onset of the rut.

Normally, one fawn (rarely two) is dropped after eight months of gestation. The most vulnerable period in the life of the gazelle is the period of parturition. But nature's scheme of protection by camouflage, and literally getting a fawn up on its legs in four to six hours, helps the newborn infant to follow its mother to safety. But its principal survival strategy is to manage in situations of total absence of free water. It manages even where rain is a rare and chance occurrence and year after year may pass without even a trace of water vapour in the atmosphere. The gazelle is able to survive in these conditions because it has an inbuilt adaptive

age resources of the desert and, therefore, its water dependence has discouraged its distribution in the heartland of the Thar. It is actually the female that is called nilgai (blue cow) and the male, blue bull, though they have no resemblance to or relationship with the sacred cow. The bull is strong, with spiky horns totally out of proportion to its body size; they are more like spurs set in the wrong place. However, they are effective and efficient in ripping open a rival male during courtship quarrels. The fights between bulls are highly ritualized, starting with an arching of bodies, straining of necks, holding tails erect like

system to produce metabolic water in the physiological process of digestion. Its kidney chemistry is such that it can excrete highly concentrated urine, thus helping the body to economize on water. The gazelle is well distributed throughout the desert. There are some pockets where it is much less wary than elsewhere because it has received protection from the desert's human inhabitants, especially the Bishnois, and even the meat-eating Muslims.

The third member of the antelope group (not the family) is the nilgai *(Boselaphus tragocamelus)*, the largest antelope of India. Ecologically, the animal's heavy demand on forage is not in the interest of the meagre for-

flags, and looking slyly at each other from the corner of their eyes. They move in closing circles, finally falling on their knees, trying to get at each other's vulnerable points. The vanquished is chased out of the victor's territory enclosing the cows in oestrus. Though the right of exclusive mating is fully demonstrated by the leader, recessive males sneak in to cover the cows while the dominant male is busy chasing away his rivals. After eight months of gestation, when grasses and cover are sufficient, one, two or three fawns (generally two) are dropped. The increasing number of nilgai in certain areas, in the absence of a predator, is becoming a problem.

The pale-chestnut-coloured wild ass *(Asinus hemionus khur)* of the desert is a fascinating creature – for its survival capacity, if for nothing else. Its body cells are capable of withstanding dehydration and also have the capacity of holding reserves of water when it is available – a perfect adaptive strategy in the harsh environment of the desert. The wild ass, an animal of the open sandy desert, is now confined to the Little Rann of Kutch. Its withdrawal from the sandy tracts to the *bet* (islands) in the Rann is recent. These 'islands' within the temporary marshes provide a protected habitat to this endangered population, and hence its withdrawal there. Unfortunately, even from these *bets* the cattle of the Maldharis are edging the wild ass out. They now live mostly in *Prosopis juliflora* bushes, a modified habitat, on the fringes of the Rann. The bushes provide a good cover and their dry pods a sugar-rich diet. Normally, the ass feeds on grasses, salt-tolerant bushes and even the dry leaves of aak *(Calotropis procera)*. Like the antelope, this species relies on its keen sight and speed for its safety. It is capable of running at 60 km (40 miles) an hour. The wild ass lives in herds of 30 to 40 members (sometimes as many as 100) under the leadership of a stallion who guides the direction of movement. Their current population is estimated to be somewhat over 4,500 animals, all in the Little Rann.

Underground dwellers

The desert gerbil *(Meriones hurranae)* has adapted itself to living in extreme climates with temperatures of over 50°C (120°F) in summer and freezing nights in winter. The hot winds, called *loo*, enhance desiccation, and cold winds from the Himalaya increase the chill at night. The gerbil's strategy for desert living is to burrow in the ground, where its living chambers are cooler by 40 percent and more humid by 45 percent than at the surface in summer and warmer by 20°C (70°F) in winter. It is active in the late evening, when the temperature is comfortable. It changes its feeding timetable in winter by becoming totally diurnal. Dr Ishwari Prakash and his team experimented on the desert gerbil, feeding their sample on 100 percent dehydrated food for 21 months, without

any adverse effect on the rodent's health. The secret of living without water, for months and even years, is its metabolic chemistry which, during the process of digestion, produces water.

The gerbil lives in colonies, sometimes in open fixed dunes, but mostly under khair or zizyphus bushes. The burrows are interconnected and have many escape routes. It feeds on grass seeds, fallen fruits and even stems. It also eats insects. Its long bushy tail is its rudder to balance and guide its direction while taking long leaps. The rich population, 800 burrows per 1 hectare (2½ acres), provide sufficient food as well as water (since 65 percent of its body is water) to its predators.

Other common rodents of the desert are the desert hare *(Lepus nigricollis dayanus)* and the hedgehog *(Hemiechinus auritus)*. The hare is a fast runner and depends on its camouflage colouration when an enemy approaches. The hedgehog is purely nocturnal and rolls itself into a spiny unappetizing ball. The hare is purely vegetarian and the hedgehog an insectivorous rodent. Both live in burrows. The common hare *(Lepus nigricollis)*, with a grey or black nape, needs proximity to water. It is distributed on the fringes of the desert. The crested porcupine *(Hystrix indica)* occurs in the hilly terrain of Jalore and Siwana. It is totally nocturnal.

LEFT: male chinkaras.
RIGHT: painted sand grouse.

Predators

The main predator of the desert is the peninsular Indian wolf *(Canis lupus pallipes)*, once widely distributed over the desert, preferring hilly and broken country. After massive destruction of the antelope, the wolf was forced to take to preying on sheep and goats and it soon became the shepherd's nightmare. It was therefore singled out for destruction, to be killed by any means, including smoking mothers and their pups to death in burrows. This very nearly dropped the final curtain for the species in the desert. It is now reduced to a dangerously low number, ex-

tremely limited in its distribution.

The Indian wolf preys not by chase but by surprise attack, and, therefore, does not need the company of other wolves. It lives in pairs or family packs and sometimes organizes cooperative hunting. In the Indian desert they shelter from the heat in burrows dug in the sand dunes, or they remain above ground, lying up in fields or patches of scrub and thorn forest – they will hunt wild goats, sheep and deer, but will also live off rodents during the lean periods.

The golden jackal *(Canis aureus)*, widely believed to be strictly a scavenger, is also an effective predator, especially when helpless does are parturient and the fawns are too weak to stand. It is absent in the core area of the desert owing to its need for water.

The common fox *(Vulpes bengalensis)* and the desert fox *(Vulpes vulpes)* are both widely but thinly distributed throughout the desert region. The common fox, distinguished by the black tip on its tail, is aggressive. It attacks gazelle and kills fawns and even grown females. The desert fox preys only on rodents, gerbils, desert hare, birds and reptiles like the spiny-tail lizard. A fox hole, especially when it has pups in it, is often located under the same bushes as those of the gerbils and in the midst of hundreds of their burrows. Why predator and prey live in such deadly proximity is still unexplained. The fox hunts during the cooler hours of the day to avoid over-consumption of water, which it obtains only from its prey.

There are also the predators of the air. The blackwinged kite *(Elanus caeruleus)*, crested honey-buzzard *(Pernis ptilorhynchus)*, shikra *(Accipiter badius)*, tawny eagle *(Aquila rapax)* and laggar falcon *(Falco biarmicus jugger)*, stay all the year round and nest in the desert. The owls and nightjars take over at night. The short-eared owl *(Asio flammeus)* and spotted owlet *(Athena brama)* are common. But the majority of the avian predators arrive almost with the influx of the prey birds. They include the goshawk *(Accipiter gentilis)*, sparrowhawk *(Accipiter nisus)*, long-legged buzzard *(Butea rufinus)*, desert buzzard *(Butea vulpinus)*, Bonelli's hawk-eagle *(Hieraetus fasciatus)*, steppe-eagle *(Aquila nipalensis)*, greater spotted eagle *(Aquila clanga)*, lesser spotted eagle *(Aquila pomarina)*, Lanner falcon *(Falco biarmicus cherrug)*, peregrine falcon *(Falco peregrinus)*, oriental hobby *(Falco serverus)* and kestrel *(Falco tinnunculus)*.

The Thar is overcrowded with cattle, and hundreds of them die every day, leaving enough for the vultures to scavenge. The common among them are the white-backed *(Gyps bengalensis)*, long-billed *(Gyps indicus)* and Egyptian vulture *(Neophron percnopterus)*. The king vulture *(Aegypius calvus)* is present in small numbers, mostly in pairs. The vultures cope with the arid climate and high temperature by shifting vertically. After a hefty meal, they sometimes soar at 900–1,200 metres (3,000 to 4,000 ft) in the cool air and descend in the evening to roost.

Desert Conservation

The wide faunal spectrum of the Indian desert – insect to antelope and wolf – and its unique life-style, represent a finely balanced biological pyramid. But in the present context of "development plans", and the dream of "making the desert bloom", the Indian desert is in danger. It is already the most crowded desert in the world. The additional water, more cattle and more people being introduced in large numbers will increase congestion and destroy its essential nature. Much has already been destroyed by excessive cattle grazing, the reckless killing of wild animals, the removal

natural wildlife, needs a better deal since it is India's only gene pool of drought-resistant species. It needs greater care in handling than other ecosystems, since it is one of the most fragile. An attempt to salvage a tiny dot of 3,162 sq km (1,220 sq miles) out of 700,000 sq km (270,000 sq miles) of natural desert, was made by establishing the **Thar Desert National Park** 32 km (20 miles) west of Jaisalmer, to preserve a sample of the discipline of the desert. An initial encouraging start took steps to rebuild populations of vanishing species like the desert fox and the great Indian bustard, and preserve the spectacle of

of the natural vegetation for fuel and even the depletion of its underground water. Traditional patterns of human habitation fitted into their own niche within this complex and delicate ecosystem, but these have been discarded in the face of economic and population pressures.

This landscape, with its impressive and inspiring philosophy of living on a bare minimum – a lesson in ecological humility – deserves to be understood better. The Great Indian Desert, colourful and living with its

the landing sand-grouse and flocks of houbara but there has subsequently been some slackening of effort. Renewed and intensified action, including an expansion of the area of the park, is urgently called for if the initial progress is to be consolidated (indeed, if it is not to be lost).

Indian conservationists have suggested that the Desert National Park be declared a Biosphere Reserve. Most of the major ecosystems of India have biosphere reserves, except the desert. The Thar Desert has all the features to acheive the status of Biosphere Reserve. Desert-dweller communities are an integral part of this park and they should not be displaced. ❏

LEFT: jackal with kill.
ABOVE: desert fox.

COMMUNITY CONSERVATION AREAS

The ancient traditions of India have given widespread protection to sacred sites,
trees and animals and may continue to play an important conservation role

India's first wildlife protected areas were not set up by the government, or by kings and sultans. They were created by ordinary people, by indigenous or tribal communities who set aside parts of the landscape for cultural, ethical or economic reasons. But community conserved areas (CCAs) are not only a historical fact, they are a reality of present times, ignored till recently by urban wildlifers, but nevertheless a living, vibrant reality.

Perhaps the original CCAs were sacred sites – patches of forest, waterbodies or grasslands that were considered by communities to be inhabited by gods, ancestors or totems, and therefore strictly protected from any resource extraction. Many of these, still existing, may be several thousand years old. Among the youngest of the CCAs are those where communities, having faced scarcity of water or fuel or fodder, or having become alarmed by the rapid decimation of wildlife, have declared natural ecosystems near them as sites for protection and/or conservation with restrained use.

The Range of CCAs

There are literally thousands of such areas in India and other countries, but there is precious little documentation on them, and little recognition of their value. Sacred sites and species were once extremely widespread across India, according to one estimate covering perhaps about 10 percent of many regions. These included forest groves, village tanks, Himalayan grasslands and individual species (such as langur, nilgai, elephant and ficus species). Unfortunately, the forces of commercialization, cultural change, population increase and development projects have destroyed many of these sites. But though considerably less in number and coverage, they are still common; Maharashtra, for instance, still has several thousand.

Many of the sacred groves have preserved remnant populations of rare and endemic species, sometimes in their original and undisturbed form, that have been wiped out elsewhere. In general such areas are quite small (sometimes only a handful of trees), but there are also large ones like the Mawphlang Sacred

Grove in Meghalaya which covers 75 hectares (185 acres). In fact researchers B.K. Tiwari, S. Barik and R.S. Tripathi from the Noth East Hill University have recorded 79 sacred groves in Meghalaya, ranging in size from 100 sq metres (1,000 sq ft) to 1,200 hectares (3,000 acres), of which about 40 range between 50 hectares (123 acres) to 400 hectares (988 acres). Interestingly, in some parts of India, communities have designated new forest areas as sacred in order to protect them. For example in Uttaranchal in the late 1990s, a number of village communities devoted parts of their forests to the goddess till such time that the forests are completely regenerated.

PRECEDING PAGES: Indian grassland.
LEFT: Bishnoi woman nursing goat kid, Rajasthan.
RIGHT: the landscape of Cherrapunji, Meghalaya .

Dozens of heronries are being protected by communities that live around them. Trees in or near village ponds are often the favourite nesting and roosting sites for pelicans, storks, herons, egrets, ibises and other waterbirds. Well-known examples include Kokkare Bellur in Karnataka; Nellapattu, Vedurapattu, and Veerapuram in Andhra Pradesh; Chittarangudi and Vedanthangal in Tamil Nadu, and many others (some of which have become officially protected sanctuaries). Many of these harbour globally threatened species like the spottedbilled pelican.

Wintering water bird populations also find a safe haven in many wetlands within or adjacent

to villages whose residents zealously guard them. Mangalajodi village in Orissa, on the edge of the Chilika lagoon, harbours several hundred thousand migratory ducks and waders. From being a village full of bird catchers (with substantial income coming from selling these birds), the residents are now offering complete protection against hunting and other disturbances. In Uttar Pradesh, Amakhera village of Aligarh district is home to a large number of migratory birds, which the villagers are careful not to disturb even while withdrawing irrigation and drinking water. Patna Lake in Etah District of the same state, can support up to 100,000 water birds in a favourable season. The lake was

declared a wildlife sanctuary in 1991 but has been protected for centuries by the locals as a sacred pond. Sareli village in Kheri District of Uttar Pradesh supports a nesting population of over 1,000 openbill storks, considered harbingers of a good monsoon. As they feed on snails, villagers also consider them useful in controlling the spread of diseases.

Quite a few species of plants and animals are protected across the landscape, because of their spiritual, religious, cultural or economic value. The blue bull (nilgai), rhesus macaque, and blackbuck are the most commonly protected animals virtually across India. So, too, are plants like many Ficus species such as banyan and peepal. In central India, the Mahua tree *(Madhuca indica)* is almost never cut even while clearing land for cultivation. In Rajasthan, the khejdi *(Prosopis cineraria)* is considered a *kalpavriksh* (tree that grants all wishes) and zealously protected by many communities. In some communities, elephants or tigers are considered sacred and left strictly alone.

A few Examples

In Orissa, Andhra Pradesh and other states, tens of thousands of hectares have been regenerated and/or protected by village communities, usually by their own efforts (including many cases of setting up all-women forest protection teams, as at Dengejheri village), or through government-supported programmes like joint forest management. The biodiversity value of these forests is considerable, including several threatened mammal and bird species. In the Ranpur range, elephants are reported to be frequenting the community conserved forests, having moved here from their former ranges disrupted by highways, railway lines and industries. In Orissa alone there are believed to be more than 10,000 village forest protection committees. In the Ranpur block near Bhubaneshwar, 180 conserving villages (many of them adivasi settlements) have together created a federation. This is to enable the combining of their initiatives at a landscape level, to maximize harmony and reduce conflicts, and to provide a unified organization for discussions with the government or outsiders.

LEFT: sambar, Bharatpur.
RIGHT: local women's community conservation group, Panchayat, Uttaranchal.

● In Nagaland, several dozen villages have over the last decade or two conserved natural ecosystems as forest or wildlife reserves, the latter dedicated exclusively or predominantly to wildlife conservation. One of the biggest is the Khonoma Tragopan and Wildlife Sanctuary, spread over 20 sq km (8 sq miles), where hunting and resource extraction is completely prohibited; in another 50 sq km (20 sq miles) or so, very minimal resource use for home use only is allowed. Amongst the earliest initiatives were the forest and wildlife reserves set up by Luzophuhu village in Phek district, and the Ghoshu Bird Sanctuary declared by Gikhiye village in Zonheboto

area forms an important corridor between, Nanda Devi Biosphere Reserve and Askot Wildlife Sanctuary, which are critically important for highland biodiversity. Together with Nandadevi, Askot and areas conserved by the Van Panchayats the total area under protection in this ecologically sensitive area comes to about 88 percent of the entire river basin. In addition, villages such as Jardhargaon, Lasiyal and Nahin Kalan in Tehri Garhwal district, influenced by the Chipko movement, have regenerated and protected hundreds of hectares (several acres) of forests and helped renew populations of leopard, bear and other species.

district, both in the 1980s. Many of these are recognized as Important Bird Areas. Given the indiscriminate hunting that this state has witnessed in the last three decades, these efforts are crucial in giving Nagaland's unique biodiversity a renewed lease of life.

● In Uttaranchal, some of the state's best forests are under the management of Van Panchayats (VP) set up several decades ago, mostly in the Kumaon area. Some of these are very large, for example Makku Van Panchayat covers roughly 2,000 hectares (5,000 acres). Of the 2240 sq km (865 sq miles) stretch of Gori Ganga River Basin 1439 sq km (556 sq miles) is under the management of the village Van Panchayats. This

● In Bongaigaon district of Assam, the villagers of Shankar Ghola are protecting a few hundred hectares of forest which contains, amongst other things, a troupe of the highly threatened golden langur.

● With help from the NGO Tarun Bharat Sangh (TBS), several dozen villages in Alwar district (Rajasthan), have reconstructed the water regime, regenerated forests and helped revive populations of wild herbivores, birds and other wildlife. Bhaonta-Kolyala villages have even declared a "public wildlife sanctuary" over 1,200 hectares (3,000 acres).

● Youth clubs from the villages around the Loktak Lake (Manipur), have formed a Sangai Protection Forum to protect the greatly endangered brow-antlered deer, which is found only in this wetland. They take part in the management of the Keibul Lamjao National Park, which forms the core of the lake.

● In 1,800 hectares (450 acres) of deciduous forest, Gond adivasis of Mendha (Lekha), Gadchiroli district (Maharashtra), have warded off a paper mill bent on destroying the bamboo stocks, stopped the practice of lighting forest fires, and moved towards sustainable extraction of non-timber forest produce. Despite some continued hunting, the area harbours considerable wildlife, including the endangered central race

of the giant squirrel. The initiative has spread to several neighbouring villages. Also in Vidarbha, many other villages are conserving forests with significant wildlife potential. For instance, the forests of community-conserved Satara Tukum form an important buffer to the Tadoba Tiger Reserve. At nearby Saigata village, a Dalit youth club has led a 20-year movement to regenerate and conserve several hundred hectares of forest.

● Many traditional practices of sustainable use helped in wildlife conservation. For instance, pastoral communities in Ladakh, Rajasthan, Gujarat and many other states had strict rules regarding the amount and frequency of grazing

on specified grasslands. Ornithologists have recorded that these helped to maintain viable habitats for threatened species like bustards and floricans.

● At Khichan village (Rajasthan), villagers provide safety and food to the wintering Demoiselle cranes, which flock there in huge numbers of up to 10,000. Several lakh rupees are spent by the residents on this, without a grudge or grumble.

● The Bishnois, a community in Rajasthan and Punjab famous for its self-sacrificing defence of wildlife and trees, continue strong traditions of conservation. Blackbuck in particular are found in plentiful numbers in their settlements. Blackbuck conservation is also taking place as a traditional practice in some other parts of India; the Buguda village of Ganjam district in Orissa has even left fallow a considerable part of its agricultural land for blackbuck to roam and graze on.

● In Goa, Kerala and Orissa, important nesting sites for sea turtles such as Galjibag and Rushikulya beaches, have been protected through the action of local fisherfolk, with help from NGOs and the Forest Department. In 2006, over 100,000 turtles were reported to have nested at Rushikulya, on the Orissa coast, where the Rushikulya Sea Turtle Protection Committee, formed by the youth of Puranabandha village and a youth committee of Gokharkuda village, zealously protect the nesting beach. They also help prevent mass casualties of hatchlings that often wander towards inland areas attracted by the lights of villages.

People Power

In addition to pro-active conservation initiatives such as the ones above, there are also very many instances of local communities saving natural ecosystems and wildlife populations from certain destruction. As examples, several big dams that would have submerged huge areas of forest or other ecosystems, have been stopped by people's movements. This includes proposed dams like the Bhopalpatnam-Ichhampalli in Maharashtra and Chhattisgarh, which would have submerged a major part of the Indravati Tiger Reserve, Bodhghat in Chhattisgarh, and Rathong Chu in Sikkim. Along hundreds of kilometres of India's coastline and the adjoining marine waters the National Fishworkers' Forum has staved off destructive trawling, fought for the implementation of the Coastal Regulation Zone and assisted in movements against industrial aquaculture – all of it leading to the protection of marine wildlife. Many such movements have saved areas that are equal in size and sometimes bigger than official protected areas.

Quite a few sites conserved by communities have been recognized to be of such wildlife value that they have been declared sanctuaries or national parks by state governments. In Punjab, lands belonging to the Bishnoi, with considerable blackbuck and chinkara populations, have been declared the Abohar Sanctuary. Several heronries in southern India, such as Nellapattu, Vedanthangal and Chittarangudi, are now wildlife sanctuaries. Many grassland areas which had traditional pastoralism that sustained threatened bird populations, have been declared bustard sanctuaries (such as Karera in Madhya Pradesh). In some cases this has helped to stave off outside threats, but in several cases, it has transferred the responsibility of conservation away from villagers to government agencies who don't always have the resources or the zeal to carry out their duty, as a result of which the areas have suffered neglect and decline.

Many CCAs provide corridors and linkages for animal and gene movement, frequently between officially protected areas. Studies by the NGO Foundation for Ecological Security show that in the Himalayan state of Uttaranchal, two critical protected areas (the Nanda Devi National Park and Biosphere Reserve, and the Askot Sanctuary) are linked by hundreds of square kilometres of community forest land managed under the traditional Van Panchayat (Village Council) system. Together they form a contiguous forest swathe, which would make it one of India's biggest protected areas if the village forests were recognised as equivalent to Protected Areas (PAs).

CCAs can thus be a powerful tool for enhancing the formal PA network of a country. However, they are not given this recognition in most countries. Exceptions to this include Australia, Canada, Colombia and Madagascar. At the IUCN World Parks Congress in 2003, the President of Madagascar committed his country to tripling

the land area under protection in five years. But rather than do this through conventional models alone, the country's wildlife agency has drawn up plans to use a range of PA governance types, including a large number of CCAs, and to "democratise" the governance of PAs in general. Some other countries already recognize indigenous protected areas as part of the PA system.

The Dynamics of Community Conservation

CCAs are managed in many different ways, for different purposes, with differing results. The starting point may have been an ethical concern

for wildlife, a spiritual or religious motivation, the necessity to conserve scarce resources or regenerate water sources, or the need to secure control over an area to withstand outside threats. Whatever the initial motivations, it is clear that at many sites, the initiatives are helping to conserve and enhance wildlife and biodiversity. They are also helping towards more secure livelihoods and ecosystem benefits for local people. The precise dimensions of this are, however, not clear, as there is precious little documentation available on CCAs.

The range of mechanisms used by communities in CCAs is fascinating. At virtually all sites, the community has formed rules and regulations,

LEFT: a Tamil Nadu villager hugs one of the trees that saved his village from the December 2004 tsunami.
RIGHT: olive ridley nesting, Orissa.

and penalties for anyone violating these. At some places the penalties differ depending on the nature of the violation, or even on the class of the offender (with poorer people being fined less). Usually, there is also an institutional mechanism set up to protect the area, such as forest protection committees, youth groups, wildlife protection groups, women's committees or even *gram sabhas* (village assembly) as a whole.

Another critical aspect of many CCAs is the availability of knowledge within the community. As well as their own traditional and local knowledge, inputs from outsiders with a scientific background have greatly helped to

vulnerable, once the leaders are no longer on the scene, unless the effort has meanwhile become institutionalized so that other members can continue it.

Problems and Prospects

CCAs continue to face a host of problems. One of the greatest is that India does not have a supportive policy environment. Recently a category of "community reserves" was added to the Wild Life (Protection) Act, and could have helped provide much-needed legal backing to CCAs. Unfortunately, it is very restrictive, as it is allowed only on community or private lands,

empower people. In some cases local mobilization in other arenas (development, empowerment) has helped in conservation; in others, local mobilization for conservation has helped in efforts at livelihood improvement and more sustainable developmental inputs.

Security of tenure of the land/resources being conserved, or the confidence that the community could continue with its initiative irrespective of the legal ownership of the land, is key to a successful initiative. Finally, we have found that strong leadership from within the community, and often a catalytic or supportive role from outside, is crucial to successful conservation. This also sometimes make the initiative

whereas most common lands where CCAs are located are in government hands. The new Biological Diversity Act could provide some support if its category of "Biodiversity Heritage Sites" is appropriately defined. Additionally, the proposed Tribal (Recognition of Forest Rights) Bill, if it becomes an Act, could provide powerful legal backing to forest CCAs.

This is urgently needed, for many CCAs are threatened by mining, hydro-electric/irrigation projects, urban expansion, industrialization, Special Economic Zones, and other so-called "development" projects. The locally sustained economies of CCAs are not seen as contributing to the economic growth of the country. For example, the proposed Utkal Coal Project at Raijharan in Orissa for open cast coal mining is in an area densely covered with Sal forests. Four villages (Raijharan, Nandijhor, Goalgadia and Similisahi) have been conserving these forests for at least 15 years. In another example from Orissa, Sterlite Group's Vedanta Alumina proposes to blast the Niyamgiri hilltop for bauxite ore. Niyamgiri hill range is sacred for the Dongaria Kondh tribe and is rich in biodiversity. The blackbuck habitat in the Bishnoi land in Punjab has been divided into two by a canal constructed despite protest from the villagers.

The conserving communities are highly influenced by processes outside of the community or the village, including the neo-liberal economic policies and open market systems. Communities remote in location and rich in natural resources are now dependent on the markets and money. However, the markets with which these communities interface are often highly exploitative. Government policies often end up supporting the exploitation. For example, many villages surrounded by an abundance of non-timber forest products (NTFP) would like to develop a sustainable market for these produce or items made from them. However, tendu patta (*Disopyros melanoxylon*), mahua (*Madhuca indica*) and other NTFP that they collect have been nationalized by the government and cannot be sold in the open market. This makes collectors dependent on the government-approved contractors or government-run purchasing centres. Neither of these give the collectors desired prices.

Despite a widespread community forestry movement in states like Orissa, there is still no state-level policy to facilitate or support these initiatives. These forests are either reserved forests under the Forest Department's control, or disputed forests which can be claimed by the government at any point in time.

CCAs also suffer the undermining of traditional institutions by centralized political systems. Even well-intentioned government policies, such as the community reserves or Joint Forest Management, involve taking over functions and powers, or establishing uniform and parallel institutional bodies based on representative politics. A better approach would be

to understand and help overcome the weaknesses and strengths of the community institutions themselves, and build on these.

Wider market forces and "modern" lifestyles are changing aspirations and rendering traditional value systems ineffective amongst the youth. Modern education does not inculcate a respect for local values and rubbishes the knowledge systems that formed the basis for traditional conservation. Youth are getting more and more isolated from local realities and drifting away, threatening the human and institutional base of many CCAs.

Often a great amount of effort and time is spent by the villagers in protection and

patrolling of the forests. This is at the cost of wages that they could have earned. The remoteness of the areas does not bring about other employment opportunities easily. In some cases, because of appropriate support, the livelihoods of local people have been improved and strengthened but in many cases the communities are still struggling to achieve this. At sites such as Mangalajodi and Rushikuliya in Orissa, or many CCAs in Nagaland, communities are very keen on initiating eco-tourism. In areas where NTFP is easily available they would like to start sustainable, organic forest-based enterprises. However, the resources, know-how and appropriate policy conditions are lacking. ❑

LEFT: protests against the Sardar Sarovar Dam project, Bhopal.
RIGHT: construction on the Sardar Sarovar Dam.

PLACES

A detailed guide to a selection of parks and sanctuaries of the region, with accompanying maps

The concept of the unity of all life, and its roots in and dependence on the environment, is an ancient one in South Asia. All life is deemed sacred and each creature has its place and function in nature's mosaic. This view lay at the root of the advocacy of compassion for all living creatures and *ahimsa* (non-violence) preached by the Buddha and Mahavira. In the 3rd-century BC Emperor Ashoka issued his edicts concerning human behaviour towards animals and set up sanctuaries for wild animals. This designation of protected wild areas is perhaps the first such governmental decree on record anywhere. But even before this, in Vedic literature from a thousand years earlier, there is mention of sacred groves in which life was protected. The Buddha himself preached his first sermon in a Deer Park near Sarnath, a few kilometres from Varanasi.

With the passage of the centuries, much of the strength of this tradition was, in practice, lost, though the percepts were never wholly forgotten. In more recent years, it was, paradoxically, the hunters, the *shikaris* of the subcontinent, who played a major role in the preservation of forests and wildlife. It was essentially for sport that the Mughal emperors declared large tracts of forest as reserves. Both prior to and during British rule, other princes did the same in territories they controlled: the "Princely States" that were permitted to survive under British control and protection. Many enlightened British administrators in India who started as *shikaris* turned into pioneer conservationists and earnest naturalists, as did many Indian *shikaris*.

The years of World War II and those that immediately followed brought devastation at an ever increasing rate to the region's forests and wildlife. To the insistent clang of alarm bells and pressure from public opinion, led by informed and active conservationists, governments have established national parks and sanctuaries all over the region. India now has over 90 national parks and 500 sanctuaries. Thanks to these, many species that would otherwise have disappeared by the end of the 20th century have been assured a future, and a number are thriving again in parks and sanctuaries in which habitats favourable to them have been preserved and even, in some cases, extended by reclamation.

A selection of these parks and sanctuaries and what can be seen in them is presented in the pages that follow. The variety is fascinatingly rich and the settings are among the most beautiful to be seen anywhere. ❑

PRECEDING PAGES: sambar in velvet; chital herd; a magnificent display of blackbuck, Velavadar, Gujarat; startled chital.
LEFT: chital or spotted deer with langur, Bandhavgarh.

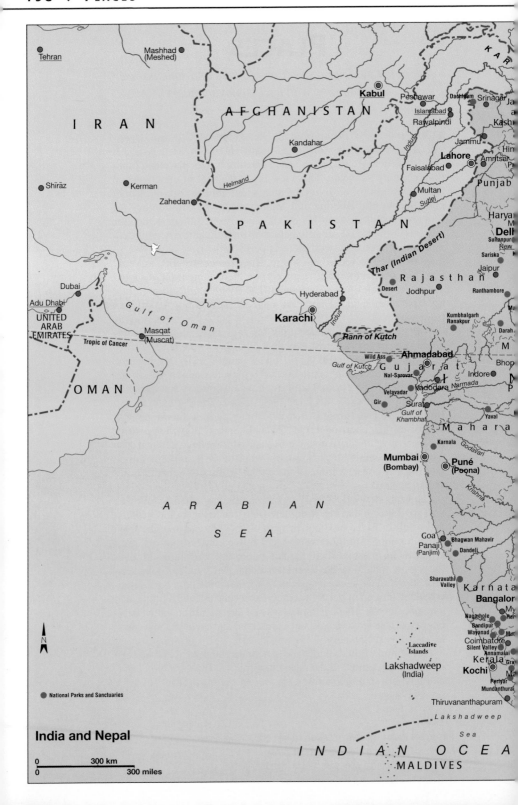

India and Nepal

0	300 km
0	300 miles

● National Parks and Sanctuaries

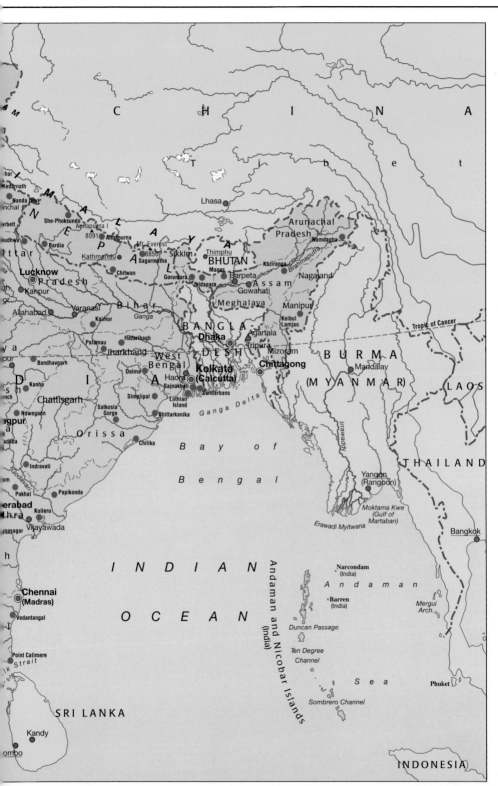

Map on page 204

NANDA DEVI

Guarded by high ridges and overlooked by India's second highest peak, unspoilt forests and the alpine pastures of the Valley of Flowers are home to the snow leopard

The Nanda Devi Biosphere Reserve, situated in the Kumaon and Garhwal regions of the Western Himalayas, in the districts of Chamoli, Pithoragarh and Almora, was established in 1982. It covers an area of 5,860 sq km (2,262 sq miles) with two core zones: the **Nanda Devi National Park** (625 sq km/241 sq miles) and **Valley of Flowers National Park** (8,800 hectares/21,745 acres), and an outer buffer zone of 5,149 sq km (1,988 sq miles). Nanda Devi is one of the most spectacular wilderness areas in the Himalaya.

Nanda Devi (7,817 metres/25,646 ft), a natural monument and India's second highest peak, stands high above the basin of the Rishi Ganga river, which has cut for itself one of the finest gorges in the world. Unlike many other Himalayan areas, it is largely free from human settlement and has remained unspoiled due to its inaccessibility, particularly the forests of the lower Rishi Valley. Nanda Devi National Park could easily become a World Heritage Site based on its exceptional natural beauty and populations of rare and threatened mammals. Access to Nanda Devi National Park is very difficult, due to a series of high ridges with peaks such as Lata, Jhandidhar, Dunagiri, Kalanka, Rishiparvat, Nanda Devi East, Nanda Khata and Trishul, which also form the boundary of the core zone. Thus, not only is Nanda Devi protected by law, but its geographic features act as an effective obstacle to human and livestock entry.

Nanda Devi Biosphere Reserve mainly consists of montane wet temperate forest, sub-tropical pine forest and sub-alpine dry scrub. The elevation ranges from 2,100–7,817 metres (6,889–25,646 ft).

Snow Leopards

The most spectacular mammal here is the snow leopard *(Uncia uncia)*, which occurs in the alpine and subalpine zones. This well built, muscular cat can bring down prey much larger than itself, though, unlike its distant neighbours the tiger and leopard, the snow leopard is generally not aggressive toward man. Its main natural prey are blue sheep *(Pseudois nayaur),* musk deer *(Moschus moschiferus)* and Himalayan tahr *(Hemitragus jemlahicus),* as well as marmots and other small rodents. Its proportionately long tail helps it maintain its balance on the often steep slopes of its mountainous environment and large furred feet, like those of the lynx, act as snowshoes. They ambush prey from above when possible and can jump up to 15 metres (50 ft). Solitary and very circumspect in its habits, the snow leopard is seldom seen, though it does become troublesome to herders of domestic stock. The first

close-up footage captured by a human (as opposed to remote cameras) was taken in 2006, for the BBC TV series, *Planet Earth*.

Most of the eco-region's mammals are small species scurrying among the boulders and undergrowth – the Himalayan palm civet, pale weasel, Himalayan weasel, pikas and voles. Also here are bharal, goral, serow, Himalayan musk deer, Himalayan tahr, Himalayan black bear, leopard, brown bear and common langur.

Other large carnivores are common leopard *(P. pardus)* Himalayan black bear *(Selenarctos thibetanus)* and brown bear (Ursus arctos), the existance of which has yet to be confirmed. The only primate present is common langur *(Presbytis entellus)*, although Rhesus macaque *(Macaca mullata)* has been sighted outside the park boundaries.

Birds

A total of 112 bird species has been recorded from Nanda Devi, 83 within the biosphere reserve and 29 around Joshimath and the oak forest at Auli. Bird species

richness is highest in temperate forests with 47 species, 24 of which were seen only in this habitat dominated by oak, fir, birch and rhododendron. Sub-alpine forest has about 43 species, 18 of which were seen only in this habitat type. Nine species, from a total of 32 recorded, were exclusive to the alpine pastures. Almost all species of avifauna in the Himalaya show altitudinal migration, ascending to sub-alpine and alpine areas in summer to breed, and descending to temperate and tropical areas in the winter.

Three species of pheasants are reported from this park: cheer pheasant *(Catreus wallichi)*, Himalayan monal *(Lophophorus impejanus)* and koklass pheasant *(Pucrasia macrolopha)*. While the former is globally threatened, and considered vulnerable by BirdLife International, the latter two are still common in the Western Himalayas. Other Galliformes include snow partridge *(Lerwa lerwa)* and Himalayan snowcock *(Tetraogallus himalayensis)*. The cheer pheasant is reported from slopes near Reni village.

LEFT: tragopa one of severa beautiful Himalayan pheasants.

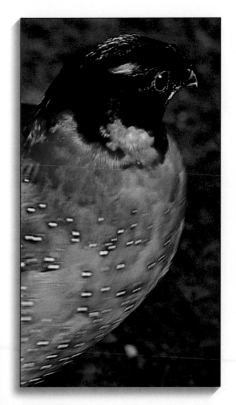

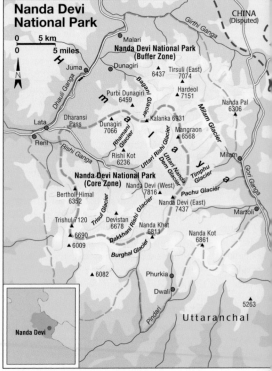

Nanda Devi
National Park

0   5 km
0   5 miles

N

CHINA
(Disputed)

Girthi Ganga

Malari
Nanda Devi National Park
(Buffer Zone)

Juma
Dunagiri
Tirsuli (East)
6437   7074

Purbi Dunagiri
6459
Hardeol
▲7151
Nanda Pal
6306

Lata
Dharansi
Pass
Dunagiri
7066
Kalanka 6931
Mangraon
▲6568

Reni
Rishi Ganga
Rishi Kot
6236

Nanda Devi National Park
(Core Zone)
Nanda Devi (West)
7816▲
Pachu Glacier

Berthol Himal
6352
Nanda Devi (East)
7437

Trishul 7120
Devistan
6678
Nanda Khat
6811
Nanda Kot
6861

▲6690
▲6009
Burghal Glacier

▲6082
Phurkia

Dwali

Pindari

Uttaranchal

5263

Nanda Devi

Map
n page
204

Nanda Devi is considered an Important Bird Area by BirdLife International and the Bombay Natural History Society. It is also considered as Endemic Bird Area of the Western Himalayas.

Poaching, especially of musk deer and snow leopard is the constant threat. Mountaineering expeditions were not allowed for many years due to the pollution left behind by such activities, but now limited expeditions are allowed under strict rules. The lower temperate and tropical forests are perhaps the most vulnerable habitats in the Himalayas due to human habitation and deforestation.

Valley of Flowers National Park

The Valley of Flowers National Park, its buffer zone, and Khiron Valley are located in the Chamoli district of Garhwal Himalaya. The park was established in 1982. The River Pushpawati originates from the Tipra glacier in the valley, flows through the park, joins the River Bhyundar and drains into the Alaknanda at Gobindghat, forming a major tributary of the River Ganga. The park is surrounded by the snow-clad summits of Nilgiri Parvat (6,407 metres/21,020 ft), Gauri Parvat (6,590 metres/21,621 ft), Rataban (5,400 metres/17,717 ft), Sapta Sringa (5,025 metres/16,486 ft), and Kunt Khal (5,855 metres/19,209 ft). The altitude ranges from 3,200–6,590 metres (10,500–21,620 ft). A British mountaineer, Frank Smythe, is credited with having discovered this valley. The upper Bhyundar Valley became internationally known following its exploration by Smythe, first as a member of the successful Kamet Expedition in 1931 and later in 1937, when he made an extensive herbarium collection. Overawed by the profusion of wild flowers he named it Valley of Flowers. He recorded that the flora was as rich as or probably richer than any valley in Sikkim, with many plants of restricted distribution.

The park is located in the newly established state of Uttranchal, which was carved out from the earlier Uttar Pradesh. Its alti-

LOW: snow
●pard.

tude varies from 3,200–6,590 metres (10,500–21,620 ft), and the temperature - 7–17 °C (19.5–63 °F). The total area of the park is 8,750 hectares (21,622 acres).

As the valley received tremendous attention from tourists and plant explorers from all over the world, the Government of Uttar Pradesh designated its 8,750 hectare (21,622 acre) area as a national park in 1982 for the conservation of its rich biodiversity. Forests constitute 529 hectares (1,307 acres), alpine pastures 1,863 hectares (4,604 acres), and 6,358 hectares (15,711 acres) is estimated to be under permanent snow.

Vegetation

There are three main vegetation zones in the park and its surroundings, namely temperate, sub-alpine and alpine. The temperate zone (2,400–3,000 metres/7,900–9,800 ft) is characterized by broadleaf and coniferous forests. Sub-alpine forest (3,000–3,300 metres/9,800–10,800 ft) is dominated by *Betula utilis, Rhododendron campanulatum, Abies pindrow, Acer caesium* and

Prunus cornuta. The alpine zone begins at the treeline (3,500 m/11,500 ft) and is dominated by herbaceous vegetation with some small shrubs.

Over 500 vascular plants have been recorded, of which 31 are rare and endangered, including 13 medicinal plants.

About 82 bird have been identified from the Valley of Flowers. Except for the yellow-rumped honeyguide *(Indicator xanthonotus)*, which is Near Threatened according to BirdLife International, no other bird of conservation concern is found at the site. It must be added here, that detailed studies on the bird life of this floral paradise have not been conducted. This site is one of the only two completely protected alpine grassland and scrub habitats in India, the other being Nanda Devi NP.

Birdlife

Although the Valley of Flowers is better known for its alpine pastures, at lower elevations it has Sino-Himalayan Temperate Forest, where many representative birds of

BELOW: Himalayan orchid

Map on page 204

this biome occur, such as the black-throated tit *(Aegithalos concinnus)*, grey-hooded warbler *(Seicercus xanthoschistos)* and black-faced flycatcher-warbler *(Abroscopus schisticeps)*. Surveys in the alpine zone may reveal good breeding populations of pipits and rosefinches, and such species as the spotted bush-warbler *(Bradypterus thoracicus)*, typical of alpine breeding bird communities in Garhwal Himalaya. The Alpine habitats are under-explored and are likely to be excellent alpine bird habitats in view of their strict protection from grazing. The Valley of Flowers has been identified as an Important Bird Area by BirdLife International and the Bombay Natural History Society.

Mammals

The resident fauna of the park includes the Himalayan musk deer *(Moschus chrysogaster)*, the serow *(Nemorhaedus sumatraensis)*, the Himalayan tahr *(Hemitragus jemlahicus)*, the Asiatic black bear *(Ursus thibetanus)*, the bharal *(Pseudois nayaur)*, the mouse hare *(Ochotona roylei)*, the red fox *(Vulpes vulpes)* and the Himalayan weasel *(Mustela sibirica)*.

Environmental Threats

The Vishnuprayag Dam in the upper Alaknanda Valley is the most serious threat to the park. In order to boost its generating capacity, it is proposed to divert water from the Pushpavati River via a 7.5 km (4¾ miles) long tunnel. The construction of the tunnel, as well as a motorable road to the shrine at Hemkund Saheb, would not only have geographical impact on the Bhyundar Valley, but also change its biodiversity values for ever.

Another conservation threat in the area is the overexploitation of rare medicinal herbs. Grazing and trampling by large herds of domestic livestock, including cows, buffalos, horses, sheep, goats and yak, are beginning to severely degrade the natural habitat. Several species are threatened, including the snow leopard, serow, Himalayan tahr, argali, and Himalayan goral. ❑

LOW: Nanda Devi East Base Camp.

Map page 212

CORBETT

*India's first National Park was the setting for both
F.W. Champions' celebrated photography of Tigerland
and Jim Corbett's tales of maneaters*

Just short of 300 km (190 miles) northeast of Delhi, cradled in the foothills of the Himalaya lies the Corbett National Park. It is India's first national park and also one of her finest.

This park has quite a history. Long ago, on the banks of the River Ramganga, there lived a flourishing community. Today, some evidence of their culture is found in fragments of terracotta and the remains of their temples along the river. This community lived by clearing some of the forest in the *duns* (valleys) and had to fight a constant battle to keep their farmlands free from the invading jungle.

The first in a series

The 40 years following the arrival of the British in this area in 1820 were disastrous. Trees were felled mercilessly for timber and these virgin forests were devastated. It was a Major Ramsay who took the first real systematic measures which, in years to follow, were to restore the forests to their former health. Cattle stations were removed, cultivation was stopped, a fire-fighting force was established and, most important, the removal of timber without a license was totally prohibited. Then, in 1907, the possibility of creating a game sanctuary in this area was first mooted but was rejected outright. Two forest officers, E.R. Stevens and his successor, E.A. Smythies, were to take up this cause again. However, it was only later, when Smythies was a conservator, that he consulted Major Jim Corbett who knew this area well, regarding the possible boundaries for a proposed national park.

During the 1930s, tiger shooting was in vogue and many viceroys, governor-generals and other dignitaries visited this area – the famous terai and bhabar tracts of then United Provinces – to kill tigers from the safety of an elephant's back or

high *machan*. However, in a strange twist, it was through the efforts of other hunters, who abhorred this form of sport and massacre, that Sir Malcolm Hailey, then Governor of the United Provinces, keenly accepted the recommendation that an area of 256.59 sq km (99.07 sq miles) be set aside for the park. It was a welcome case of poachers turned gamekeepers. Thus, on 8 August, 1936, the Hailey National Park, the first in India, was established.

Tribute to an enlightened hunter

In 1952, a few years after India attained independence, the park's name was changed to Ramganga National Park, after the life-giving Ramganga river that

PRECEDING PAGES: early morning, Corbett National Park.
LEFT: great horned owl.
RIGHT: the cloven-footed goral.

flows through almost the whole length of it. In 1957, it was renamed once more, Corbett National Park, in honour and memory of the late Jim Corbett, the legendary hunter-naturalist turned author and photographer, who helped in demarcating the park's boundaries and setting it up. It was in this area that he had shot the "maneaters" who had been carrying off local villagers, the notorious Kanda Maneater being one of them. His books on these thrilling, if somewhat gung-ho, adventures, *The Maneaters of Kumaon* and *The Maneating Leopard of Rudraprayag*, are perennial best-sellers, well known all over the world.

Perhaps the real hero was the man who had influenced Jim Corbett most to hang up his guns and take to the camera, a forest officer called F.W. Champion, the pioneer of wildlife photography in India. His photographic masterpieces, *With a Camera in Tiger-land* and *The Jungle in Sunlight and Shadow*, were photographed and written in these very same jungles.

In the late 1960s and the early 1970s, the world was hit by the awareness that the Indian tiger *(Panthera tigris tigris)* was on the brink of extinction and that of an estimated 40,000 at the turn of the 20th century, less than 2,000 survived in the wild. A far reaching project was envisaged. Its philosophy was that if the tiger and its habitat were totally protected in tiger reserves, then other species of fauna and flora would flourish too, as nature would maintain her own balance. Thus, with the help of the World Wildlife Fund (WWF), Project Tiger was launched at Dhikala in the Corbett National Park on 1 April, 1973. This national park was one of the first tiger reserves, along with seven others in the country; today, there are 27 such reserves. After initial gains (up to 4,000 tigers were recorded in 1984) the present-day population has dropped alarmingly to around 1,200, under pressure from poaching and the continuing damage done to India's forest cover.

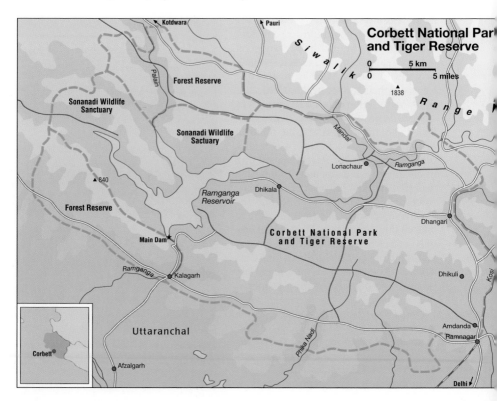

Topography

The Corbett National Park, or just "Corbett" as it is also popularly known, is situated in the hilly districts of Pauri Garhwal and Nainital of the Uttranchal. It lies between latitude 29° 13' – 29° 35' N and longitude 78° 33' – 78° 46' E. The park comprises an area of 520.5 sq km (201 sq miles). Of this, an area of 320 sq km (123.5 sq miles) is the core – the *sanctum sanctorum*, where no kind of disturbance is permitted. There is a move to expand the park by another 1,100 sq km (425 sq miles). However, so far only an area of 300 sq km (116 sq miles) is to be added to the northern area of the park. A buffer zone of 900 sq km (348 sq. miles) is also planned. These expansions are keenly sought by conservationists as it will link the park with other forests through corridors. This is important to help the overflow of animals to level out, prevent inbreeding and ensure that viable gene pools are maintained.

The area in the Himalayan foothills in which the park is situated is known as the South Patlidun. In elevation the park ranges between 400 metres (1,312 ft) at its lowest to 1,210 metres (3,970 ft) at its highest. Corbett is, in fact, a large valley with its long axis from east to west. Through this valley run three thickly forested ridge systems, roughly parallel to one another and in the same direction. Small offshoots of these ridges run north to south and the valleys formed in between are known as *sots*. The ridge to the north forms the boundary of the park in that direction and Kanda, the highest point, with its magnificent panoramic view of the park, is here.

Between the northern ridge and the longer median ridge, is the Ramganga river, which enters the park from the northeast, flows through the park into the reservoir and makes its exit at Kalagarh towards the southwest. The southern ridge is a bit lower and this area of the park is drier and is notable for its more deciduous type of vegetation and its own rugged charm.

A topographic change of significance that took place in the park was the inundation of 42 sq km (16 sq miles) of prime habitat when almost a tenth of the park's area was lost to the waters of a multi-purpose hydroelectric dam at Kalagarh. This is the largest earthen dam in Asia and lies at the southwestern fringe of Corbett. The construction of the dam certainly was not in the best interest of the park. Conservationists had feared that the changes that would come with such a dam would bring about adverse effects, but the changes by and large have been absorbed by the remarkable resilience of nature.

The waters first started to fill up in 1974. In 1976, when they had inundated a greater part of the reservoir, the elephant migration routes linking the park with the western and northwestern reserved forests were cut off. Not for long though. Those great, accomplished trail-blazers and surveyors of gradients soon established other routes.

There was a shift of animals from the affected areas to higher ground. There

HT: a grey gur takes a tious look.

will also be changes that are less apparent at this stage, and though some research has been done, much more is needed and it is planned to study these changes in detail. The lake, besides just its scenic charm, has added to the park in a few ways. A large number of species of water birds, both migrants and others, have begun to frequent its waters, though mainly in winter. Crocodiles – both the long-snouted, fish-eating gharial *(Gavialis gangeticus)* and the mugger *(Crocodylus palustris)* have found new homes here and their numbers have increased. They can often be seen sunning themselves on the sand banks. Sporting fish such as the mahseer *(Tor putitora)* and malee *(Wallago attu)*, abound in the lake and in the river.

Flora and climate

Vegetation in the park is confined chiefly to the bhabar tract type of the Siwalik hills; different kinds of vegetation are found all along the varied topography, which comprises hilly and riverine areas, temporary marshy depressions, plateaus and ravines. The park is known for its almost pure sal *(Shorea robusta)* stands in the lower hilly ridges and flat valleys. Some associates of sal here are haldu *(Adina cordifolia)*, rohini *(Mallotus philippinensis)*, and karipak *(Murraya koenigi)*.

The riverine area is clothed in shisham *(Dalbergia sissoo)*, khair *(Acacia catechu)* and others. In early summer it is an unforgettable sight to witness the soothing green of the shisham islands in new leaf.

On the higher ridges we find bakli *(Anogeissus latifolia)*, which enriches the hues of the park with its reddish leaves and pale bark. The chir *(Pinus roxburghii)*, anauri *(Legestroemia parviflora)*, and gurail *(Bauhinia racemosa)* are some others that find root-holds at these contours, along with bamboos. The common shrub is *Clerodendrum viscosum* and a weed which is causing some

BELOW: Early morning on the Ramganga.

Map
n page
212

concern is the lantana *(Lantana camera)*.

The chaurs, the savannah grasslands, are covered with a variety of grasses like *Themeda arundinacea*, *Vetiveria zizanioides* and *Thysanulena maxima*.

A hundred and ten species of trees, 51 species of shrubs and over 33 species of bamboo and grass are found here.

There are three distinct seasons in Corbett: cold – November to February; hot - March to June; and rainy (monsoons) – July to October. In winter the nights are cold, at an average of 5°C (41°F), with frost and some fog which lasts till late morning, but the sun is pleasant and the day temperature averages 25°C (77°F).

In the hot season, June is the hottest month, with day temperatures going up to an unbearable 44°C (112°F) but the nights are pleasant with an average temperature of 21°C (70°F). In the monsoon season, from June to October, the park remains closed to tourists.

There is very heavy rain, between 150–280 cm (60–112 in). The roads are washed away by the heavy downpours and when the sun does shine the jungle steams with humidity. The animals move to the hilly areas of Corbett at this time for the cool breeze and to avoid the daans, a blood-sucking fly, which plagues them in the lowlands. Surely, these few months are times of a well deserved rest from the attention of humans for the denizens of the jungle.

Mammals

Over 50 mammal, 580 bird and 25 reptile species have been listed in Corbett. The insect life in itself is astounding and though not much work has been done in this respect even the lay person will be amazed at its abundance, mainly after the monsoon.

Corbett is well-known as a haven for its tigers. There is plentiful prey – four kinds of deer, wild boar and other lesser animals – for them to live on. With a bit of luck, it is possible to see a tiger on the road as you enter the park and travel

LOW: Corbett renowned its tigers.

down to Dhikala. Pug marks are seen in abundance on the roadsides, paths and animal trails. It is by tracing these pug marks, which bear individual characteristics, that the population is estimated, which has shown a marked increase from 40 in 1972 to 90 tigers in 1984, and up to 128 in 1995, although poachers have been caught within the park itself.

Leopards *(Panthera pardus)* are found in the hilly areas of the park. They do sometimes venture into the lower jungle, but at much risk to themselves from tigers. There have been many cases of leopards being killed and eaten by tigers. The leopard is, however, a great survivor and can sustain itself on even small birds and rodents.

The lesser cats such as the leopard cat *(Felis bengalensis horsfieldi)*, the jungle cat *(Felis chaus)*, the rare fishing cat *(Felis viverina)* and some others are found here, but, being nocturnal, are rarely seen. Civet cats that have been spotted in the park include the Himalayan palm civet and the linsang or tiger civet.

The sloth bear *(Melursus ursinus)* is found in the Bijrani-Malani areas of the park. It can be seen on the roadsides in the early morning or late evening, busily demolishing termite mounds for the grubs, or in the mahwa *(Madhuca indica)* trees, relishing the sweet sticky flowers, which ferment in the hot season and are intoxicating.

The Himalayan black bear *(Selenarctos thibetanus)* is seen in the higher hills towards Kanda, but only rarely and only during the cold winters.

The dhole *(Cuon alpinus)*, the wild dog, is also rare and seen in the southern areas of Corbett towards Bijrani. The golden jackal *(Canis aureus)* is commonly seen around all the campus areas. During the fawning season, jackals are most active and can be seen killing and carrying off newly dropped chital fawns.

The yellow-throated marten *(Martes flavicula flavicula)*, the Himalayan palm

BELOW: elephants bathing in the Ranganga River.

Map
n page
212

civet *(Paguma larvata grayi)*, the Indian grey mongoose *(Herpestes edwardsi)*, the common otter *(Lutra lutra)* and the black-naped hare *(Lepus nigricollis rufi-caudatus)* are some of the smaller resident mammals. The porcupine *(Hystrix indica)* can also be seen at night near the rubbish dumps of the park buildings at Dhikala.

Elephants *(Elephas maximus)* are one of the main attractions of Corbett. The whole jungle belongs to them. It is possible to see a lone tusker or even a herd crossing the road. Corbett's elephants by and large are well behaved, but one must always remember that, "Elephants have the right of way". The park's elephant population varies from about 200 to 300 and more in summer, when the sub-herds amalgamate and form large herds.

Of the four species of deer that are found here the chital *(Axis axis)* is the well-known spotted deer and considered one of the most beautiful in the world. This is one of the chief prey animals of the carnivora. A smaller cousin of the chital, the para *(Axis porcinus)* is found in the more open grassland and riverain areas. The sambar *(Cervus unicolour)* is the largest Asiatic deer and is sought after by the larger adult tigers of the park. The kakkar *(Muntiacus muntjak)*, also called the barking deer, is the smallest of the four. Nervous and shy, it warns the jungle's denizens of danger from predators with its hoarse, dog-like bark.

The goat-antelopes are represented by the ghoral *(Nemorhaedus goral)* in Corbett. Ghorals can be spotted on a drive up the hilly road to Kanda.

Wild boar *(Sus scrofa)* are found in the forests as well as in the grasslands, sometimes seen in sounders of 10 to 30 pigs. Even the tigers respect the large male boars – it is not unknown for an encounter between a tiger and one of these stalwart beasts to end in the tiger's death.

The langur *(Presbytis entellus)* and the rhesus *(Macaca mulatta)* are well

ow:
tal herd in
g grass.

distributed throughout the park and also warn the jungle with their alarm calls, when they see either tiger or leopard from their tree-top perches.

Avian attractions

Corbett has many attractions for the bird watcher, with over 580 species found here. Most of the water birds are migrants and arrive in winter. These include the greylag and the barheaded goose, ducks of many kinds, and great crested grebe, snipe, sandpiper, plover, gull and wagtail. There are also resident are darters, cormorants, egrets, herons, blacknecked stork and spur-winged lapwing. The commonly seen raptors in Corbett are the osprey, crested serpent eagle, blackwinged kite, shikra, Pallas's fishing eagle, greyheaded fishing eagle, spotted eagle and harrier.

Some of the other birds found in the forests include minivets, shrikes, babblers, doves, drongos, cuckoos, parakeets, barbets, 17 kinds of woodpecker, thrushes, peafowl, kalij pheasants and the red junglefowl – the ancestor of all domestic fowl.

On elephant rides, the mahouts used to keep a wary eye open for the circling vultures as they used to help in pinpointing a carnivore's kill. Sadly, they are now gone due to the killer drug diclofenac which has almost completely wiped out a staggering 85 million griffon vultures, The species once commonly-found were the Indian white-backed or white-rumped, slender-billed and the king or red-headed vultures.

The nocturnal birds are the nightjars, thick-knees, owls and owlets and, by the river, the great stone plover and stone curlew hunt at night.

Reptiles

The Ramganga is the home of the descendants of the prehistoric reptiles, the gharial and the mugger. The gharial is the rare fish-eating, long-nosed crocodile, only just saved from extinction in the park through captive breeding and

BELOW: pytho swallowing a chital.

Map
on page
212

release to augment the few survivors there. Both the gharial and the mugger have been helped by the creation of the lake of the Kalagarh dam. A few species of turtles and tortoises are also found in and around the lake.

There is a wide variety of snakes in the park. As well as harmless varieties, the Indian python, viper, cobra, krait and king cobra, the largest of poisonous snakes, also inhabit Corbett. There are also monitors and other lesser lizards.

Facilities

The park is open from 15 November to 15 June. The best time to visit depends on one's priorities of interests. For wildlife photography, the best months are April to June.

There is a wide variety of accommodation available at Corbett, much of it very comfortable and well-maintained – options include Tiger Tops Corbett Lodge, Corbett Hideaway and Corbett Jungle Resort in Ramnagar *(see also* *page 337)* The park authorities also maintain lodges within the park itself, though it is often difficult to book these, and reservations may only be made with an advance payment. For some of these you will have to bring your own food and bedding.

It is possible to take jeep and, better, elephant rides around the park – booked through the park administration at Dhikala. These are for morning and evening viewing and the elephant rides provide the best opportunities for wildlife viewing as the visibility is excellent, and silent and close approach to wild animals is possible. It is not safe to walk through the park as in the past there have been attacks on people by tigers and elephants.

At the park administration and centre at Dhikala there is also a good library, shop and restaurant. Dhikala itself is a very picturesque location, and the areas around it, including the famous Dhikala Chaur, abound in wildlife. ❏

LOW:
though large,
the gharial is
built for speed
not strength.

Map
on page
222

DUDHWA

*These spectacular sal forest and grasslands on the border with Nepal
began as a sanctuary for the swamp deer but Dudhwa is
also known for tiger and wetland birds*

Dudhwa National Park, which emerged from a struggle against a welter of vested interests, is even now threatened by a surge of ever increasing demographic pressure. A viable pattern of coexistence between humans and other forms of life is urgently required if the latter are not to be overwhelmed.

The North Kheri Forest Division, as the area in which the park is located was previously called, has the finest quality sal *(Shorea robusta)* in India; the Forest Department, in its eagerness to exploit this commercially, opposed the establishment of the park, oblivious of their simultaneous responsibility of protecting India's wildlife. "Sportsmen" too were reluctant to surrender the right to kill the so-called game animals that lived there in substantial numbers. The surrounding population protested that they would be denied building materials for their homes and grazing areas for their cattle.

Thanks to the avid lobbying by the well-known conservationist Arjan Singh, and the firm conviction of a conservation-minded prime minister, the late Mrs Indira Gandhi, the division was declared a wildlife sanctuary in 1965 and a national park in 1977, despite opposition and objections.

Barasingha country

Dudhwa National Park, covering (490 sq km (190 sq miles) of grassland and woodland, consists, as mentioned, mainly of sal forest. The Neora river and the bed of the Soheli, which is dry before the confluence, run along the southern edge, from here until the sal forest to the north lie the grasslands that are the barasingha's, or swamp deer's, preferred habitat, about 100 sq km (40 sq miles) of which have been preserved in the park. The rest of the *terai* have been taken over by cultivation.

By far the largest numbers of barasingha, for which the park is best known, occur in the Sathiana, Salukapar and Kakraha blocks, in the southwest and southeast sectors respectively, which together comprise some 44–46 sq km (17–18 sq miles). Sathiana is the wetter area, much of it being inundated for at least short periods during the monsoon season. Grasses are generally tall and coarse, sometimes forming dense thickets that are difficult to penetrate even by elephant. Several swampy depressions, which contain water for all or most of the year, cross the land from north to south, and numerous jamun trees *(Syzygium cuminii)* attest to the wetness of the habitat; the high-water marks on the trees

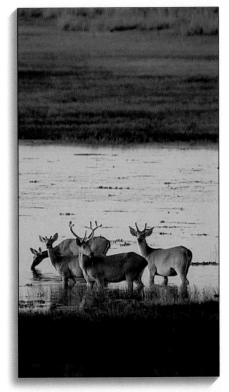

LEFT: spotted deer are often seen with gurs.
RIGHT: barasingha, or swamp deer.

close to the Neora river may be up to 2 metres (6½ ft) and in some years more. The western end of the Sathiana is better drained than the east; the grasses appear to be shorter, and there are large stands of *Imperata cylindrica*, but the various-aged plantings of sisam trees *(Dalbergia sissoo)* obscure the animals. Other timbers of specialized utility are semal *(Bombax ceiba)*, khair *(Acacia catechu)*, sirsa *(Albizia procera)*, haldu *(Adira cordifolia)* and tun *(Cedrela toona)*.

Some of the grasslands are infested with the weed *Cymbopogon martinii*, known as East Indian geranium, Indian rosha or motia. Dense mats of *Tiliacora* species, another weed, has developed in large portions of the sal forests. The fast-growing *Lantana Camara* shrub has progressively destroyed large areas of forestland and disturbed the normal movement of wildlife species. This tough evergreen shrub with red flowers, of South American origin, is destroying the local palatable grasses and reeds which are the main food of several species of herbivorous animals. These weeds are inedible and are spreading rapidly, making the affected areas inhospitable for herbivores. As these animals are displaced, tigers and leopards also step out of the park area.

Tigers and leopards

The tiger, originally the glamorous objective of every sport killer's rifle sight, and now the cynosure of every wildlife tourist's questing eye, exists in fair number in the park. Unfortunately, there is hardly any buffer zone, and the forested area is surrounded by agricultural crops, mainly sugar cane, which has replaced the tall grasses that tigers used to inhabit in earlier years. With the decimation of their prey species by firearms, the tigers have come into conflict with the adjoining human population.

Dudhwa is celebrated for the successful hand-rearing by Arjan Singh of a tiger cub, Tara, from virtual domestication to free, self-sustained life in the wild. After

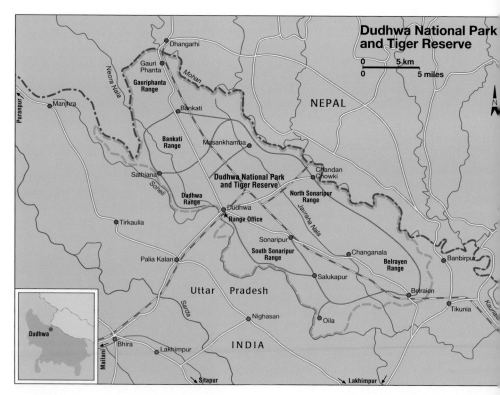

Map
on page
222

20 months of hand-rearing, Tara was launched into the jungle in 1978.

Leopards are few in Dudhwa, as is usually the case in habitats supporting tigers, where competition from the senior predator depresses their population, in spite of the fact that the prey overlap between the two species is limited.

Since Dudhwa provides the optimum habitat for barasingha, or swamp deer *(Cervus duvauceli duvauceli)*, the remnants of the once prolific deer species is crowded into the wetlands of the park, which has the distinction of having the largest population of this threatened species in the subcontinent. Mirchia Jheel, once infamous for its *battues* of the barasingha, in which it was common for as many as 30–40 stags to be gunned down in a morning's "sport", is now under cultivation, as are other previous habitat areas. Herds of 200 and more may, however, still be seen in the southern grasslands, their presence rendered more spectacular by the propensity for segregation of the antlered males.

Human habitation surrounds the park, resulting in the usual man-animal conflicts. Crop-raiding by ungulates wandering into adjacent fields of wheat or sugar cane – particularly in winter when grasses inside the park are coarse – makes them vulnerable to poaching. Livestock-lifting by carnivores, who have sometimes followed the above-mentioned prey species, then provokes reprisals by villagers: on one occasion, villagers poisoned a cattle carcass which resulted in the death of a tigress and her three cubs.

Return of the rhino

An exciting innovation is the attempted reintroduction into Dudhwa of the great Indian one-horned rhinoceros, made possible as a gift to conservation by the late Indira Gandhi. Two males and five females were translocated from Assam in 1984, of which one female died just after reaching Dudhwa, and another subsequently. Two more females rhinos were brought from Nepal. Currently, the num-

ber has increased to 22 but unfortunately, all the young ones born in Dudhwa are sired by one dominant male called Banke. Thus the population is severely inbred and urgently needs new blood lines. Initially, visitors were not allowed inside the rhinos' enclosure, but now one can enjoy the sight of these beasts wallowing in the puddles or peacefully grazing on the abundant grasses.

Elephant

Previously only seasonal visitors, wild elephant were driven to cross over to Dudhwa by massive habitat destruction in Nepal during the 1960s and 70s and a herd of over 30 animals spent nearly 10 years in the park. Being wide-ranging animals they have since returned to Nepal to remnants of their habitat still surviving in Sukla Phanta and Bardia Wildlife Reserves across the border. Further visits would be welcome, especially as the magnificent herd bull has been put at more than 4 metres (11 ft) tall at the shoulder. Several animals are lost each year to collisions with trains, which regularly speed along the tracks cutting through the park.

Other Animals

Other animals seen in Dudhwa in fair to dwindling numbers are sloth bears, ratels, civets, jackals, fishing cats, jungle cats and leopard cats. Among the deer, in addition to the barasingha, are the sambar, the chital or spotted deer (considered the handsomest deer in the world), the hog deer and the barking deer. An occasional nilgai or bluebull (the largest antelope in India) is seen, particularly in the open parts of the park. Wild pigs are common.

In winter, basking on the sandy banks of the Soheli-Neora river, running along the southern boundary of the park, the mugger (also known as the snub-nosed crocodile or marsh crocodile) may be seen. It prefers fairly shallow, calm waters and grows to a length of 4–5 metres (13–16 ft). Otters are fairly common, as also are pythons and monitor lizards.

BELOW: Brahminy kite

Avian variety

Birdlife is prolific, and one ornithologist has said that Dudhwa could establish its claim to fame merely on account of its owls and storks. Among the night birds of prey are the great Indian horned owl, the forest eagle owl, the brown fish owl, the tawny fish owl, the dusky horned owl, and the brown wood owl. The collared scops owl and the jungle owlet are among the more vociferous of the lesser varieties. Apart from the sarus crane, there are black-necked storks, white-necked storks, black storks, painted storks, white storks, open-billed storks and lesser adjutant storks (distinguishable from greater adjutant by smaller size, uniform wing, and lack of gular pouch). Storks are strong fliers and several species migrate over large distances. They are experts at soaring on thermals and often circle high in the sky, gaining height for easy travel, or searching for likely feeding places.

Raptors are of infinite variety and occasionally species of hawks and eagles appear which tax the talent of the most gifted of ornithologists. Six vultures, including the cinerious, are present at times. Among the bustards, the Bengal bustard and the similar florican still hold on in greatly diminished numbers. The swamp francolin has a transitional habitat, with the black and the grey partridges occupying higher grasslands and sandy soils.

Among the colourful birds are varieties of woodpeckers, orioles, pittas, kingfishers, minivets, flycatchers and sunbirds; also hornbills, bulbuls, prinias, chats and warblers (whose innumerable species were obviously named by an ornithologist with a sense of humor).

Migratory birds are plentiful, especially waterfowl, and as Dudhwa is close to the Himalayan foothills, various species stop over in the course of their migration to the plains in winter. However, national as well as international pressures are becoming manifest. The white ibis has vanished, and the ethereal trumpeting of the fighting demoiselle cranes is heard no more. ❑

Map
n page
222

LOW:
se-up of
hon snake.

Map on page 230

CHITWAN

*Chitwan offers exceptionally rich and varied opportunities –
view rhino from elephant-back or take a boat down
the Narayani spotting dolphin and gharial*

One possible meaning of Chitwan is "Heart of the Jungle" and it could not be more aptly described. With its tropical creeper-clad forests, great meandering rivers, lush seas of tall elephant grass, and the magnificent backdrop of the Himalaya in the distance, Chitwan is a most romantic jungle. And for its 960 sq km (370 sq miles), it has a richness and variety of wildlife matched by few other parks.

Until the 1950s, a virulent form of malaria prevalent in the region kept Chitwan relatively free of human settlement. Between 1846 and 1950, when Nepal was ruled by the Rana prime ministers, Chitwan was a hunting reserve, exclusively for the ruling classes. It was jealously guarded, if only to preserve it for more hunting. During that period, Chitwan was the venue of many a vicious hunt to which the royalty of Europe and India, and the top brass of the British Raj, were often invited. These hunts were lavish operations, with several hundred elephants and beaters being employed to round up and drive big game towards the shooters.

Massive slaughter

However, several years were often allowed to lapse between such massive hunts; they were not always held in the same area, and the habitat was left relatively intact, so the hunted species recovered their losses fairly rapidly. In the last hunt of 1938–39, in which the then Viceroy of India, Lord Linlithgow, also took part, a record bag of 120 tiger, 38 rhino, 27 leopard and 15 bear was taken. That so much big game was still there to shoot in spite of two previous hunts in the same decade indicates what an amazingly vital and thriving area Chitwan must have been for wildlife.

In 1950 the Ranas fell from power and the new government opened up Chitwan for settlement. A malaria eradication programme was launched in 1954 to attract settlers from the overpopulated hills, and by 1960 Chitwan was declared free of malaria. The human population rose from 36,000 in 1950 to 100,000 in 1960 and extensive forest areas were cleared for cultivation. Poaching was rampant, both for the pot and for money, with the rhino being the main target since its horn fetched a handsome price.

When in 1962 a rhino sanctuary was declared south of the Rapti river the barasingha *(Cervus duvauceli)* and the wild buffalo *(Bubalus bubalis)* had already become extinct here. And despite the efforts of the 130-strong armed

guards, called Gainda Gasti or Rhino Patrol, poaching continued and by the 1960s about 100 rhinos remained, down from 800–2,000 in 1950.

Chitwan was finally gazetted as Nepal's first national park in 1973 and a few years later a contingent of the Royal Nepalese Army was called in to combat poaching. Ever since, poaching of rhino within the park has been almost unheard of, although some does take place outside its limits.

The park headquarters are at Kasara Durbar, where an old hunting lodge houses the offices and a small museum. Near Kasara is the Gharial Project. There are several excellent places to stay, both inside and outside the park. One of the best ways to get around the park is by elephant and there are seven different stables operated by the park authorities. A different view of the park can be had from a trip down the Narayani River, with excellent opportunities for spotting gharial.

Topography

Along the length of Nepal, in the middle, runs the Mahabharat Range; viewed from the plains, it is a blue mass of mountains. To its south, and almost parallel to and hugging it, runs a lower range of broken hills called the Siwalik. At times, such as in Chitwan, the two ranges separate and enclose huge flat valleys known as doons.

The park straddles the Siwalik range, the highest point in it being about 600 metres (2,000 ft). Although much of it is hilly, a portion lies on the floodplain of three large rivers, the Reu, the Rapti and the Narayani, at an elevation of about 140 metres (465 ft).

Much of the park is bounded by these rivers and their tributaries. Both the Rapti and its tributary, the Reu, are low during the dry months (December to April) and are fordable for four-wheel-drive vehicles at a few places. But during the monsoon, after a heavy downpour, flash floods turn them into raging tor-

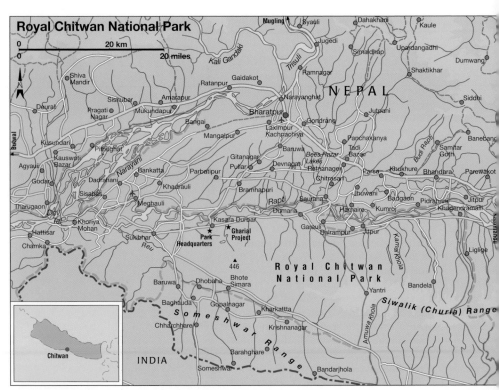

Map on page 230

rents and hundreds of trees may be washed downriver. During such times even the bravest of elephants will refuse to cross them. These two rivers meet about 1 km (½ mile) east of where they link with the huge Narayani river, which has its origins high up in the Tibetan plateau. It meanders through the flat valley floor and forms a series of large gravel islands, known as bandarjhula, from Sigraulighat to Amaltarighat. The Narayani eventually cuts a narrow gorge in the Siwalik and becomes the Gandak in India before joining the holy Ganga – the Ganges in India.

Climate

Chitwan has a monsoonal climate with high humidity most of the year. In March and April the air is relatively dry. Apart from the cool months of December to February, the weather is generally hot during the day, particularly from May to September. Mid-June heralds the coming of the monsoon, which is the most dramatic time of year, with heavy showers and occasional floods. After the monsoon the jungle is lush and green and the sky crystal clear, with the snow-covered Himalaya 80–100 km (50–60 miles) away clearly visible, especially in the evening. During the winter months a thick mist descends on the forest around 10pm and persists into the late morning. The humidity reaches its peak in the early hours of the morning and the dew dripping from the trees onto the forest litter below makes a sound loud enough to convince newcomers to Chitwan that it is raining.

Two types of forest

The vegetation of Chitwan is tropical moist deciduous and two main types of forest may be recognized; the sal forest and the floodplain forest. On high ground and in the hills, where drainage is good and flooding does not occur, is the sal forest, so called after the dominant tree, sal *(Shorea robusta)*. This forest covers roughly 75 percent of the park area and attains a height of 40 metres (130 ft) or more at the base of the hills,

but becomes stunted higher up. A common associate of sal is saj *(Terminalia tomentosa)*, another large tree, easily recognized by its grey bark that resembles the skin of a crocodile.

The kusum tree *(Schleichera trijuga)* bursts into a riot of red when the new leaves sprout in February–March, later turning to green, and the large-leaved tantari *(Dillenia pentagyna)*, a medium-size tree, bears clusters of bright yellow flowers in the late spring. Other components of the sal forest are the sturdy karam or haldu *(Adina cordifolia)* and the middle-sized sandan *(Ougenia dalbergioides)*.

Giant vines and creepers, such as debre lahara *(Spatholobus parviflorus)* and bhorla *(Bauhinia vahlii)* twine upwards, using the larger trees for support. Sometimes a branch or a whole tree may collapse under their weight. The trees and their limbs also harbour several species of orchid and other epiphytes. On the very high ridges of the Siwalik grow

sallo or chir pine *(Pinus roxburghii)*.

On the floodplain, which is prone to waterlogging and flooding during the monsoon, patches of grassland and riverine forest occur. Dense stands of elephant grass, often 6 metres (20 ft) high, are composed of *Saccharum* species, *Phragmites karka, Themeda villosa, Arundo donax* and *Arundinella nepalensis*. Some grasses are shorter, usually under 2 metres (6½ ft) tall, such as *Imperata cylindrica* and *Bothriocloa intermdeia* and are commonly found in old village sites, although taller species are gradually displacing the short grasses. In Chitwan, most grasses flower between August and November, different species at different times – and there are many species. The change of colour of the grass canopies from white to purple to yellow and various shades of pastel is a memorable sight.

Interspersed in the grassland are trees such as shisham *(Dalbergia sissoo)*, Khair *(Acacia catechu)* and simal *(Bombax ceiba)*, especially on mid-river gravel islands and on the sandbanks of the Reu, Rapti and Narayani rivers. Both shisham and khair average about 14 metres (45 ft) in height but the simal is the largest tree in the park. Its flowers attract a variety of birds in the spring and during the course of a day dozens of species may be spotted in a single tree.

Mature riverine forests are often dense with a great variety of shrubs and other trees. In moist places, such as the Itcharni Tappu and other areas near Sauraha, there are thick patches of bheller *(Trewia nudiflora)*. The dark crooked skeletons of dhak *(Butea monosperma)* suddenly burst into flower in February and are aptly called "Flame of the Forest".

The beautiful white flowers of bhanti *(Clerodendron viscosum)*, seen in March and April, have a lovely fragrance and attract numerous colourful butterflies and bees. Also in moist spots, several kinds of strangler figs *(Ficus spp.)* may be seen draped over their hosts, at varying stages

BELOW: strangler fig growing over host trees.

Map
n page
230

of takeover. Foxtail orchids decorate some trees with their purple blossom in April, and the magnificent orange flowers of sungawa *(Dendrobium densiflorum)* in June–July.

Fire, an ecological factor

Apart from rainfall and flood, an important factor in the ecology of Chitwan is fire. Each year, some time in December and January, some 50,000 to 100,000 villagers enter the park for two weeks to collect thatch grass and reeds, both vital building materials for their houses. Having reaped their harvest, they set fire to the grassland and the fire spreads into the hills. Burning is intermittent and continues until the end of April or the beginning of May, when the pre-monsoon showers put an end to it. These fires have been an annual event, perhaps for hundreds of years, and this must surely affect the composition of the forest. Perhaps it explains the predominance of fire-tolerant species, such as sal and simal, and also why tall coarse grasses are gradually replacing the short grass from old village sites.

Burning effectively "opens up" the grassland and the forest and the leaf-fall of spring improves visibility even further, so wildlife sightings at this time of the year are particularly good. Regrowth of grass is fast and herbivores concentrate on the once burnt grassland to graze on the succulent new grasses. Chital herds a hundred strong may sometimes be seen.

In and around the "Tals"

The floodplain is crisscrossed by numerous seasonal water channels and dotted with marsh, swamp and lakes. Only a handful of lakes are of any size: Tamar Tal and Lame Tal near Kasara Durbar; and Dhakre Tal, Lame Tal and Devi Tal near Tiger Tops. The latter is the largest and most spectacular of all.

These lakes are the rhino's favourite haunts and also support a number of

.OW: tiger
mark.

water birds, fish, turtle and marsh mugger *(Crocodylus palustris)*. The mugger may grow to over 3 metres (10 ft) long and with its blunt nose and huge jaws lined with yellow teeth is sinister-looking, the wavy outline of its mouth giving the impression of a nasty smile. The mugger will eat anything that it can overpower and kill, from birds and amphibians to deer, wild boar and even python. They prefer enclosed waters but are also found in rivers.

The gharial *(Gavialis gangeticus)*, on the other hand, lives only in rivers and feeds largely on fish. Easily recognized by its slender snout, it is larger than the mugger and may reach 5 metres (16 ft) in length. The Narayani, with about 40 adults, has the largest single concentration of wild gharial anywhere. Several young gharial, artificially hatched and hand reared at the Gharial Project near Kasara Durbar, have been released in batches since 1980 and many have survived. The gharial is, however, very wary

of humans and will slither into the river even when as far as 45 metres (150 ft) away. But look for their tell-tale eyes and nostrils gleaming over the surface of the water. The best time of year to see crocodiles is winter (October–February), when they come out of the water and bask in the sun, often all day long.

Another peculiar aquatic predator in the Narayani river is the rare Gangetic dolphin *(Platanista gangetica)* – the most threatened cetacean. About 2 metres (7 ft) long when adult, this spindle-shaped mammal feeds on crustaceans and fish on the riverbed and breaks the surface every minute or so to breathe. Its hissing sound is unmistakable and it may be seen at the Narayani-Rapti confluence from July to September and at Amaltarighat for most of the year, except when the water is low from January to April. The smooth-coated otter *(Lutra perspicillata)* is another common aquatic predator and to watch a family playing outside its den is an endearing sight.

BELOW: Indian python swallowing axis deer.

Map
page
230

Indian pythons *(Python molurus)* are common near large bodies of water and these heavy reptiles, which may reach 5–6 metres (16–20 ft) in length, sometimes waylay deer, which come to drink. An adult python can swallow a full-grown hog deer *(Axis porcinus)*, weighing 20 kg (45 lbs) and then go without food for months.

Birds, Resident and Migratory

Chitwan is a bird-watcher's paradise. It is not unusual to spot 100 species in a single day, depending of course on the time of year. Over 440 species of birds have been recorded, of which a little under half are year-round residents. These include the beautiful Indian peafowl *(Pavo cristatus)* common in the floodplain, asian openbill *(Anastomus oscitans)* near marshes and lakes, small pied kingfisher *(Ceryle rudis)* over open rivers, and three-toed golden backed woodpecker *(Dinopium shorii)* in the sal forest. The blackheaded oriole *(Oriolus*

xanthornus) fills the forest with song, and the loud honking of the giant hornbill *(Buceros bicornis)* may be heard.

Of the many winter visitors, such as ducks, geese, waders and leafwarblers, the brahminy duck *(Tadorna ferruginia)* is the most conspicuous, not only because of its numbers but also its colours and call. Another distinguished winter visitor is the huge black-necked stork *(Ephipphiorhynchus asiaticus)*, a rare bird seen on open river banks. By comparison, the summer visitors are much fewer but include such colourful birds as the paradise flycatcher *(Terpsiphone paradisi)* and the golden oriole *(Oriolus oriolus)*, which arrive in February–March, and the Indian pitta *(Pitta brachyura)* and green-breasted pitta *(Pitta sordida)* in April–May.

Among the rarities of Chitwan's birds are the greyheaded fishing eagle *(Ichthyophaga ichthyaetus)*, seen near swamps and lakes; the great slaty woodpecker *(Mulleripicus pulverulentus)* near

OW: sunrise
r the river.

the forested hill streams; and the yellow bittern *(Ixobrychus sinensis)* in tall marsh grass. In late spring the rare Bengal florican *(Houbaropsis bengalensis)* males may be seen in the grassland, displaying to their mates, their white wings in sharp contrast to their black bodies.

The best months for bird-watching are February and March, when the winter visitors are still around, the summer visitors have started to arrive, and the breeding birds become very vocal and conspicuous. Also, the visibility is at its best because of burning and leaf-fall, and the trees are in blossom, which attracts the birds.

Spotting the mammals

In terms of seeing wildlife, the floodplain belt is the best as it harbors a larger concentration of animals than the sal forest. Chitwan's estimated 450 rhinos *(Rhinoceros unicornis)* are found almost wholly in the grassland and riverine forest. Chitwan is one of the two last strongholds for this endangered rhino (Kaziranga in Assam being the other) and it harbours a quarter of the world's total.

In the Siwalik hills is the gaur *(Bos gaurus)*, the most magnificent among hoofed animals. During the spring the gaur descend to the grassland in search of new shoots after the fires. The forests around Devi Tal, Tamar Tar, Dumaria and Khagendramalli are particularly good spots for seeing them in February–April.

Of the four species of deer found in Chitwan, the hog deer *(Axis porcinus)* is restricted almost exclusively to the grassland, and the chital *(Axis axis)* to the lowland parts as it avoids sloping ground and hilly terrain. The sambar *(Cervus unicolour)* and the barking deer *(Muntiacus muntjak)* are found throughout the park.

Also common throughout the park, but mainly in the floodplain, is the wild boar *(Sus scrofa)*, which often lives in large groups of 20, even 30 or more animals, although 6–10 is the average. The wild boar and the four kinds of deer all form impor-

BELOW: chital hind.

Map
page
230

tant prey species for the tiger *(Panthera tigris)* and the leopard *(Panthera pardus)*.

Monkeys also feature strongly on the leopard's menu and two species occur in the park. The handsome grey langur *(Presbytis entellus)* with long limbs and tail and a black face, lives mainly in the sal forest in troops of 10–20 individuals. Langurs are not particularly shy and will allow a fairly close approach, but not the Chitwan rhesus macaque *(Macaca mulatta)*. Unlike their counterparts found near railway platforms and temples, who show complete contempt for people, the rhesus of Chitwan is extremely shy.

The rare ones and the great cats

Although Chitwan has over 50 species of mammals, they are often not easily seen because of their nocturnal and secretive habits. Rare mammals in Chitwan include the wild dog *(Cuon alpinus)*, the serow *(Capricornis sumatraensis)*, the hyena *(Hyaena hyaena)*, the spotted linsang *(Prionodon pardicolour)* and the ratel *(Mellivora capensis)*.

The two large predators in the park are the tiger and the leopard. They do not tend to mix well – the tiger may attack and even kill the leopard. The leopards are often forced out to live on the edge of the park. However, the two can live side by side. Good camouflage aids the leopard, and by altering its schedule and becoming more diurnal it becomes easier for it to share the same area as the tiger.

Moreover, competition between the two is further reduced by the tiger's preference for larger prey species than those of the leopard. Chitwan has a fair number of leopards but they are not often seen. It is estimated that about 40 breeding adult tigers exist in the park, which makes a total of up to 120 including cubs, sub-adults and transients. You may sometimes see a tiger, a pair, or exceptionally a family of female and cubs, but despite such numbers tiger sightings are not common. ❏

ow: leopard
tree.

Map page 240

BARDIA

Larger, more remote and less humid than Chitwan, security and poaching problems inflicted heavy losses on the park but scenic Royal Bardia offers stunning river trips and rewarding jeep safaris

About 400 km (250 miles) to the west of Khatmandu, in far western Nepal, lies the Royal Bardia National Park, also known as Karnali because of the great river of that name that drains the region. Royal Bardia National Park, like Royal Chitwan, is located in the Terai of Nepal – the lowland band along the long south-western edge of the country. It is both hill country and part of the plain of the River Ganges. Until the 1950s, most of this region was uninhabited due to virulent malarial mosquitos. But the Nepali government reduced the swarms of mosquitoes with DDT in the 1950s and 1960s paving the way for hill people to move down into the lowlands and clear away the forest to farm. By 1960 more than half of the forest had disappeared to make room for agricultural fields and the human population had risen from 36,000 to 100,000. Uncontrolled poaching also erupted and the rhino population fell from at least 800 (perhaps as many as 2,000) to a mere 100.

The Royal Bardia National Park is the largest and most undisturbed wild area of the Terai region of Nepal. Bardia encompasses riverine grassland and sal forests similar to Chitwan park, but has a drier climate and a more remote location. The area was initially set aside as a royal hunting preserve during the Rana regime (1846–1950), with an area of 348 sq km (134 sq miles), and was declared a wildlife reserve in 1976. This was expanded to 968 sq km (374 sq miles) in 1985 and, in 1988, became the Royal Bardia National Park.

The reserve is bounded to the west by the Karnali river and its distributary, the Girwa, and to the east by a section of the Nepalgunj–Birendranager highway. A large part of the reserve is hill country as it drapes the southern flanks of the Churia or Siwalik hills, the outermost range of the Himalaya. The crestlines of the Churia form its northern boundary.

From the base of the Churia the ground slopes gradually southward for about 8 km (5 miles), and this highly porous ground is called the *Bhabhar*. Thereafter, it flattens out as far as the eye can see. This is part of the Gangetic plain, and the strip between the Bhabhar and the Indian border is known as the terai. The southern edge of the reserve is mainly bhabhar, with a small piece of terai at the southwest.

Flora and fauna

Bardia, with its stately sal *(Shorea robusta)* trees, its tall termite mounds, and its *phantas* (old village sites), is very reminiscent of Dudhwa in Uttar Pradesh. The forests are tropical dry deciduous. Since a great part of the park is high ground with

T: hikers in nla Karnali ey, Nepal. **HT:** many of dia's tigers e been lost oaching in ent years.

good drainage, it is dominated by the sal, a hardwood tree. The sal associates with many other trees, notably saj or asna *(Terminalia tomentosa)*, and on the highest ridges of the hills, with chir pine *(Pinus roxburghii)*. The sal forest and its shaded ravines are the home of sambar, barking deer, porcupine, sloth bear and kaleej.

On the lower ground is a mosaic of grassland and riverine forest with the simal trees *(Bombax ceiba)* standing above all others. The simal, when old, are gigantic in size and develop huge buttresses at their base for extra support. Their large red, sometimes orange, flowers are a memorable sight in the early spring. The *phantas* are old village sites where a small herd of barasingha *(Cervus duvauceli)* and large numbers of chital *(Axis axis)* may still be seen.

The waters of the Karnali emerge from the narrow gorge at Chisapani, fan out over a gentle slope and eventually slow down to a sluggish pace on the plains. A few kilometres downriver of the gorge it branches out into two main channels or distributaries – Karnali to the west and Girwa to the east. Here shisham *(Dalbergia sissoo)*, khair *(Acacia catechu)* and simal flourish (such an assortment of trees is common on all riverine sites). These islands are the favourite haunts of the nilgai, the subcontinent's largest antelope.

But much of the park is drained by another smaller river, the Babai, which courses down the Siwalik range and collects spring and rainwater from its numerous seasonal and perennial tributaries. The Karnali-Girwa and the Babai attract a large number of migratory waterfowl.

Wildlife viewing

The best place for this is the old reserve area between the Karnali-Girwa and the Babai river, especially along the former, and the adjoining phantas such as Baghora and Lamkoili.

At present the only concessions in Bardia are run by Tiger Tops. Their Karnali Lodge *(see page 336)* is not far from the

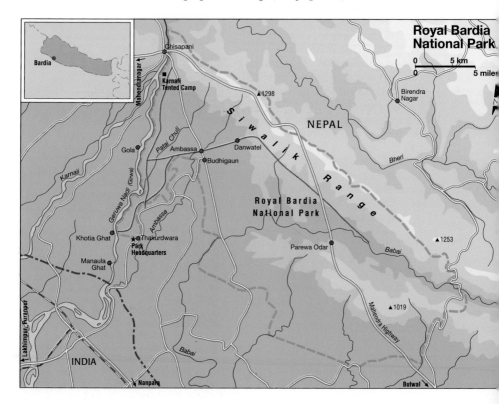

Map
on page
240

park headquarters at Thakurdwara – where elephant safaris can be booked – and Karnali Tented Camp is south of Chisopani on the bank of the Karnali-Girwa. There are also a few forest lodges around the park headquarters at Thakurdwara.

You need four to five nights to fully appreciate the jungle and its sights in Bardia. A trip there is a mixture of wildlife, culture and adventure. All, even any one, of the following day-trips will confirm this.

Floating Down the Girwa

Taking a boat or canoe ride down the park's rivers is an excellent way of spotting wildlife, as well as being scenically stuning. On this river trip you will see many species of birds – ducks, herons, gulls, terns, kingfishers, cormorants and osprey; and perhaps also rhesus monkey *(Macaca mulatta)*, langur *(Presbytis entellus)*, nilgai *(Boselaphus tragocamelus)* and smooth coated otter *(Lutra perspicillata)*. If you are lucky, you may even glimpse the Gangetic dolphin as it surfaces for air – Manu Tappu is a particularly good place for this. On your drive back to camp, via the phantas, you will add more animals to your spotting list, such as chital and wild boar.

Trek out and float back

Take an early morning walk up to Chisapani gorge, bird-watching as you go. Cross the river by ferry or by raft, then follow the old trading route that runs along the west bank of the Karnali. The road has been cut out of stone into a steep hillside and is well worn by centuries of use by traders and their pack animals. You may meet traders from Dailekh and Achham to the north, heading for Chisapani with their produce and then returning home with salt, kerosene and other goods. These are hardy men and women, with even hardier beasts of burden, mainly goat and sheep, each laden with a 55 kg (25 lb) load on its back. The hillside is forested and during the mid-morning, bird-watching conditions are excellent.

After about 2½ hours of walking, you descend to the riverbank for lunch just short of the small village of Kachalipur. Travel-

ling back through the gorge by boat, you will be struck by the peculiar rock formations along the banks, which provide excellent hideouts for otters, and good vantage points for crocodiles to bask in the sun.

Wallcreeper *(Tichodroma muraria)*, with its grey body and conspicuous crimson wings, is a common winter bird in the gorge. They fly about on the vertical cliffs and here and there white droppings of cormorants and darters decorate the black rock. As you come out of the gorge, a spectacular view of the floodplains opens up in front of you.

Jeep and foot safari

Take a jeep southeast (with a packed lunch), for about 13 km (8 miles) and near Amreni turn northwards towards the base of the hills. The forest here becomes dense and dark, giant creepers drape the sal trees and the "tentacles" of the strangler figs literally squeeze the life out of their hosts. You may see evidence of the passage of wild elephant – droppings, tracks, uproot-

HT: dhole, an wild dog.

ed trees, and trees stripped of their bark. Carry on to Danawa Tal guard post and trek into the hills for a couple of hours. On the stream beds look for the tracks of the animals that have passed here – tiger, leopard, monkey, porcupine, civet and others.

Stop by a pool for a picnic lunch and then drive back to the base of the hills and take the road to the Babai river. Peafowl and red jungle fowl are common here and you may also see gharial or mugger crocodiles. On your return, visit the phantas again. Towards late afternoon, the jungle comes alive with the activity of its denizens and you may spot sambar, barasingha and wild boar, not to mention the abundant chital.

Insurgents and Poachers

When Maoist insurgents detained and assaulted four members of a rhino monitoring team in 2004 it became too dangerous to send park staff into Bardia. The ceasefire between the government of Nepal and the Maoists in April 2006 has allowed conservationists (park staff and personnel from the IUCN and WWF) to conduct a study of the wildlife for the first time in two years. The findings show that during the past two years of armed conflict most of the endangered tigers and rhinos inside the Bardia National Park have been wiped out by poachers.

Field visits found evidence of only three tigers (down from a 2001 estimate of 13) and only three rhinos in the area of the park surveyed. More than 70 rhinos have been translocated there since 1986 and if left undisturbed the rhino population should have numbered around 100. Two poachers were apprehended along with weapons and a large cache of ammunition plus the smoked meat of various deer – important prey species for tigers and other carnivores. Virtually all the guard posts inside the Babai Valley were found to be destroyed.

Anti-poaching units recently began patrolling parks like Bardia again – and so far, none of the units has been attacked by

BELOW: sambar and egret.

Map
on page
240

Maoist rebels. WWF is calling upon the Government of Nepal to take advantage of the new climate of peace to focus on anti-poaching operations to help turn the tide. It is also vital that the international community works hard to stem the demand for tiger parts and rhino horn, which is decimating these species around the globe.

Spotter's luck

What you see, and how much, depends on chance, and in any of these three outings you could see leopard, sloth bear, wild elephant and tiger. The rhinos introduced here in early 1986 flourished for a time and were one of Bardia's star attractions. When the park had a healthy population of tigers baiting – the laying out of food to attract the animals – was allowed (unlike in Nepal's other national parks and sanctuaries) which made Bardia one of the best places in Nepal to spot tiger. Other predators of Bardia include hyena, wild dog, jackal, the large and the small Indian civet, mongoose, python, mugger and gharial. The tall grass also harbours some hispid hare, believed, until recently, to have become extinct. Over 350 species of birds have been recorded.

The tourist season here is from November to May; for the rest of the year the reserve is inaccessible because of the monsoon floods. The weather is generally warm, but gets cold in the early morning and evening in December and January. During these two months, each year, local villagers are allowed to enter the park for a couple of weeks to collect thatch grass and reed to use as building materials for their houses. Having collected their harvest, the villagers set fire to the grassland and forest, and much of the undergrowth is burnt to ashes. But regrowth is quick and numerous herbivores congregate on the now open phantas to feed on the new succulent grasses. Thus the best wildlife sightings in Bardia are between January and April when the vegetation is "open" and visibility better than at other times. ❑

LOW: sunset
er Royal
rdia.

KAZIRANGA

The stronghold of the Indian rhino, even one day during Kaziranga's short season will reward the visitor with unrivalled sights of the region's large mammals

Map
on page
248

No two places could be more diverse in their physical appearance and character, yet the twin sanctuaries of Assam, which would form a perfect triangle with Guwahati, are together completely representative of the Indian northeast. While Kaziranga is flat country with elephant grass and shallow swamps interspersed with large patches of semi-evergreen forest, Manas lies at the foot of the Bhutan hills and through it flows the Manas river, which spills into the plains, splitting into two streams, the Beki and the Hakua. On either side of the Manas river, plentiful wildlife and magnificent scenery combine to form one of the world's best and undoubtably most picturesque wildlife reserves.

Like Manas, Kaziranga, too, lies on the banks of a river – the mighty Brahmaputra. The name, literally translated, means "son of Brahma", who according to Hindu mythology is the creator of the universe, but the massive river could just as easily have been named after Shiva – the destroyer. Each year, with the onset of the monsoon in June, it overspills its banks and the surrounding areas are ravaged. In Kaziranga, the river forces people and wildlife to take shelter on whatever high ground they can find, and, according to a local estimate, it washes away almost 1,000 hog deer each year. In 1998 and 2000 the floods were devastating and a substantial part of the park's animal population was killed, including (in 1998) 35 rhinos and 30 percent of the hog deer. In 2004, many animals again were lost and others took refuge in the the Karbi Hills south of the park. However, when the river withdraws, leaving *bheels* (swamps) with a shallow spread of water, Kaziranga comes into its own, offering the visitor some of the best views of the Indian one-horned rhinoceros and wild buffalo.

Kaziranga

The monsoon and the Brahmaputra leave Kaziranga with a comparatively short season – January to May. Approachable from either Guwahati or Jorhat, it is sandwiched by the highway to the south and the river to its north. The reserve sprawls over 430 sq km (165 sq miles) of grassland and impenetrable vegetative luxuriance comprising close-tangled and thorny rattan cane, elephant grass and tall trees of the evergreen forests. Until 1908, Kaziranga was a sport hunter's and poacher's paradise, but the rapidly declining population of rhino forced the authorities, in 1926, to designate it a reserve forest, closed to shooting. Some estimates put the rhino population at that time at about a

PRECEDING PAGES: elephants crossing the Manas River. LEFT: capped langur. RIGHT: rhinoceros and cattle egret.

dozen and the subsequent revival of this massive and powerful animal, reminiscent of prehistoric creatures, has been one of the more notable feats of faunal conservation. In 1940, Kaziranga was officially declared a wildlife sanctuary.

Good accommodation is available just outside the park, especially the excellent Wild Grass Resorts *(see page 337–8).* Both park authorities and private operators provide jeep hire. Better still is an elephant safari, booked through the Forest Range Officer.

In almost all wildlife reserves in India, the visitors need to give themselves a few days to have a reasonable chance of seeing wildlife at close quarters. Kaziranga, however, is the exception, where one can hope to see most of the mammals for which it is known in a single day. During the day, especially in the morning, Kaziranga has a thick ground mist that blurs the distant horizon and creates a very special atmosphere in the area – covering its creatures with a ghostly

haze; undoubtedly, Kaziranga is one of the few unspoilt floodplains of the Brahmaputra.

In the 1930s, Kaziranga was virtually a closed book and the sanctuary was opened to tourists only around 1938. The rhino, the main attraction in the park, was then unused to humans and would quite blindly (they are notoriously shortsighted and charge whatever they perceive as a challenge) take on any intruder. Fortunately, at the last minute they tended to veer off, leaving almost everything in the area badly shaken but rarely hurt. The rhino is now a lot more used to humans, and though a mother with a calf may demonstrate in front of a riding elephant, they often let people get amazingly close to them.

The only natural enemy of the rhino is the tiger, of which there is a sizable population in the park (a recent estimate put the figure at 80). The tall grass and the patches of forest provide excellent cover for the big cats, which are therefore rarely seen. In August 2006 Kaziranga was

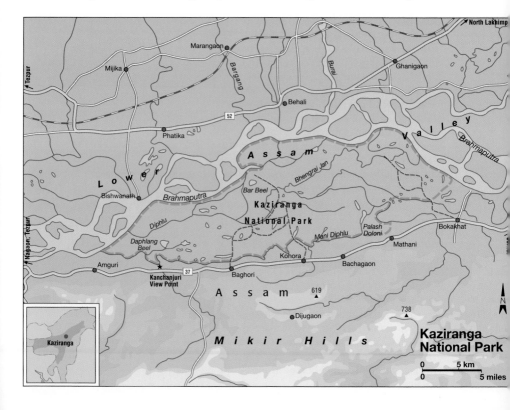

Map
on page
248

declared a tiger reserve under the Project Tiger scheme. This new status will provide better funding for field staff and more publicity, benefitting all the wildlife.

Sometimes a tiger will attack and kill a rhino calf despite the mother's aggressive vigilance, but the rhino suffers more at the hand of man. Its horn, believed to be an aphrodisiac by the ancient Indians and highly sought after by Chinese medicine men, is a lucrative target for poachers, who usually operate from the Darrang district across the Brahmaputra river and sometimes from the Mikir hills where the animals retreat during the floods. The rhino, being a creature of set habits, follows well-worn trails and even defecates at the same spot each day. Taking advantage of its regular habits, a pit large enough to accommodate its body is dug by the poachers in its usual path and then covered with leaves and grass. The unwary animal falls into the pit where it is killed and its horn hacked off with a *dao* (sharp knife). Other parts of the body

also command sale value. As both sexes carry the horn, the threat is doubly compounded.

The wild buffalo herds in Kaziranga, like the rhino, have also got relatively used to humans and can be approached on elephant-back with little danger. By and large, buffalo herds are shy of humans, and mothers canter off with their wooly calves if threatened. However, solitary bulls are often bad tempered and quick to charge with or without any provocation. If a good elephant holds its ground, the bull will usually pull up short, a picture of wild defiance. These bulls often stay in the vicinity of herds, and sometimes mate with domestic buffalo cows as well. The Kaziranga buffalo have over the years suffered from domestic genes invading the wild stock, and unlike the wild buffalo of Manas, the animals are thought to be interbred in most cases.

The presence of buffalo and rhino make walking in the sanctuary a difficult prop-

LOW:
tle egrets
d on insects
red up by
ffalo.

osition. A third species ensure that visitors enter only riding elephants or in vehicles. Herds of up to 200 wild elephants can be seen migrating from the Mikir hills to the *bheels* and, like the buffalo, it is again the solitary bull elephant that is prone to create trouble. The large number of untusked males *(mukhnas)* in the northeast often causes confusion, for what is taken to be a large female turns out to be a male. A riding elephant, on occasion, can wander into a herd of wild elephants; moreover, a wild elephant will even caress a trained one with its trunk, oblivious of the dreaded human cargo on its back.

As one starts from Mihimukh, the Himalaya, which are more than 160 km (100 miles) to the north, can be seen on some days. Small herds of barasingha (swamp deer) and the odd wild boar are usually among the first animals seen. A subspecies of the barasingha of Kanha and of the other variety found in the terai of Uttar Pradesh, these deer of Assam have slightly splayed hooves and are

found on high ground in the proximity of water. When the stags are regenerating their antlers, it is not uncommon to find all-male herds.

The chital does not extend beyond the Brahmaputra, its eastern range in India being Manas, but there are plenty of *para*, as hog deer are referred to in this region. Mixed herds, of both sexes, are often scattered around the various bheels, and these small deer are among the main prey species of the tiger in Kaziranga. Solitary hog deer are often seen.

Among the other animals found in Kaziranga, the wild boar is fairly common. Some gaur (NB: the word gaur in Assamese refers to the rhino, while the gaur is called a bison) are also found here, but are scarce and rarely seen. Leopard cats and otters are not uncommon, while the odd leopard may be chanced upon. A wide variety of snakes, including rock python are also found, while the prehistoric monitor lizard is relatively easily seen.

BELOW: barasingha herd.

Map
n page
248

Birds

Grasslands are often excellent raptor country, and Kaziranga is no exception – the crested serpent eagle is common, Pallas's fishing eagle and the grey-headed fishing eagle are frequently seen. Dawn is welcomed by the loud calling of the swamp francolin, which shatters the misty silence of the morning, while red jungle fowl tentatively step onto a jeep track before taking off at a mad run in front of a jeep. The Bengal florican and a variety of waterfowl, of which the bar-headed goose and the lesser whistling teal are the most frequently seen, are among the other birds found in the sanctuary. A large number of pelicans nest close to Mihimukh on large semul trees and the clumps of forest are alive with the screeching of the rose-breasted parakeet and an assortment of birds common to the northeast. As one would expect, the swamps are home to a diverse avifauna of the shallow watersides. Black-necked, lesser, greater and open-billed storks, egret and heron of all shapes and sizes and other waders can be found around the *bheels*, which are clogged with water hyacinth. When this once exotic plant first appeared in Kaziranga, no animal would condescend to feed on it except the wild boar, which ate the roots during the dry season. Now buffaloes as well as elephants browse on it, though somewhat reluctantly.

Firmly entrenched on the Indian tourist map, Kaziranga has its problems, natural and man-made. Floods drown many animals annually or force them to risk crossing the highway to higher ground where poachers may be waiting. Poaching has been reduced dramatically however – about 18 rhinos were killed in the last five years, as compared to at least 50 slaughtered annually in the early 1990s. A disproportionate increase in human populations along the highway and the sanctuary has created socio-economic problems and Assam is still tackling the effects of political turmoil. On the other hand, regular transport links have made travel easier, and the northeast is no longer as inaccessible as it used to be. ❑

LOW:
phant in
h of burning
ssland.

Map
n page
254

MANAS

*After a troubled past, Assam's Manas National Park can again tempt
visitors with an unsurpassed diversity of exciting wildlife encounters
but is famed for its primates, buffalo and elephant*

This sanctuary, in contrast to Kaziranga, is far removed from the National Highway and the mainstream of human life passes it by. Barpeta Road, the railhead that also serves as the sanctuary's headquarters, is almost three hours by road or rail from Guwahati. The park was closed for many years due to insurgency. Although officially opened now, it is advisable to contact the park authorities before travelling.

Manas has a much longer season than Kaziranga, the only wet period is from mid-May to September, but the best period to visit the area is either in November or February. Unlike the open swamps and grasslands of Kaziranga, where the visitor may see a large number of animals, wildlife viewing in Manas is never regular – or easy. But when one is confronted by an animal, it is usually at close quarters and, invariably, exciting and dramatic.

Few places can hold a visitor in its grip the way Manas can. Over 2,600 sq km (1,000 sq miles) in area, the Manas river at Mothanguri forms the boundary between India and Bhutan, and one of the great attractions of the park is the golden langur that inhabit the park's tall flowering trees.

The topography of the reserve is dramatically diverse: the river spilling out of the foothills; the lower sandy stretches where islands of trees stand like sentinels over herds of wild buffalo, with fishing eagles and ospreys searching the fast flowing streams for fish; there are the great forests of mixed deciduous vegetation, which shut the light off at ground level and finally, small glades of grassland where elephant herds leave their calling card by uprooting every invading sapling that tries to encroach into the glades.

In terms of diversity in animal life, Manas again stands alone. Most of the animals found in Kaziranga are also found in Manas. There are 45 species of birds and animals here that are listed under Schedule I (highly endangered) in the IUCN Red Data Book and of these species some, like the hispid hare and the pigmy hog, are today found only here. Both these remarkable animals have been reduced to a rarity, so much so that their extinction was once thought to be just a matter of time. The situation today seems to be less desperate.

There were over 80 rhinos in Manas National Park in the late 1980s when the Bodo agitation hit the Park. This was followed by a period of severe political unrest in the region, during which time protection camps were attacked, watchtowers and bridges burnt and park staff killed. Though

insurgent groups were involved, the main culprits again were organized poaching gangs spreading terror in the park and plundering trees for timber, rhinos for horns, elephants for ivory and tigers for bones and claws. Illegal timber was floated down the Manas and Beki rivers out of the park with the complicity of officials and local political leaders. In less than a decade the rhino population was more or less wiped out.

With the return of relative peace, Manas National Park will be the first to receive rhinos translocated from Kaziranga and Pabitora under Indian Rhino Vision 2020, a new initiative put together by the Government of Assam, International Rhino Foundation (IRF), World Wildlife Fund (WWF) and other NGOs. Manas will be one of three new secure protected areas which will be established. These will be secured by constructing new anti-poaching camps, establishing communication networks, and employing anti-poaching staff. One hundred rhinos will be relocated between the new reserves over a 6-year period.

Hispid hare

As one travels into Manas from Barpeta Road, leaving the long semul-lined drive and the Bansbari tea estate behind, the gravel road snakes through open grassland that is said to be prime country for the hispid hare (*Caprolagus hispidus*), which is also known as the Assamese rabbit or "bristly rabbit" (it is a rabbit not a hare). When the grassland and associated forest are set on fire, the hare moves to forested foothills, or to cultivated fields and shelters on the embankments of dried up streams. When the thatch becomes too waterlogged during the height of the monsoon, it prefers the forested areas of the foothills. During the late evenings, just as dusk gives way to darkness, the beam from a vehicle's headlights sometimes spotlights the scurrying figure of this elusive and rare animal.

Facilities

When the park is open, Mathanguri is the best place to stay and although the lodges offer quite basic accommodation they are

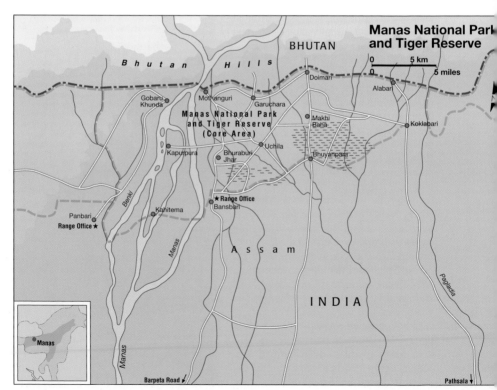

Map
n page
254

clean and in an excellent position *(see page 338)*. Situated on a rise overlooking the Manas river, there could be few places so endearing to a naturalist. From the balcony of the rest house, one overlooks Bhutan, while on the Indian side the forests are tinged with pink, especially in February when the semul trees are an explosion of colour. The Project Tiger people have a number of riding elephants that provide the ideal means to move about and give the visitor the best approach to wildlife, but the saddles or *howdahs* are quite different from the broad seats of North and South India. Here, one needs to straddle the animal or sit sideways on the saddle, which can be a little painful after a while. Red ants, notorious for a rather painful sting, drop onto you from their leaf nests in trees, and there is little one can do other than watch out for them.

Primates

While the golden langur are usually approachable on foot from the boat landing on the Bhutan side, the colourful capped langur is only approachable from elephant back. Extremely shy, these primates usually move away, but if one were to watch them quietly for half an hour, they seem to forget your presence and go about their business of eating and grooming with the nonchalance so typical of the langur family. The Assamese macaque is rarely seen in the forests, but they inhabit the islands downstream and move in large troupes from place to place. The slow loris and the Hoolock gibbon also extend into Manas, but sightings are rare.

Water buffalo

Two of the main attractions, however, are the water buffalo and the elephant. The ideal way to observe buffalo is to try and hire a boat at Mothanguri and spend the better part of the day drifting downstream before being picked up by motorized transport some 35 km (22 miles) away. The herds come to the river during the day to cool off and they stare

curiously at the drifting boat, their sweeping and majestic horns thrown back in graceful arcs. The lone bull, eager to maintain his territory, will toss his head as only a bull can and sometimes he will follow along the side, presenting a sight that is rarely forgotten. On elephant-back too, one sometimes succeeds in surprising a herd in the water, which then struggles to the bank through the mist and the water.

Elephant

Locating elephants in the thick forest is never an easy task, but once a herd is found, the riding elephant often manages to get into the herd. To be surrounded by a herd of trumpeting wild elephants can leave one weak around the knees, and to be charged by a lone bull is by no means an uncommon occurrence here. Fortunately, the trained elephants are adept at making a quick getaway, but the image of a charging tusker with its ears fanned out is a memory that never fades.

Other Mammals

A lot more elusive and shy is the Indian bison, or gaur, which stands taller than a buffalo at the shoulder. Sometimes, one can see a large herd in the grassy glades, but at the slightest sound or movement, they thunder off into the cover of the forest. Another method of looking for gaur is to drive along the foothills on jungle tracks that are hemmed in by tall grass on either side.

The area is full of hog deer and sometimes a tiger can be seen plodding along the tracks, looking for a chance to kill. This stretch is good for the other big cats too. When fires are lit to burn the grass, a clouded leopard may emerge from behind a smoldering tree trunk where he had been feeding off the insects that are forced out by the smoke. Manas provides an ideal habitat for the sloth bear, yet another species inseparably linked with Manas, and they too can usually be seen at dawn or dusk. In fact, the sloth bear is often seen when the light is too poor for photography. Picked up by a spotlight, it will scuttle

BELOW: wild buffalo are restricted to a few pockets of northeastern India.

Map
n page
254

away, but sometimes curiosity prevails, and animals will come close to the jeep, staring at it with myopic eyes.

Deer

Manas is the eastern range of chital, but the Field Director of the park fears that the small surviving population is hardly breeding, for reasons that are not known. The muntjac, or barking deer, hog deer, sambar and, in places, swamp deer, represent the deer family in fairly good numbers. The sambar is perhaps the most widely distributed of all Indian deer and though only one species is recognized, there are changes in colour and the average size of antlers from one region to another. If one were to sweep across the top half of India from west to east, the Rajasthan sambar is a dull brown, which changes to a slightly deeper shade of red as you approach Bihar, which also has some of the best stags. The reddish tinge gets even more pronounced as we move further east. Another notable thing in Manas is the raw patch sambar develop on their

throat – it looks quite a bit like a sore. This interesting phenomenon is common to all the large deer in eastern India.

Birds

For insects, butterflies and reptiles, the northeast is prime country and the blaze of colour at ground level in the jungle inspires breathless wonder. In the canopy above, winged stars steal the show; scarlet minivets flash their orange and yellow towards the watching heavens; a bee-eater clicks its beak as it grabs a bee; magpie, robins and bulbuls fill the air with their constant chatter. It is famed for its hornbills – the common grey, Indian pied, wreathed and rufous-necked, and great pied – which share more or less the same habitat and which whoosh their way from tree to tree. Red jungle fowl and kaleej pheasants scratch for their food from under the fallen leaves, while the great river offers ornithologists its own brand of avifauna with mergansers and brahminy ducks, egrets, pelicans and herons, eagles and pratincoles.   ❏

LOW: rhino
d water
acinth.

SUNDARBANS

The world's largest mangrove forest is synonymous with its notorious maneating tigers and estuarine crocodiles but also harbours the gangetic dolphin and spectacular birdlife

Map
n page
260

The Sundarbans, at the confluence of the Ganga, Brahmaputra and Meghna rivers, is the largest delta in the world, covered with mangrove forests and vast saline mud flats. It got its name from the mangrove plant locally known as Sundari *(Heritiera minor)*. The Sundarbans stretches from the Hooghly (India) on the west to the Meghna (Bangladesh) in the east, both of which are major streams of the River Ganga. It spreads over the southern part of three districts, namely 24-Parganas (India), Khulna and Backarganj (Bangladesh). The boundary of Sundarbans within West Bengal is demarcated by the Raimangal and Hooghly rivers in the East and West respectively, and the Bay of Bengal in the south. The northern limit cannot be clearly defined due to the progressive reclamation of land.

The Sundarbans covers an area of 9,630 sq km (3,718 sq miles), of which 2,585 sq km (998 sq miles) was demarcated as the Sundarbans Tiger Reserve in 1984, and 1,330 sq km (513 sq miles) as the national park (core area). Sajnakhali Wildlife Sanctuary (362 sq km /140 sq miles) lies within the buffer zone, to the north of Netidhopani and Chadkhali forest blocks. There are two small sanctuaries within the Biosphere Reserve: the 583 hectare (1,441 acre) Halliday Island Wildlife Sanctuary, and the 3,885 hectare (9,600 acre) Lothian Island Wildlife Sanctuary. The temperature ranges from 5–45 ℃ (41–113 °F), and elevation 0–5 metres (0–16.4 ft). The total area of the IBA extends over 4,262 sq km (1,645 sq miles), of which 2,320 sq km (895 sq miles) is under mangrove forest and the remaining is under water.

Sundarbans is the largest continuous mangrove forest in the world with an area of about 10, 000 sq. km of which 62 percent falls within the territory of Bangladesh. On the Indian side alone,

this forest equals 60 percent of India's total mangrove population. It also probably has the largest tiger population in the world. It is a World Heritage Site and Biosphere Reserve, both in India and Bangladesh. The Bangladesh Sundarbans is also a Ramsar site – 'Sundarbans Reserved Forest' – and it is hoped that the Indian Sundarbans will soon be. This World Heritage site is known for its rich biodiversity, especially fish, crustaceans, reptiles and birds.

Flora

As reported earlier, *Heritiera minor*, locally known as Sundari, is a predominant feature of Sundarbans. It has moist tropical seral forest, comprising beach for-

FT: a tiger
nning
ough surf.
GHT:
angroves.

est and tidal forests. Characteristic plants include various species of *Rhizophora*, *Bruguiera gymnorhiza*, *Ceriops*, and *Avicennia officinalis*. *Heritiera minor* is scattered over areas of higher elevation, along with *Sonneratia apetala*, *Excoecaria agallocha*, and *Phoenix paludosa*. Low mangrove forest (3–6 m/10–29½ ft high) occurs between Matla and Muriganga, to the west of the national park and tiger reserve. This area is devoid of fresh water because its rivers are cut off from the ramifications of the Hooghly in the north. The soft mud of the intertidal zone supports a dense forest, very similar in composition to salt-water *Heritiera* forest. Various trees and other plants were introduced, including some exotics.

Tiger

Although seldom seem, the Bengal Tiger (*Panthera tigris tigris*) is the star attraction of Sundarbans. Elsewhere, cases of tigers killing humans are very rare, but the tigers of the Sundarbans have long

been notorious man-eaters. Man enters the park to collect wood, honey and to fish. The number of casualties have been reduced from more than 40 to less than 10 per year. A number of explanations for this unique behaviour have been suggested. The saltiness of the tiger's drinking water in this area puts them in a state of constant discomfort, leading them to be extremely aggressive (freshwater lakes have been artificially made but to no avail). The high tides in the area destroy the tigers' scents that serve as territorial markers – thus another possibility is that the only way for a tiger to defend its territory is to physically dominate everything that enters. Floods in this part of India kill thousands, and the bodies drift out into the swampy waters, where tigers scavenge on them, thereby aquiring a taste for human flesh. In the marsh-like and slippery environemnt, the cats may consider man an easier catch than their main prey – chital (spotted deer), wild boar and rhesus macaque,

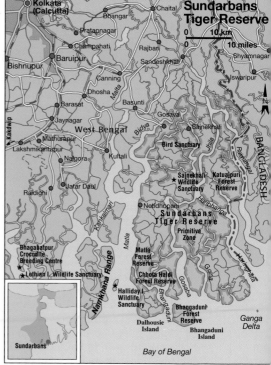

Map on page 260

though crabs and fish are also eaten by Sundarbans tigers.

Though the danger of tiger attacks is a deterent, poaching continues, both of tigers and their prey species. This may cause tigers to stray towards human habitation to prey on livestock, leading to conflict.

Other fauna

The Sundarbans also has the largest population of the estuarine crocodile *(Crocodylus porosus)* and is home to salvator lizard or water monitor *(Varanus salvator)* and river terrapin *(Batagur baska)*.

The horseshoe crab, or king crab, *(Limulus polyphemus)* is found here. Almost unchanged for 350 to 450 million years, and often referred to as "living fossils", the trilobite-like horseshoe crab is more closely related to spiders and scorpions than crabs and is different to most other animal life. It has blue blood due to copper-based hemocyanin instead of the iron-based hemoglobin found in mammals and, like the starfish, has the rare ability to

regrow lost limbs. It has no fewer than 10 eyes and is able to detect ultraviolet light. They are of great value to the medical and pharmaceutical industry.

The area also serves as the nesting ground for endangered marine turtles like olive ridley *(Lepidochelys oliveacea)*, green turtle *(Chelonia myda)* and Hawk's bill turtles *(Eretmochelys imbricata)*. The endangered gangetic dolphin *(Platanista gangetica)* thrives within mangrove creeks. A number of heronries form here during monsoon and in winter. The forest provides a good habitat for honey-bees, sometimes seen in huge swarms.

A hundred years ago the Sundarbans Forests were the home of many wild animals, including the Javan rhinoceros *(Rhinoceros sondaicus)*, swamp deer *(Cervus duvauceli)*, and wild buffalo *(Bubalus arnee)*. It is said that barking deer *(Muntiacus muntjak)* existed on these swamp islands, but it has not been recorded in recent years from the Sundarbans Forests that lie in West Bengal.

LOW: estuarine or saltwater crocodile.

Birds

Sundarbans is a birdwatchers paradise with more than 220 species. Although the whole of the Sundarbans mangrove is a bird watcher's paradise, Sajnakhali Wildlife Sanctuary is best known for its bird life, with 16 species in a breeding colony, including darter *(Anhinga melanogaster)* and black-necked stork *(Ephippiorhynchus asiaticus)* (both presently listed as Near Threatened by BirdLife International).

In India, Sundarbans is the most important site for the vulnerable masked finfoot *(Heliopais personata)*. It is difficult to estimate the total number of this elusive bird, but it is fairly common in suitable areas. Earlier, greater adjutant *(Leptoptilos dubius)* was commonly seen but now sightings are rare due to a drastic decline in its numbers.

Another uncommon species is the Spoon-billed Sandpiper *(Eurynorhynchus pygmeus)*, which is regularly reported from this site. As can be expected, Sun-derban is famous for its waterbirds and water-dependent birds, such as the kingfishers. Out of the 12 kingfisher species found in India, six are found in this IBA. They are the common *(Alcedo atthis)*, brown-winged *(Halcyon amauroptera)*, stork-billed *(Halcyon capensis)*, ruddy *(Halcyon coromanda)*, white-throated *(Halcyon smyrnensis)*, black-capped *(Halcyon pileata)*, collared *(Todiramphus chloris)* and pied kingfishers *(Ceryle rudis)*. About 30 species of small waders (sandpipers, stints, plovers and curlews) and nine species of gulls and terns are found here.

Sundarbans is one of two sites where the mangrove whistler *(Pachycephala grisola)*, is definitely found. It is widely distributed in south and southeast Asia, but its narrow, ribbon-like habitat along the coasts is under tremendous human pressure all over Asia, which would put this species at risk in future. Incidentally, this is the only bird species that is entirely restricted to mangroves.

BELOW: white breasted king fisher.

Map
on page
260

Threats

Despite its status as a World Heritage Site, Biosphere Reserve, Tiger Reserve, National Park and Wildlife Sanctuary, the Sundarbans suffers from many anthropogenic problems. Illegal fishing, cutting of mangroves, poaching and encroachment are the biggest chronic threats.

Illegal settlers are causing widespread destruction of mangroves, particularly on Jambu Dweep, the furthermost of the cluster of islands. The Supreme Court of India has banned human habitation on this island, but over 20,000 people reside here, mostly in a place called Charso Bees. The fishing business here, run mostly by Bangladeshis from Chittagong, records a turnover of about Rs.1.5 billion annually. Many settlers on the island are unaware that fishing in the protected area is prohibited. Experts have repeatedly warned that the destruction of the mangroves is one of the major causes of devastation caused by the cyclones and floods every year. Moreover, mangroves have a signif-

icant role to play in climate change. The mangrove swamp's ability to sequester carbon dioxide from the atmosphere far exceeds that of any other ecosystem. Little carbon is released through decay as dead leaves fall into the water where they are covered in sediment and preserved in an anaerobic environment.

Poaching in the Sundarbans is a persistent and uncontrollable problem because thousands of people are moving in the reserve all the time. Poachers go mainly for tiger and deer and often use snare traps.

Unmanaged tourism is another problem for the sensitive ecology of Sundarbans. There are plans to build a large tourist resort on 303 hectares (750 acres) of land spread across the five islands of Sagar, Kaikhali, Fraserganj, L-Plot and Jharkhali. There will be floatels, water sports and arrangements for excursions to different creeks in the delta. Such a massive project, in the name of "eco-tourism", would give rise to anthropogenic problems and irreversibly damage the ecology.   ❏

BELOW:
stilt-rooted
mangroves.

Map on page 268

KEOLADEO GHANA

*A man-made lake at Bharatpur has flourished into a
world-famous bird sanctuary – breathtaking at any
time of year by either boat or bicycle*

Only 176 km (110 miles) from Delhi and 50 km (31 miles) west of Agra and the Taj Mahal, Keoladeo Ghana, or Bharatpur Bird Sanctuary as it is commonly known, is a wonder of the natural world no less worth seeing than the marble tomb of Shahjahan's queen. Keoladeo Ghana National Park (KNP) is a Ramsar site under the Ramsar Convention. Over 400 species of birds find a refuge in the 29 sq km (11 sq miles) of shallow lakes and woodland that makes up the park. A third of them are migrants, many of whom winter in Bharatpur before returning to their breeding grounds as far away as Siberia and Central Asia. Some 120 species nest in the park and the heronry at Keoladeo Ghana is said to be one of the finest in the world. The park is open throughout the year, although most visitors choose to come between the months of October and March when wintering wildfowl assemble in their thousands on the lakes or *jheels*.

History

The name 'Keoladeo' is derived from the name of an ancient Hindu temple devoted to Lord Shiva, located in the sanctuary's central zone. Old records show that the area supported thick forest, which in local parlance is called 'Ghana'. While many of India's parks have been developed from the hunting preserves of princely India, Keoladeo Ghana is perhaps the only park where the habitat has been created by a maharaja. The park, a little way from Bharatpur town and still commonly known as "Bharatpur" rather than by its official name, is the handiwork of the royal family of Bharatpur. The maharaja developed the area in the late 19th century. Until then it was no different from the arid scrub woodland of the surrounding countryside except that it formed a slight depression, which collected rainwater

during the monsoon and attracted wildfowl for the period before it dried up. The maharaja recognized the area's potential and augmented the water supply by diverting water from a nearby irrigation canal. He also constructed small dams, dykes and shooting butts to turn the area into the finest wildfowl hunting preserve in north India. In a few years the new ecosystem so flourished that it was able to support thousands of water birds. The park is unique in being bound by a stone-masonry wall and agricultural fields and villages in immediate surroundings, thus lacking a buffer zone.

The maharaja celebrated his success in style, with extravagant shooting parties for the bloodthirsty dignitaries of British

and princely India. Their kills are recorded to this day on a sandstone inscription in the park.

Perhaps surprisingly, the birds survived these depradations and still came to Bharatpur in huge numbers. In 1956 the hunting preserve became a sanctuary, but the VIP shoots continued until 1964 and the maharaja himself retained his personal shooting rights until 1972.

The end of the shooting parties did not mean the end of Bharatpur's problems. The viceroys and maharajas were replaced by a large number of tourists and hundreds of domestic cattle and buffaloes belonging to local villagers. In order to control these problems Bharatpur was upgraded to a national park in 1981 and renamed Keoladeo.

Geography and habitat

Keoladeo Ghana lies 370 metres (1,214 ft) above sea level and, besides the wetland for which it is famous, contains various other habitats from woodland, scrub

and pasture to denuded saline patches. The lakes are fed entirely by rain and river water brought by canal from the Gambhir and Banganga rivers. In the monsoon some 11 sq km (4 sq miles) of the park can be inundated. One waterway, the Ghana Canal, bisects the park, running northeast to northwest.

One main metalled road runs through the centre of the park from the northern entrance, through the main wetland area on the eastern side of the park, where it follows the course of the Ghana Canal. At intervals along the road raised paths lined with babul trees *(Acacia nilotica)* lead off into the wetland. Babuls are the dominant tree in the park and these paths and undergrowth along them provide excellent blinds for birdwatching. There are many good paths in the park and several trails, beginning and ending at various points on the road, are recommended to visitors.

Bharatpur forms part of the vast Indo-Gangetic Plain and its climate is therefore **LEFT:** hot in summer (max 47°C/116°F, min. purple heron

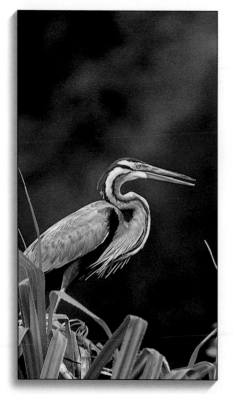

Map
page
268

35°C/95°F), humid in the monsoon (July–September) and comparatively cool in the winter (max 35°C/95°F, min 5°C/41°F), becoming quite chilly at night. Average annual rainfall is 66 cm (26 in).

Flora

Keoladeo Ghana contains a bewildering variety of flora, representing 64 families, 181 genera and 227 subspecies. Besides the babul, other native species of tree include ber, kadam, khajur and khejri. Dozens of species of grasses and reeds abound, providing rich grazing for birds and mammals alike. The wetland habitat of the park has been described by naturalist Anne Bastille as "a living soup of frogs, toads, water snakes, snails, leeches, turtles, pondweeds, carp, water hyacinth, catfish, water beetles, duckweed, lilies, protozoans, wild celery and plankton". Even this description is by no means a comprehensive list of ingredients. Among the fish are rohu *(Labeo rohita),* bata *(Labeo bata),* calbasu *(Labeo calbasu),* catla *(Catla catla),* mrigal *(Cirrhina mrigal)* and sarana *(Barbus sarana).* Some grow to a good size and a 15 kg (33 lb) sarana has been caught in the park. Predatory fishes include murrel *(Ophiocephalus strictus)* and freshwater shark *(Wallago attu).*

Visiting the park

Although many people visit Keoladeo Ghana for the day and stay at Bhaaratpur, it is recommended to stay at least one night in one of the hotels, which provide accommodation within or just outside the park *(see page 338).* This gives the visitor the chance to see Keoladeo Ghana at its best – in the early morning and evening. Entry tickets to the park are available at its main entrance. One can drive motor vehicles from the entrance as far as the Forest Lodge and the offices of the warden located in Shanti Kutir, formerly a hunting lodge of the maharaja. However, from there on, the only vehicles allowed are bicycles and cycle rickshaws. Both are available for hire from the Forest Lodge and the "rickshaw wallahs" take

a genuine interest in the birdlife and have been trained to recognize the different species. Boats are also available to take groups of visitors on a circular tour of the wetland starting from the jetty near Shanti Kutir, and a boat trip shortly after dawn is perhaps the most enchanting introduction to the park.

Birds

At the start of the peak tourist season in October the heronries are still occupied, although breeding begins shortly after the onset of the monsoon. Thousands of birds nest together in mixed heronries, dominated by different species in different parts of the sanctuary. Some of the most spectacular heronries are situated near the road and can be approached by the raised paths running off it. The crowded and noisy colonies are constructed in babul trees that stand half submerged in water. As many as eight or nine species of birds may nest in one tree. Painted storks, white ibis, open-

LEFT: bronze-winged jacana.

bills, spoonbills, egrets, herons, cormorants and shags are in abundance, while thousands of moorhens and jacanas breed in the floating vegetation on the water surface. The amount of food necessary to support the heronries is enormous. It has been estimated that 2,000 painted storks breeding in an area of no more than 2.5 sq km (1 sq mile) require 4–6 tons of food each day to support themselves and their nestlings. In the 30 to 40 days they breed they consume at least 1,200 tons of food – and this is only one section of the population of one species breeding in the park. The painted storks, like many other birds in Bharapur during the monsoon, are local migrants that come to the park between July and October to breed.

In October birds from further afield gradually begin to arrive. Among the ducks, geese and waders that come to Keoladeo are gadwal, wigeon, shovelers, garganey, marbled, common and northern pintail, and the red-crested, common and white-eyed pochards. Unmistakable as they fly overhead are the musical whistling teal. Greylag and bar-headed geese also appear in large numbers and waders include various species of plover, sandpiper and snipe. Two species of pelican, the rosy and dalmatian, join the resident grey pelican.

The Bombay Natural History Society carried out a programme of ringing birds at Keoladeo Ghana. Common teal, garganey and wigeon have been recovered in the former-USSR as far as 4,600 km (2,858 miles) away. A shoveler was found in Samarkand, and ruff and reeve as far as 5,850 km (3,635 miles) away in Yakutian in Russia. The ringing operation has also provided evidence that has helped to prove that Keoladeo Ghana is a staging post for many migrants, who build up their reserves of fat in the park before departing for their final destinations in places such as South India.

Besides the waterfowl, there are many terrestrial migrant species. Warblers, pip-

BELOW: egr in the lake.

Map
↑ page
268

its, wagtails and buntings are also winter visitors. But of all migrants the most sought-after is the Siberian crane.

Although Siberian cranes had been known to visit India for centuries (Ustad Mansur, a court artist of the Emperor Jahangir, made a detailed painting of the crane in the 17th century), it has never been a common species.

There is only one wintering place left for the western race of this extremely rare species: Feredunkenar in Iran, where only three Siberian Cranes were sighted in the winter of 2005–6. The last Sib, as this species is fondly called by bird-watchers, was seen in Keoladeo in the winter of 2001, when only two birds appeared. Since then, no Sib has come to Keoladeo. The journey here used to be nearly 6,400 km (4,000 miles) from their earlier breeding grounds in Siberia. They used to arrive by the end of November or December and would stay till early March. These impressive, pure white birds, with their black primaries and

crimson bills and facial patches, were one of the four cranes in the park.

The demoiselle and common cranes too are visitors, the sarus being the only resident. The Sarus crane is the tallest of the cranes, standing nearly 2 metres (6 ft) tall and with a wingspan of 2.4 metres (8 ft).

Unlike other Indian cranes, the Siberian crane is entirely vegetarian. It feeds on underwater aquatic roots and tubers in loose flocks of five or six. Some birds, however, remain in their breeding pairs and establish their own territories. They see off intruders with a spectacular display, throwing their heads backwards and forwards, accompanied by loud cries. These pairs often have one chick with them on arrival, whose immature brown and white plumage changes to pure white and black during the winter. The inability of these cranes to produce more than one chick is one reason given for their scarcity.

Many species at Bharatpur are specialist feeders like the Siberian crane. It is this that allows so many birds to flourish in

OW:
onbill in
eding
nage.

such a small area. Each helps itself to one ingredient of the wetland soup. Flamingos sieve the water for plankton, spoonbills rake the mud with their lower mandibles for mollusks, tadpoles and fish, while egrets and herons spear their prey, and geese and brahminy ducks graze at the water's edge.

An indication of the strength of the food chain in the sanctuary is the number of birds of prey, migratory and resident, which it contains. At least 32 species of birds of prey and seven species of owl have been observed. Among notable migrants are the steppe eagle, greater spotted eagle, pale and marsh harriers, osprey and peregrine falcon. Resident Indian species are no less striking. These include the tawny eagle, ring-tailed fishing eagle, crested serpent eagle, and Brahminy and black-winged kites. Four species of vultures can be seen, notably the less common king or black vultures.

The migrants leave for their breeding grounds around March, when many of the small, terrestrial birds in the park are preparing to nest. Even without migrants, there are many birds still to be seen and, although the spectacle of the winter season is missing, the visitor has the pleasure of having the park more or less to themselves. Egrets, herons, cormorants, storks, plump purple moorhens and elegant pheasant-tailed jacanas are all residents.

Pied kingfishers hover dramatically overhead before plunging into the water after their prey and darters perch like cormorants, hanging their wings out to dry. In the hot weather, before the monsoon breaks, red-wattled lapwing and stone curlew hatch their eggs in well-camouflaged nests on the ground, and pairs of sarus cranes, seen in India as symbols of fidelity, perform their courtship dances. Terrestrial birds too are in abundance. At the onset of the monsoon, weaver birds begin to construct their elaborate pendulous nests from date palms and other trees.

BELOW:
female nilga

Map
n page
268

Mammals and pythons

The most easily sighted of the mammals at Keoladeo Ghana (besides the lively little ground squirrels) are the sounders of wild boar, which root around the jungle near the Forest Lodge and in thickets. Sambar and nilgai can be seen near or in the shallow waters of the wetland, although chital or spotted deer are restricted to the park's dry area towards the south and west. Until the mid-1980s there was a small population of blackbuck numbering 22–25 animals but they disappeared when livestock grazing was completely stopped once the sanctuary became a national park.

The common mongoose can often be seen running across the road or in the undergrowth at its edges, and smooth otters are another attractive and entertaining animal to look out for on the lakes. Three types of wild cats, the jungle cat, leopard and fishing cat, are present, as are the Indian and common palm civets. Golden Jackals can be very vocal at night and striped hyenas, foxes, por-cupine, hare and a variety of smaller mammals have also been seen.

A bonus to visitors fond of reptiles are the large rock pythons that can be seen sunning themselves, especially at Python Point beyond the Keoladeo Temple.

Threats

In 2004 local politics denied water supply to the Bharatpur district and KNP from the Panchana dam. KNP's administration responded to this death-blowing move by digging bore wells to draw water from the ground. However, water from the River Gambhir carries essential fish fry that resident and migratory birds require. In addition, the ground water is alkaline and assists the proliferation of Prosopis – an exotic tree introduced into the region to reduce soil erosion. Experts fear that drought-like conditions in the park, year after year, would turn the place into a dry land/grassland. The park now faces the danger of being converted to woodlands and a glorified cattle grazing ground. ❏

LOW:
nted stork.

RANTHAMBORE

The bold tigers of Ranthambore have suffered through poaching and corruption but the historic fort and ruins lend the forest a unique atmosphere

Map
page
276

The great jungles of Central India were an awesome gift of nature that have been vandalized and largely destroyed over the years. What survives is but a small portion of its northwestern extremity.

This region, with its relics, is a historically important reminder of the misty past. The fort of Ranthambore was the centre of a Hindu Kingdom that was beseiged by Allaudin Khilji's army in AD 1301. He later defeated its king, Raja Hamir, and the Rajput women are reputed to have committed the terrible ritual of *sati* in the fort.

However, the area soon slipped back into the hands of the Rajputs and again became a powerful kingdom. The Mughal Emperor, Akbar, attacked it in 1569, the year after he took the fort at Chittaurgarh, and conquered it in 40 days of warfare. The event was important enough to be commemorated with five magnificent miniature paintings by the emperor's renowned artists, Miskina, Paras, Khem Karan, Mukund, Shankar and Lal, in the imperial copy of Abul Fazl's *Akbar Nama*, the official chronicle of Akbar's reign.

The Kachchwaha rulers of the principality of Amer (later known as Jaipur state) received the fort from the Mughals and it remained with them till 1949 when Jaipur state was merged into Rajasthan. The forests around the fort, then known by the name of the nearby township of Sawai Madhopur, were the private hunting grounds of the maharajas of Jaipur. Among the most infamous of their hunting parties was one organized for Queen Elizabeth II and the Duke of Edinburgh in 1961 – by which time royalty, both local and visiting, should have known better. It was due to the desire to preserve game for sport that the forest and its inhabitants first received protection and thus survived long enough to be rescued by Project Tiger.

In 1972, it was estimated that there were 1,927 tigers in India, of which Rajasthan had 74 and the number of tigers estimated in the Ranthambore Sanctuary's 155 sq km (60 sq miles) was 14. That year saw the launching of Project Tiger, and this sanctuary, named after the fort, became one of the eight sanctuaries and national parks of the new project. Over the years, the sanctuary has become a national park with a core area of 410 sq km (158 sq miles).*In 1984, an additional area of 104 sq km (40 sq miles) of adjoining forest was designated the Sawai Man Singh Sanctuary, after the late Maharaja of Jaipur.

However, in the early 1990s tigers disappeared from the Ranthambore Tiger Reserve. After the shocking revelation in

LEFT: tigers at Ranthambore have become more active during the day.
BELOW: young rhesus macaque.

2005 that the tigers had vanished from the Sariska reserve, also in Rajasthan, Ranthambore is approaching a similar crisis once again. The park authorities admitted last year that the official estimate of 47 tigers for 2004–05 was incorrect and that it had only about 26 tigers. An independent survey conducted by NGO Tiger Watch estimated this year that there could be no more than 15 tigers left. There are some hopes that the situation will get better now that the state government has announced 4,000 additional posts in the Forest Department. In the meantime, the department is concentrating on the relocation of villages along the periphery of the core areas and the buffer zones of the park.

Friendly tigers

Ranthambore is famous for its tigers and justly so. Over the last few decades tigers have become more and more active during the day, challenging the earlier belief that they are nocturnal animals. More than in any other park or sanctuary in India, tigers are now encountered here in broad daylight. They have lost some fear of humans and seem quite unperturbed by their presence.

Besides hunting in broad daylight as well as at night, some other unique aspects of tiger behaviour have been observed and photographed. Once, for instance, a magnificent large male hunted openly from the thickets on the edge of the lakes and ran down its sambar prey in the water. A tigress, too, indulged in similar behaviour. There have been instances when a tiger and a crocodile from the lake have confronted each other. On one memorable occasion a tiger battled with a crocodile over a sambar carcass and finally took possession of it in broad daylight, after a long fight.

Tigresses with cubs were seen only rarely and it was generally believed that tigers are solitary creatures and only the mothers take care of their cubs so long as these are unable to care for themselves. Here too their behaviour seems to have undergone a change. In 1986, two tiger

LEFT: forest track.

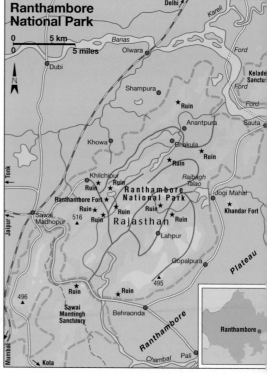

Map
n page
276

families, one with two cubs and another with three, were extremely trusting of human presence in jeeps and were observed for long stretches of time in jungle clearings in broad daylight, even when the cubs were a few weeks old. The family with three cubs included a large male, which seemed to have chosen to live with the cubs without being aggressive. In fact, this male was also seen with another tigress in the same Bakaula nala region from time to time.

Because of such tiger activities, Ranthambore is probably the best park in which to photograph them. In recent times it has become a centre of attraction for wildlife photographers from all over the world. Sighting a tiger can never be a sure shot, but here one comes as close to it as it is possible.

Other predators

This park also has a large population of leopards, or panthers, which are the second largest predators of this forest. The prey species of tigers and leopards overlap, and because of possible conflicts between them, the latter are found more often on the periphery of the park. Kachida Valley accounts for the highest number of sightings of these cats. They do not appear to be as fearlessly diurnal as tigers have become and therefore their sightings are not as frequent.

Another interesting feature of the park is the visibility of marsh crocodiles in and around the lakes. Over the years, their number has increased and these reptiles, 2.5–3 metres (8–10 ft) in length, are not uncommon. They are easily seen in the water or basking on the shore of the lakes. Often they are seen crossing from one lake to another. Interestingly, they eat dead sambar on land and try to drag the carcass into the water, even during daylight hours.

Other predators in Ranthambore are hyenas, jackals and jungle cats. Caracal, too, have been recorded. The last sighting of wild dogs was way back in 1954; it is not known why they have disappeared from these forests completely.

LOW:
rring
nbar stags.

Other Animals and Birds

Driving through Ranthambore one may encounter sloth bears. Lakarda and Anantpura are the areas where they are seen most often.

Sambar are seen everywhere and in large herds around the lakes. They are in hard horn and at their best during the rutting period in the winter months, though their antlers tend to be smaller than those of their counterparts in Central India. Sambar are known to wallow in and like water, but here they can be observed in water for hours, eating and swimming in the lakes. Behaviour one would expect from swamp deer (barasingha) rather than sambar.

Chital are extremely common throughout the park and they come to water in their hundreds, particularly in the warmer months. Nilgai, too, are found all over the park, with the greatest concentration around the lakes, they roam in smaller herds than those of sambar and chital.

Sounders of wild boar can be seen around the lakes with an occasional chinkara (Indi-an gazelle) also coming along. Among others, Indian hare and mongoose are most visible on the edge of the water. Monitor lizards are common though shy; they are usually quick to notice vehicle movement and, by the time one notices them, they are scuttling off to their burrows.

Though this park is famous for its animals, it is rich in birdlife as well. Bonelli's eagle, crested serpent eagle, great Indian horned owl, grey francolin, painted partridge, sangrouse, quail, spur fowl, common pea fowl, tree pie, paradise flycatcher, pheasant-tailed jacana, painted stork, white-necked stork, spoonbill and green pigeon are among the resident birds of the park. In addition, during the winter months, the park receives migrant visitors, primarily a variety of some raptors and ducks.

These forests are around the Aravalli and the Vindhya ranges, each of which has distinctive geological features. The forest is of typically dry deciduous type, with dhok being the most prominent tree.

BELOW: blac naped hare.

Map
n page
276

Ronj, ber, salai, occasional mango groves, palm trees, banyan and pipal trees give it a character all its own.

Photographer's dream

The entry point to the national park from Sawai Madhopur town takes the visitor to the foot of the Ranthambore fort and the Jogi Mahal. India's second-largest banyan tree rules supreme here, with its visiting langur troupe. Close by is Padam Talao (tank), which takes its name from the water lilies in it. At the far end is the Raj Bagh Talao followed by Milak Talao, which dries up in summer. These lakes attract considerable concentrations of ungulates, which in turn attract tigers. On several occasions they have been seen from the edge of the lake, hunting or resting in the water. Trips around these lakes are a wildlife photographer's dream.

From the lakes one can take fascinating trips to Nal Ghati and Lahpur through the enchanting Dhok Avenue, to Bakaula and Anantpur via Lakarda, or to Kachida val-ley and Anantpura. These are the most frequented routes visitors take and both morning and evening outings are rewarding as animals are active at that time. A jeep is a must as the forest roads make it rather tough going in places.

The park is studded with remnants of its historic past. Old defensive walls, wells, mosques and other structures bear mute testimony to kingdoms and battles long forgotten. Overgrown with pipal trees, they blend with their natural surroundings, thus lending to it an incomparable charm. Raj Bagh, a quadrangle with *baradaris* (sitting areas) between Padam Talao and Raj Bagh Talao, is a mixture of architectural styles, with ruins of fountain systems and apartments. Tigers have often been seen roaming about freely in these ruins, and some visitors have been lucky enough to be able to photograph them in these unlikely surroundings. The whole forest is dominated by the massive battlements of Ranthambore fort – worth a visit for its own sake, but doubly so within the park. ❑

LOW:
ster beetle.

Map on page 282

GIR

The Gir is the last refuge of the lion outside Africa – a beautiful deciduous forest which the big cats share with the Maldhari buffalo herders, astounding birdlife and many ancient temples

The lion has always occupied a unique position in India. More than 2,000 years ago Emperor Ashoka chose to inscribe some of his edicts on the famous lion capital of Sarnath, which is today the emblem of the Republic of India. This magnificent animal once roamed all over North India up to Bihar, but in the last hundred years it has been wiped out elsewhere, and today the only surviving population of lions outside the continent of Africa is found in the Gir forest. The Asiatic lion was once widespread from Bangladesh and India across the Middle East to Turkey – and was perhaps the European lion of the Mediteranean. Considered royal game by rulers in India from time immemorial, lions were protected, but large prides and daylight activity made them easier to poach than tigers or leopards. Hunting, and to some extent disappearance of their habitat has left them with only the Gir, their last habitat, and their last refuge.

Home of the asiatic lion

In the southwest of the Saurashtra peninsula of Gujarat state, an area of 1,412 sq km (545 sq miles) of forest and grassland survives amid increasing pressure of human and cattle population. The forest area itself has shrunk by half since the turn of the 20th century and what remains is the Gir Sanctuary with a core area of 300 sq km (116 sq miles), which has been declared a national park. It is no longer connected to even the Girnar Mountain where, until the mid-20th century, lions were often reported on the outskirts of Junagadh city. Sasan, with a lodge, is the headquarters of the sanctuary.

The Gir is a mixed deciduous type of forest with teak, ber, flame of the forest, jamun, a variety of acacia, particularly babul – and an occasional banyan tree. It is a hilly tract with many rivers and

offers to the visitor long pleasant outings of quiet beauty.

At the turn of the 20th century there was a disastrous famine, which lives in local memory as the "chappanio kal". The lion's prey population fell drastically and lions took to man-eating and their numbers declined drastically. It is believed that they were on the verge of extinction by the 1910s, with only two dozen lions left in Gir.

However, the Nawab of Junagadh, in whose domain most of the Gir forest fell, protected them vigorously. Since independence in 1947 protection has continued and lion hunting has been totally banned since the mid-1950s. As the Gir was the only home of the Asiatic lion,

LEFT: Asiatic lion, Gir Forest.
RIGHT: three striped palm squirrel.

there was an urgent need to establish their status. Consequently, the first systematic census of large mammals in India was conducted in the Gir in 1950 by the late M.A. Wynter-Blyth and the late R.S. Dharmakumarsinhji, both naturalists of outstanding ability. This set the trend for such censuses elsewhere in India, particularly those of tigers. By the mid-1990s, there were over 300 lions in the Gir forest as against 205 in 1979. As of summer 2006 the figure is approximately 350 animals.

The best way to observe lion is, of course, in their natural surroundings at dawn and dusk, when these predators are on the move. This can be done from a jeep as, owing to the protection given to them, they are not shy of motor vehicles. Nevertheless, one cannot be certain about seeing them on all occasions and some visitors are disappointed. The Forest Department has set up a "safari park" in a fenced-off area of about 400 hectares (1,000 acres) of the forest

where seeing the lions is more certain. The enclosure contains four to five lions that are easily viewed.

The Asiatic lion *(Panthera leo persica)* is slightly smaller than its African cousin – mature males reach a weight of 150–225 kg (330–500 lbs) and females 120–160 kg (265–350 lbs) – and its mane is smaller too. Nonetheless, a large male lion of the Gir is indeed a sight to behold. A former Nawab, Sir Mahabat Khanji of Junagadh ordered a series of Gir lion postage stamps for his state way back in 1929, thus making the Asiatic lion the first wild animal to figure philatelically in India.

A few lions from Gir were reintroduced in Chandraprabha Wildlife Sanctuary in Uttar Pradesh, but, due to the non-scientific approach and lack of follow-up, the experiment failed. The Gujarat State Government did propose to establish a second home for lions in the Barda hills near Porbandar. It has been proposed to set aside a 180-sq-km

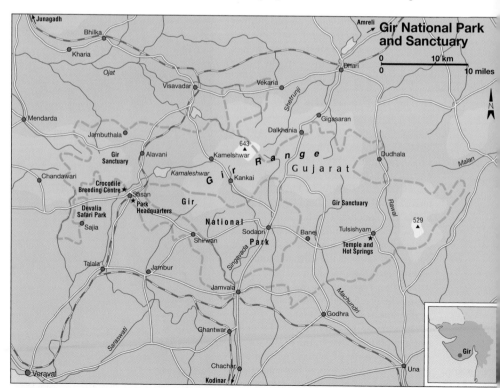

Map on page 282

(70-sq-mile) area for the purpose. The success of this enterprise would depend on the availability of prey animals and sufficient area for the lion population to take root undisturbed. It was the obvious lack of these conditions which saw the end of the lions in this area some 80 years ago. Today the Barda hills area is no longer connected to the Gir, as was the case then, and the scheme has not yet been realized, even though it was proposed over 20 years ago. The Gir, therefore, remains the sole haven of the Asiatic lion, which, above all, is its unique attraction.

In a major step, the state government has decided to set up a new lion sanctuary at Jesar Hills in the Bhavnagar-Amreli forests. The alarming number of lion deaths – at least 100 in the last four years – and pressure from the central government to shift the lion sanctuary to Madhya Pradesh for better conservation spurred the state authorities into action. The new sanctuary will allow the lion population to expand where previously it had been overcrowed, and is also insurance against epidemics hitting a single lion population in Gir.

The Hunters and the Hunted

The Gir has always had a large population of leopards (or panthers) too and they are more visible here than in other Indian forests. In 1985 there were 201 panthers as against 261 in 1979, but now the figure is approximately 500. These are the Indian leopard *(Panthera pardus fusca)*. If one is lucky, they can be encountered while driving through the forest.

According to the latest census data of 2001, sambar number 2,300, chital 46,000, nilgai 1,200, four-horned antelope 850, chinkara *(Indian gazelle)* 550, wild boar 2,500, and unknown numbers of langur. These are the prey population for the big cats, along with domestic cattle. Chital and sambar are the main natural prey of lions and leopard. While chital is more common in comparatively

LOW: landscape.

open areas of the sanctuary, sambar prefers dense vegetation and so are more common in the park where cattle grazing is strictly restricted. Perhaps the number of nilgai is greater as this large antelope also prefers open scrub jungle.

Among the other carnivores are the wild cat, the jackal and the hyena. The sloth bear is conspicuous by its absence from the Gir. Pythons and many other species of snakes have been recorded. The Gir is an excellent area for seeing marsh crocodiles in its rivers and particularly in the lake of Kamaleshwar dam. There is a crocodile breeding farm at Sasan. It is from this farm that these reptiles are taken to restock the lakes and rivers of Gujarat.

Birds

The forest is remarkably rich in birdlife too. Paradise flycatcher, black-headed cuckoo shrike, grey drongo, pied woodpecker, coppersmith, Indian roller, crested swift, fish owl, 6 species of vulture, shaheen falcon, Bonelli's eagle, crested serpent eagle, painted sandgrouse, rock bush quail, grey francolin and white-necked stork, are among the many species of birds found here.

Wildlife viewing in the Girs is best done by driving around the forest. The best drives from Sasan are to Baval Chowk and Kankai, to Chodavdi and Tulsishyam, and to Kamaleshwar dam. The roads are manageable by a sturdy car, but a jeep is definitely advisable. The best time for viewing is at sunrise and sunset, as the animals are most active at these times.

The sanctuary usually remains closed from June to October and the best time to visit the forest is between December and March. The summer temperature can be as high as 40°C (104°F) while in winter it can be as low as 6°C (43°F).

Lions and Humans

The Gir is steeped in history and folklore. It has temples of great antiquity

BELOW: lione and cubs wit chital kill.

Map
on page
282

like Kankai Mata and Tulsishyam, a place of pilgrimage with hot springs. The forest is famous for its cattle herders, the Maldharis, whose buffaloes form a substantial part of the lions' food. These herders live in small thorn-fenced settlements called *nes*, which are well worth visiting. The Maldharis' lives have changed little over the years and their folklore and traditions are a unique record of coexistence of human beings with lions.

A major problem of the sanctuary continues to be the human population and their cattle herds, despite certain steps being taken to meet this situation. For example, a rubble wall around the sanctuary prevents some herders and their cattle from entering the sanctuary, but sizable human and cattle populations remain within it. The number of cattle within the sanctuary is estimated at 20,000, and these compete for food and territory with the wild ungulates. Because of such disturbances, one does not see such animals as sambar, chital and nilgai in the Gir in such numbers and concentrations as one does in better-protected sanctuaries and national parks. Actually, cattle form a very substantial part of a lion's diet today, and, in seeming paradox, unless the Maldharis and their cattle are progressively removed, the Gir's natural prey population cannot increase. In fact it will continue to remain under constant threat of epidemics and a sudden drastic reduction in numbers.

Both illegal electrified fences and wells pose threats to wildlife. Saurashtra is an arid zone and people are compelled to dig wells, which they abandon after they have run dry. Wells are death traps for unsuspecting Asiatic lions and leopards, who fall into them and either end up maimed or dead. In the area outside the forest, there are over 1,000 wells – often 5 metres (15 ft) wide and equally as deep – for which it is impossible to assign responsibility. ❏

BELOW:
leopardess.

KANHA

Famous long before it became the setting for Kipling's Jungles Book and the site of the swamp deer's rescue from the brink of extinction, there is no better place in the world than Kanha for viewing tigers in the wild

Map
page
290

Kanha in Madhya Pradesh (five hours driving from Jabalpur, six from Nagpur) has sometimes been called the N'Gorongoro of India. The simile is apt, though Kanha is far greener and its cordon of hills far more densely wooded. Unlike Tanzania's N' Gorongoro, the Kanha Valley is not a volcanic crater, but the enclosing hills are a consequence of geologically ancient volcanic activity. The horseshoe-shaped Kanha Valley, which accounts for nearly a third and is the oldest part of the Kanha National Park, is bound by two distant spurs emanating from the main Mekal ridge, forming its southern rim. The spurs, in their gently tapering traverse, nearly close in the north leaving a narrow opening for the meandering Sulkum or Surpan river – the valley's main drainage. Herds of the Kanha miscellany, the axis deer *(chital)*, the swamp deer *(barasingha)*, the blackbuck *(hiran)*, the wild pig and occasionally the gaur, throng the central parkland of the valley, providing the basis for the comparison with N'Gorongoro. With its confiding herds and relatively tolerant predators, Kanha offers almost unrivaled scope to a keen photographer of Indian wildlife.

The forests of the Banjar Valley and the Halon Valley, respectively forming Kanha's western and eastern halves, had, even at the turn of the 20th century, been long famous for their deer and tiger. Expectedly, therefore, they were reserved as the exclusive hunting grounds for the most privileged, the British Viceroy, as early as 1910. The ups and downs in the ensuing decades gave an interesting conservation history to Kanha, which celebrated its golden jubilee in 1983. It all started with an area of some 250 sq km (96 sq miles) in the Kanha Valley being gazetted as a sanctuary in 1933. This was followed by 300 sq km (116 sq miles) of the Haron Valley around Supkhar also being declared a sanctuary in 1935. However, because of extensive deer damage to tree saplings in the forests and crops in nearby villages, the Supkhar sanctuary was denotified within a few years. Both these areas at that time still harboured teeming populations of the Central Indian barasingha *(Cervus duvauceli branderi)*. This majestic cousin of the nominate swamp deer *(Cervus duvauceli duvauceli)* of the sub-Himalayan floodplains had adapted itself to the hard-ground grasslands and until the turn of the 20th century dominated the Central Indian highlands.

Mounting pressures on the wilderness notwithstanding, the Kanha Valley sur-

vived as a sanctuary into the 1950s. Excessive stock-grazing had, however, jeopardized the barasingha's grassland habitat and its numbers had greatly declined. Yet a few thousand still found a home in Kanha Valley's central maidans – meadows with sporadic groves of trees. Then in the early 1950s, in a scandalous act of butchery, a rich hunter was allowed to shoot 30 tigers in and around the sanctuary. The furore that followed led to special legislation and the Kanha Valley was declared a 249-sq-km (96-sq-mile) national park in 1955. Since then, the gains have been steady. In 1962, the park was expanded to 318 sq km (123 sq miles). In 1970, the area south of the Mekal ridge and down to the River Banjar was added, raising it to 446 sq km (172 sq miles). Finally, Project Tiger paved the way for the integration of the eastern Halon Valley into the park system, initially on a sanctuary status in 1974 and as a full national park since 1976. This gives Kanha National Park its present area of 940 sq km (363 sq miles) which is further buffered by an additional area of 1,000 sq km (388 sq miles). The total conservation unit encompasses 1,945 sq km (750 sq miles) and is called Kanha Tiger Reserve under Project Tiger.

Rich habitat

Kanha's topography and geology combine variously to give it its rich habitat diversity. The range of elevation is 450–900 metres (1,480–2,950 ft) above sea level. The bauxite-capped hills sport extensive plateaux, locally called *dadar*, which carry extensive grasslands with only sparse tree growth. Folds at their fringes, where bauxite yields to basalt, have perennial springs.

This combination is an ideal habitat for gaur *(Bos gauras)*, the largest of the world's cattle, sambar *(Cervus unicolour)*, the largest of the Indian deer, and chausingha *(Tetraceros quadricornis)*, the only four-horned ungulate in the world. Nilgai antelope (bluebull) are

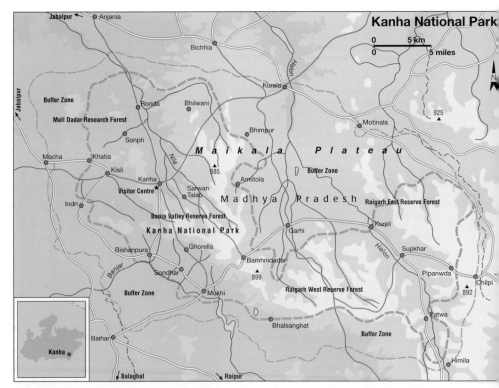

Map
on page
290

RIGHT: golden langur in flame the forest.

common here and sloth bear are frequent visitors. You may see a pied or a marsh harrier *(Circus melanoleucus or C. aeruginosus)* hovering in the air and swooping onto a cluster of bush quail *(Perdicula asiatica)*.

The rims of the plateaux have steep rocky slopes and, often, escarpments. The latter prove a rare stance for breathtaking views of the valleys below and the hills beyond. Many of these plateaux are large enough for runways and indeed Bamhnidadar, 850 metres (2,780 ft) above sea level, on the southeastern rim of the Kanha valley had one operative airfield until 1976. A late afternoon visit to Bamhnidadar to see some of these animals is greatly recommended. Watching from here the changing hues of the verdant Banjar Valley below, against the backdrop of a gradual, glorious sunset, is an enthralling experience indeed.

The trip down from these plateaux is through exquisite wild country. Huge trees, including bija *(Pterocarpus marsupium)*, haldu *(Adina cardifolia)* and dhaora *(Anogeissus latifolia)*, along with a host of other large and small trees, comprise the thick forests on the slopes. Garlands of massive mahul *(Bauhinia vahlaii)* climbers span the spaces between trees. Dense bamboo *(Dendrocalamus strictus)* thickets occupy the understory. Much of these mixed forests in such difficult terrain have escaped any form of exploitation and are a picture of raw wilderness. Sighting the red jungle fowl, the painted spurfowl, some gaur and sambar, and a shy barking deer *(Muntiacus muntjak)* pausing at the roadside glade is common. What may distinguish such a drive is a leopard hurtling down a tree or one simply walking along the road.

Water is generally scarce on the slopes during the dry season. But in the upper reaches of the major *nullahs*, where they flow through gorges carved in basaltic rock, the flow is perennial. There are also some seepage springs scattered amid the slopes. These water holes are the focal points for numerous animals and birds, large and small. In the lower slopes the forest cover changes, often abruptly, from mixed deciduous to lush green sal *(Shorea robusta)*, with or without bamboo. The valleys with rich alluvium carry a mixed interspersion of stately, near pure stands of sal and extensive meadows. It is this characteristic parkland appearance of the valleys that typifies the Kanha landscape.

The large grassy clearings are a consequence of old, abandoned cultivation, although many were formed as a result of a massive village relocation operation under Project Tiger. This important operation was undertaken with great success in order to meet the twin objective of preventing wild animal damage to the crops and cattle of the interior settlements in the park and to release wildlife habitat from human occupation and disturbance in this prime conservation area. Significantly, the operation was smooth and with full involvement of the affected people, who were provided adequate and viable alternatives in the form of agricultural land and newly organized

housing at sites of their choice outside the park. This has been hailed as a major management success of the Kanha National Park in conservation circles the world over.

In recent years, however, concern has been raised about the degree of involvement in conservation of those peoples living on the park's fringes. They are mostly Adivasi groups who have traditionally relied on forest produce as a major source of income. Their important role as protectors of the forest buffer zone is compromised if they feel they have no stake in the running of the park and the benefits that conservation can bring. This is perhaps the most pressing issue facing the park authorities as motivated and informed local people can form one of the most effective barriers against poaching. While Kanha is one of the best protected and most successful national parks in India, poaching is not unknown and the pressures on the wildlife population, particularly tigers, can only increase in the face of huge demand for tiger parts from East Asia.

Kanha's jewel

The swamp deer, or barasingha, is the jewel of Kanha and its rescue from the brink of extinction is the crowning glory of its conservation achievements. The enlargement of grassland habitat through village relocation has been the main basis of this breakthrough. Barasingha feed almost exclusively on grasses, and tall grass meadows are essential to the security of their fawns from minor and major predators from August to September, when they are dropped, to late November. By this time, the fawns are strong enough to keep pace with the herds and are well initiated into the art of security through herding. Cultivation of the valley grasslands had appropriated the bulk of the grassland habitat while excessive stock grazing did not allow grasses to grow tall enough in the remainder. In consequence, the rate of

BELOW: chital herd in a typical Kan meadow.

Map on page 290

success at raising young steadily declined and in Kanha Valley itself the barasingha numbers fell from nearly 3,000 in the early 1950s to just 66 in 1970. This was the last surviving population of this sub-species in the world. Fortunately, as a result of measures taken, including village relocation, their population continues to show a steady increase and has now crossed the 500 mark, which has been maintained.

With its multitined beams of antlers bent forward and adorned by crowns of grass, tufts, the proud carriage of a dominant barasingha stag, silhouetted in profile through mist against sunbeams breaking through stately sal trees on an early winter morning, can be an all-quenching feast to the eyes of a nature lover. Peak winter, December–January, is the barasingha's rutting season and large congregations are seen in the Kanha and Sonph meadows. It is difficult to paint a picture in words of the impressive display of the big breeding stags, the rivalry among them leading to serious fights amid clouds of kicked-up dust, the almost unconcerned females grazing away, the youngsters looking askance, the chase by the victor, the run for life by the vanquished and the finale in the form of the majestic re-entry of the victor into the herd after a thorough wallow in mud. All this, while stag bellows echo from all directions.

Blackbuck is not an animal of the moist deciduous forests of the hills or the sal forests of the valleys. Kanha meadows used to carry a small number of blackbuck. It entered Kanha valley from the plains outside, probably with the extension of cultivation along the Sulkum river. Now that the cultivation is gone and the overgrazed short grass meadows are changing over to taller grasses, the blackbuck has disappeared. Its numbers, near 80 in 1972, had dropped to under 10 in 1986 and blackbuck are now not seen within the park.

Jackals, normally scavengers but oppor-

LOW: barasingha stag in rutting season.

tunistic predators, have accentuated the jeopardy. When, following strict protection and intensive conservation measures in the 1970s, all wild animal populations showed a rapid increase, including the most populous chital, the jackal took to hunting the rich crop of chital fawns in the meadows by forming small packs. This opportunistic hunting was extended to blackbuck fawns in the central Kanha meadows, from where, unlike chital, they had nowhere else to go. However, in a 28-hectare (69-acre) tiger- and leopard-proof enclosure (raised originally for the barasingha) just south of Kanha, their number during the same period went up from about five to well over 30.

Shravantal is an ancient, small earthbound tank in the central Kanha meadows. This is an important watering source in the area. It even attracts a fair number of water fowl in winter – mainly the lesser whitling teal, but also to be seen are some common teal, pintail, cotton teal and an occasional shoveler.

Sighting animals

Kanha has a distinct monsoonal climate. Over 90 percent of its annual precipitation of 160 cm (64 ins) arrives between late June and late September. The park remains closed from 1 July to 31 October, but an early downpour, washing away portions of fair-weather roads, may enforce an earlier closure (though seldom before 20 June). November is mildly cold while December and January are the coldest and given to severe frost, late night temperatures in valleys dipping to -2°C (29°F). February and March is pleasant spring-like weather. April starts warming up while May and June is the hottest period.

Premonsoon showers in late June kill the heat and herald massive deer congregations in the maidans, which quickly shed their brown-yellow and don the rich green of the new flush of grasses. This coincides with the second peak of the chital rutting season. Their rut starts in late March and stretches well into July,

BELOW: swamp deer.

Map on page 290

IGHT:
ʒung tiger.

the first peak being from mid-April to mid-May. The valleys reverberate with the loud, sharp and long-drawn bugling of stags. The maidans are dotted with dominant stags displaying to and courting females and fighting rivals for them.

Jeep safaris in the park are permitted only by daylight. The best time is in early mornings and late afternoons. Kanha animals are confiding and a little care in approach can yield prolonged pleasure observing interesting animal behaviour within a species and interaction among different species. As soon as a group of animals is sighted, the vehicle should slow down and stop at a distance where the animals take note but do not run away. Soon they resettle, whereafter advances may be made gradually. With patience a vehicle can be positioned between groups of animals on both sides of the road. Vehicles are not allowed to leave the road. Nor is walking allowed while on excursions.

The best chances of seeing gaur are at Bamhnidadar in the late afternoons or in the early mornings in the Bishanpura-Sondhar-Ghorella area in the Mukki range. All these areas are good for sighting wild dog *(Cuon alpinus)*, or dhole (locally called *sonha kutta*) too. The dhole may also be often seen in Kanha and Sonph maidans. Observing langurs – the species here is *Presbytis entellus* – is absorbing in itself, but their interaction with other herbivores is even more interesting. Langurs are often locally referred to as the chital's herders because seeing a herd of chital under a tree being foraged by langurs is a common sight. Chital and, sometimes, also wild boar *(Sus scrofa)* follow the foraging langurs and greedily feed on the leftovers of fruits and leaves generously thrown to the ground by the latter. The association is further advantageous to the deer and the boar because langurs, from their high stance on trees, can see or detect a predator from suspicious movements much earlier and raise the alarm in good time. Langurs are quite serious in such observations and seldom sound a false alarm.

Birds

Kanha's birdlife is rich, the tally of species being close to 300. Mornings are full of rich bird calls. Peafowl, and sometimes dancing peacocks during March to June, are seen all over. The Indian roller, racket-tailed drongo, red and yellow wattled lapwings, green bee-eater, various doves (five species), grey hornbill, tree pie, myna, munias, bushchat, warblers, flycatchers, babblers and woodpeckers are commonly seen. Blackheaded and golden oriole, paradise flycatcher, pied Malabar hornbill, Indian pitta, Indian stone curlew, common gray and painted partridge and yellow-legged green pigeon are often seen on drives. Black ibis, white-necked and lesser adjutant storks, white-breasted and pied kingfishers, different egrets and occasionally cormorants are seen around water bodies or streams near Kanha, Sonph, Kisli and Mukki. The main birds of prey, often seen swooping down on and catching or feeding on small mammals,

snakes and birds, are the crested serpent eagle, crested honey buzzard, white-eyed buzzard, black-winged kite, shikra, lagger and shaheen falcon, kestrel and a number of owls and owlets including the barn owl, brown fish owl and the nightjar. Often white-backed and scavenger vultures and occasionally black and longbilled vultures can be seen scavenging on tiger, leopard and wild-dog kills. For bird-watchers staying at Mukki, the area along the Banjar river, and for those at Kisli, going round the Kisli and Kanha campuses, can prove highly rewarding. Penetrating into woodland on foot even around the campus is neither advisable nor permitted for reasons of safety.

Tiger land

The raw beauty of the Kanha wilderness is satisfying because a comparison of the condition of the forests outside with that of those inside is a strong pointer to "conservation in action" in the park.

Kanha's diverse miscellany of mammals and birdlife is without many parallels because so much is seen so well in so short a time. Yet Kanha is better known as a good place to see tigers, of which there are presently believed to be around 100 individuals.

Sighting tigers on drives here is not uncommon, but seeing and photographing tigers depends very much on the skill and knowledge of your guide. The best time is very early in the morning for tiger tracking from Kisli, Kanha or Mukki.

As the dense sal forest makes sightings of tiger difficult, one of the most promising places for a sighting is a flattish nullah bed or a grassy glade amid stately sal trees. Pug marks, the drag of a kill, the various vocalizations of the predator, the crowing and shuttling of the crows, and the alarm calls of the langur and deer are signs that could lead to a rendezvous with the secretive tiger. The evaluation of these signs enables the guide to decide

BELOW: wild boars at a waterhole.

Map
n page
290

the right course. On a drive through the park, a good guide will suddenly stop and peer through the canopy of bamboo, ban-rahar *(Flamingia sop)* or sindur *(Mallotus philippinensis)* bushes lower down. He will adjust the jeep's position for a better view and point out what he has seen – the remains of a kill or the unmistakable stripes. Having made sure of a predator's presence in the area, he will avoid disturbing it.

While awaiting the tiger's arrival it is essential to remain quiet and still. Too much movement and noise might scare away the tiger. One strategy is to take advantage of the cat's urge to laze as the day advances. With the arrival of other jeeps, the game of out-flanking the tiger, hide and seek, begins and finally the tiger gets reconciled to being watched – a bit of a nuisance, but harmless. It is this relentless persuing of tigers that can potentially ruin a day's wildlife watching, however – the jeeps running about the jungle scare off the more timid and

equally interesting species that the park contains. A good course of action is often to pick a site with a good view and sit quietly and wait. Sometimes a tiger is sighted within 2 or 3 hours, and at others in less than an hour. On some days tigers are sighted at more than one area, on other days at none. Once a tiger settles down, it can be viewed for several hours.

The game of tracking is thrilling and affords a real feel of the dynamic wilderness, something happening or expected to happen all the time. Many a time a leopard is seen, though unlike the tiger, not for a prolonged view. Other rare sightings may include a monitor lizard, a porcupine or a python. Of course a host of birds and often gaur, sambar and muntjac are seen too.

Although elephant rides had been discontinued at Kanha, it seems they are now being used for tiger viewing again. When a tiger is sighted, the jeeps converge on the spot and the visitors are then transferred to elephants to approach the tiger. ❑

OW:
leopard's
aids
ance.

Map
page
300

BANDHAVGARH

*A young park at an historic site, with carvings, temples and fort,
Bandhavgarh is small but has plenty to see – and is easily accessible
by train or from the nearby temples of popular Khajuraho*

Bandhavgarh is a national park with a very long history. Set among the Vindhya hills of Madhya Pradesh with an area of 437 sq km (168 sq miles), it contains a wide variety of habitats and a high density of animals, including a large number of tigers.

Geography, flora and climate

When originally formed in 1968, Bandhavgarh was a comparatively small park of only 105 sq km (40 sq miles), but in mid-1986 it was extended to include two large areas of forest adjoining it on the northern and southern sides. These extension areas consist mainly of sal forest. In the north a series of ridges, intercut by perennial streams, run parallel to the main Umaria road, which runs through the park. To the south, gently undulating forest is interspersed with grazing areas, formerly agricultural land.

Currently the central area of the park – the original 105 sq km (40 sq miles) – remains the principal viewing area. There are 32 hills in this part of the park, which has a large fort at its center. The fort's cliffs are 800 meters (2,625 ft) high, 300 meters (1,000 ft) above the surrounding countryside. Over half the area is covered by sal forest although on the upper slopes it is replaced by mixed forest of sali, saj, dhobin and saja. Towards the north there are large stretches of bamboo and grassland. Most of the bamboo flowered in 1985 and the old clumps died, leaving the ground covered with new bamboo growth. Many streams run through the valleys, but only three are perennial. One of them, the Charanganga, has its source at the fort.

Winter temperatures (November–mid-February) vary from almost freezing at night to around 20°C (68°F) in the daytime. Summer nights are also cooler than the daytime temperature, which rises to 40°C (104°F). The park is closed during the monsoon (July–October), which coincides with the breeding season of many resident birds and most ungulate species.

History

Bandhavgarh has been a centre of human activity and settlement for over 2,000 years. Legend has it that Rama, hero of the Hindu epic, the *Ramayana*, stopped at Bandhavgarh on his way back to his homeland after defeating the demon king Ravana of Lanka. Two monkey architects, who had engineered a bridge between the isle of Lanka and the mainland (Rama's Bridge or Adam's Bridge), are said to have built Bandhavgarh's fort. Later Rama handed it over to his brother Lakshmana who became known as band-

havdhish, "the lord of the fort" – a title still used by the present "lord of the fort", the former Maharaja of Rewa. Lakshmana is the particular god of the fort and is regularly worshipped in a temple there.

The oldest signs of habitation in the park are the caves dug into the sandstone to the north of the fort. Several contain Brahmi inscriptions dating from the 1st century BC. From that time onwards Bandhavgarh was ruled by a succession of dynasties, including the Chandela kings of Bundelkhand who built the famous temples at Khajuraho. The Baghel kings, the direct ancestors of the present royal family of Rewa, established their dynasty at Bandhavgarh in the 12th century. It remained their capital until 1617, when the centre of court life moved to Rewa, 120 km (75 miles) to the north. Without royal patronage Bandhavgarh became more and more deserted until forest overran the area and it became a royal hunting reserve. This helped to preserve the forest and its wildlife, although the maharajas made full use of their rights. Each set out to kill the auspicious number of 109 tigers.

At Independence, Bandhavgarh remained the private property of the maharaja until he gave it to the state for the formation of a national park in 1968. After the park was created, poaching was brought under control and the number of animals rose dramatically. Small dams were built to solve the problem of water shortage. Grazing by local cattle was stopped and a village within the park boundaries was relocated. The tigers in particular prospered and the 1986 extension provided much-needed forest to accommodate them

Within the park

Bandhavgarh is justifiably famous for its tigers, but it has a wide range of other animals. The undergrowth is not as dense as in some northern terai forests, but the best time to see the park's inhabitants is still the summer months when water becomes more scarce and the undergrowth dies back.

LEFT: sal tree in blossom.

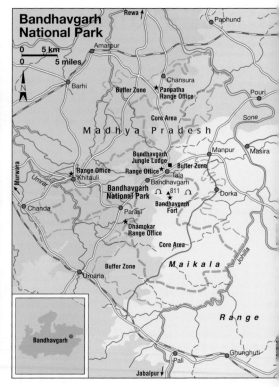

Map
◄ page
300

The most effective way to search for tigers is on elephant back. Government elephants belonging to the Forest Department can be boarded from a point near the Forest Rest House, not far from the park entrance. It is advisable to book your elephant in advance and to wear plenty of warm clothing if going for an early-morning ride in winter. The mahouts are kept well-informed of the whereabouts of the nearest tigers but will generally only go for comparatively short trips into the jungle on the north side of the main viewing area. However, there are many tigers in the park and elephants are able to take you up steep, rocky hillsides and down marshy riverbeds that are impassable to vehicles.

There are several good-weather roads in the park. Jeeps are definitely recommended over other vehicles and can be hired from the White Tiger Forest Lodge or the Bandhavgarh Jungle Lodge *(see page 336)*. Other places to stay include the Bandhavgarh Jungle Camp, Tiger Trails and the Patel Lodge. It is also advisable to take a guide. Good, English-speaking guides are also available from the lodges and rest houses. A forest guard must accompany all visitors into the park. Entry into the park is allowed only during daylight hours. For both elephant and jeep rides the hours immediately after dawn and before sunset are best.

Fauna

Chinkara, still rather shy, can be sighted on the grassland areas of the park, particularly on formerly cultivated land in the southern extension area, on the edges of the main viewing area. Also to be seen in the grasslands are nilgai, chausingha and sounders of wild boar, as well as the occasional jackal or fox. In March and April gaur, or Indian bison, move down from the higher hills to the southeast of the park and make their way through the southern extension area to the central meadows of the park to graze. The need for water and good grazing draws them

ow: tiger
d fallen sal
es.

to the park and they return to the south-eastern hills at the onset of the monsoon.

Muntijac and sambar prefer denser vegetation. The main prey animal, however, for the tigers and the park's rarely sighed leopards are the chital, which now number a few thousand.

There are two types of monkey common in the park – the rhesus macaque and the black-faced langur. Drives can also reveal jungle cats, hyenas, porcupines, ratels and a variety of other mammals. At least one small pack of wild dogs inhabits the central area of the park.

Birds

As the park is relatively new, there is still a good chance of adding birds to the checklist of some 242 species already compiled. Bandhavgarh attracts many migratory birds in the winter months, including birds of prey like the steppe eagle and a variety of wildfowl. However, as it has limited water surfaces it cannot compete with parks with large areas of

wetland. While you are not allowed to go into the park on foot, the park headquarters and the Jungle Lodge and Camp offer excellent opportunities to watch the smaller birds. Attracted by flowering and fruiting trees, some very attractive and less common birds can be seen – for example the blue-bearded bee-eater, the white-bellied drongo, Tickell's blue flycatcher, the white-browed fantail, both the gold-fronted and Jerdon's leafbirds, minivets and woodshrikes. Any large fruiting tree generally reveals a population of yellow-legged green pigeons and some of the noisiest residents – blossom-headed parakeets. Grey and, less often, the magnificent black and white Malabar hornbills fly across. On roads through the sal forests it is worth looking out for the large racket-tailed drongo and the dipping plumes of the paradise flycatcher.

The Fort

The fort still belongs to the Maharaja of Rewa and permission is required to visit it. However, permission is available locally and no trip to Bandhavgarh can really be complete without making the effort to climb up to the fort.

There are two ways up on to the plateau, a jeep track and a footpath – both steep. It is far easier to see the fort by jeep but much more rewarding to make the journey on foot. There is a convenient place to park vehicles on the southern side of the fort in the lush jungle that surrounds its base. This point is known as Shesh Saya, named after a unique 11 metre (35-foot) long statue of a reclining Vishnu carved around the 10th century, from whose feet the Charanganga is said to flow.

A rectangular pool of spring water lies just beneath the statue and the path to the main gate of the fort, the Kart Pol, leads off to the left of the pool. On the other side of this imposing gateway lie 227 hectares (560 acres) of grassland, over which are scattered turtle-filled tanks and the many remains of the human inhabitants of the fort – from ancient statues to the barracks occupied by Rewa's troops up to Independence.

LEFT: green beat-eater.

Map page 300

At a brisk pace the walk from the Shesh Saya to the southern side of the fort need only take an hour, but if you stop to see the statues and temples on the way it can easily take much longer.

As you follow the path southwards, the most remarkable sights are the 10th-century rock images of the incarnations of Vishnu. A statue of Narasimha (half-man half-lion) towers almost 7 metres (22 ft) above the grass. There is a carving of Barah Bhagwan (the boar incarnation) and a small temple enshrining a large image of Vishnu in his fish avatar. The tortoise incarnation stands unenclosed and flanked by later carvings of Ganesh, the elephant god, and other deities. The charm of this walk lies in discovering these monuments in the jungle, unspoilt and unexploited. Some of the statues lie off the main path and so it is best to take a guide. Apart from the avatars, well worth seeing are three small temples of around the 12th century. These temples are deserted but the fort is still used as a

place of worship. Kabir Das, the celebrated 16th-century saint, once lived and preached here.

The natural ramparts of the fort give breathtaking views of the surrounding countryside. Vultures wheel around the precipice, which also attracts blue rock thrushes and crag martins. The fort has a small population of blackbuck, which have been reintroduced and to some extent protected from tigers in the park below by repairs to the masonry walls at the edges of the fort.

Thus Bandhavgarh offers excellent wildlife and bird viewing plus a historical interest that most other parks lack. It is a comfortable drive from Khajuraho and so visitors can enjoy both the spectacular 10th-century temples of the one and the wildlife of the other in one trip. And for those who enjoy train travel Bandhavgarh has two railway stations within reach – Umaria and Satna – and jeeps that can collect visitors from the station and deposit them on elephant back before breakfast. ❏

ow: langur, ping.

THE NILGIRI BIOSPHERE

*The Nilgiri in the Western Ghats is India's premier biosphere reserve,
with a range of forests and habitats, it includes the protected areas of
Bandipur, Nagarahole, Mudumalai, Wayanad and Silent Valley*

Map
n page
308

Tall trees, swaying bamboos and grassy expanses. Calls of mynas and drongos that pierce the gentle murmur of forest streams. A herd of gaur in the morning sun, with massive horned heads and pale green eyes that stare back at you. A blazing afternoon. A pack of wild dogs cornering a chital stag in a forest pool. An elephant herd frolicking in water as the setting sun bathes it in gold. As night falls, the haunting cry of a peacock retiring to the top of a tall, leafless tree. A sambar calling in alarm. A tiger is on the move, leaving its tracks on a dusty trail. This is typical South Indian jungle. Most of it is gone forever. Yet in the vast forests of the Mysore plateau in Karnataka state, which stretch between the towering Western Ghats and Nilgiri mountains, the experience comes alive even now.

Administered separately, Nagarahole (pronounced Naagara-holay) and Bandipur are but two faces of a single spectacular ecological continuum that also includes Mudumalai and Wayanad wildlife sanctuaries in the neighbouring states. The 865-sq-km (33-sq-mile) Bandipur National Park lies south of the Kabini river, which meanders through the jungle, while Nagarahole 640 sq km (247 sq mile), including proposed expansion) is to its north. The old royal capital city of Mysore is the gateway to both parks. Due to their geographic proximity the two parks share many features. The balmy climate is common to both. So are most of the plant and animal species. Yet, there are differences too.

The Bandipur that the tourist sees is an open, grassy woodland, while the jungles of Nagarahole are taller and denser. Bandipur has superb scenery of mountains, gorges and undisturbed forests. Nagarahole has an astonishing abundance of wildlife. Together, these two parks cover more than 1,500 sq km (580 sq

miles). About a third of this area has been demarcated as the "Wilderness Zone" in which all disturbances, including tourism and forestry, are prohibited. The facilities for wildlife tourism have been developed in the three "tourism zones". Two of these, called Nagarahole and Karapura, are in Nagarahole National Park while the third is in Bandipur. Two more tourism zones, at Begur in Bandipur and Moorkal in Nagarahole are being planned.

These parks have had some of the most troubled recent histories of any of the Indian parks. A couple of years ago, they were periodically closed to visitors due to depredation by poachers and sandalwood smugglers – most notably the infamous Veerappan and his gang. Veerappan was

ECEDING
GES:
phants at
terhole
T: common
gur.
HT: egrets
re once
ted for their
mes, used
decorate
oans and
es' hats.

so brazen that he even kidnapped the late Kannada actor Rajkumar. Subsequently, Veerappan was shot dead in a police encounter, leaving forest and police staff in peace. Now there is no threat to tourists from such criminals but visitors are still advised to check the current state of access with the parks' authorities.

A major problem plaguing Bandipur and Nagarahole is vacancies in the forest guard cadre, where as many as 50 percent of the posts are not filled. Further, the average age of the forest guards is about 55 years and their workload is heavy. Non-governmental organizations point out that the morale of forest guards is low since they are not paid on time and members of the anti-poaching camp are poorly equipped.

A further problem has been forest fires. These occur both because the dry grasslands of the parks are naturally prone to fire, and because of arson – which provides a cover for poaching and expoitation of the forest for firewood and other resources. The park authorities are very overstretched and unless there is a concerted effort to stamp out poaching and encroachment on to forest land the intolerable pressures the parks face may prove fatal for these precious environments.

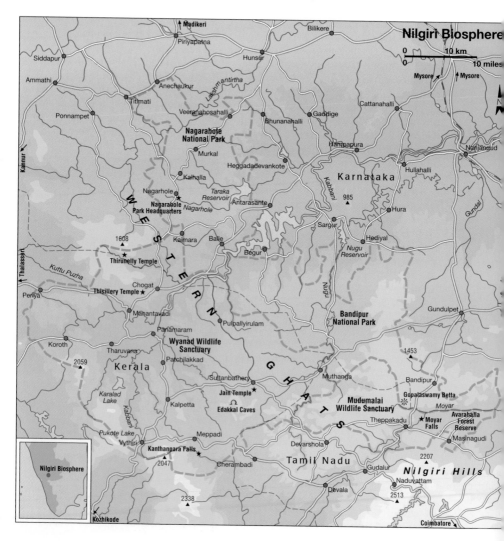

Map on page 308

Climate and landscape

Three seasons are usually recognized. The wet season, or monsoon, lasts from June to September. The cool season that follows lasts up to January. The hot season, or summer, extends from February to May. However, seasonal variations of temperature are quite moderate, ranging between 15°C (59°F) at the coldest to about 28°C (82°F) at the hottest. Annual rainfall is lowest at the eastern edge of Bandipur – 80 cm (32 ins). It increases gradually going in a north-westerly direction, reaching about (150 cm (60 ins) at the western edge of Nagarahole. The landscape is generally one of gentle slopes and shallow valleys at an average altitude of 700 metres (2,300 ft). A few peaks are higher, Gopalaswamy Betta 1,454 metres (4,770 ft) in Bandipur Park being the highest.

Kabini, a tributary of the mighty Cauvery, is the largest river draining this tract. Other important rivers are the Moyar and Mulehole (both in Bandipur), the Lakshmana Teertha and Nagarahole – the last name meaning "Cobra River". An irrigation dam was built across the Kabini in 1974, creating the picturesque lake that separates the two parks.

Two basic types of tropical, mixed deciduous forests clothe the region. The moist deciduous type, usually occurring in localities getting a rainfall higher than 120 cm (48 ins), is found in the northern and western parts of Nagarahole Park as well as on the western fringes of Bandipur. The dry deciduous type covers the southeastern part of Nagarahole and most of Bandipur. Interestingly, unlike the temperate-zone forests, these tropical deciduous forests are leafless in summer rather than in winter. The period of leaf fall, essentially an ecological adaptation to cope with water stress, is relatively shorter in the moist type when compared to the dry.

The most deciduous forests are tall and dense. The tree canopy is usually two-storied. The upper canopy, about 30 metres (98 ft) tall, is dominated by valuable timber trees such as mathi *(Terminalia tomentosa)*, nandi *(Lagerstroemia lanceolata)*, honne *(Pterocarpus marsupium)* and tadasalu *(Grewia tilaefolia)*. These jungles are reputed as the home of the two most expensive timbers – dark, shiny rosewood *(Dalbergia latifolia)* and the rich, grainy teak *(Tectona grandis)*. The lower forest canopy has the prolific fruit yielders – nelli *(Phyllanthus emblica)*, kooli *(Gonclina arborea)*, kadu tega *(Dillenia pentagyna)* and the Randia S – all of which attract a host of animals and birds. Bende *(Kydia calycina)*, whose bark is a great favourite with elephants, is ubiquitous.

Lower down, the shrub layer is usually very dense and varied in composition. However, in recent decades runaway exotic shrubs like lantana and eupatorium have established dominance, aggressively invading openings created by logging. In the moist deciduous forests grass growth is not very profuse where the trees and shrubs are dense. But in cleared openings a variety of grasses grow.

A unique feature of these moist deciduous forests, particularly in Nagarahole, are the open grassy swamps locally called hadlus. Here the soil is clayey, perenni-

ally moist, and supports a luxuriant growth of green grass all the year round. These are ideal spots to watch large concentrations of ungulates, particularly gaur.

The dry deciduous forest type is strikingly different. The canopy is lower, trees are more widely spaced and their trunks are usually stunted and crooked. Many species of the moist type are present but their relative dominance varies. Dindalu *(Anogeissus latifolia)* is usually the commonest tree. Kakke *(Cassia fistula)*, "flame of the forest" *(Butea monosperma)* and bamboo *(Dendrocalamus strictus)* are all common. The second canopy is barely discernible. There are open grassland patches and the entire habitat has a woodland savannah-like appearance. In summer, forage and water scarcity pose serious problems to the herbivores.

An even more harsh environment is found around the Moyar Gorge at the easternmost edge of Bandipur. In this region of lowest rainfall, dry deciduous forest gives way to an even poorer, stunted scrub

type. The soil is rocky and barren and the vegetation dominated by thorny plants.

Elephants and others

The Nagarahole-Bandipur forests are perhaps one of the best remaining habitats of the Asian elephant *(Elephas maximus)* in the world. Over a thousand of these mighty beasts are estimated to range over this tract. A striking ecological feature of these elephant populations is their seasonal migration. In the wet season when water and forage are plentiful everywhere, the elephants are evenly distributed. This is the best time to see huge herds of them in the open forests of Bandipur. As the cool season ends and summer sets in, water and forage availability becomes restricted. Elephants congregate around specific localities like the banks of Mulehole river, Nagarahole Tourism Zone, and, above all, the banks of the Kabini.

Setting out on a jeep ride from Karapura Tourism Zone you can reach a place called Mastigudi on the banks of the Kabini around sunset to witness a scene reminiscent of Africa rather than Asia. A breathtaking panoramic sweep of a 1.5 km (1 mile) stretch of the river is dotted with elephants – over a hundred of them. If you are lucky you might even see a herd swimming across, the adults carefully chaperoning the "little" babies. During the 19th century, G.P. Sanderson developed the *Khedda* (stockade) method of capturing elephants at this site. Though the medieval barbarity of the *khedda* is mercifully a thing of the past in this conservation-conscious age, we get a glimpse of it when the waters of the Kabini recede and the remnants of the old stockade are revealed.

Gaur *(Bos gaurus)*, largest of the wild bovids, are another attraction in these parks. They suffered a major population crash due to rinderpest disease in 1968 and it took almost a decade for numbers to recover. At Bandipur, they are still not as common as before. Herds of 20–30 animals, or sometimes massive solitary bulls, can be seen placidly grazing as you pass by in a jeep.

Four species of deer inhabit these forests. The largest of them is the sambar

LEFT: sambar have remarkably acute hearing

Map
on page
308

(Cervus unicolour), a shy creature preferring thick cover and becoming active late in the evening. One usually tends to underestimate their abundance in any area. The usual sighting is of two or three animals, normally a mother with her young. During the wet season large temporary associations of 10–20 sambar are occasionally seen. Very large stags with fine antlers are also seen in Bandipur.

The commonest deer in both parks is the chital or axis deer *(Axis axis)*. These handsome spotted deer are so numerous around the park headquarters at Nagarahole and Bandipur that one tends to ignore them after a while. They are also the least shy species, congregating around the tourist rest houses at night, perhaps to avoid predators. Being partial to open grassy areas, chital are most often seen in the cleared "view-lines" bordering the "game roads". Human intrusions, such as opening up dense forests, clearing view-lines and creating water holes, have all obviously benefited chital, which tend to

be less numerous in the denser more "natural" forests.

Muntjac *(Muntiacus muntjak)* are small goat-sized, reddish-fawn-coloured deer with a surprisingly loud bark that carries long distances in the stillness of the night, warning everyone about predators on the prowl. So the muntjac is also known as the barking deer. This alert little sentinel of the forest prefers the edge of dense cover, venturing out only to graze or eat fallen over-ripe fruit. Usually, one gets only a fleeting glimpse of muntjac dashing for cover. But on the Nagaraja Game Road in Nagarahole muntjacs have become accustomed to tourists and can be seen at close quarters.

Chevrotain or mouse deer *(Tragulus meminna)* are a tiny, rabbit-sized, evolutionarily-early kind of deer. Though they appear to be reasonably common, going by the evidence of their tracks, they are rarely seen by tourists because of their entirely nocturnal habits.

The four-horned antelope *(Tetracerus*

LOW:
elephant
counter in
garahole.

quadricornis) is perhaps the most interesting ungulate in these parks. About the size of the muntjac, but with longer legs, it has a duller, brownish coat. The male four-horned antelope has two spiky horns in the usual place and two extra rudimentary knobs set a little forward, giving the species the unique distinction of being the only wild four-horned animal in the world. It is a thinly distributed species that prefers open, dry, hilly terrain and is uncommon everywhere. Very little is known about its ecology, but it is not found in the denser moist forest of Nagarahole. Unfortunately, some park staff who accompany the tourists do not distinguish it from the muntjac, though it is seen often on the Russel Fireline Road of the Karapura and Moyar area of Bandipur.

Wild pig *(Sus scrofa)* and blacknaped hare *(Lepus nigricollis)* are two other common species. The Indian porcupine *(Hystrix indica)* and pangolin *(Manis crassicaudata)* are two other species not commonly seen because they are noctur-nal. The former is a rodent with a catholic diet that includes the antlers that deer shed annually. The latter relies on an exclusive diet of ants and termites. Other mammals worth mentioning are the handsome red giant squirrel *(Ratufa indica)*, large brown flying squirrel *(Petaurista petaurista)*, giant fruit bat *(Pteropus giganteus)*, and the secretive slender loris *(Loris tardi-gradus)*. Except the giant squirrel, these are all nocturnal and are usually heard rather than seen.

Living up in the tree canopy are two kinds of monkeys. The Hanuman langur *(Presbytis entellus)* is a longtailed leaf-eating species, extremely common in both parks. The bonnet macaque *(Macaca radiata)* is a versatile feeder common around human settlements but rare in deep jungle.

The hunters

Among carnivores the least predatory animal is the sloth bear *(Melursus ursinus)*. It feeds mainly on termites, vegetable matter, honey and, occasionally, carrion. This

BELOW:
leopard
disturbed
on its kill.

Map
n page
308

HT:
rusty
tted cat.

short-sighted creature is sometimes preyed upon by the other large carnivores. Though bears are seen in all the areas, the best place to sight them is the Karapura Tourism Zone. If you are lucky you may see a mother sloth bear carrying her cubs piggy-back.

With such a large and diverse assemblage of prey species, the Nagarahole-Bandipur forests naturally harbour many predators. Tigers *(Panthera tigris)*, leopard *(Panthera pardus fusca)*, and the Asiatic wild dog *(Cuon alpinus)*, also called dhole, all coexist in these parks.

Though Bandipur is one among the nine originally constituted Project Tiger Reserves (with 74 tigers reported in 1995), interestingly it is Nagarahole that is the stronghold of the tiger. Protection, high concentrations of large ungulate prey and dense cover, ideal for the stalking predator, have all combined to create what is perhaps the finest tiger habitat in South India. Heavy predation on gaur, including large solitary bulls, by the tiger is a special feature of Nagarahole. Yet you must remember that even here seeing a tiger in daylight is not as easy as it is in some North Indian parks. Strict avoidance of artificial baiting and the consequent lack of acclimatization to tourism is perhaps one of the reasons why an encounter with a tiger is a chancy event in Nagarahole. Tiger sightings are even more difficult in Karapura and quite extraordinary events in Bandipur.

However, if you are interested in the leopard, Karapura is undoubtedly the place to go. The forest there supports a high density of the leopard's favourite prey – the langur monkey. Leopards can be usually seen at fairly close range during an evening jeep drive, unless you are very noisy.

The wild dog is a reddish, spaniel-sized, pack-hunting canid. Unlike tigers and leopards, which stalk their prey in dense cover, wild dogs course after their prey, which is usually chital or sambar. Because wild dogs hunt mainly during the day and prefer open areas suitable for coursing, they are seen fairly often by tourists. Bandipur is the best place to see them, followed by Nagarahole and Karapura. The striped hyena *(Hyaena hyaena)*, another large carnivore, is found very rarely in the scrub forests of eastern Bandipur. Reported to be more a scavenger than a hunter, it is generally not seen by tourists.

A host of smaller carnivores is also present. The diminutive jackal *(Canis aureus)* is the only other canid, apart from the dhole. There are three species of lesser cats: the jungle cat *(Felis chaus)*; the leopard cat *(Felis bengalensis)*; and the rare rusty spotted cat *(Felis rubiginosa)*, all being nocturnal. There are two species of civets – the perfume-yielding small Indian civet *(Viverricula indica)* and the arboreal palm civet *(Paradoxurus hermaphroditus)* – which are also nocturnal, and four species of mongooses: the common *(Herpestes edwardsi)*; the stripe-necked *(Herpestes vitticollis)*; the brown *(Herpestes fuscus)*; and the ruddy *(Herpestes smithii)*. All the mongooses are found in the tract but identifying them in the field takes some practice. The common otter *(Lutra lutra)* is the only mustalid recorded from the rivers of these forests. Groups of otters can sometimes be seen in the Kabini reservoir.

Birds

The Nagarahole-Bandipur region is rich territory for bird watchers. An incomplete checklist of birds exceeds 200 entries. The backwaters of the Kabini sustain huge gatherings of cormorants, teal, ducks, herons and waders. The abundance of fish there, including the large masheer *(Tor tor)*, attracts a number of ospreys *(Pandion haliaetus)* and grey-headed fishing eagles *(Icthyophaga ichthyaetus)*. Among other birds of prey, the crested hawk eagle *(Spizaetus cirrhatus)*, serpent eagle *(Spilornis cheela)* and honey buzzard *(Pernis ptilorhyneus)* are all common. The shaheen falcon *(Falco peregrinus)*, hobby *(Falco subbuteo)* and the spectacular king vulture *(Sarcogyps calvus)* are some rarer birds of prey seen in the area.

Among pheasant species, peafowl *(Pavo cristatus)*, grey jungle fowl *(Gallus sonneratti)* and the quarrelsome red spurfowl *(Galloperdix spadicea)* are usually seen in the forest, while the grey francolin *(Farancolinus pondicerianus)*

prefers the scrub on the fringes.

The other colourful or uncommon birds seen in these forests are Malabar trogon *(Harpactes faciatus)*, blue-bearded bee eater *(Nyctyornis athertoni)*, Malabar pied hornbill *(Anthracoceros coronatus)*, great black woodpecker *(Dryocopus javensis)*, Alexandrine parakeet *(Psittacula eupatria)*, lesser coucal *(Centropus toulou)*, Indian pitta *(Pitta brachyura)*, scarlet minivet *(Pricrocotus flammeus)*, fairy blue bird *(Irene pullea)*, scimitar babbler *(Promatorhinus horsfieldii)*, paradise flycatcher *(Tersiphone paradisi)*, Malabar whistling thrush *(Myiophonous horsfieldii)*, green imperial pigeon *(Ducula aenea)* and yellow-legged green pigeon *(Treron phoenicoptera)*. The racket tailed drongo *(Dicrurus paradiseus)* and hill myna *(Gracula religiosa)* are the noisy birds of the day while the owls and nightjars are heard at night.

Unfortunately, the tourist cannot wander around on foot in the forests to watch birds. Considering the dangers of encounters with elephants, the park authorities have wisely forbidden such explorations. So the bird-watching is generally confined to the vicinity of rest houses and to the jungle safaris on vehicles. An early morning coracle ride from Karapura provides absolutely fantastic opportunities for bird-watching.

LEFT: Mudumalai in the dry months.

Reptiles

Coracle rides on the Kabini may occasionally also yield sightings of marsh crocodile *(Crocodilus palustrus)*. The other large reptile, the monitor lizard *(Varanus bengalensis)* is sometimes seen in the forests. Several species of snakes including rock python *(Python molurus)*, cobra *(Naja naja)*, rat snake *(Ptyas mucosus)*, wolf snake *(Lycodon aulicus)*, vine snake *(Anaetulla nastus)*, common krait *(Bungarus caeruleus)*, Russel's viper *(Vipera russelli)*, green keelback *(Macrophisthadon plumbicolor)* and bamboo pit viper *(Trimeresurus gramineus)* are also found.

The reptilean and amphibian fauna of the region also include a variety of turtles and frogs. To complete the picture there is a tremendous abundance and

Map
n page
308

diversity of insect life, including many colourful butterfly species.

Getting the most out of your trip

Of the three choices there are available to you to sample the splendours of the wildlife of the region (Bandipur, Karapura and Nagarahole), it is preferable to choose one or two if you have only limited time at your disposal – indeed this may be chosen for you by the current access status of the different parks. Two to three days are needed to derive full benefit from a visit to any one of the three.

If your visit coincides with the peak of the monsoon, Bandipur is the best choice because of its better accessibility and wildlife viewing possibilities. In June and July Nagarahole and, to a lesser extent, Karapura become rain-soaked and the roads often become so muddy that you may find yourself confined to your rest house. The forests are lush and green in the wet season.

The skies are bright blue and the weather sunny and cool between October and January. But the animals are widely dispersed and, because of the dense undergrowth, are harder to view, particularly in Nagarahole and Karapura. During the dry season, animal sightings are excellent in Nagarahole and Karapura, but generally poor in Bandipur. However, the forests are leafless and bone dry in this season.

It is important to plan your trip well in advance because accommodation is very limited in these parks and at least a month's advance reservation is advisable. It is better to avoid weekend visits to Bandipur or Nagarahole because the heavy influx of tourists will detract from the quality of the experience for the keen wildlife observer. Accommodation is hardest to get in Nagarahole, followed by Bandipur and Karapura in that order. The first two cater for the needs of a large number of domestic tourists and are priced accordingly.

On the other hand, Karapura, though more expensive, is fully geared to meet the

_OW:_ tiger,
rtled by
mera.

needs of a more exclusive clientele. The Kabini River Lodge *(see page 339)* there, with its vast wooded compound, splendid lakeside scenery and gracious old-world air is well organized and uncrowded when compared to the rest houses in Nagarahole or Bandipur. Reservations are also easier to make because of its connections with the network of private travel operators. In Bandipur and Nagarahole reasonably priced Indian food is available at a couple of hours' notice. At Katapura there is usually an excellent Indian or Western menu to choose from. There is also a well-stocked bar, unlike the other two places where you will have to carry your own alcohol. The quality of rooms and service is also far superior at the Kabini Lodge. If you have booked your accommodation at Nagarahole, you risk the occassional last-minute cancellation because of visiting VIPs.

Bandipur is about 80 km (50 miles) from Mysore city (recently renamed *Mysuru*) and is on the excellent highway that goes to Ooty. It is well connected by buses to both

places. There are only one or two buses a day that run between Mysore and Nagarahole, covering the distance in about 3 hours. Karapura is the most difficult to reach on such public transport. Though a few buses running between Mysore and Manandawadi in Kerala pass through it after a painful 3 to 4-hour journey from Mysore, a walk of 1.5 km (1 mile) to the Kabini Lodge awaits you. For a visitor short on time a 2-hour taxi ride from Mysore is the most convenient way to reach any one of these three places. Even though Bandipur and Karapura can be reached at any time of the day, you will have to enter Nagarahole before six in the evening because the route is closed to all traffic at night. In any case, it is better to reach there before evening to avoid encountering an elephant roadblock.

In all three places, tourists are taken into the forest to see wildlife in jeeps or vans between 6 and 9am and between 4 and 6pm. These trips are on specially laid-out dirt roads called "game roads", which usually pass close to grazing areas, salt licks and water holes. The undergrowth is cleared to a distance of about 30 metres (32 yards) on either side to improve visibility and to attract herbivores to the sprouting grass. Usually an excellent view of most common species can be had at a range of 14–18 metres (15–20 yards) particularly if total silence is observed by all the passengers in the vehicle. The experienced drivers of these vehicles generally keep at a safe distance from elephants. A park guard accompanies the visitors and is reasonably good at spotting large animals. As a rule he is quite useless at identifying birds and smaller mammals. The trained naturalists of the Kabini Lodge who accompany tourists in Karapura are far better in this respect. You are strictly prohibited from getting down from the vehicle. The jungle ride usually lasts about an hour and a half and payment is on the basis of distance travelled.

Kabini Lodge offers facilities of coracle rides on the river. (A coracle is a round country boat made of bamboo and buffalo hide.) Special permission from the park authorities is needed for the use of watchtowers in the forests.

LEFT: crested serpent eagle

Map
on page
308

Those who are keen on photography should carry at least a 200mm telephoto lens. Because of the low light levels under the forest canopy, a big aperture setting and fast film (200–400 ASA) will give you more photographic success.

Special attractions

In Bandipur, a spot called Rolling Rocks, where you get a superb panoramic view of the Moyar Gorge, is well worth a visit. An hour's drive in your own transport during the non-wildlife viewing hours will take you to Gopalaswamy Betta, from where a wonderful vista of the entire region stretches before you. There is also an interesting temple on the hill.

You can profitably combine your trip to Bandipur-Nagarahole forests with visits to the Ranganathittu Bird Sanctuary and other interesting tourist spots near Mysore city. About 13 km (8 miles) from Mysore is the battle-scarred town of Shrirangapattanam, once Tipu Sultan's capital.

Wayanad

The large area originally known as Wayanad on the northeastern slopes of the Nilgiri mountains now holds three parks in three states: the Wayanad sanctuary in Kerala to the west; Bandipur Tiger Reserve in Karnataka to the north; and Mudumalai in Tamil Nadu to the South.

An integral part of the Nilgiri Biosphere Reserve, Wayanad Wildlife Sanctuary is contiguous to the protected areas of Nagarhole and Bandipur national parks. The vegetation chiefly consists of lush moist deciduous forests with a few patches of semi evergreen forests. The sanctuary has excellent covers of teak forests and marshes dominated by thick bamboo groves and other tall grasses. Established in 1973, the sanctuary is also a Project Elephant site and has a rich population of these wonderful pachyderms. The sanctuary shelters a wide variety of wildlife which includes leopard, tiger, guar (Indian bison), giant squirrel, jungle cat, civet cat, langur, wild dog, and deer.

LOW: a glossy gaur.

Mudumalai has the same meaning – "the ancient hill range" – in each of the languages of these three states. The Moyar river flows north through the park and then turns east to form the northern boundary of Mudumalai National Park, separating it from Bandipur. The park is split by the Mysore-Ootacamund highway running north–south and following the left bank of the Moyar river. Despite being only 300 sq km (116 sq miles) in area, Mudumalai has a great variety of attractive habitats.

As with the parks at Nagarahole and Bundipur, Mudumalai is periodically closed due to the activities of smugglers, dacoits and poachers. Check with the park authorities before you travel.

Birdlife

The birdlife is rich and extensive. The variety includes the beautiful Malabar trogon, the Malabar grey hornbill and the Malabar great black woodpecker, with its magnificent crimson crest contrasted by its black body. The leading avian predator

in the drier and more open forest areas of Mudumalai, where it is fairly common, is undoubtedly the crested hawk-eagle. The crested serpent eagle is also found. Although rarely seen, many owls can be found in the different forest types. The common scops owl and the little scops owl are more often heard, while the tiny-eared owl uses its brown marking to merge with the trees. During the summer, many of the resident song birds, such as barbets, mynas, parakeets and cuckoos, fill the forest with their calls.

Elephants, predators and prey

While the Moyar river forms a political and administrative division, the herds of elephant, gaur and other animals move freely between Bandipur, Mudumalai and the neighbouring forests. The great feline predators are only rarely seen, although the tiger is present throughout the sanctuary. Leopards are most often seen, in the Kargudi area. The other important predator in the area is the wild dog or dhole *(Cuon alpinus)*, which hunt in packs.

In 1968 an epidemic of rinderpest reduced the great herds of gaur to a few scattered groups in the outlying forest. As in Bandipur, these small groups are now returning to their old grazing haunts. Although the large herds of over 80 that used to be found at Theppakkadu are regrettably no longer seen, smaller composite herds are regrouping, with two or more master bulls leading their respective groups.

The elephant population, seen in various herds throughout Mudumalai, is made up of animals migrating through the area on a seasonal basis looking for fresh fodder. Many of the old migratory trails along the Western Ghats are now cultivated hillsides and valleys. Those routes through Nagarahole, Bandipur and Mudumalai reserves continue south and west into the remnants of the great forest areas of Kerala.

The two most common species in the sanctuary are the chital or spotted deer and the sambar. Both have definite local variations. The chital are usually seen in small groups throughout the sanctuary except in

LEFT: black giant squirre

Map
n page
308

Benne to the southwest. In the southeast, however, near the well-watered open grasslands of the Masinagudi area, larger herds are found. At Viewpoint, near Masinagudi, herds of over a hundred are often seen.

Sambar are found throughout the park, but except for those in the Avarahalla–Manradiar area, they are quite small. In the Avarahalla area, however, the stags have a very distinct local identity, being much darker than usual but with smaller antlers. Another deer seen here is the solitary barking deer, or muntjac, which lives in the same forest habitat as the chital. An unusual sight, but more often seen here than elsewhere in India, is the tiny mouse deer or Indian chevrotain *(Tragulus meminna)*, usually camouflaged with the light-cream mottled pattern on its brown coat.

Of the other mammals, the wild boar is the one most often seen, especially along the streams, on the banks of pools or crossing a culvert. In the clearings near Theppakkadu in the north and at Kargudi at the centre, both bonnet macaques and common langurs are found. Occasional sightings of the giant squirrel are made, although they are more often only heard. Flying squirrels, being nocturnal, are rarely observed.

The only reptile regularly seen is the monitor lizard, especially along the road to Mayar powerhouse in the northeast corner. As in most of the region, the best period for wildlife-viewing is the summer months (March–June).

Silent Valley

North from Palakkad on the Coimbatore–Kannur National Highway, you finally reach **Attappadi**, a centre of the Irular, Mudugar and Kurumbar peoples. Another 12 km (7 miles) is **Silent Valley**, one of the few tropical evergreen rainforests left in the country. Elephant, tiger, wild dog, flying squirrel and lion-tail macaque are found in this valley, in addition to a wealth of plant life. Entry into the area is strictly regulated by permits issued by the Forest Department. ❑

ow:
nt Valley.

Map
n page
322

PERIYAR

*Leave the jeep behind and enjoy the calm beauty of Periyar Tiger Reserve
- you can trek in the forest but a boat on the lake gives
unbeatable views of the elephants*

The Periyar Wildlife Sanctuary, now one of the 27 Project Tiger Reserves in India, is an interesting example of how development need not be incompatible with the requirements of wildlife. Over a hundred years ago, a British engineer, Colonel J. Pennycuick, conceived a design to dam the Periyar river, which runs through some of the most spectacular forests of the Western Ghats in Kerala state in South India. The dam was constructed in 1895 and the adjoining forests protected by the Maharaja of Travancore. Today the 777-sq-km (300-sq-mile) sanctuary is a Tiger Reserve. The actual reservoir is 55 sq km (21 sq miles) and it meant that the best valley forests were submerged and lost. The black stumps still to be seen jutting out of the water, which are an eerie and wonderful sight in the early winter mornings as the mist rises, are the only remains of the richly vegetated valley. But the dam also made some compensations. Periyar has become one of the most picturesque wildlife sanctuaries in the world and is enjoyed by over 300,000 tourists every year. For the animals, the reservoir and surrounding forests provide protection and a perennial water supply.

Getting the most out of your trip

The best time to visit Periyar is between October and April, thus missing the southwest monsoon period. During March and April, when water gets low and the grass dries out, animals have to spend more time near the lake and elephants are especially dependent on the lake during this period. This is the time of year when they can often be seen bathing and swimming, both to cool off and to get from one feeding area to the next. The grass is also short during this time of year and animal visibility is thus increased.

Hotels include, Aranya Nivas and Periyar House in the tourist complex area, the Taj Garden Retreat and the Spice Garden, and the Lake Palace at Eddapaliyam *(see page 339)*. There are several rest houses in prime wildlife areas, which may be booked in advance at very reasonable prices.

Since boat travel is the only means of transport within the sanctuary (cars can go only up to the tourist centre), large areas can be covered in a short time and a three or four-day stay is satisfactory, with boat rides in the morning and evening and animal and bird watching on the lake shores in between. Sitting on the steps at Eddapaliyam, the visitor can regularly watch gaur, elephant and wild pig on the opposite bank.

FT: elephant, ewing.
GHT: Malabar ed hornbill.

However, for the more deeply interested visitor or naturalist who has the time and inclination, a longer stay is certainly worthwhile: Periyar is a truly spectacular sanctuary. Although walking into the sanctuary is discouraged by the Forest Department, it is possible to go on treks with guides and there are watchtowers overlooking pools that can be used. It must be remembered, however, that the animals feel most comfortable and allow the closest approach by boat – though do pick a boat with the smallest number of people, the larger boats are very noisy and scare the animals away.

If you express a particular interest – for example birds or primates – the Forest Department is most helpful and the guide provided for trekking, usually from the Manan people and with a vast knowledge of the natural history of the area, will be able to point out things of particular interest. Daytime as well as night-time periods can be spent on watch-towers, away from the main tourist activity. Shy, timid animals like the gaur, India's largest

bovine, prefer the seclusion of the swampy grasslands near Eddapaliyam and other areas associated with watchtowers.

With special permission and an accompanying guide, one can trek or boat to the source of the Periyar Lake – the Periyar river. This is in the core area of the park, normally not open to visits, and the rest house situated there is known as Thannikudi. From here, armed guards patrol a huge 220-sq-km (85-sq-mile) beat to guard against animal and wood poachers. The Periyar is a beautiful, clear river and it is not uncommon to see the dark shapes of metre-long mahseer, a fish made famous by hunter-writers such as Jim Corbett, gliding just beneath the surface. Here in Thannikudi the sloth bear is common; its signs are everywhere. This is also where tigers can live in peace, away from the main forest activities that are still permitted within the sanctuary.

Spending a few days in Periyar is a unique and unforgettable experience. Here is one sanctuary where you never travel

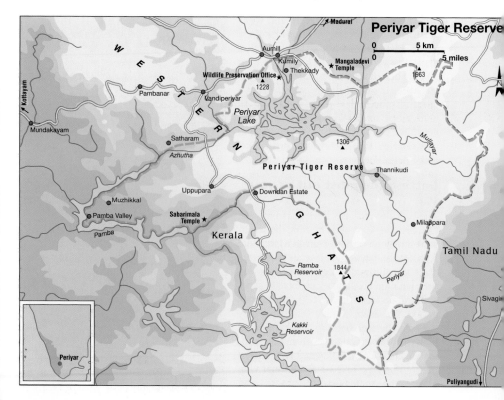

Map
on page
322

by road; no traffic noise, no dust, no bumps. Most importantly, one is not disturbing the animals' territory.

Geography, flora and climate

The only flat areas of Periyar are the marshy grasslands at the ends of the fingers of the lake. Most parts of the Sanctuary consists of grass-covered rolling hill peaks and densely forested hillsides, giving the appearance typical of the Western Ghats – forested *sholas* interspersed with grass slopes. Lower reaches of hills and valleys are covered with tropical and semi-tropical forests, with numerous seasonal and perennial streams. Dense forest provides food and shade in the hot months, while adjoining grasslands provide good browse to herbivores.

The forests of Periyar can be divided into four broad categories. The open grasslands, studded with fire-resistant vegetation, harbour many species of grasses, such as elephant grass. This is the common dining hall of all the herbivores, from the gaur and elephant to the small wild boar and barking deer. Then we have the moist deciduous forest type, dominated by trees like Terminalia and teak (*Tectona grandis*), which lose their leaves seasonally. The semi-evergreen forest occurs along wet stream areas and is often adjacent to the tropical evergreen forests. And lastly, the climax forests: the *sholas* or tropical evergreen jungle that occurs in the valleys and where one can see trees 30–40 metres (100–130 ft) high. The dense tree-canopy allows only a limited stream of sunlight through and in the moist, dark corridors, ferns, orchids and epiphytes abound. Also to be found here is the small but efficient parasite, the leech. Leeches live on blood and prey mostly on warm-blooded animals that periodically pass through their territory. However, there are obviously not enough game animals to go around and a juicy human limb is always welcome, as visitors may find to their dismay.

Elephants

There is probably no sanctuary in the world where elephant behaviour can be watched in such absolute comfort and

safety. It was here that this writer and her colleagues first appreciated the great repertoire of elephant sounds, some of which are startlingly human. The total elephant population is about 800 and one can approach to within 20 metres (20 yards) of placid groups feeding, bathing and swimming. Often, after a swim, elephants indulge in their own brand of mudslinging – trunkfuls of dust are sprayed on their backs, an activity which may decrease parasite infestation and protect them from the sun. Whatever the reason, it is a spectacular sight.

Unlike their African cousins, female Indian elephants have no tusks. In fact, not all bulls have tusks either. Tuskless males are called *maknas*. A male tusker is, of course, a magnificent animal, but it may be that the *maknas* are the lucky ones, because sustained poaching for ivory has wiped out most of the big tuskers in South Indian jungles. The high stakes involved make poachers increasingly daring and bold, and forest officials

have an almost insurmountable problem on their hands. The ivory criminals have in recent years started hanging live wires to electrocute elephants. Also, tuskers are singled out and crippled by a shot in the knee; the helpless animal is then closely approached and killed. It is equally tragic when a wounded elephant manages to get away from its killers.

Poaching and human encroachment are the biggest problems that the 150-strong Forest Department staff have to contend with. Kerala has the highest human density figures in India, and Periyar is an island surrounded by human habitation. Cattle grazing has become a serious problem. Cattle within the park disturb the wildlife, stop effective grass growth and compete with the herbivores for food. But their presence in the reserve can have much more serious consequences. In 1974–75, the dreaded rinderpest disease (or cattle plague), which fatally affects bovines and which is spread by cattle, reached epidemic proportions in South India. A thousand gaur died from it in Periyar. The Forest Department is working out a plan to ensure, through a system of ear tags, that all cattle in adjoining areas are immunized against rinderpest.

Birdlife

A typical sight in Periyar are the darters and cormorants that bask on the remnant poles of the submerged forest, and allow tourist boats to approach to within metres of them without fear. The depth of the lake excludes wading birds but offers splendid opportunities for anglers such as ospreys, kingfishers and kites. Otters, also expert fishers, are a common sight, fishing in the shallows or bounding along the shore with their wet fur gleaming in the sun.

Both the great hornbill and the grey hornbill can be easily seen in Periyar. Several fruit trees just around the boat landing area attract these hornbills, hill mynas, orioles and racket-tailed drongos. Very often, the first sign of a great hornbill is the whoosh, whoosh, whoosh of its wings

BELOW: Periya Lake, Kerala.

Map
on page
322

as the heavy bird flies overhead. Both hornbills have a somewhat hysterical laughing call, one of the loudest sounds of the forest. Above the forest office at the boat landing, a family of lesser adjutant have nested for decades in a very tall tree.

Other animals

Apart from elephants, another herbivore commonly seen is the wild pig. Sounders of 30 or 40 animals are common in Periyar. With its stiff upright mane and disgrunted expression, the pig lends a comic touch to the Periyar scene. The wild pig is an opportunistic feeder and not wholly vegetarian; at Point Calimere on the Tamil Nadu coast, they even dig up and eat the eggs of sea turtles. Sambar, barking deer and mouse deer are the representatives of the deer family in Periyar; interestingly, the spotted deer or chital is absent. An experiment was tried several years ago and a group of chital released on an island in the sanctuary, but they apparently didn't survive. Some of the high hill crests

within Periyar are inhabited by the last Nilgiri tahr in the area, but they are generally too shy and elusive to be seen.

On rocky shelves called *paarai* along the lakeshore one may see a large dark monitor lizard basking in the midday sun especially in the cooler months. Pythons are fairly regularly seen by the trekking guides and in the evergreen areas an occasional king cobra is sighted. Among the smaller reptiles, two spectacular species are the flying lizard and the flying snake. The flying lizard is hard to see because of its cryptic lichen-like colouration but gliding from one tree to another, its wings are brilliant yellow or orange. An observant naturalist can spot them on a sunny tree trunk by patiently looking for the male, who flaps a tell-tale yellow throat flap, or dewlap. The flying snake on the other hand is one of the most colourful snakes in the country, with a brilliant pattern of yellow and black, with reddish rosettes. Flying snakes don't really fly, of course, but can launch themselves and flatten

LOW: a
mouse deer.

their bodies to make an extended 'flight' to a lower branch or tree. Yet another flying creature is the flying frog, not uncommon in parts of the sanctuary especially during the rains. It 'flies', or glides, by extending its toes, which are all connected by extra-wide webbing.

Among the predators of Periyar is the wild dog, or dhole, which is fairly commonly seen along the lakeshores and adjoining forests. There are about 50 packs of these carnivores here and they hunt deer, wild pig and other game collectively and alone. Sometimes you may hear the high-pitched, eerie whistle of a wild dog on the hunt. Prey animals typically run to the lake to escape. Wild dogs are much maligned for their so-called "cruelty" and in the past were shot as vermin even within sanctuaries. In fact, wild dogs are important predators in the food chain of the jungle. As for their cruelty: every carnivore, from tigers to spiders, must kill for food.

There are several animals that can be seen around the rest houses and other habitations within the sanctuary. After dark, porcupines and wild pig scuffle around rubbish dumps and vegetable patches. There are four species of monkeys here: the rare and endangered lion-tailed macaque, the Nilgiri langur, the common langur along the eastern boundaries, and the bonnet macaque around peripheral areas of the sanctuary. The beautiful Malabar squirrel allows fairly close approach at times and one can often hear its loud, excited chatter in the trees. Another large squirrel that lives here is the flying squirrel but, being nocturnal, you will have to watch and listen for it on bright moonlit nights. It makes spectacular glides between trees, which may extend to 180–280 meters (200–300 yards). Flying squirrels make a fairly loud, plaintive cooing sound that is distinctive if you know what to listen for.

The lucky tourist may even see a tiger, which is at the apex of the food chain – and still in danger of becoming extinct. At the turn of the 20th century there were

BELOW: golde flying snake.

Map
on page
322

over 40,000 tigers in India. But sport hunters and commercial interests persecuted the animal so relentlessly that by 1972 less than 2,000 animals survived. Together with the World Wildlife Fund, the Government of India launched Project Tiger, with a million dollars raised by the WWF to save the animal and its habitat. There are now an estimated 26 to 36 tigers in Periyar, which seem to be holding their own better than tigers elsewhere, though no tiger in India is really safe from the poachers' bullets, traps and poisons.

Eco-tourism

There are a few Adivasi villages near the sanctuary. Among the Adivasi peoples in this area are the Manans and the Oralis. The latter still build tree dwellings, these days not so much as residences but as watchtowers to keep animals like wild pig, sambar and elephants from their crops. The Manans are expert fishermen and fish the lake and the clear streams that run into it for mahseer. A few Manans tra-

ditionally practice the dangerous exercise of collecting the honey of hill bees. These are large and potentially dangerous bees that build massive hives high in the branches of rainforest trees such as the silk cotton (*Bombax*). For climbing to these often 30-metre (100-ft) high honeycombs, they carve bamboo spikes, which they hammer into the tree with a wooden mallet. They only do this at night to avoid being stung, and sometimes collect 25 kg (55 lbs) of honey at a time from one tree.

The main threat to the park is from the 4 million people who enter the reserve every year, (from November to January) on pilgrimage to the Sabarimal temple. Nearly half a million tourists visit the park each year but a successful eco-tourism project is managed by the local people, with local women and ex-poachers educating visitors, and money being pumped back into the local community. There are 22 eco-development committees in the fringe area, and these are also helpful in forest protection also.   ❏

BELOW: mating damsel flies.

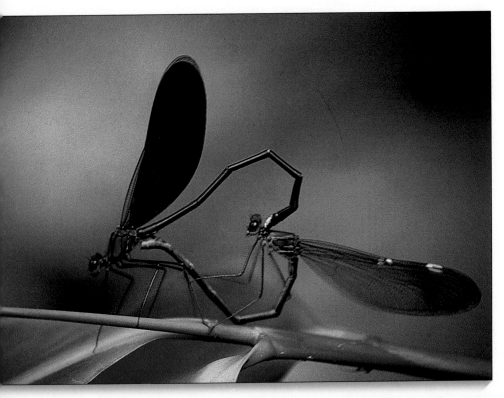

INSIGHT GUIDES

TRAVEL TIPS

Indian
WILDLIFE

TRAVEL TIPS

TRANSPORT

GETTING THERE
AND GETTING AROUND

GETTING THERE

By Air

The vast majority of visitors arrive in India by air. Mumbai and Delhi airports are the major entry points with fewer international flights from Europe using Kolkata and Chennai. Kolkata and Chennai especially have flights to and from East Asia. The national carrier is Air India (www.airindia.com), but other carriers which have regular flights between the UK (where many transatlantic passengers can change) and India are British Airways (www.ba.com), Virgin Atlantic (www.virgin-atlantic.com) and Jet Airways (www.jetairways.com).

Other international airports are: Ahmadabad, with flights to and from the UK and the USA as well as the Gulf region; Thiruvananthapuram, with flights to and from the Gulf region, the Maldives and Sri Lanka; Hyderabad, with fewer flights to and from the Gulf region; and Dabolin (Goa), with charter flights from Europe.

Agra, Varanasi, Kanpur, Patna, Kozhikode, Kochi and Bangalore are airports with limited international air access and customs and immigration facilities, and are not international airports in the real sense of the term. Agra serves charter flights from the UK. Varanasi, Kanpur and Patna have daily flights from Kathmandu in Nepal and there are connecting flights to Delhi. Kozhikode and Kochi have flights to and from the Gulf region.

Discounts are often available during the off-peak season, so it is worth making enquiries. Many long-

Cut Your Carbon

Air travel produces a huge amount of carbon dioxide and is one of the main contributors to global warming. Where possible, take the train while in the country *(see page 334)* as this produces less CO_2. Although nothing can repair the immediate damage of your flight out, it is possible to offset your "carbon load" by, for example, having trees planted as a "carbon sink". A number of organisations can do this for you and many have online "carbon calculators" which tell you how much you need to donate. In the UK travellers can try www.climatecare.org or www.carbonneutral.com, in the US log on to www.climatefriendly.com or www.sustainabletravelinternational.com

haul flights arrive between midnight and 6am, apparently to suit the night landing regulations of European and East Asian cities but, in reality, to help a full plane taking off in the thin air of an Indian summer.

Once you have bought a ticket, check with the airline to confirm your booking well in advance. **NB**: It is advisable to check in for flights to and from India as early as possible, as planes are often full and/or overbooked.

The four major airports are constantly improving and all have left-luggage facilities. Porters and licensed taxis are available. Delhi, Mumbai, Kolkata and Chennai all have duty-free shops in both the arrival and departure halls. Airport banks are open 24 hours for currency exchange.

International airport contacts

IGI **(New Delhi)**
Airport Manager, tel: 011-2569 6179
Terminal 1A, tel: 011-2569 6150
Terminal 1B, tel: 011-2567 5315
International Airport Mumbai
Airport Manager, tel: 022-2838 7046
Terminal 1A, tel: 022-2615 6400
Terminal 1B, tel: 022-2615 6500
International Airport Kolkata
Airport Manager, tel: 033-2232 0501
International Airport Chennai
Airport Manager, tel: 044-2552 9172

By Sea

A few cruise ships do call in at Cochin and Mumbai, but India is not a regular cruise destination. Some freighters offer passage to India and excellent accommodation is available. Great Eastern Shipping (www.greatship.com), Lloyd Triestino (www.lloydtriestino.it) and the Shipping Corporation of India (www.shipindia.com) have sailings to Mumbai, Kolkata and Chennai.

Overland

It is theoretically possible to take the train from the UK to India. The Eurostar takes you from London to Paris, from there you can get to Istanbul via Vienna and Sofia. A train leaves once a week from Istanbul to Tehran, from where you can make your way to the Pakistani border at Quetta (the line between Kerman and Zahedan on the Iranian side is nearing completion, thus adding the last section of track between Europe and South Asia).

Land services have now resumed between India and Pakistan. The train from Lahore in Pakistan to Delhi in India crosses the Wagah-Attari border. The Samjhota Express to Delhi via Amritsar leaves Lahore at 11am (check in 8am) on Mondays and Thursdays. There is also a direct bus from Lahore to Delhi leaving at 6am from outside Faletti's Hotel on Egerton Road Tues–Wed, Fri and Sat. The trip takes about seven hours and the fare includes all your food. The new bus between Muzaffarabad and Srinigar is for Kashmiris only.

The border with Nepal is only open for non-Indian or Nepalese nationals at Birganj/Raxhal, Bairwa and Kakarbitta/Naxalbari.

GETTING AROUND

Boats

Apart from the river ferries there are very few boat services in India. The Andaman Islands are connected to Kolkata, Chennai and Vishakapatnam by boat, as well as to each other. There is a catamaran service between Mumbai and Goa run by Samudra Link Ferries (www.sam-link.com). Kerala has a regular passenger boat system and a number of services operate from Alappuzha and Kollam (formerly Alleppey and Quilon), including the popular backwater trip between the two. There is also a boat service to and from the Lakshadweep islands from Kochi (see http://lakport.nic.in).

Buses

Almost every part of the country is connected by an extensive and well-developed bus system with the railway stations being the natural hubs for both local and regional services. Some of the more rural routes are serviced by noisy dilapidated vehicles, but an increasing number of deluxe and air-conditioned expresses ply the trunk routes.

Many of the trunk routes are now operated by video coaches – if you have never been to an Indian cinema, a night bus journey, for better or (usually) worse, is a highly amplified introduction to the popular variety of Hindi or regional film.

There are many parts of the country where the bus service is the only means of public transport – the Himalayas in particular – and at times may be more convenient (for instance, between Agra and Jaipur).

On many routes, even local ones, reservations can be made. Most large baggage is carried on the bus roof, so all bags should be locked

and you might want to check on it at intermediate stops.

Almost all cities have a bus service; Mumbai's bus service is excellent, the ones in Chennai and Kolkata are not too bad, and the service in Delhi is steadily improving. It is advisable not to use city bus services during rush hour when they become unbearably crowded.

In most cities, however, it is generally preferable to use taxis or three-wheeled "auto-rickshaws".

Regional road transport websites

Most states have a road transport executive responsible for regional bus services. A few have websites (given below) with general information and timetables for useful routes.
Andhra Pradesh
www.apsrtc.net
Assam
www.assamtransport.com
Gujarat
www.gujaratsrtc.com
Himachal Pradesh
www.himachal.nic.in/hrtc
Karnataka
www.ksrtc.org
Kerala
www.keralartc.com
Rajasthan
www.rsrtc.org
Tamil Nadu
www.tn.gov.in/transport/stu.htm
Uttar Pradesh
www.upsrtc.com

Cars and Taxis

Chauffeur-driven cars, costing about Rs1,500–2,000 a day, can be arranged through tourist offices, hotels or travel agents.

Taxis are both air-conditioned and non-air-conditioned (cheaper and sometimes more comfortable). Charges vary, ranging from about Rs350 for eight hours and 80 km (50 miles) to Rs500 for an air-conditioned car. For out-of-town travel, there is a per km charge, usually around Rs3–4 per km in the plains (in the hills this rate is often Rs6 per km), with an overnight charge of around Rs100. Package tours, sold by travel agencies and hotels, include assistance, guides and hotel accommodation, in addition to taxi charges.

The local yellow-top black taxis are metered, but with constant hikes in fuel prices, charges may often be higher than indicated on the meter. If so, this will be prominently stated in the taxi and the driver will have a card showing

the excess over the meter reading that can be legitimately charged.

When taking a taxi or bus into town from the airport, it is advisable to change money in the arrival hall. In Delhi, Mumbai and Bangalore, a system of prepayment for taxis into the city is operated by the traffic police. This saves considerable anguish when the occasional unscrupulous driver takes a long route or tries to overcharge. Elsewhere, enquire at the information desk for the going rate for a journey to your destination before getting into the taxi; and make sure the meter is "down" before you embark. It is alright to share a taxi even if the destination may not be the same (although in the same area). In some cities, for example Mumbai, taxis have fare charts which, when applied to the amount on the meter, give the correct fare. There is often a night surcharge of 10 percent between 11pm and 6am and a rate of Rs1 to Rs2 per piece of baggage.

The fare for three-wheelers is about half that of taxis. Do not forget to ensure that the meter in the three-wheeler is flagged down to the minimum fare.

Driving in India

The best advice to anyone who is thinking about driving in India is, **don't**. Roads can be very congested and dangerous and there are many unwritten rules. It is much easier, safer and often cheaper to hire a car and driver.

However, if you do have to drive you will need your domestic licence, liability insurance, an international driver's permit and your vehicle's registration papers. Information regarding road conditions can be obtained from national and state automobile associations which periodically issue regional motoring maps, general information regarding roads and detailed route charts.

Contact: the **Automobile Association of Upper India** (AAUI), C-8 institutional Area, South of IIT, New Delhi - 110016; tel: 11-26965397; www.aaui.org; the **Western India Automobile Association** Lalji Narainji Memorial Building, 76 Vir Nariman Road, Mumbai 400 020, tel: 22-2041085; www.wiaaindia.com; the **Automobile Association of Eastern India** 13 Promothosh Barna Sarani, Kolkata 700 019, tel: 2475 5131; **Automobile Association of Southern India** 187 Anna Salai, Chennai 600 006, tel: 44-2852 1162; www.aasindia.in; and the **UP Automobile Association** 32-A Mahatma Gandhi Marg, Allahabad, tel: 260 0332.

Railways

Rail travel is safe, comfortable and by far the best way to get around the country. Trains are slow compared to those in the West, so if you are in a hurry, stick to the expresses. Fares are generally low. Indian Railways has a number of different classes, of varying degrees of comfort. In descending order of price, they are:
● First class AC, very comfortable with lockable cabins of four berths each.
● AC II tier, partitions arranged in groups of 6 berths with curtains that pull across to provide privacy.
● AC III tier, partitions with groups of 9 berths, the middle berths fold down for sleeping.
● AC chair car.
● First class (unfortunately now rare), non-AC but with ceiling fans. Has lockable cabins of four berths each. There is one cabin of two berths halfway down each carriage.
● Sleeper class, partitions of 9 berths with ceiling fans.
● Second class, unreserved with no berths and hard seats.

In the summer months it is best to go AC. When the weather is cooler then first class can be an excellent option as it is possible to see the passing countryside without having to stare through the darkened windows of AC. All carriages have both Western and Indian-style toilets. If you are up to squatting on a moving train always use the Indian toilet as they are invariably cleaner and better maintained.

Bedding consisting of two sheets; a pillow and a blanket is provided in first class AC, AC II tier and III tier, and is also available from the attendant for Rs 20 in first class. In theory, if they want bedding, first-class passengers should contact the station manager before travelling, but extra bedding is often available. If travelling sleeper class then it is a good idea to take a sheet sleeping bag (any Indian tailor will run one up for you).

Food can usually be ordered through the coach attendant. On Shatabdi and Rajdhani trains the fare covers food, drinks and snacks as well.

Retiring rooms (for short-term occupation only) are available at over 1,100 stations on a first-come first-served basis, but these are usually heavily booked. All first-class waiting rooms have couches for passengers using their own bedding. At both New Delhi and Howrah stations, a Rail Yatri Niwas has been built for transit passengers. Rooms can be booked in advance.

Cloakrooms are available at most stations where travellers can leave their luggage, but bags must be locked, and don't lose the reclaim ticket. Check opening times of the cloakroom for collection.

Very useful pre-paid taxi and/or auto-rickshaw services are available at most large stations.

Remember to check which station your train departs from and do allow at least half an hour to find your seat/berth. Lists of passengers with the compartment and seat/berth numbers allotted to them are displayed on platforms and on each carriage an hour before departure. The station superintendent and the conductor attached to the train are usually available for assistance.

Reservations and Passes

Reservations are required for all classes other than second class and reserving well in advance is strongly recommended. Many stations now have very efficient computerised booking counters from where you can book any ticket for any route. Reservations may be made up to 60 days in advance.

In the larger cities, the major stations have tourist sections with English-speaking staff to reduce the queues for foreigners and non-resident Indians buying tickets; payment is in pounds sterling or US dollars (travellers' cheques or cash).

If reservations are not available then certain trains have a tourist quota that may be available. Other options are to take a waitlisted ticket or the more assured reservation against cancellation (RAC); the booking clerk should be able to advise you on how likely you are to get a reservation. Tatkal trains (marked with a "T" in timetables) have a certain number of reservations held back, which become available one day in advance for an extra charge. It is also possible to make bookings from abroad through Indian Railways representatives *(see below)*. They will accept bookings up to six months ahead, with a minimum of one month for first class, three months for second.

To buy your ticket you must first fill in a **Reservation Requisition Form**, which will be available from one of the windows in the booking office. The form is in the local language on one side and English on the reverse. In addition to the obvious information, such as where you wish to leave from and go to and when, to fill in the form you also need to know:
● The train number and name. You can get this from a timetable, or, if the train departs from the station you are booking from, it is usually displayed on a board in the booking office.
● The class you wish to travel and whether you require a berth (for overnight journeys, or any journey between 9pm and 6am), or only a seat.
● Whether you require a lower, middle or upper berth. An upper berth is a good idea as it can be used throughout the day, whereas the other two may only be used for sleeping 9pm–6am.

Foreign travellers should also fill in their passport numbers in the column that asks for your Concession Travel Authority Number, which is needed if the ticket is issued under the foreign tourist quota.

Cancellations can be made with varying degrees of penalty depending on the class and how close the cancellation is made to the time of departure (you will need to fill in the same form as for a reservation.

The **Indrail Pass**, gives unlimited travel on the entire rail network for periods of between 12 hours and 90 days and can be good value if you plan on travelling nearly every day They are available to foreign nationals and Indians resident abroad and are paid for in foreign currency. They can cut down on time getting reservations, you pay no reservation fees and no sleeper berth surcharge for night journeys for any class of accommodation.

In the UK the pass can be obtained through the very efficient and highly recommended:
S.D. Enterprises Ltd
103 Wembley Park Drive, Wembley, Middlesex HA9 8HG
Tel: (020) 8903 3411
Fax: (020) 8903 0392
www.indiarail.co.uk
They can also book single-journey tickets in advance for you. The Indrail Pass can be bought in India at the tourist counters at Railway Central Reservations Offices in Chennai, Kolkata, Mumbai Central, Mumbai CST and New Delhi.

Timetables

Tourist offices at railway reservation centres are helpful in planning itineraries and obtaining reservations (International Tourist Bureau, New Delhi railway station, tel: (011) 2334 6804). There are tourist offices at New Delhi (tel: 2340 5156, 2336

1732), Mumbai Churchgate, Kolkata Fairlie Place, Chennai Central, and some other popular tourist destinations. Railway timetables available at Indian Tourist Offices abroad also contain much useful information.

Each regional railway prints its full timetable in Hindi, English and the regional language. There is also the monthly *Indian Bradshaw*, which lists all services across the country, or the concise but comprehensive *Trains At A Glance*, probably the most useful timetable for foreign tourists. These publications are also available at travel agents and information counters at all major airports and railway stations but they are updated and reprinted regularly so are periodically unavailable. In addition, a local travel magazine, Travel Links, publishes air and rail timetables. All this information (and more, including fares and details of special trains and passes) can be found on the Indian Railways websites *(see below)*.

Indian Railways Websites

For general information:
www.indianrailways.gov.in
For timetables, fares and the current status of trains and your ticket:
www.indianrail.gov.in
To buy tickets online (you will need to register, and delivery or collection of tickets is only available in certain cities):
www.irctc.co.in
For a wide range of links and useful information go to the "rail gateway" website at:
www.raildwar.com
If you really fall in love with the railways, and become a bit obsessive, try the excellent Indian Railways Fan Club site:
www.irfca.org
A great deal of historical information is on the National Rail Museum site:
www.railmuseum.org

Regions

Indian Railways is divided into regional zones. These are given below along with their individual websites, which contain routes and timetable information:
Central Railway
www.centralrailwayonline.com
East Central Railway
www.ecr.indianrail.gov.in
East Coast Railway
www.eastcoastrailway.gov.in
Eastern Railway
www.easternrailway.gov.in
Konkan Railway
www.konkanrailway.com
North Central Railway
http://10.102.2.21
Northeastern Railway
www.ner.railnet.gov.in
Northeast Frontier Railway
www.nfr.railnet.gov.in
Northern Railway
www.uttarrailway.com
Northwestern Railway
www.northwwesternrailway.com
South Central Railway
www.scrailway.gov.in
South East Central Railway
www.secr.gov.in
Southeastern Railway
www.serailway.com
Southern Railway
www.srailway.com
Southwestern Railway
www.southwesternrailway.org
West Central Railway
www.westcentralrailway.com
Western Railway
www.westernrailwayindia.com

Special Trains

India has four, very expensive, luxury trains that provide tours through Rajasthan, Gujarat and the Deccan, stopping off at a couple of wildlife sanctuaries, such as Ranthambore, Sariska and Gir, en-route. Booking information, prices and itineraries can be found on their websites:
The Palace on Wheels
www.palaceonwheels.net

The Royal Orient
www.indianrail.gov.in/royal_orient.html
Deccan Odyssey
www.thedeccanodyssey.com
Fairy Queen
www.railmuseum.org

Hill Trains

India also has a number of charming "toy trains" which run from the plains up to certain hill stations. These include the narrow-gauge tracks up to Udhagamandalam (Ooty) in the Nilgiris, the line from New Jalpaiguri to Darjeeling, and the track between Neral and Matheran near Mumbai, as well as the broad-gauge line between Kalka and Simla (this service is known as the Himalayan Queen).

Rickshaws

The best, and most Indian, way of getting around town is by rickshaw. These come in two types: a cycle rickshaw (a tricycle with a seat for two people on the back), and a motorised three-wheeler known as an "auto" (all in Delhi and some in other cities have been converted to run on CNG, compressed natural gas to counter pollution). Autos are, like taxis, supposed to use a meter. You should insist on this and get out if they refuse. Meter rates are subject to periodic changes, and extras for late-night journeys etc., which the driver should show you on a card. In popular tourist spots, during rush hour and bad weather, you may find it impossible to persuade the drivers to use the meter. A tactic that might work is to suggest "meter plus five" (the cost plus Rs5). If not, you'll have to negotiate the fare. After a short while in the country you will get a feel for what is acceptable and, given that as a relatively well-off foreign tourist you are expected quite reasonably to pay a little more, what is not. Due to high oil prices fares have recently gone up.

In many it is common for auto drivers to suggest that, for a fixed amount, they take you around the sites for a whole day. This can be convenient and, if you bargain well, good value. Make sure that both of you understand what the price is and where you want to go (i.e. not via endless shops) before you set off.

Cycle rickshaws are more convenient in some places, like the very congested streets of Old Delhi. With these you should negotiate the fare before you set off.

Note: rickshaws are not allowed into central Mumbai and the only options are to use either the well-developed bus service, or the reasonably-priced taxis.

Indrail Pass Fares in US Dollars

	First Class AC		Other AC and 1st Class (Non-AC)		Sleeper Class 2nd Class (Non-AC)	
	Adult	Child	Adult	Child	Adult	Child
Half-day	57	29	26	13	11	6
1 Day	95	47	43	22	19	10
2 Days	160	80	70	35	30	15
4 Days	220	110	110	55	50	25
7 Days	270	135	135	68	80	40
15 Days	370	185	185	95	90	45
21 Days	396	198	198	99	100	50
30 Days	495	248	248	126	125	65
60 Days	800	400	400	200	185	95
90 Days	1060	530	530	265	235	120

A CCOMMODATION

HOTELS AND LODGES

BANDHAVGARH

Bandhavgarh Jungle Lodge
Umaria
Tel: 07627-265 317
www.welcomheritagehotels.com
Modern thatched cottages
set in pleasant grounds
with a central dining area.
Very close to the park
entrance. Nature tours
and excursions can be
arranged through the
lodge. £££££
Churhat Kothi
Tel: 07627-265 358
www.churhatkothi.com
This highly recommended
resort was founded by the
naturalist K.K. Singh and is
one of the finest jungle
lodges in India. It's
comfortable and stylish,
and the very knowlegable
staff can arrange excellent
trips into the nearby park.
Credit cards not accepted.
£££££
Tiger Trails Resort
Tala
Tel: 07655-265 325
www.indianadventures.com
Simple but comfortable
cottage accommodation
close to the park and
overlooking a small lake.
Quiet and well run. £££
White Tiger Forest Lodge
Tel: 07627-265 308
www.mptourism.com
Slightly run down but good
value accommodation from
the Madhya Pradesh state
tourism authority. There is
also a reasonable
restaurant and bar. ££

BANDIPUR

Bandipur Safari Lodge
Melkamanahalli
Tel: 08229-633 001
www.junglelodges.com
Very well run basic
accommodation in
modern cottages (no
air conditioning) close
to the park entrance.
Knowledgeable staff
and good jeep safaris for
watching the wildlife.
Recommended. £££
Country Club Bush Betta
Mangala
Tel: 08229-236 090
www.countryclubindia.net
Recently taken over and
renovated this resort now
has over 60 rooms and a
large swimming pool. A
little way from the park
entrance but good for
families. £££–££££
**Forest Department
Cottages**
For reservations contact:
The Field Director, Project Tiger,
Aranya Bhavan, Ashokapuram,
Mysore 570 008
Tel/fax: 0821-248 0901
www.karnatakatourism.org
Basic accommodation,
some of it in very cheap
dormitories, in good
locations. £–££
Hotel Mayura Prakruti
Melkamanahalli
Tel: 08229-233 001
www.karnatakatourism.org
Simple budget
accommodation but one of
the best options near the
park. Good value cottages

and a decent outdoor
restaurant. £
Tusker Trails
Mangala
Tel: 0821-263 6055
Basic (no air conditioning)
but clean and comfortable
accommodation in a nice
forested setting. Good
opportunities for wildlife
spotting and safaris are
conducted twice daily.
££££

BARDIA

Nepal Wildlife Resort
Reservations: PO Box 1044,
Thamel, Kathmandu
Tel: 01-425 8492
The resort offers cottage-
style accommodation, a
viewing tower and a wide
range of activities,
including a Dolphin Tour
and cultural shows. £££££
Rhino Lodge Bardia
Thakurdwara
Reservations: P.O.Box 5026,
Thamel, Kathmandu
Tel: 01-470 1200
www.nepal-safari.com
A collection of simple
cottages. £££–££££
Tiger Tops Karnali Lodge
Reservations: Tiger Tops, PO Box
242, Kathmandu
Tel: 01-436 1500
www.tigermountain.com
The lodge, run by Tiger
Tops, is on the edge of
the forest at the park's
southern border; the Tented
Camp is on the banks of
the Karnali River. Both
feature comfortable

accommodation, Tiger
Tops' excellent service
and food, and a full range
of activities, including
elephant rides, jeep drives,
boat trips and guided jungle
walks. £££££

CHITWAN

Chitwan Jungle Lodge
Reservations: PO Box 1281, Durbar
Marg, Kathmandu
Tel: 01-444 2240
www.chitwanjunglelodge.com
A large lodge (36 rooms),
set in the middle of the
park east of Sauraha.
£££–££££
Tharu Safari Lodge
Reservations: Tiger Tops, PO Box
242, Kathmandu
Tel: 01-436 1500
www.tigermountain.com
Set on the edge of the
park near the Narayani
River, the resort's 11
rooms are decorated in the
style of traditional Tharu
longhouses. Swimming
pool, pony and bullock cart
rides and elephant safaris.
£££££–£££££
Tiger Tops
Reservations: PO Box 242,
Kathmandu
Tel: 01-436 1500
www.tigermountain.com
Located in the heart of the
park, this famous pioneer
ecotourism lodge operates
wildlife safaris from the
comfort of 25 elegant tree-
top rooms. Fully equipped
with elephants, trained
naturalists, jeep and boat

trips and jungle treks. A Tented Camp about 5 km (3 miles) away features 12 safari tents with twin beds. Accessible by daily half-hour flights to Meghauli airstrip, a five-hour drive or one- to three-day river trips. Prices are inclusive of all guided activities and meals. **£££££**

Royal Park Hotel
Reservations: Thamel, Kathmandu.
Tel: 01-441 2987
Nicely designed and decorated bungalows scattered amid spacious grounds, with an open-air bar overlooking the Rapti River. Good food, including a bakery. **££–£££**

CORBETT

Camp Corbett
Corbett Nagar
Tel: 05942-242 126
www.campcorbett.net
An excellent and friendly place to stay. Pleasant cottages, a good library and nearby bird watching all add to its attractions. The food is particularly good. **££££**

Corbett Ramganga Resort
Jhamaria
Book through: WelcomHeritage, 31 First Floor, Siri Fort Road, New Delhi 110 049
Tel: 011-2626 6650
www.welcomheritagehotels.com
An upmarket resort beautifully situated by the eponymous river. Well maintained grounds and attractive cottages. Not as eco-friendly as some, but with lots of activities for children. **£££££**

Forest Rest Houses
Dhikala
Must be booked through: Main Reception Centre, Ramnagar, Nainital, U.P.
Tel: 05947-251 489
Basic accommodation, from dormitories to private bungalows, in various locations within the park itself. Recommended for early morning or evening animal spotting. Book well in advance. **£–££**

Infinity Resorts
Dhikuli
Tel: 05947-251 279
www.tigercorbettindia.com

Formerly Tiger Tops Corbett, this is a classic jungle lodge. Comfortable and with a certain charm, there are at least some efforts to be "eco-friendly". The staff can arrange extended safaris in the sanctuary. **£££££**

Jungle Brook
Ramnagar
Tel: 0091-98998 89710
www.junglebrook.com
Lovely thatched cottages and "tents" in delightful surroundings. Quiet and secluded with great walks in the immediate area. **££££–£££££**

Tiger Camp
Book through:
Tiger Camp, B-9, Sector 27, Noida 201 301
Tel: 0120-255 1963
www.tiger-camp.com
Attractive, local-style cottages and rooms with en-suite bathrooms. There is a good restaurant and well-run jeep tours. **£££**

DUDHWA

Forest Rest Houses
Book through:
Chief Wildlife Warden, 17 Rana Pratap Marg, Lucknow 226 001
Tel: 0522-220 6584
www.up-tourism.com
Basic huts in different locations across the park. Those at Dudhwa and Sathiana (which have canteens) have bedding while for Bankatti, Sonaripur and Kila you will have to bring your own and also arrange food before arrriving. There is an extra charge for the generator at Sathiana and Sonaripur, there is no electricity at Kila. Book in advance. **£–££**

Tharu Huts
Dudhwa
Book through:
Field Director, Project Tiger, Palia, Dudhwa Tiger Reserve, Lakimpur Kheri 262 701, U.P.
Tel: 05872-252 106
Basic hut accommodation. Project Tiger also has a dormitory which might be available. **£–££**

GIR

Gir Birding Lodge
Bambhafod Naka, Sasan, Gujarat
Tel: 02877-255 514
www.girnationalpark.com
Straightforward and attractive accommodation set in a mango orchard. Well-run with knowledgeable staff. **£££**

Gir Lodge
Sasan, Junagadh 326 132, Gujarat
Tel: 02877-285 521
www.tajhotels.com
A well-run and attractive hotel on the edge of the park, the comfortable rooms have lovely views over the Hiran River. Jeep safaris can also be arranged. **£££££**

Maneland Jungle Lodge
Sasan, Junagadh 362 135, Gujarat
Tel: 02877-285 555
www.maneland.com
This is an excellent and well-priced option with attractive rooms and attentive staff. In a good location for wildlife spotting. **£££**

KANHA

Kanha Jungle Lodge
Mukki
Book through:
206 Rakeshdeep, 11 Commercial Complex, Gulmohar Enclave, Green Park, Delhi 110 049
Tel: 011-2685 3760
www.adventure-india.com
Quite pricey but well placed simple and well-kept accommodation. Good for bird watching and with some regard for the environment. **£££££**

Kipling Camp
Morcha Village, Kisli, Mandla 481 768, M.P.
Tel: 07649-277 218
www.kiplingcamp.com
Charming accommodation in small cottages. This well-run camp has a very knowledgeable staff of resident naturalists and the wildlife watching is excellent (good visits to the park). **£££££**

Krishna Jungle Resort
Book through:
Hotel Krishna, Bhanvartal

PRICE CATEGORIES

The rates below are for a double room (AC where available) in high season, including taxes
£ = up to Rs 700
££ = Rs 700–1,700
£££ = Rs 1,700–3,000
££££ = Rs 3,000–4,500
£££££ = above Rs 4,500

Extension, Napier Town, Jabalpur 482 001
Tel: 0761-240 1263
www.krishnahotels.com
Comfortable if dated accommodation in tents and cottages. Well organised and also has a small pool. **££££–£££££**

MPTDC Lodges
Bhagira Log Huts, Mukki; Tourist Hostel, Kisli; Kanha Safari Lodge, Mukki
Tel: 07649-277 227; Kanha Safari Lodge 07637-226 029
www.mptourism.com
A range of simple but clean and decent accommodation, from dormitories to double rooms. All of the lodges have restaurants. **£–££**

Royal Tiger Resort
Mukki 481 111, Balaghat, M.P.
Tel: 07637-226 038
www.royaltiger.com
Locally inspired cottages in large, wooded grounds. good amenities and excellent, locally grown organic food. **£££££**

Shergarh
Bahmi, Balaghat 481 111, M.P.
Tel: 07637-226 086
(in the UK Jun–Oct 07969-804 472)
www.shergarh.com
Extremely well run and professional camp, with knowledgeable guides and comfortable accommodation. There is a useful section on their website about responsible tourism. No credit cards. Recommended. **£££££**

KAZIRANGA

Aranya Tourist Lodge
Book through:
Tourist Information Officer, Kaziranga National Park, Golaghat, Assam
Tel: 03776-266 2423
www.assamtourism.org

A mix of clean and simple rooms, all with en-suite facilities. Helpful staff and a good restaurant. **£–££**

Wild Grass
Kaziranga 785 109
Tel: 03776-266 2085
www.oldassam.com
Simple but attractive huts and comfortable tents set in beautiful grounds. Excellent food and activities centred on local music and dance. Recommended. **£££**

KEOLADEO GHANA

The Bagh
Agra–Achnera Road, Bharatpur 321 001
Tel: 05644-228 333
www.thebagh.com
Elegant accommodation with excellent bathrooms. The rooms open out onto beautiful gardens. Good food and convenient for the park. **£££££**

Chandra Mahal Haveli
Peharsar, Nadbai
Tel: 05643-223 238
The turn-off for this lovely 1850s *haveli*, set in the middle of a small village, is 22 km (14 miles) out of town down the Jaipur–Agra road. There are suites with a terrace overlooking the charming garden, and a good restaurant. **££££**

Falcon Guest House
Saras
Tel: 05644-223 815
The best budget guesthouse run by the amiable Mrs Rajni Singh. The rooms are clean and the larger ones have private balconies and softer mattresses. Peaceful and homely the owner's husband is a keen ornithologist willing to share his knowledge.

PRICE CATEGORIES

The rates below are for a double room (AC where available) in high season, including taxes
£ = up to Rs 700
££ = Rs 700–1,700
£££ = Rs 1,700–3,000
££££ = Rs 3,000–4,500
£££££ = above Rs 4,500

Home-cooked meals are served in the garden restaurant. **£–££**

Hotel Eagle's Nest
NH 11
Tel: 05644-225 144
A comfortable place, close to the park, with large, clean rooms. The restaurant is very good and serves a large variety of non-vegetarian North Indian and Chinese dishes as well as beer. The owner is a reputed ornithologist. **££**

ITDC Hotel Bharatpur Ashok
Keoladeo Ghana National Park
Tel: 05644-222 722
www.theashokgroup.com
Situated inside the park, this friendly hotel has good rooms with balconies, and a restaurant. Very convenient for early-morning birdwatching. Book in advance. **££££**

Jungle Lodge
Gori Shankar
Tel: 05644-225 622
Clean rooms, running hot water, shady marble-floored verandas, a beautiful green garden and a library make this one of the best choices within the park precincts. The service is great and there is a small but nice restaurant. Cycles, binoculars and two motorcycles can be hired. **£**

Kadamkunj
NH 11
Delhi tel: 09891-458 220
A jungle lodge situated in an idyllic setting with picturesque views of the nearby bird sanctuary. The rooms are quiet, comfortable and located around a grassy quadrangle. Good meals available at the restaurant. **£££**

Kiran Guest House
364 Rajendra Nagar
Tel: 05644-223 845
Has five spacious and immaculate rooms with a lovely terrace-top restaurant serving good food and chilled beer. Great personal service, homely and good value for money. The hotel arranges rides to and from town and bikes and binoculars are available. **£**

Laxmi Vilas Palace
Kakaji ki Kothi
Tel: 05644-231 199
www.laxmivilas.com
This former palace on the outskirts of the city dates from 1899. It has attractive suites and rooms; the food is recommended and the service is excellent. **£££££**

Spoonbill
Agra Road, close to the Saras
Tel: 05644-223 571
Decent rooms with shared baths and dormitory beds. Very good food and friendly service. **£–££**

MANAS

Bansbari Lodge
Manas
Tel: 03666-296 824
www.assambengalnavigation.com
Probably the best option close to the park. This is pleasant, simple accommodation in lovely surroundings by the river. Decent food is on offer and nature walks can be arranged with a guide. **£££££**

Mathanguri Forest Lodge
Mathanguri
Book through:
Field Director, Manas National Park, Assam
Tel: 03666-261 413
Slightly run-down, basic rooms set in the park itself. Order food and make preparations in advance. **£–££**

MUDUMALAI

Bamboo Banks
Masinagudi, Tamil Nadu
Tel: 0423-252 6211
www.bamboobanks.in
A highly recommended place to stay. Well appointed cottages in wooded grounds. Good Parsi food using locally grown vegetables. Excellent value for the position and facilities. **£££**

Forest Rest Houses
Abhayaranyam, Kargudi, Masinagudi and Teppakadu
Book through:
Wildlife Warden, Mahalingam Buildings, Coonoor Road,

Udhagamandalam 643 001, Tamil Nadu
Tel: 0423-244 4098
Simple accommodation in a number of locations. Catering is provided on request. **£**

Jungle Retreat
Bokkapuram, Masinagudi 643 223, Tamil Nadu
Tel: 0423-252 6469
www.jungleretreat.com
An excellent, and very reasonable, place to stay. Straightforward and pleasant accommodation. Wonderful views from the grounds (which also have a pool). Friendly service and excellent wildlife watching. **££££**

Jungle Trails
Masinagudi
0423-252 6256
Simple but clean and decent accommodation for the true wildlife enthusiast. The resort is run by the naturalist Mark Davidar who is a mine of information on the natural history of the surrouding area. **££**

Monarch Safari Park
Bokkapuram, Masinagudi 643 223, Tamil Nadu
Tel: 0423-252 6250
www.hojoindia.com
Well-sited with some great views. Simple, raised huts with attached bathrooms. Decent food in the restaurant and good birdwatching from the grounds. **££–£££**

NAGARAHOLE

Forest Department Cottages
Book through:
Conservator of Forests, Kodagu Circle, Aranya Bhavan, Madikeri 571 201, Karnataka
Tel: 08272-225 708
www.karnatakatourism.org
Basic lodges with simple but clean rooms. food is available as are jeeps for safaris. **££–£££**

Jungle Inn
Veeranahosalli, Hunsur, Murkal–Nagarhole Road, Mysore District 570 011, Karnataka
Tel: 09822-246 022
www.jungleinnnagarhole.com
Decent rooms in a well-run resort. The wildlife

watching facilities are excellent and safaris within the park are accompanied by a knowledgeable naturalist. £££££
Kabini River Lodge
Karapur, Nissana Beltur, Mysore District 571 114, Karnataka
Tel: 08228-264 402
www.junglelodges.com
One of the best wildlife lodges India. Comfortable accommodation, decent food and excellent advice from the resident naturalists. Very good value and highly recommended. £££££–£££££
Water Woods
19 Karapur, Mysore District 571 114, Karnataka
Tel: 0821-226 4421
www.waterwoods.net
Expensive but beautifully kept and comfortable accommodation overlooking the river. Decent buffet food and good access to the park by boat or jeep. £££££

NANDA DEVI

GMVN Tourist Bungalow
Joshimath
Tel: 01389-222 118
www.gmvnl.com
Small, basic but clean rooms run by the tourism development corporation. Very cheap dormitory beds are also available. £
The **Johar Valley Trek**, that takes in part of the Valley of the Flowers, can be booked through:
Shakti
3rd Floor, E-82 Greater Kailash 1, New Delhi
Tel: 011-5173 4788
www.shaktihimalaya.com

PERIYAR

Aranya Niwas
Thekkady, Idukki 685 536, Kerala
Tel: 0486-922 2023
www.ktdc.com
Set on the banks of the lake this somewhat dated but still comfortable retreat retains some of its colonial charm. £££££–£££££
Bamboo Grove
Periyar Tiger Reseve, Thekkady

685 536, Kerala
Tel: 04869-224 571
www.periyartigerreserve.org
Set right in the park itself, these simple huts are perfect for serious wildlife observation. Book in advance. £££
Jungle Inn
Periyar Tiger Reseve, Thekkady 685 536, Kerala
Tel: 04869-224 571
www.periyartigerreserve.org
A rare opportunity to spend a night in amongst the wildlife of the park. A small, secluded hut that is ideally placed for forest treks. £–££
Lake Palace
Thekkady, Idukki 685 536, Kerala
Tel: 0486-922 2023
www.ktdc.com
Previously belonging to the Maharaja of Travancore, this small heritage resort is a great place from which to launch your wildlife spotting trips. £££££
Periyar House
Thekkady, Idukki 685 536, Kerala
Tel: 0486-922 2026
www.ktdc.com
Good-value budget accommodation near to the park, Clean and comfortable rooms and friendly staff. ££
Spice Village
Kumily Road, Thekkady 685 536, Kerala
Tel: 04869-224 514
www.cghearth.com
Traditional-style thatched cottages in beautiful grounds. Very comfortable and excellent service. Forest walks and *ayurvedic* treatments are on offer. Recommended. £££££

RANTHAMBORE

RTDC Jhoomar Baori
7 km (4 miles) from railway station
Tel: 07462-220 195
Set atop a hill, this former hunting lodge provides stunning views of the lush green forests surrounding it. The rooms are good, though a little run-down, and continental food is available. Discounts on rooms Apr–June. ££

Sawai Madhopur Lodge
3 km (2 miles) from station
Tel: 07462-220 541
www.tajhotels.com
In the past this was the Maharaja of Jaipur's hunting lodge. It has now been converted into a Taj group hotel offering all the 5-star amenities and swanky rooms and luxury tents. ££££
Sher Bagh
Park edge
Tel: 07462-252 119, Delhi tel: 011-2331 6534
Originally designed for the Maharaja of Jaipur and his guests' hunting expeditions, this forest-friendly camp has 12 luxury tents with attached bathrooms. The meals are scrumptious and special evening talks with conservationists who have dedicated their lives to Ranthambore and its animals are a real treat. Highly recommended. ££££
Vanyavilas
Ranthambore Road, 10 minutes from railway station
Tel: 07462-223 999
www.oberoivanyavilas.com
Extremely expensive luxury tent accommodation with attached colonial-style baths and spacious private compounds, set in perfectly landscaped gardens. The latest Oberoi resort is definitely extremely lavish. Highly recommended if you can afford it. ££££

SILENT VALLEY

Forest Department Rest House
Mukkali
Book through:
Wildlife Warden, Silent Valley National Park, Mannarkkad, Palakkad, Kerala
Tel: 0492-242 2056/245 3225
www.keralaforest.org
Basic accommmodation ranging from simple doubles to a dormitory. You must be accompanied by a forest guard to enter the sanctuary. £

THE SUNDARBANS

WBTDC Tourist Lodge
Sajnekhali, Gosaba, South 24 Parganas 743 331, West Bengal
Tel: 03219-252 560
www.wbtourism.com
Basic rooms and a dormitory in a secluded building run by the Tourism Development Corporation. Food available, but book in advance. £
Good tours of the Sundarbans can also be arranged through the Kolkata office of
Pugmarks:
10 Meher Ali Road, Kolkata
Tel: 033-2280 8917
www.pugmarksholidays.com

WAYANAD

Forest Rest Houses
In Tholpetty, Muthanga, Kurichat and Thirunelly
Book through:
Wildlife Warden, Wayanad Widlife Division, Sulthanbathery
Tel: 04936-262 0454
www.keralaforest.org
A series of simple huts and dormitories. All of them have a cook and a guide. £
Green Magic Nature Resort
Vythiri
Book through:
Tour India, P.O. Box 163, near S.M.V. High School, M.G. Road, Thiruvananthapuram
Tel: 0471-233 0437
www.tourindiakerala.com
Accommodation in wonderful treehouses in the heart of pristine rainforest. This is an eco-resort in the true sense of the term (bio-gas and solar power, only natural toiletries allowed, and organic food). Not cheap, but a unique experience. £££££
Jungle Park Resort
52a Vrindhavan Colony, Chevayur, Kozhikode, Kerala
Tel: 0495-552 1163
www.jungleparkresorts.com
Beautifully sited in the Fintser Hills, this eco-resort has traditional-style cottages set within the forest. ££££–£££££

A CTIVITIES

OBSERVING WILDLIFE

OBSERVING WILDLIFE

The Jungle

To most people, the word jungle conjures up images of dense, lush tropical forest with torrential rainfall, huge trees festooned with creepers, and infested with dangerous animals, snakes and insects. In its Sanskrit origins, the word jungle denotes any wild country, untamed land – a wilderness. How many trees grow on it and how tall, and what and how many creatures live in it, makes no difference. The semi-arid thorny scrub of Yala in Sri Lanka is no less a "jungle" than the steaming forest of Manas in Assam in Eastern India.

At the onset, it should be pointed out that, although the Indian subcontinent harbours a great variety of wildlife, the large assemblies of animals seen so often in the African bush are not seen here. Most jungles of the Indian subcontinent are thick and dense, with poor visibility. Animals living in such closed environments are generally shy and retiring, and live in small scattered groups, or even as solitary individuals.

Perhaps it is also necessary to explain why so many more birds than mammals are seen. Mammals are largely nocturnal, retreating into their hideouts during the day, and are usually silent. On the other hand, most birds are diurnal, not so shy of man and quite vocal. Moreover, there are far more birds than there are mammals – India alone has about 1,200 species of birds against 350 species of mammals. So, while spotting 100 species of birds in a day is not unusual, a mammal list of even 10 species is considered good. But the mystique and the romance of exploring the jungle here, perhaps for this very reason, is greater than anywhere else in the world.

Wildlife Parks

Much of India's wilderness now falls within areas giving legal protection to the many species and the flora within them. Some of these protected areas are small, obscure and extremely difficult to reach. Many have little or no facilities and are in no way capable of catering for visitors. Others have a variety of accommodation ranging from forest bungalows, rest houses and Public Works Department (PWD) bungalows to deluxe tented camps and lodges. The list that follows is as comprehensive as possible within the needs of this volume. Basic information, such as location, status, access and accommodation, is given along with an indication of the major mammal, birds, reptiles and flora that are to be found.

Even when a rest house is available, the facilities may be limited. In many areas there is only a building with basic furniture – visitors must bring their own food and bedding. A contact address is given wherever possible and bookings can be made by post. Some parks have a wider range of facilities provided by State Tourism Corporations, the Indian Tourism Development Corporation (ITDC) and private companies. Bookings for these can be made through most travel agencies.

There are about 90 national parks and more than 500 sanctuaries in India, home to hundreds of species of mammals, birds and reptiles (see also pages 19–29 and 181–7). Of these, Gujarat's **Gir Forest** is famous for its population of Asiatic lions, **Periyar** (in Kerala) for elephants, **Manas** and **Kaziranga** for one-horned rhinoceroses, Manipur's **Keibul Lamjao Park** for Thamin deer, and **Corbett** and **Kanha** for tigers. A selection of some notable wildlife sanctuaries follows.

For details of parks and sanctuaries please see the Wildlife Parks chapters.

Your safari kit

Your most invaluable companion while on a wildlife safari is a good pair of medium-size compact binoculars. For general purposes, 7x or 8x magnification is adequate, but for bird-watching 10x magnification is better as it brings out details of plumage clearly – so vital for positive identification. Many rare sightings have been missed because binoculars were not easily at hand. So carry your binoculars round your neck, and use them constantly to scan the area around you. You will be surprised how much more you will see if you do.

Another essential item is a three-yard (three-metre) tape measure, preferably the spring coil type, with both centimeter and inch calibrations, to measure anything of interest – dimensions of a den, the size of a track, the height of a claw mark on a tree, for example.

To record your observations, you will need a small notebook in which you may also want to sketch things of interest. Do not forget to mention the name of the place, time and date. In time, in this note book you will have put together an amazing variety of information.

Other items include a topographic map (if available), a compass and a lightweight torch with a red lens (your night vision will work better than with white light and it will not scare wildlife so much). (*For other items see page 354.*)

When to look for animals

A national park or reserve is a living museum of nature's creations – landscapes, rock formations, water, plants and animals. But unlike in an art or historical museum where objects are on display, here you have to seek out your animals. You have to know where they live, when they move about, how to attract and approach them. Not unlike people, animals are creatures of habit and have distinct daily and seasonal patterns of activity. An understanding of these patterns increases our chance of seeing them.

The frequency of wildlife sightings in national parks and reserves varies, depending on the time of year. The Indian subcontinent is affected by the monsoons (in some areas twice a year), and this influences the pattern of vegetation growth and the availability of food and water. This in turn affects the distribution and behaviour of animals. Since the vegetation is overgrown and lush during the monsoon and for several months after, these are not the best periods for wildlife viewing in most national parks.

Generally, the best times are from February to May. During these months the trees are often bare and the undergrowth dead or regenerating, so visibility is considerably improved. Since there is also a general scarcity of water, the animals concentrate near sources of water. In places where annual grass burning is still practised such as in Chitwan and Bardia in Nepal, regrowth of grasses attracts large concentrations of herbivores, who in their turn attract predators.

However, the time of year you choose to visit a park will also depend on what your are looking for. "Best months" usually mean those in which one is most likely to see large mammals that are the main attraction of most national parks and reserves. But in Chitwan, for instance, the best months for seeing birds are February–March, for mammals March–May, for insects and for the lush jungle June–September, and for crocodiles, who come out of water to bask in the sun, October–February. The marshes of Bharatpur present a magnificent spectacle of breeding birds during August, September and October.

There are rewards for the nature lover at every hour of the day and night, but for watching mammals you have to follow their daily cycle of activity. They are mostly nocturnal and remain active for 2–3 hours after sunrise. A night trip can be a very rewarding experience, but is not permitted in most parks and reserves, and rightly so. Animals should have at least some time to conduct their lives without human intrusion. Around 10am animals retreat for rest and lie in hiding, giving the impression during midday and in the early afternoon that the jungle is devoid of life. But they resume their activities around 4pm, filling the jungle with life and activity. Your safaris are therefore best organized during the early mornings and late afternoons. In the winter, afternoon safaris are better as there is often a thick mist in the morning.

Monkeys, like people, are creatures of the day. They are up early and feed for a few hours before their midday siesta, when they sit around contentedly on the ground or in trees. They resume feeding activity in the afternoon and by sundown are ready to go to sleep. Langurs are noisy feeders and not only their calls but also their jumping from branch to branch make a loud noise, so their presence can be detected from a distance.

Where to look for animals

Animals are most conspicuous when they are feeding or at play and the most likely spots to observe such activities are grassy meadows, the edge of forests, at salt licks or near water holes. Herbivores have to feed daily for several hours, and the heavyweights, such as rhino and elephant, have prodigious appetites and may spend 15–18 hours a day feeding, thus making themselves very conspicuous.

Open grass meadows and river banks are the favourite grounds of hoofed animals, where the short grasses provide nourishment. For ungulates the tall grasses are often inedible and therefore of little value, except as shelter. In a forest thick with trees and scant grass, hoofed animals will often be thinly spread but leaf-eaters, such as langurs, are usually common. Recently burned patches of grassland and forest attract deer, antelope, wild boar, gaur, buffalo, rhino and other herbivores who come for the new succulent grasses.

Most mammals have to drink at least once, if not twice, a day. In areas where water is plentiful, such as the floodplains of Chitwan, Manas and Kaziranga, animals are evenly spread out. But in places where water is localized, as in the Siwalik hills of northern India and Nepal, mammals usually stay close to water, especially during the afternoon when they come to drink. In arid areas with scant rainfall, water is in short supply during the summer before the rains, so this is the time to look for animals near the few remaining sources for water. Predators often lie, in cover, near a water hole and take their chances on the prey species that wander within range. This also explains why herbivores are so nervous when approaching these spots.

Large animals also use water for cooling their bodies. In the steaming months of May and June, tigers lie in secluded pools in the jungle, and elephant, rhino, buffalo and wild boar also have favourite spots to wallow in the water or mud.

Mammals also visit salt licks regularly to replenish their body stocks of vital minerals. Over the years, salt licks become well known to the animals living in the area, and elephant, rhino, gaur, deer, monkeys and others come to them from time to time. A salt lick may be part of a hillside, a patch of earth or clay, or buried in the bed of a spring, lake, river or stream.

How to conduct your safari

Dress comfortably, in clothes that permit easy movement, and avoid wearing bright colours that make you conspicuous. Jungle-green, khaki, or beige camouflage are preferred for tropical and subtropical environments, but in the Himalaya, where snow is present, light neutral colours may be most suitable. The idea is to blend with the surroundings so that you do not unnecessarily announce your presence from a distance.

Animals are very wary of the human voice. So, in order to get close to them, absolute silence is essential. Walk lightly and unless in the mountains, avoid heavy boots; sneakers or running shoes are best.

Animals living in closed environments have an exceptional sense of smell and will detect and avoid human scent. While stalking animals, it is therefore important to stay downwind of them or you will give your presence away sooner than you think, especially if there is

ABOVE: measuring pug marks.

a gentle breeze. For the same reason avoid wearing perfumes and, if using insect repellent, choose the kind that smells the least. Also, no smoking, please.

Move slowly, as this gives you more time to look around and you are less conspicuous to the animals, thereby permitting you to approach closer to them. Walking slowly is also safer. A hasty step might bring you face to face with a rhino, gaur, elephant, or tiger – encounters of a kind that is best avoided. In South India, which has a good population of poisonous snakes, it pays to look where you step. Even while in a vehicle, a slow drive gives you the time to scan the area around you.

Usually, the animals will spot you first and disappear without your knowing it. Human sightings by animals are far more common than animal sightings by humans. Occasionally you will know that you have been spotted when you hear or see animals bounding away. They may even give an alarm call which will convey a warning to other creatures.

But if you spot them first you should move cautiously, using every bit of cover to your advantage, freezing every time they look in your direction. A deer or antelope will soon get your wind and will try to pinpoint you with its nose, eyes and ears.

Some animals are inquisitive and may even come towards you. But un-der no circumstances should you stalk or go close to large carnivores and other potentially dangerous animals. Most animals will retreat at the sight of man but the large animals may have good reason not to. A leopard or bear may be guarding her cubs, for example. Under these circumstances they are likely to warn you with a noisy snarl before you come too close. If you do not heed that, it is at your own risk.

Some drivers and guides, in the heat of excitement, will take you dangerously close to potentially harmful animals. Or perhaps be-cause you want a close-up photograph. This kind of drama should be discouraged as casualties are likely to occur if you violate the personal space of wild animals and make them feel vulnerable. In a national park or reserve their wel-fare comes first and disturbing, harassing or unnecessarily provok-ing them is taboo.

On a nature walk, keep your senses on the alert. Most animals blend extremely well with their environment. The spotted fur of the leopard breaks its contours and is in-visible in the light and shadow of the jungle. Even the giant elephant merges with the gray tree trunks and the undergrowth. But don't get obsessed with sighting animals: the imagination can play tricks and you may start "seeing animals" that are not there. A rock on the mountainside may become a black bear! And a black bear a rock!

Two ways to maximize your chances of seeing animals are:
● to watch them from a hide or blind, locally known as a *machan*, where you wait for them to come near you while you are hidden from their view;
● to actually go out in search of them by vehicle, elephant, boat, or on foot.

This may sound simple, but to get the best results requires deep knowledge of the wilds and its denizens.

Machans

A *machan*, as explained, is a hide or blind in a tree or on the ground. When on the ground it resembles a hut with several peepholes to look out from. They are best made from local materials – trees, bamboo, grass, leaves, stone or mud. A good temporary or mobile machan can be made of canvas or burlap stitched to size, with custom-made windows and an exit door. It can easily be put up with the help of sticks or its own set of aluminium poles. It should be jungle-green or light brown in colour or with a camouflage pattern to break its outline.

Such a collapsible machan is es-sential to the wildlife photographer. The idea of a machan is to become so inconspicuous that animals come close to you without detecting your presence. In this respect, a tree machan has the advantage that, apart from providing a better lookout point, human scent disperses from it more rapidly into the upper air than from a ground machan.

In an area where wind or breeze is a constant factor, especially during the mornings and afternoons when you are most likely to use a machan, it is best sited downwind from where the animals appear. A machan must also not stand out from the surrounding landscape if animals are to approach it without much hesitation. If situated in a thick jungle, it is usually hidden and camouflaged by foliage; if in an open area, it may be so placed as to appear to blend with a natural structure such as a termite mound or rock outcrops.

A machan usually overlooks a natural water hole or a salt lick (either or both may be artificially created if necessary), and occasionally open ground with a long view. Unless water is plentiful in the area, machans overlooking water holes are very productive for spotting animals. Smaller animals such a porcupine can be attracted by regularly leaving some potatoes and other vegetables on a spot frequented by them during the night. Carnivores, such as tiger and leopard are sometimes baited by using a chunk of meat or by tying a buffalo calf or goat in their path.

But, whatever the advantages of machans, from them you can only hope to see the animals that chance to come by. When you go out in search of them, whether by Landrover, on elephant back, by boat or on foot, in full view of the animals that you seek, while you have the freedom to look for them in the most likely spots, you also run the risk of announcing your presence and warning them away.

Safaris by Landrover and elephant

For some unknown reason, most wild animals seem quite indifferent to the sight and sound of a vehicle and during the night the headlights seem to mesmerize them. In fact, it is amazing how close you can get to some animals by vehicle. As the sound of the engine does not seem to bother most animals, it is best to keep the engine running as this not only drowns human noises but also ensures speedy escape if your subject happens to be big and angry. Animals may accept the presence of your vehicle, but this does not mean that they will continue to "cooperate" if you step out of the vehicle. Why animals should tolerate

such an alien object as a truck, and bolt at the sight of humans, no one knows. Perhaps vehicles, although strange, do not seem dangerous to them, whereas they have a long history and tradition of the need to avoid people.

Vehicles have the advantage that you can cover a large area in a relatively short time. Tracks in the parks are rough and you may need to cross streams, rivers and muddy places and they give you quick and easy access to the best spots for viewing animals. But vehicles will only take you where there are roads and since driving off-road is usually not allowed in most national parks, you will have to resort to other means – travel by elephant, boat and on foot.

Elephants have long been used for hunting, and more recently for forestry operations, wildlife management and wildlife watching. Nepal and India must be among the few Asian countries to employ elephants for wildlife tourism.

Elephants have the advantage that they can go to places where no vehicle, boat, or man on foot can go. They will climb up hillsides, negotiate steep banks, and walk through marsh, swamp and thick jungle. In fact, were it not for the elephant, tall grasslands, like those found in Chitwan and Kaziranga, would be so much more difficult to explore safely. Elephants, however, dislike and avoid deep rivers and strong currents and quicksands. They give you a feeling of security and, although they are quite timid by nature, few animals will attack them. Rhino and tiger have been known to, under provocation, but perched on the howdah, 3 metres (10 ft) from the ground, you are quite safe. The only disadvantage is that elephants move slowly and therefore you can only cover a small area in each outing.

Despite the human smell and noise, most animals tolerate people on elephants. In fact, even the keen-nosed wild elephant will allow a man on a domesticated elephant to approach and sometimes even mingle with the wild herd.

Elephants, with their keen noses, constantly pick up smells left by other animals. Being the largest creature in the Asian jungle, they will ignore most animals but they have an instinctive dislike of large carnivores. If such an animal is nearby, an elephant might resist going towards it, but it will show no fear of an immobilized (drugged) tiger or a dead one. They also dislike going close to gaur, buffalo and rhino.

Signs in the jungle

Wildlife observation may be direct, when you actually see the animals in their natural state, or indirect, when you "observe" their presence or passage by their spoor, scats, shelters, smells, sounds and so on. The jungle is full of such signs but their interpretation is not simple, therefore only the most obvious are mentioned here.

Marks

Look for markings on trees in the jungle. Deer rub their antlers against small trees, usually to clear their velvet, and leave distinct marks of injury. And depending upon how high the marks are from the ground, between 30–120 cm (1–4 ft), you can make a good guess as to which deer species was responsible for it.

In rhino country, rhino rubbing posts are frequently encountered. They are usually about 1.5 metres (3–5 ft) above the ground on a sloping tree trunk or stump. From regular use, the rubbed area becomes smooth and devoid of bark, often with a coating of mud. In elephant country, uprooted trees and trees with stripped bark or twisted branches betray their presence. Bears and leopards leave distinct claw marks on the trees they climb and tigers habitually rake their claws on trees, leaving deep gashes, sometimes with fragments of claw in them. Other types of cat also indulge in this form of marking/cleaning.

A forest floor littered with fresh fallen leaves and twigs indicates the feeding activity of langurs. Chital often take advantage of this "free lunch" and follow the monkeys who feed in the treetops.

Wild boar rootle the ground for food and leave tell-tale patches of loose upturned earth. Sloth bears dig up termite mounds at their bases and suck up the insects. These diggings may be 1 metre (3 ft) deep, and sometimes even larger craters may be excavated by them in search of choice food.

Elephants have an exceptional nose and where water is scarce will locate it under the ground, dig a hole with their forefeet and drink the clear water that collects at the bottom. Other animals use these "water holes" after the elephants have left.

Burrows and nests

In the jungle all kinds of cavities and holes may be seen in rock, on the ground and in trees. These are often shelters or dens used by a variety of animals and birds. Most carnivores

ABOVE: otter and wader tracks.

live in burrows. They either dig these themselves or appropriate existing holes and cavities. Porcupine warrens are elaborate systems of tunnels under the ground, usually with two or more entry and exit points. They are often recognized by the gnawed horns, bones and antlers lying at the entrance. Otters live in burrows with an underwater entrance although their living chamber is above the water level. Their burrows are usually at the bases of trees, among the roots.

Even large carnivores like brown and black bears hibernate in cavities during the winter. Contrary to popular belief, tigers and lions do not live in caves or dens, although occasionally they may use them as shelter. Tiger "dens" are usually very secluded spots in the forest or tall grass where they are least likely to be disturbed.

A common sight on most steep river banks are holes used as nests by the sand martin. Bee-eaters and kingfishers also nest in burrows. The tailor bird stitches a nest out of one or more leaves, and the weaver makes a graceful nest hanging from a branch.

The most interesting nest is made by the giant hornbill. The male seals his mate in a hole in a tree, using a plaster of clay and debris, leaving a small opening through which he feeds her. When the chicks hatch and are large enough, the female breaks open the wall and emerges. The couple then replaster the opening and continue to feed the chicks through a hole until they are ready to come out, when the wall is broken once again, and the family set out into the jungle.

Droppings

The shape, size, colour and smell of mammal droppings can give clues to which animals live in the jungle. Local Adivasis and trackers are often very knowledgeable about droppings. The contents of herbivore droppings give useful indications of the plant species eaten, and carnivore droppings of the species of prey consumed. Exceptionally, you may find something particularly interesting, such as the claws of tiger cub or leopard in tiger droppings.

Some animals, such as civets and weasels, habitually defecate at "latrines" and, in time, large piles are formed. Large quantities of wolf droppings may be found near its den. Rhinos also have dung piles which, after months, even years, of use become huge accumulations. Some animals, such as the red fox and the otter, defecate at prominent spots, such as on stones, a fallen branch, or on top of a mound.

Birds of prey, herons and owls regurgitate matter from their mouths. These distinct pellets, consisting of bone, feather, hair and other indigestible matter, are often found in large numbers below a favourite perch or roosting site.

Sounds

The sounds in the jungle often give clues to the identity of the animals producing them. With training and long experience you learn to recognize the sounds of most birds and mammals. In fact, identification of a bird is sometimes easier from its call than from its sighting, and elusive birds, such as cuckoos, are far more often heard than seen. Birds of the night, such as owls and nightjars, are difficult to recognize but have very distinctive calls, making it possible to identify them instantly.

The roar of a lion, the alarm call of a sambar, the trumpeting of an elephant, the whistle of a wild dog, are all sounds betraying their identities. Some sounds will tell you more. The bugling of a hundred barasingha stags will tell you that their rutting season is on.

If you hear rhino huff and puff, snort and grunt, thundering about in the tall grass, and then a peculiar whistling sound, you know that two rhinos have had a dispute; or perhaps a male is chasing a reluctant female. The alarm call of a peafowl or a deer often indicates the presence of a tiger or leopard. The rhesus will bark agitatedly and the langur makes the distinctive call (kha-ko, kha-ko-kha) that almost invariably means tiger or leopard.

Carcasses

Carcasses of the kills of large predators are often betrayed by vultures, crows and blue magpies. By mid-morning the vultures riding the thermals in the sky spot the carcass, or the excitement of crows, and are attracted to it; within the hour dozens of vultures descend on the carcass out of the sky. If you see vultures heading in a particular direction and follow them you will certainly come upon a dead beast or its remains.

Approach a carcass with caution, especially if the vultures are in the nearby trees or on the ground at a distance. This often indicates that a large carnivore is nearby. Hungry tigers can be possessive of their kills and, although they usually retreat at the sight of man, they might not.

Tracks around the kill will indicate which carnivore or scavenger has been feeding on it. Leopard and tiger kills may be distinguished by the size of canine punctures and the gap between them, these being always larger and wider in the case of a tiger. The tiger begins to eat from the hindquarters, the leopard from the stomach or chest. The tiger's feeding is quite clean, with the alimentary canal left unpunctured, but the leopard is a messy feeder.

Leopards usually take their kills into trees, especially when in open areas, in order to protect them from other predators and scavengers. Tigers, on the other hand, stay near the kill for up to several days, depending upon the size of the carcass, and will resent intrusion and often rush at the vultures and manage to kill one or two. In order to hide the carcass from competitors, the tiger covers it with earth, twigs and other debris. Lions are communal feeders and usually finish the kill in a single sitting and so do not need to guard or stay near it.

Tell-tale tracks

All terrestrial animals leave impressions of their feet on the ground as they go about their business. A good tracker, by looking at the tracks and trail (a sequence of tracks), can often tell the species, age, sex and speed with which the animal was moving.

Adivasi groups, who will supplement their diet by hunting, are very knowledgeable about the natural history of their area and have the knack of reading tracks and other signs with accuracy. A reliable interpretation of the signs in the wild gives them clues as to where to put traps, what kind of traps and what bait to use at what time of year and day.

Roads, banks of rivers and lakes, the seashore and snow are the best places to look for tracks. But not all tracks reproduce faithfully and in fact those made by the same animal may look different, depending upon the hardness of the ground and the gait of the animal at the time. In deep mud and soft sand or snow the tracks are indistinct and larger than life, whereas on harder ground they will be more realistic and show details of the contours of the feet. If the animal is running, the tracks will show a slide mark in the direction of travel, the slide being more pronounced on soft ground. The toes or hooves will often splay for better traction and the impact itself will cause the tracks to be larger. In deep snow

or sand a running animal will leave quite unrecognizable tracks.

An early morning walk is the best time to study tracks as at that time they are fresh and well preserved. As the day wears on, tracks are gradually obliterated by the action of the elements, and by the activities of people.

In an Indian jungle the most conspicuous tracks are those of the tiger, and by following a fresh tiger trail you can learn about its activities of the previous night. Track one with the help of a professional tracker or guide and you will be amazed at the information they will be able to infer on the animal that made them.

From the size of the tracks they will perhaps infer that it is a male and, if they have tracked tigers regularly in that area, even identify which male. Soon you will be shown where the tiger sat for a while, where he started to run, and began to stalk. From time to time, you will scent a strong musky smell and a closer examination will reveal that the tiger has been marking his trail with a spray of urine. Here the tiger has scraped the ground with his hind paws and defecated, leaving evidence of what he has eaten. Halfway down the road his trail mixes with those of a female and as the tracks of both are equally fresh, we know they were together. Tracking, if expertly done, will sometimes lead to the animal itself, its kill or den.

When you see a track you may want to sketch it, but this is easier said than done. A simple method is to use a rectangular plate of glass 20 cm x 30 cm (8 in x 12 in), in a wooden frame, the molding of which is about a 6mm (¼ in) above the surface of the glass.

When you place this tracer flat on the ground over the track, the glass will be slightly raised and the track will remain intact. Now with a medium-point black felt pen and with your eyes vertically over the track, trace its outlines on the glass exactly as you see them. Then trace the track from the glass on to thin tracing paper, and you have a permanent, lifesize record of a track.

In a national park or reserve, ideally, nothing should be removed. Even such seemingly valueless things as antlers on the forest floor, or a dead log, have their role in the scheme of nature. In a way they are as much a part of the jungle as the deer and the tree that shed them. The antler will provide minerals to porcupines, rodents and so on, and the deadwood will sustain a number of insects. Later, when the antler and the deadwood have disintegrated, they will

return the minerals to the soil. And so, in a cycle of life and death, nature in all its glory should survive intact as we see it in the jungle.

PHOTOGRAPHY

Any recommendations with regard to equipment given by one professional is liable to be disputed by another. There are, though, certain pieces of advise that can be given without fear of contradiction.

Considerable skill is required to photograph insects, flowers and trees in their natural environment and lengthy preparation is often required. Animals, on the other hand, are, perhaps surprisingly, easier to photography. Most travellers use one of the many makes of 35 mm SLR cameras, each of which has a facility to change lenses. Unless otherwise stated, all comments refer to this type of equipment.

Unlike the Galapagos islands or Antarctica, nowhere in South Asia are standard lenses adequate for photographing wild animals. Telephoto lenses from 180 mm upward are required for most animal photographs, 35 mm or 28 mm wide-angle lenses are extremely useful for striking scenic or environmental pictures. Also, a tripod or monopod is very handy, especially when using telephoto lenses.

There are few places in South Asia where prompt and reliable camera servicing can be had, so equipment should be checked before leaving for India. If your equipment is new, it is advisable to shoot a test roll before leaving home to ensure you are familiar with the equipment and that everything is working as expected. Carrying an extra body not only gives flexibility in using alternative lenses or film types, but also acts as a back-up in case of mechanical or electrical failure.

Outside of the major cities good quality film is generally not easily available and when found, may not be of the type you are used to. Carry more film than you think you'll need. Surplus film can be used as presents and is always greatly appreciated.

Having to use telephoto lenses and the poor light conditions of the jungle often means that excellent high-resolution film such as Kodachrome 25 or 64 is not fast enough. Higher speed Ektachrome or Fujichrome lack a certain quality but do give flexibility in poor light. The same applies to print or negative film.

A – Z

A HANDY SUMMARY OF PRACTICAL INFORMATION, ARRANGED ALPHABETICALLY

A rrival

Once through customs the visitor is often besieged by porters, taxi drivers and others. Choose one porter and stick to him. There is a system of paying porters a fixed amount per piece of baggage before leaving the terminal: a tip of Rs5, once the bags are aboard the taxi or bus, is sufficient. If a travel agent or a friend is meeting you, he or she may be waiting outside the building.

Some major hotels operate courtesy buses, and a public service known as EATS (Ex-Serviceman's Transport Service) operates an airport bus service in Delhi, Mumbai and Kolkata, with stops en route to the city centre. There are also offical, pre-paid taxis and coaches.

B egging

Visitors to India will encounter people asking for alms, especially in the cities, around holy shrines and on railway journeys. Many of these beggers are physically disabled and they have few other options for survival. Although you should use your discretion, giving small amounts of money (one or two rupees) will be gratefully received and will generally be helping someone out. Try to give discretely or you might attract unwanted attention. If you are unsure about whether to give or not, it is fine to follow what other people around you are doing.

C hildren

Indians love children and are very tolerant and indulgent with them, making India a very easy place to travel with children, and children will find the sights and sounds just as rewarding as adults. The problem is that children can be more easily affected by the heat, unsafe drinking water and unfamiliar food seasoned with chillies and spices. In case of diarrhoea, rehydration salts are vital. Keep the child away from stray animals, especially dogs and monkeys. To avoid the risk of rabies, it may be safer to give children an anti-rabies vaccine. For infants, it is difficult to find nappies and places to change them. Consider bringing a supply of disposables, or changing to terries which, after rinsing, can be given to the hotel laundry or *dhobi*. A changing mat is essential, as is powdered milk of a brand that your child is familiar with. For touring, walking and hiking, a child-carrier backpack is well worth the weight.

Climate

India's climate ranges from the permanent snows of the Himalayas and the tropical conditions along the coasts, to the continental climate of inland areas. There are also many regional and seasonal variations. In general, the best time to visit is after the southwest monsoon.

October to March is the cool season and the best time of year in Peninsular India. The weather is beautifully predictable in winter, with blue skies and bright sunshine in most areas. Parts of the south and east see a brief spell of rain from the northeast monsoon, while snow and sleet make the extreme north very cold and often inaccessible.

Summer, from April to June, is very hot and dry for most of the

Annual Temperature and Rainfall Chart

		Jan	Feb	Mar	Apr	May	June	July	Aug	Sep	Oct	Nov	Dec
Agra	Max/Min °C	22/7	26/10	32/16	38/22	42/27	41/29	35/27	33/26	33/25	33/19	29/12	24/8
	Rainfall mm	16	9	11	5	10	60	210	263	151	23	2	4
Ahmadabad	Max/Min °C	29/12	31/15	36/19	40/23	41/26	38/27	33/26	32/25	33/24	36/21	33/16	30/13
	Rainfall mm	4	0	1	2	5	100	316	213	163	13	5	1
Bangalore	Max/Min °C	28/15	31/16	33/19	34/21	33/21	30/20	28/19	29/19	28/19	28/19	27/17	27/15
	Rainfall mm	4	14	6	37	119	65	93	95	129	195	46	16
Bhopal	Max/Min °C	26/10	29/13	34/17	38/21	41/26	37/25	30/23	29/23	30/22	31/18	29/13	26/11
	Rainfall mm	17	5	10	3	11	137	499	308	232	37	15	7
Bhubaneshwar	Max/Min °C	29/16	32/19	35/22	38/26	38/27	35/26	31/25	31/25	31/25	31/23	29/18	28/16
	Rainfall mm	12	25	17	12	61	223	301	336	305	266	51	3
Chandigarh	Max/Min °C	20/7	23/9	29/14	34/19	38/24	39/26	34/24	33/23	33/22	31/17	27/10	22/7
	Rainfall mm	56	25	26	10	13	62	277	263	226	82	5	18
Chennai	Max/Min °C	29/20	31/21	33/23	35/23	38/28	37/28	35/26	35/25	34/25	32/24	29/23	28/21
	Rainfall mm	24	7	15	15	52	53	83	124	118	267	309	139
Darjeeling	Max/Min °C	9/3	11/4	15/8	18/11	19/13	19/15	20/15	20/15	20/15	19/11	15/7	12/4
	Rainfall mm	22	27	52	109	187	522	713	573	419	116	14	5
Delhi	Max/Min °C	21/7	24/10	30/15	36/21	41/27	40/29	35/27	34/26	34/25	35/19	29/12	23/8
	Rainfall mm	25	22	17	7	8	65	211	173	150	31	1	5
Guwahati	Max/Min °C	23/10	27/12	30/16	32/20	31/23	32/25	32/26	32/26	30/25	27/22	25/17	27/12
	Rainfall mm	17	9	73	136	276	351	373	294	190	86	8	7
Hyderabad	Max/Min °C	29/15	31/17	35/20	37/24	39/26	34/24	30/22	29/22	30/22	30/20	29/16	28/13
	Rainfall mm	2	11	13	24	30	107	165	147	163	71	25	5
Jaipur	Max/Min °C	22/8	25/11	31/15	37/21	41/26	39/27	34/26	32/24	33/23	33/18	29/12	24/9
	Rainfall mm	14	8	9	4	10	54	193	239	90	19	3	4
Jaisalmer	Max/Min °C	24/8	28/11	33/17	38/21	42/25	41/27	38/27	36/25	36/25	36/20	31/13	26/9
	Rainfall mm	2	1	3	1	5	7	89	86	14	1	5	2
Kolkata	Max/Min °C	26/12	29/15	34/20	36/24	36/26	34/26	32/26	32/26	32/26	31/24	29/18	27/13
	Rainfall mm	13	22	30	50	135	263	320	318	253	134	29	4
Leh	Max/Min °C	-3/-14	1/-12	6/-6	12/-1	17/3	21/7	25/10	24/10	21/5	14/-1	8/-7	2/-11
	Rainfall mm	12	9	12	7	7	4	16	20	12	7	3	8
Lucknow	Max/Min °C	23/9	26/11	33/16	38/22	41/27	39/28	34/27	33/26	33/23	33/20	29/13	25/9
	Rainfall mm	25	17	9	6	12	94	299	302	182	40	1	6
Mumbai	Max/Min °C	31/16	32/17	33/20	33/24	33/26	32/26	30/25	29/24	30/24	32/23	33/20	32/18
	Rainfall mm	0	1	0	0	20	647	945	660	309	117	7	1
Nagpur	Max/Min °C	29/13	33/15	36/19	40/24	43/28	38/27	31/24	30/24	31/23	32/20	30/14	29/12
	Rainfall mm	15	2	25	20	10	174	351	277	181	62	9	2
Panaji	Max/Min °C	31/19	32/20	32/23	33/25	33/27	31/25	29/24	29/24	29/24	31/23	33/22	33/21
	Rainfall mm	2	0	4	17	18	580	892	341	277	122	20	37
Patna	Max/Min °C	24/11	26/13	33/19	38/23	39/26	37/27	33/27	32/27	32/26	32/23	29/16	25/12
	Rainfall mm	21	20	7	8	28	139	266	307	243	63	6	2
Pune	Max/Min °C	31/12	33/13	36/17	38/21	37/23	32/23	28/22	28/21	29/21	32/19	31/15	30/12
	Rainfall mm	2	0	3	18	35	103	187	106	127	92	37	5
Simla	Max/Min °C	9/2	10/3	14/7	19/11	23/15	24/16	21/16	20/15	20/14	18/10	15/7	11/4
	Rainfall mm	65	48	58	38	54	147	415	385	195	45	7	24
Tiruvananthapuram	Max/Min °C	31/22	32/23	33/24	32/25	31/25	29/24	29/23	29/22	30/23	30/23	30/23	31/23
	Rainfall mm	20	20	43	122	249	331	215	164	123	271	207	73
Varanasi	Max/Min °C	23/9	37/11	33/17	39/22	41/27	39/28	33/26	32/26	32/25	32/21	29/13	25/9
	Rainfall mm	23	8	14	1	8	102	346	240	261	38	15	2

TRANSPORT

ACCOMMODATION

EATING OUT

ACTIVITIES

A – Z

country, and humid along the coasts. The hills are particularly lovely at this time of the year.

The southwest monsoon begins to set in along the western coast towards the end of May, bringing respite from the heat and varying amounts of rain as it moves across the rest of the country through June and July and withdraws by late September. Northeastern India has heavy rain during this season, making it one of the wettest regions in the world.

Customs and Entry

Customs procedures have recently been simplified. Visitors fill in declaration forms on the plane, and then proceed to the relevant red or green channels. Keep the slip in your passport for when you disembark.

Currency declaration
At present, forms for bringing in amounts of cash in excess of US$10,000 must be completed at customs on arrival.

Duty-free imports
These include 200 cigarettes (or 50 cigars), 0.95 litres (1 pint) of alcohol, a camera with five rolls of film and a reasonable amount of personal effects, including binoculars, laptop and sound recording instruments.

Professional equipment and high-value articles must be declared or listed on arrival with a written undertaking to re-export them. Both the list and the articles must be produced on departure. As this formality can be a lengthy process, allow extra time, both on arrival and at departure. For unaccompanied baggage or baggage misplaced by the airline, make sure you get a landing certificate from customs on arrival.

Entry Regulations
Tourist visas for all nationalities are issued for three or six months from the date of issue (not entry). It is preferable to take a multiple-entry visa, in order to have the option of visiting a neighbouring country. Get a visa from the embassy or high commission in your country of residence, rather than risk the complications and delays involved in applying for one in neighbouring countries.

Tourist visas cannot be extended; you must leave the country and re-enter on a new one. It may be difficult to apply for a new visa from neighbouring countries. Five-year visas are also issued to business people and students. In addition to visas, special permits are required for certain areas, while other areas

are out of bounds to foreigners altogether (see Restricted & Protected Areas, page 349).

If you stay for more than 180 days, before leaving the country you must have a tax clearance certificate. These can be obtained from the foreigner's section of the income tax department in every city. Tax clearance certificates are free, but take bank receipts to demonstrate that you have changed money legally.

Exports
Export of antiques (over 100 years old), all animal products, and jewellery valued at over Rs2,000 (in the case of gold) and Rs10,000 (for articles not made of gold) are banned. When in doubt about the age of semi-antiques, contact the office of the Archaeological Survey of India in Delhi, Mumbai, Kolkata or Chennai (www.asi.nic.in).

Prohibited articles
These include certain drugs, live plants, gold and silver bullion, and coins not in current use. All checked luggage arriving at Delhi airport is X-rayed before reaching the baggage collection area in the arrival hall.

D eparture

It is absolutely essential to reconfirm your reservations for all outward-bound flights at least 72 hours before departure, especially in the peak season, when most of the flights are overbooked. Security procedures can be intensive and time-consuming, so allow at least 2 hours for check-in.

An airport/seaport tax is charged on departure (Rs75, Rs550 for neighbouring SAARC countries). This should be included in your ticket, but make sure you check with your airline or look on your ticket.

For visitors with entry permits, exit endorsements are necessary from the office where they were registered. Should a stay exceed 180 days, an income tax exemption certificate must be obtained from the Foreign Section of the Income Tax Department in Delhi, Mumbai, Kolkata or Chennai.

Disabled Travellers

Although disability carries little social stigma in India compared to many other countries, there are very few special toilets or provisions for wheelchairs. The roads are full of potholes and kerbs are often high and without ramps. If you have difficulty walking, it may be hard to

negotiate Indian streets. On the other hand, people will always be willing to help you in and out of buses or cars, or up stairs. Taxis and rickshaws are cheap and the driver, with a small tip, will probably help. You could employ a guide who will be prepared to help with obstacles. Another option is to go with a paid companion. In the UK, **Holiday Care**, 7th Floor, Sunley House, 4 Bedford Park, Croydon, Surrey CR0 2AP (tel: 0845 124 9974; www.holidaycare.org.uk), can put you in touch with someone.

E lectricity

The voltage system in India is 220V AC, 50 cycles. DC supplies also exist, so check first. Sockets are of the two round-pin variety normally, but do vary. Take a universal adaptor for British, Irish and Australasian plugs. American and Canadian appliances will need a transformer.

Embassies and High Commissions

Australian High Commission, Australian Compound, 1–50G Shantipath, Chanakyapuri (P.O. Box 5210), New Delhi Tel: (011) 5139 9900 Fax: (011) 5149 4491 www.ausgovindia.com
British High Commission Shantipath, Chanakyapuri, New Delhi Tel: (011) 2687 2161 (24 hrs) Fax: (011) 2687 0065 www.ukinindia.com
Canadian High Commission 7–8 Shantipath, Chanakyapuri (P.O. Box 5207), New Delhi Tel: (011) 2687 6500 www.dfait-maeci.gc.ca
Irish Embassy 13 Jor Bagh, New Delhi Tel: (011) 2462 6714 Fax: (011) 2469 7053 www.irelandinindia.com
New Zealand High Commission 50N Nyaya Marg, Chanyakapuri, New Delhi Tel: (011) 2688 3170 Fax: (011) 2688 3165 www.nzembassy.com
US Embassy Shantipath, Chanakyapuri, New Delhi Tel: (011) 2419 8000 Fax: (011) 2419 0017 http://newdelhi.usembassy.gov

Indian Missions Abroad
Australia
High Commission of India 3–5 Moonah Place, Yarralumla, Canberra ACT-2600 Tel: (616) 273 3774/273 3999

Fax: (616) 273 3328/273 1308
www.highcommissionofindiaaustralia.org
Canada
High Commission of India
10 Springfield Road, Ottawa,
Ontario KLM 1 C9
Tel: (613) 744 3751–3
Fax: (613) 744 0913
www.hciottawa.ca
Great Britain
High Commission of India
India House, Aldwych,
London WC2B 4NA
Tel: (0891) 880 800 (24-hours
recorded visa information);
(020) 7836 0990 (visa enquiries);
(020) 7836-8484 (general)
www.hcilondon.org
United States
Embassy of India
2107 Massachusetts Avenue NW,
Washington DC 20008
Tel: (202) 939 7000
Fax: (202) 939 7027
www.indianembassy.org

Emergencies

Generally speaking, India is a safe
place to travel, but a tourist is a
natural target for thieves and pick-
pockets, so take the usual
precautions and keep money, credit
cards, valuables and passport in a
money belt or pouch well secured
with a cord around your neck. A
protective hand over this in a
crowded place could save you a
lot of heartache and hassle.

Do not leave belongings
unattended, especially on a beach.
Invest in good strong locks (available
in India) for your bags. Chaining
luggage to the berth on a train, or
to your seat on a bus, is another
precaution that travelling Indians
often take. Watch your luggage
carefully, especially during loading
and unloading.

Credit card frauds do exist so make
sure that shops and restaurants
process your card in front of you.
Another sensible precaution is to keep
a photocopy of your passport and visa,
travellers' cheque numbers and
receipts, ticket details, insurance
policy number and telephone claims
number, and some emergency money
in a bag or case separate from your
other cash and documents. If you are
robbed, report the incident
immediately to a police station (be
patient, this can take hours).

Etiquette

● Removing one's shoes before
entering a temple, mosque or
someone's house is essential.
Overshoes are provided in some

places of worship at a nominal cost
and stockinged feet are usually
permissible.
● The *namaskaram* greeting with
joined hands, is the Indian form of
salutation and its use will be
appreciated, though men, especially
in the cities, will not hesitate to
shake hands with you if you are a
man. A handshake would even be
appreciated as a gesture of special
friendliness. Most Indian women
would be taken aback at the
informality of interaction between the
sexes common in the West and
physical contact between men and
women is to be avoided. Men should
not shake hands with a woman
(unless she first offers to).
● Avoid taking leather goods of any
kind into temples as these can often
cause offence.
● Always walk around religious
shrines clockwise.
● Photography is prohibited inside
the inner sanctum of many places of
worship. Do obtain permission before
using a camera. Visitors are usually
welcome to look around at their
leisure and can sometimes stay
during religious rituals. For visits to
places of worship, modest clothing is
essential. In mosques, women
should cover their head and arms
and wear long skirts. A small
contribution to the temple donation
box *(hundi)* is customary.
● In private, visitors are received as
honoured guests and your
unfamiliarity with Indian ways will be
accepted and understood. When
eating with your fingers, remember
to use only the right hand.
● Avoid pointing the soles of your
feet towards anyone as this is
considered a sign of disrespect.
Don't point with your index finger:
use either your extended hand or
your chin.
● Central Government has passed a
law banning smoking in all public
places, and this has now been
enacted by most State governments.

G ay and Lesbian Travellers

Homosexuality is still a taboo subject
for many Indians. Sexual relations
between men are punishable with long
prison sentences and cruising in public
could come under public disorder laws.
There is no similar law against
lesbians. While general attitudes are
discriminatory, things are changing
slowly, and at least the issue of gay
and lesbian rights is starting to be
discussed, due in no small part to
Deepa Mehta's 1998 film *Fire*, which
depicted an affair between two
married women, and the 2004 film

Girlfriend. Attacks on cinemas by the
religious right brought counter
demonstations onto the streets of
major cities. However, gay and lesbian
travellers should be discreet and avoid
any public displays of affection (as
should heterosexual couples). On the
plus side, hotels will think nothing of
two men or women sharing a room.

The male sites http://webbingsystems.
com/humsafar and www.gaybombay.org
have useful information and links. For
women, there is **Sangini**
(www.sanginii.org), who campaign for
lesbian and women's rights.

H ealth

Altitude sickness
This can occur above 2,500 metres.
Watch for symptoms of breathless-
ness, palpitations, headache,
insomnia and loss of appetite.
With total rest, travellers usually
acclimatize within 48 hours. It is
important that fluid intake is
maintained; at least 4–6 litres (7–10
pints) per day is recommended.

Inhaling a few breaths from an
oxygen cannister can provide
immediate relief in a mild attack. A
severe attack, brought on by climbing
too high or too quickly is marked by
dizziness, nausea, vomiting,
convulsions, severe thirst,
drowsiness, blurred vision,
weakness, or hearing difficulties.

The only cure is to descend to a
lower altitude at once. Lung damage
from lack of oxygen can be
permanent if untreated. Allow several
days to acclimatize before attempting
to reascend in easy stages. In acute
cases, as well as immediate descent,
it may be useful to give the additional
treatment of 250mg of actazolamide
twice a day for three days.

A previous trip with no symptoms
does not mean that a traveller is
immune to altitude sickness. It can
strike anyone, and being fit does not
prevent the problem.

Two other, extremely serious and
potentially fatal, conditions can occur
at high altitude, primarily to
mountaineers: pulmonary oedema
and cerebral oedema. The first is the
filling of the lungs with fluid
(symptoms include coughing up frothy
fluid, irrational behaviour and fatigue),
the *only* cure and treatment is to
descend *immediately*. The second is a
swelling of the brain (symptoms here
include headache, hallucinations and
disorientation, eventually resulting in
coma); immediate descent is
essential to prevent death. To reduce
the swelling it is also possible to give
4mg dexamethasone three times per

ABOVE: a pond heron, or paddy bird, takes flight.

day, although this is a very powerful drug and should only be given with medical supervision or in an extreme emergency.

Diarrhoeas

Traveller's diarrhoea

Usually caused by low-level food poisoning this can be avoided with a little care. When you arrive, rest on your first day and only eat simple food; well-cooked vegetarian dishes and peeled fruits are perhaps best. An upset stomach is often caused by eating too many rich Indian meat dishes (usually cooked with vast amounts of oil and spices) and failing to rest and let your body acclimatise.

Drink plenty of fluids, but never drink unboiled or unfiltered water. When in doubt, stick to soda, mineral water, or aerated drinks of standard brands. Avoid ice as this is often made with unboiled water. All food should be cooked and eaten hot. Don't eat salads and always peel fruit.

With all cases of diarrhoea, including dysentery and giardia described below, it is not a good idea to use imobilising drugs such as loperamide (Imodium) and atropine (Lomotil) as they prevent the body ridding itself of infection. These should only be used if you have to travel. The most important thing to do in cases of diarrhoea and/or vomiting is to rehydrate, preferably using oral rehydration salts.

Dysentery and Giardia

These are more serious forms of stomach infection and should be suspected and treated if the diarrhoea lasts for more than two days.

Dysentery is characterized by diarrhoea accompanied by the presence of mucus and blood in faeces. Other symptoms include severe stomach cramps and vomiting. Bacillic dysentery comes on quickly and is usually accompanied by fever. It may clear up by itself but its usual treatment is with 500mg of ciprofloxacin or tetracycline twice daily for five days. Do not take the powerful antibiotic chloramphenicol as it can have dangerous side effects. Amoebic dysentery has a slower onset and will not clear up on its own. If you suspect you have amoebic dysentery you should seek medical help as it can damage the gut. If this is not available then self-treat with 400mg of metronidazole (Flagyl) three times daily with food for seven days. You must not drink alchohol when taking metronidazole.

Giardia is a similar infection caused by a parasite. Like amoebic dysentery it comes on slowly and its symptoms include loose and foul-smelling diarrhoea, feeling bloated and nauseous, and stomach cramps. Giardia will not clear up on its own and will recur; its treatment is the same as for amoebic dysentery.

Fungal infections

Prickly heat is a common complaint caused by excessive perspiration. Try to keep the skin dry by using talcum powder and wearing loose-fitting cotton clothes. Fungal infections are also common, especially during the monsoon, and can be treated by exposure to the sun and/or by the application of Caneston cream.

Hospitals

In an emergency your first call should be to **East West Rescue**, 38 Golf Links, New Delhi; tel: 011-2469 8865; www.eastwestrescue.com. They operate over the whole country and have an extremely good reputation. Other hospitals include:

Delhi
All India Institute of Medical Sciences, Ansari Nagar
Tel: 2686 4851
Kripalani Hospital, Panchkuin Road
Tel: 2336 3788
Safdarjang General Hospital, Sri Aurobindo Marg
Tel: 2616 5060

Hyderabad/Secunderabad
General Hospital, Nampally
Tel: 2234 344
Newciti, Secunderabad
Tel: 2780 5961

Kolkata
Birla Heart Research Centre, 1–1 National Library Avenue
Tel: 2479 2980
Medical College Hospital, 88 College Street
Tel: 2241 1891

Mumbai
Prince Ali Khan Hospital, Nesbit Road
Tel: 2375 4343

Malaria

This moquito-borne disease is very serious and potentially fatal. There are two common strains in India, *P. falciparum* and *P. vivax*, both carried by the Anopheles mosquito. Symptoms are similar to acute flu (including some or all of: fever, shivering, diarrhoea and muscle pains) and an outbreak may come on as much as a year after visiting a malarial area. If malaria is suspected then medical attention should be sought as soon as possible.

Prophylaxis is essential for all areas except those above 2,500m (8,200 ft). The usual anti-malarial protection for India consists of a combination of daily proguanil (Paludrine) and weekly chloroquine/chloroquin (Avoclar, Nivaquin). These are now bought across the counter in the UK, and your pharmacist will advise you on the correct dosages (usually 200 mg of proguanil daily and 300 mg of chloroquin weekly). This is at present the only safe prophylaxis during pregnancy. However, the combination is at best 70% effective and it may be that medical advice will change soon.

An alternative drug is mefloquine (Lariam), taken weekly. However, this should not be taken by people with a history of epilepsy or mental illness and there has been much anecdotal evidence of long-lasting and serious side effects. In the UK mefloquine is only available as a private prescription.

A newly approved drug is the atavoquone-proguanil combination marketed as Malarone. This is recommended for areas of chloroquine resistance (such as Assam) and is taken once a day. It is expensive and at present only some Health Authorities offer it as an NHS prescription. Other drug regimes are not effective against both strains of the disease.

The best, and only certain, protection against malaria is to not get bitten. Sleep under a mosquito net impregnated with permethrin, cover up in the evenings and use an effective insect repellent such as DEET (diethyltoluamide). Burning mosquito incense coils, which are easily obtainable in India, is also a good idea.

Medical supplies

Bring along a personal medical kit to take care of minor ailments. This should include anti-diarrhoea medication, a broad spectrum antibiotic, antihistamines (for allergies) aspirin, clean needles, and something for throat infections would be a good idea. Take your regular medications, tampons and pantyliners, contraceptives and condoms, as these may be difficult to find.

Also include plasters, antiseptic cream and water purification tablets. All cuts, however minor, should be cleaned and sterilised immediately to prevent infection. Locally available oral rehydration powders (such as Vijay Electrolyte) containing salts and dextrose are an ideal additive to water, especially when travelling in the summer months or when suffering from diarrhoea. If oral rehydration salts are not available then one teaspoon each of salt and sugar in 500 ml of water is a useful substitute.

Sun exposure

The dangers of sunburn are now well-publicized. Cover up and use a high factor sunscreen, even if it is cloudy. The power of the sun is obvious on the plains and in tropical India, but also be careful in the mountains, where thinner air makes the sun very powerful, even if it feels cooler. Overexposure can also lead to the two conditions below:

Heat exhaustion is common, indicated by shallow breathing, rapid pulse, pallor, and is often accompanied by leg cramps, headache or nausea. The body temperature remains normal. Lying down in a cool place and sipping water mixed with rehydration salts or plain table salt will prevent loss of consciousness.

Heatstroke is more serious, and more likely to occur when it is both hot and humid. Babies and elderly people are especially susceptible. The body temperature soars suddenly and the skin feels dry. The victim may feel confused, then pass out.

Take them quickly to a cool room, remove their clothes and cover them with a wet sheet or towels soaked in cold water. Call for medical help and fan them constantly until their body temperature drops to 38°C (100°F).

Vaccinations

No inoculations are legally required to enter India, but it is strongly advised that you get inoculations against typhoid (Typhim Vi gives protection for 3 years), hepatitis A (Havrix gives immunity for 1 year, up to 10 years if a 6-month booster is given; the combined hepatitis A and typhoid injection gives immunity for 10 years), polio, diptheria and tetanus (a booster of Revaxis will give immunity for 10 years). India has recently had serious outbreaks of meningitis and you should get an inoculation against meningitis A, C, W and Y. You may need to show proof of a yellow fever inoculation if arriving from an infected area. Other diseases against which vaccinations might be considered, particularly for longer trips, include rabies and Japanese B encephalitis. There is no vacccination against Dengue fever, occasionally contracted in India. The only protection is to avoid being bitten (see also Malaria).

M aps

Obtaining good maps of India can be difficult. For security reasons the government forbids the sale of detailed maps in border areas, which includes the entire coastline; those which can be bought may not be exported. The Bartholomew's 1:4,000,000 map of South Asia and Lascelles map of the same scale and Nelles Verlag maps can be useful. The most detailed are held by the Survey of India, Janpath Barracks A, New Delhi 110 001. Other highly recommended maps are the Eicher series of detailed city maps, including those of Delhi, Chennai and Bangalore, and their India Road Atlas. Many of these maps are available from www.indiamapstore.com.

Media

Newspapers & Magazines

Among the better-known national English language dailies are the Times

of India, The Indian Express, The Hindu (highly-recommended, though this tends to concentrate on the South) and The Hindustan Times (all available online). There are also two Sunday papers, The Sunday Observer and The Sunday Mail. The main newspapers in Delhi are the Asian Age (good for political gossip) and Pioneer.

The top news magazines include India Today, Outlook and the exemplary Frontline (also online). There are also excellent general-interest magazines such as Sanctuary which specializes in South Asian natural history.

International newspapers are available in Mumbai and Delhi within 24 hours and some international magazines are also available.

There are several glossy magazines in English, including women's magazines such as Femina. Indian editions of Cosmopolitan and Elle magazines are also for sale.

Television & Radio Stations

Doordarshan is the government television company and broadcasts programmes in English, Hindi and regional languages. Local timings vary, but generally the news in English can be heard daily at 7.50am and 9.30pm.

Satellite television is available almost everywhere, including the Star TV's network incorporating the BBC World Service and MTV. NDTV is a local 24-hour news channel that provides good coverage of Indian news and politics. Over 50 channels can be picked up, given the right equipment.

All India Radio (AIR) broadcasts on the short-wave, medium-wave and, in Delhi, Mumbai and Chennai, on FM (VHF). The frequencies vary, so check with your hotel.

Money

All encashments of travellers' cheques and exchange of foreign currency used to have to be recorded on a currency declaration form, or receipts kept as proof of legal conversion. The laws have eased, but some businesses and hotels may still insist. Visitors staying more than 180 days will have to produce proof of encashment of traveller's cheques or exchange of currency for income tax exemption and show they have been self-supporting.

Indian currency is based on the decimal system, with 100 paise to the rupee. Coins are in denominations of 10, 20, 25 and 50 paise and 1, 2 and 5 rupees. Notes are in 10, 20, 50,

100 and 500 rupee denominations. Indian rupees may not be brought in nor taken out of the country. Exchange rates fluctuate against other currencies.

Credit cards are increasingly accepted by hotels, restaurants, large shops, tourist emporia and airlines. It is preferable to have a well-known card such as American Express, MasterCard or Visa. A number of banks will now issue rupees against a Visa card while Amex issues rupees or travellers' cheques to cardholders against a cheque at their offices. More conveniently, ATMS that issue cash against a variety of cards are found in many places. The ATMs of local banks may only issue cash against their own cards so try and find a machine on an international bank. Travellers' cheques are not worth the hassle.

P lace Names

Some places have changed their names, in many cases away from Anglicizations, including the following:
Alleppey (Alappuzha)
Badagara (Vadakara)
Baroda (Vadodara)
Bombay (Mumbai)
Calcutta (Kolkata)
Calicut (Kozhikode)
Cannanore (Kannur)
Changanacherry (Changanassery)
Cochin (Kochi)
Cape Comorin (Kanyakumari)
Madras (Chennai)
Mahabalipuram (Mamallapuram)
Mercara (Madikeri)
Ooty (Udhagamandalam)
Palghat (Palakkad)
Panjim (Panaji)
Quilon (Kollam)
Sulthan Battery (Sulthanbathery)
Tanjore (Thanjavur)
Tellicherry (Thalassery)
Trichur (Thrissur)
Trichy (Thiruchirappalli)
Trivandrum (Thiruvanathapuram)

Postal Services

The internal mail service is efficient in most areas. It is advisable to personally affix stamps to letters or postcards and hand them over to the post office counter for immediate franking rather than to post them in a letterbox. Indian stamps do not stick very well so make sure you use the pot of "gum" (glue) that is almost always available.

Sending a registered parcel overseas is a complicated and time-consuming process. Most parcels should be stitched into cheap cotton cloth and then sealed (there are people outside major post offices

offering this service). Two customs forms need to be completed. Once the parcel has been weighed and stamps affixed, make sure it is franked and a receipt of registration is issued. Important or valuable material should be registered.

Many shops offer to dispatch goods, but not all of them are reliable. It is usually only safe when handled by a government-run emporium. Generally, poste restante works well, but make sure your name is clearly written. The government's **Speedpost** service delivers quickly at a similar time and price to other international courier services.

Public Holidays

There are many festivals in India, but only a few of these are full public holidays:
26 January: Republic Day.
15 August: Independence Day.
2 October: Mahatma Gandhi's Birthday.
25 December: Christmas Day.

Other holidays generally follow the individual State Government's list, though many business establishments work during several of these holidays.

R epairs and Tailors

Traditionally, India's use of resources is very efficient, reflected in the way almost everything can be recycled and/or repaired. Since travelling around India can be hard on your shoes, baggage and clothes, this is very useful. Chappal-wallahs (shoe repairers) can be found everywhere, usually sitting by the side of the road with their tools in a wooden box. For an embarrassingly small charge, they will be able to glue, nail or stitch almost any pair of shoes or sandals back into shape.

Tailors will be able to repair your existing clothes, even badly torn ones, and – just as useful – can stitch up rucksacks which are on the point of collapse.

Indian tailors are very skilful and can run up a set of clothes quickly. Although they can do fair copies of Western fashions, they are, obviously, much better at stitching sari blouses or shalwar kamiz. The process of buying fabric is one of the great pleasures of visiting India, and if you want it made up, most shops will be able to recommend a good tailor.

Restricted and Protected Areas

The country is generally open to tourism, apart from sensitive border

regions (essentially those with China and Pakistan), certain areas of the Northeast and some of the islands.
Andaman and Nicobar Islands Individual tourists may visit the following areas: Port Blair, Havelock Islands, Long Island, Neil Island, Jooly Buoy, South and North Cinque, Red Skin Island, and the entire island of Middle Andaman (excluding the reserves). All islands in the Mahatma Gandhi Marine National Park except Boat, Holiday, Twin Islands and Pluto Islands need special permission from the Union Territory Administration. The following places may only be visited for the day: Mount Harriet, Mayabunder, Diglipur, Rangat, Ross Island, Brother Island, Sister Island, Barren Island.
Arunachal Pradesh Itanagar, Ziro, Along, Passighat, Deporijo Miao, Namdapha, Tipi Sejusa (Puki), Bhalukpong, Bomdilla-Tawang are open to tourists, as are the following trekking routes: Passighat–Jengging–Yingkiong; Bhalukpong–Bomdilla–Tawang; Roing–Mayodila–Anini; Tezu–Hayuling. Individual tourists are not allowed. Tourist groups must travel on identified tour circuits only. Maximum period of stay is 10 days.
Lakshadweep Only Agatti, Bangaram and Kadmat are open to foreign tourists. Kavaratti may be used as for transiting.
Manipur Foreigners are permitted to visit the following areas for a maximum of six days only in a group of four or more: Loktak Lake, Imphal, Moirang INA Memorial, Keibul Lamjao Deer Sanctuary, Waithak Lake, Khongjom War Memorial.
Mizoram Vairangre, Thingdawl, Aizawal are open to tourists. Individual tourists are not allowed and groups must travel on identified tour circuits only. Maximum period of stay is 10 days.
Nagaland Kohima, Mon, Phek, Tuensang, Zunheboto may be visited by individual tourists. A 10-day permit, which may be extended, is needed.
Sikkim Gangtok, Rumtek, Phodong, Pemayangtse Khecepen and Tashiding are open. A permit is needed for Zongri (West Sikkim), Tsangu (East Sikkim), Mangan, Tong, Singhik, Chungthang, Lachung and Yumthang.

T elephones

India's telephone system is steadily improving and international calls can now be dialled direct to most parts of the world or booked through the operator. Calling from hotels can be extremely expensive, with surcharges up to 300 percent, so check rates first. Mobile telephones are widely used in India and your own phone may well work while you are there.

Privately run telephone services with international direct-dialling facilities are widespread. Advertising themselves with the acronyms STD/ISD (standard trunk dialling/international subscriber dialling), they are quick and easy to use. Some stay open 24 hours a day. Both national and international calls are dialled direct. To call abroad, dial the international access code (00), the code for the country you want (44 for the UK, 1 for the US or Canada), the appropriate area code (without any initial zeros), and the number you want. Some booths have an electronic screen that keeps time and calculates cost during the call. Prices are similar to those at official telecommunications centres.

To call India from abroad, dial the international access code, followed by 91 for India, the local code minus the initial zero, then the number. Indian telephone numbers change often and although those in the book have been checked carefully they may well change in the future. NB. Indian telephone numbers are now all 10 digits long (including the area code minus the initial zero). The vast majority of numbers now start with a "2", if you encounter an old-style number (eight digits long) add a "2" to the beginning and it should work.

Home country direct services are now available from any telephone to the UK, US, Canada, Australia, New Zealand and a number of other countries. These allow you to make a reverse-charge or telephone credit card call to that country via the operator there. If you cannot find a telephone with home country direct buttons, you can use any phone toll-free by dialling 000, your country code and 17 (except Canada, which is 000-167). US international access codes are: MCI 000 127; Sprint 000 137; and AT&T 000 117.

Many privately run telephone services have fax machines and most large hotels have a fax.

E-mail and the internet are now very popular and widely available. All large cities, and many smaller places, have internet cafés or similar places where you can surf the net or send e-mails. Charges are usually around 60 Rs per hour.

Time Zones

India is 5½ hours ahead of GMT.

Tipping

There is no harm expressing your appreciation with a small tip. Depending on services rendered and the type of establishment, this could range from Rs2–Rs10.

In restaurants, the tip is customarily 10–15 percent of the bill. Leading hotels add a 10 percent service surcharge and tipping in such places is optional.

Although tipping taxis and three-wheelers is not an established norm, it does not go amiss. Here again, 10 percent of the fare or leaving the change, if not substantial, would be adequate. Porters at railway stations would expect around Rs2 a bag. At airports, a rupee per bag in addition to the fee charged by the airport authority would be welcome.

If you have been a house guest, check with your host before tipping any of the domestic helpers (for instance, a chauffeur who may have driven you around).

Tourist Information

The Ministry of Tourism has a good website (www.tourismofindia.com or www.incredibleindia.org) with a lot of useful information on obtaining visas, places to visit and tour operators.

Indian Tourist Offices abroad

Australia
Level 2 Piccadilly, 210 Pitt Street, Sydney, New South Wales 2000
Tel: (02) 9264 4855
Fax: (02) 9264 4860
Canada
60 Bloor Street West, Suite 1003, Toronto, Ontario M4N 3N6
Tel: (416) 962 3787–8
Fax: (416) 962 6279
UK
7 Cork Street, London W1X 2AB
Tel: (020) 8812 0929 (24-hour tourist information); (020) 7437 3677 (general)
Fax: (020) 7494 1048
US
1270 Avenue of America, Suite 1808, New York 10020
Tel: (212) 586 4901–3
Fax: (212) 582 3274

State Tourism Websites

These have much useful information:
Andaman and Nicobar Islands
http://tourism.andaman.nic.in
Andhra Pradesh
www.aptourism.com
Arunachal Pradesh
www.arunachaltourism.com
Assam
www.assamtourism.org
Bihar
http://bihar.nic.in
Chandigarh
www.citco.nic.in
Chattisgarh
http://cgtourism.nic.in
Daman and Diu
http://daman.nic.in
Delhi
http://delhitourism.nic.in
Goa
www.goatourism.org
Gujarat
www.gujarattourism.com

Haryana
http://htc.nic.in
Himachal Pradesh
http://himachaltourism.nic.in
Jammu and Kashmir
www.jktourism.org
Jharkhand
http://jharkhand.nic.in
Karnataka
http://kstdc.nic.in
Kerala
www.keralatourism.org
Lakshadweep
http://lakshadweep.nic.in
Madhya Pradesh
www.mptourism.com
Maharashtra
www.mtdcindia.com
Manipur
http://manipur.nic.in
Meghalaya
www.meghalayatourism.com
Mizoram

http://mizoram.nic.in
Nagaland
www.nagalandtourism.com
Orissa
www.orissa-tourism.com
Pondicherry
www.tourisminpondicherry.com
Punjab
http://punjabgovt.nic.in
Rajasthan
www.rajasthantourism.gov.in
Sikkim
http://sikkim.nic.in
Tamil Nadu
www.tamilnadutourism.org
Tripura
http://tripura.nic.in
Uttar Pradesh
www.up-tourism.com
Uttaranchal
www.uttaranchaltourism.gov.in
West Bengal
www.wbtourism.com

Water

Many water supplies in India are contaminated and are a common source of disease for travellers who have no immunity to water-borne bacteria such as giardia. Bottled water is available. However, there is no guarantee that this is safe and, perhaps more importantly, it is extremely bad for the environment (India is accumulating an enormous plastic bottle mountain). It is much better to carry your own water bottle (those made by the Swiss firm Sigg are very tough and hygienic) and fill it from safe water sources (the best is boiled water). This is not always available and portable water filters are an excellent solution. Those made by Katadyn (www.katadyn.com) are considered the best.

Weights and Measures

The metric system is uniformly used all over India. Precious metals, especially gold, are often sold by the traditional *tola*, which is equivalent to 11.5 grams. Gems are weighed in carats (0.2 grams).

Financial outlays and population are usually expressed in *lakhs* (100 thousand) and *crores* (100 *lakhs* or 10 million).

What to Bring

Clothing

When travelling in India it is best to wear cotton. Avoid synthetics. Cotton shirts, blouses and skirts are inexpensive and easily available in all towns and cities. Remember to bring underwear (especially bras) and swimwear.

In winter a light sweater might be necessary as the early mornings can be a little chilly. Comfortable footwear is essential. "Trekking" sandals are excellent for wearing in India as they are tough and provide good protection to your feet. Teva and Reef are good brands.

For their own convenience, women should not wear sleeveless tops, mini skirts or short, revealing dresses. It's a good idea to cover-up in the Indian sun anyway. Locally available *shalwar kamiz* (also known as *churidar* or a Punjabi suit), a long tunic top worn over loose trousers, are ideal.

Other Essentials

If travelling away from the major cities or big hotels, take a sheet sleeping bag, pillowcases and medical kit among other items. Sun cream and sun block are not readily available so they should be brought with you, along with toiletries and tampons. A hat or scarf to cover your head is a sensible item, as is an umbrella. A mosquito net and a basin/bath plug are also useful in smaller hotels, which often do not have them.

It is always advisable to obtain good travel insurance to cover the worst possible scenario. Take a copy of your policy and keep it separately as a safeguard.

Wildlife Societies

The Bombay Natural History Society (BNHS): Despite its name, the BNHS covers the whole of South Asia. Established in 1883, it has become the foremost organization of its type in Asia. It collects data from throughout South Asia. Its museum and library have perhaps the best collections in the continent. Much of its work in recent years has been on bird migration and, more recently, a series of studies on certain endangered species and their habitats. It publishes, three times a year, an important journal and a popular magazine, *Hornbill*, quarterly. Membership is open to all. Address: Hornbill House, Dr. Sálim Ali Chowk, Shaheed Bhagat Singh Road, Mumbai 400 023, India; tel: (0091) 022-2282 1811; www.bnhs.org.

Centre for Science and Environment (CSE): Founded by Anil Agarwal in 1981 to study the social and economic impact of science and technology. CSE organizes a feature and service for newspapers and publishes a comprehensive report, *The State of India's Environment*, each alternate year. It has recently run a high-profile campaign against pesticide levels in Coca-Cola and Pepsi. Address: 807 Vishal Bhawan, Nehru Place, New Delhi 110019; www.cseindia.org.

Indian Ministry of Environment and Forests: This is the ministry which is in overall control of India's environment, its website – www.envfor.nic.in – has many useful links to other governmental organizations, such as **The Wildlife Institute of India** (www.wii.gov.in) and **Project Tiger** (www.projecttiger.nic.in).

Sanctuary Asia: India's most widely read and influential wildlife magazine. Published bi-monthly, it has in-depth reporting on all aspects of India's environment and wildlife. Address: 145/146, Pragati Industrial Estate, N.M. Joshi Marg, Mumbai 400 011; tel: (0091) 022-2301 6848; www.sanctuaryasia.com.

Wildlife Conservation Society: Based in Bangalore, this institute carries out research into, and runs protection programmes for, India's large mammals. Address: Centre for Wildlife Studies, 823, 13th Cross, 7th Block West, Jayanagar, Bangalore 560 082, India; tel: (0091) 080-2671 5364; www.wildlife.in

Wildlife Preservation Society of India: For over 30 years the society's journal, *Cheetal*, has published articles and papers on many aspects of India's wildlife. Address: 7 Ashley Hall, Dehra Dun, Uttaranchal.

The Wildlife Protection Society of India: Set up in 1994 by the film-maker and environmentalist Belinda Wright, this organization campaigns to preserve India's biodiversity and, particularly, against poaching. Address: S-25 Panchsheel Park, New Delhi 110 017, India; tel: (0091) 11-4163 5920; www.wpsi-india.org.

Wildlife Trust of India: Established in 1998, the Wildlife Trust of India specializes in crisis management and providing a rapid response to environments and wildlife that are in particular danger. Address: A-220, New Friends Colony, New Delhi 110 065, India; tel: (0091) 011-2632 6025; www.wildlifetrustofindia.org.

Worldwide Fund for Nature – India: Started in 1969, it has undertaken a wide variety of projects. WWF-India assists and provides technical support for research projects. It publishes a regular newsletter for its members. They have an excellent library and many regional and field offices *(see website for details)*. Address: WWF-India, Secretariat, New Delhi Main Office, 172-B Lodi Road, New Delhi 110 003, India; tel: (0091) 011-4150 4797; www.wwfindia.org.

Women Travellers

"Eve-teasing" is the Indian euphemism for sexual harassment. Take the normal precautions, such as looking out for yourself on crowded local public transport (crowds are a haven for gropers). Do not wear clothes that expose legs, arms and cleavage; *shalwar kamiz* are ideal, and a shawl is handy to use as a cover-all when required.

More serious sexual assaults on tourists are rare and tend to occur in popular tourist areas, but in case something should happen, call for help from passers-by.

On the up-side, there are "ladies-only" queues at train and bus stations, and also "ladies-only" waiting rooms at stations and compartments on trains.

LANGUAGE

UNDERSTANDING THE LANGUAGE

With 18 official languages, hundreds of others and countless dialects, India can present a linguistic minefield. Luckily for the traveller, English is often understood and it is usually possible to get by. However, attempts to speak the local language are always appreciated. The language most widely spoken in the North is Hindi, while in the South, Tamil has the highest profile. Hindi is the language spoken in Rajasthan, with variations in dialect across the state.

Indian languages are phonetically regular, based on syllables rather than an alphabet. Important differences are made between long and short vowels, and reteroflex, palatal and labial consonants – listen hard to get a feel for the vocabulary below. There are various systems of transliteration and you may see many of the words below spelt different ways in English. Where a consonant is followed by "h" this is an aspirated sound, "c" is usually pronounced "ch" (followed by "h", "chh").

Travellers' Hindi

Basics

Hello/goodbye *Namaste*
Yes *Ji ha*
No *Ji nehi*
Perhaps *Shayad*
Thank you *Dhanyavad/shukriya*
How are you? *Ap kaise hai?/Ap thik hai?*
I am well *Me thik hu/thik hai*
What is your name? *Apka nam kya hai?*
My name is (John/Jane) *Mera nam (John/Jane) hai*
Where do you come from? *Ap kahan se aye?*
From (England) *(England) se*
How much (money)? *Kitna paise hai?*
That is expensive *Bahut mahenga hai*
Cheap *Sasta*
I like (tea) *Mujhe (chai) pasand hai*
Is it possible? *Kya ye sambhav hai?*
I don't understand *Mujhe samajh nehi*
I don't know *Mujhe malum nehi*
Money *Paisa*
Newspaper *Akhbar*
Sheet *Chadar*
Blanket *Kambal*
Bed *Kot/palang*
Room *Kamra*
Please clean my room *Mera kamra saf kijie*

Clothes *Kapre*
Cloth *Kapra*
Market *Bajar*

Pronouns

I am *Mai hun*
You are *Ap hain*
He/she/it is *Voh hai*
They are *Ve hain*

Verbs

To drink *Pina*
To eat *Khanna*
To do/make *Karna*
To buy *Kharidna*
To sleep *Sona*
To see *Dekhna*
To hear/listen to *Sunna*
To wash (clothes) *Dona*
To wash (yourself) *Nahana*
To get *Milna*

Prepositions, adverbs and adjectives

Now *Ab*
Right now *Abhi*
Quickly *Jaldi*
Slowly *Dirhe se*
A bit *Bahut*
A little *Tora*
Here *Yaha/idhar*
There *Vaha/udhar*
Open *Khola*
Closed *Bund*
Finished *Khatm hai*
Big/older *Bara*

Small/younger *Chota*
Beautiful *Sundar*
Old *Purana*
New *Naya*

Questions

What is? *Kya hai?*
Where is? *Kahan hai?*
Why? *Kyun?*
Who is? *Kaun hai?*
When is? *Kab hai?*
How? *Kaisa?*

Most straightforward sentences can easily be turned into a question by putting *"kya"* on the front and raising the pitch of the voice at the end of the sentence, e.g. *"Dhobi hai"*, "There is a washerman", *"Kya dhobi hai?"*, "Is there a washerman?"

Days of the week

Monday *Somvar*
Tuesday *Mangalvar*
Wednesday *Budhvar*
Thursday *Guruvar*
Friday *Shukravar*
Saturday *Shanivar*
Sunday *Itvar*
Today *Aj*
Yesterday/tomorrow *kal*
Week *Hafta*

Months

January *Janvari*
February *Farvari*

March *March*
April *Aprail*
May *Mai*
June *Jun*
July *Julai*
August *Agast*
September *Sitambar*
October *Aktubar*
November *Navambar*
December *Disambar*
Month *Mahina*
Year *Sal*

Hindi numbers

1 *ek*
2 *do*
3 *tin*
4 *char*
5 *panch*
6 *che*
7 *sat*
8 *arth*
9 *nau*
10 *das*
20 *bis*
30 *tis*
40 *chalis*
50 *pachas*
60 *sath*
70 *setur*
80 *assi*
90 *nabbe*
100 *sau*
1,000 *hazar*
100,000 *lakh*
10,000,000 *kror*

Relatives

Mother *Mata-ji*
Father *Pita-ji*
Sister *Behen*
Brother *Bhai*
Husband *Pati*
Wife *Patni*

BELOW: a Brahminy myna.

Maternal grandmother *Nani*
Maternal grandfather *Nana*
Paternal grandmother *Dadi*
Paternal grandfather *Dada*
Elder sister (term of respect) *Didi*
Daughter *Beti*
Son *Beta*
Girl *Larki*
Boy *Larka*
Are you married? *Kya ap shadishuda hai?*
Are you alone (male/female)? *Kya ap akela/akeli?*
How many children have you got? *Apke kitne bache hai?*
How many brothers and sisters have you got? *Apke kitne bhai behen hai?*

Health

Doctor *Daktar*
Hospital *Aspatal*
Dentist *Dentist*
Pain *Dard*
I am ill *Main bimar hun*
I have been vomiting *Ulti ho rahi thi*
I have a temperature *Mujhe bukhar hai*
I have a headache *Mere sir men dard hai*
I have a stomach ache *Mere pat men dard hai*
I have diarrhoea *Mujhe dast ar raha hai*

The English word "motions" is a common expression for diarrhoea.

Travel

Where is (Delhi)? *(Dilli) kahan hai?*
Bus station *Bus adda*
Railway station *Tren stashan/railgari*
Airport *Hawai adda*

Car *Gari*
How far is it? *Kitna dur hai?*
In front of/opposite (the Taj Mahal) *(Taj Mahal) ke samne*
Near *Ke nazdik/ke pas*
Far *Dur*
Ticket *Tikat*
Stop *Rukh jaiye*
Let's go *Chele jao*
I have to go *Mujhe jana hai*
Come *Ayie*
Go *Jayie*

Food

I want (a thali) *Mujhe (thali) chahiye*
Without chilli *Mirch ke bina*
Little chilli *Kam mirch*
Hot *Garam*
Cold *Tanda*
Ripe/cooked *Pukka*
Unripe/raw *Kucha*

Basics

Mirch *Chilli*
Namak *Salt*
Ghi *Clarified butter*
Dahi *Yoghurt*
Raita *Yoghurt with cucumber*
Chaval *Rice*
Panir *Cheese*
Pani *Water*
Dudh *Milk*
Lassi *Yoghurt drink*
Nimbu pani *Lime water*
Tandur *Oven*
Pilao *Rice cooked with ghi and spices*
Biryani *Rice cooked with vegetables or meat*
Mithai *Sweets*

Breads (Roti)

Puri *Deep-fried and puffed-up wheat bread*
Chapati *Flat, unleavened bread*
Nan *Leavened flat bread*
Tanduri roti *Similar to nan*
Paratha *Chapati cooked with ghi*

Vegetables (Sabzi)

Palak *Spinach*
Allu *Potato*
Gobi *Cauliflower*
Bindi *Okra*
Pyaz *Onion*
Sarsun *Mustard greens*
Mattar *Peas*
Tamata *Tomato*
Baingain/brinjal *Aubergine*
Dal *Dried pulses*

Meat

Ghost *Lamb*
Murg *Chicken*
Machli *Fish*

Fruit

Kela *Banana*
Santra *Orange*
Aum *Mango*

Travellers' Tamil

Basics

Hello *Vanakkam*
Goodbye *Poyvituvarukiren*
(Reply *Poyvituvarungal*)
Yes *Amam*
No *Illai*
Perhaps *Oruvelai*
Thank you *Nandri*
How are you? *Celakkiyama?*
What is your name? *Ungal peyar yenna?*
My name is (John/Jane) *Yen peyar (John/Jane)*
Where is the (hotel)? *(Hotel) yenge?*
What is this/that? *Idu/Adu yenna?*
What is the price? *Yenna vilai?*
That is very expensive *Anda vilai mikavum adikum*
I want (coffee) *(Kapi) Vendum*
I like (dosa) *(Dosai) Pudikkum*
Is it possible? *Mudiyuma?*
I don't understand *Puriyadu*
Enough *Podum*
Toilet *Tailet*
Bed *Kattil*
Room *Arai*
Train *Rayil*
Sari *Pudavai*
Dhoti *Vesti*
Towel *Tundu*
Sandals *Ceruppu*
Money *Punam*
Temple *Kovil*

Verbs

Come (imperative) *Varungal*
Go (imperative) *Pongal*
Stop (imperative) *Nillungal*
Sleep *Tungu*
Eat *Sappidu*
Drink *Kudi*
Buy *Vangu*
Pay (money) *Punam kodu* (literally "give money")
See *Par*
Wash (clothes) *Tuvai*
Wash (yourself) *Kazhavu*

Prepositions, adverbs and adjectives

Quickly *Sikkirum*
Slowly *Meduvaka*
A lot *Mikavum*
A little *Koncam*
Here *Inge*
There *Ange*
This *Idu*
That *Adu*
Now *Ippodu*
Same *Ade*
Good *Nalla*
Bad *Ketta*
Hot *Karam*
Cold *Kulirana*
Dirty *Acattam*
Clean *Cattam*
Beautiful *Azhakana*
Sweet *Inippu*

ABOVE: a gharial at rest.

Big *Periya*
Small *Cinna*
Old *Pazhaiya*
New *Pudiya*

Days of the week

Monday *Tingal*
Tuesday *Cevvay*
Wednesday *Putam*
Thursday *Viyazhan*
Friday *Velli*
Saturday *Ceni*
Sunday *Nayiri*
Today *Inraikku*
Week *Varam*
Month *Matam*
Year *Varutam*

Numbers

1 onru
2 irandu
3 munru
4 nanku
5 aindu
6 aru
7 yezhu
8 yettu
9 onpadu
10 pattu
11 patinonru
12 pannirandu
20 irupadu
30 muppadu
40 rarpadu
50 aimpadu
60 arupadu
70 alupadu
80 yenpadu
90 tonnuru
100 nuru
100,000 latcam
10,000,000 kodi

Questions & "and"

How? *Yeppadi?*
What? *Yenna?*
Who? *Yar?*
Why? *Yen?*
Where? *Yenge?*
When? *Yeppodu?*
How much? *Yettanai/Yevvalavu?*

Questions in Tamil are usually formed by adding a long "a" to the last word of a sentence (usually the verb), such as "*Ningal venduma?*" "What do you want?". "And" is formed by adding "um" to the end of the nouns (with an extra "y" if the noun ends in a vowel), e.g. "*Kapiyum, dosaiyum*", "Coffee and dosa".

Pronouns and relatives

I *Nan*
You *Ningal*
He/She/It *Avan/Aval/Avar*
We (including addressee)/ (excluding addressee) *Nam/Nangal*
They *Avakal*
Man *Manidan*
Woman/Girl/Daughter *Pen*
Boy/Son *Paiyan*
Children *Pillaikal*
Baby *Pappu*
Mother *Amma*
Father *Appa*
Husband *Kanavan*
Wife *Manaivi*

Health

I am sick (vomiting) *Utampu cariyillai irukkiradu*
I have a pain *Vali irukkiradu*
I have diarrhoea *"Motions" irrukkiradu*
Doctor *Taktar*
Help! *Utavi cey!*

Food (Sappadu)

Tunnir Water
Sadum Rice
Puzham Fruit
Kaykuri Vegetables
Pal Milk
Mor Buttermilk
Minakay (iilamal) (without) chilli
Tengay Coconut
Mampazham Mango
Valaippazham Banana
Kapi Coffee
Ti Tea
Iddli Steamed rice cakes
Dosai Pancake made from fermented dough
Vadai Deep fried snack made of *dal*
Rasam Thin, spicy soup, usually with a tamarind base
Sampar Thick soup made from *dal*
Poriyal Dry vegetable curry
Kolikarri Chicken curry
Attukkari Lamb curry
Mils "Meals", similar to a North Indian *thali*, traditionally served on a banana leaf
Payasam Sweet milk-based dish served at festivals

FURTHER READING

General Natural History & Mammals

Environmental Awareness and Wildlife Conservation edited by R.C. Basu, R.A. Khan and J.R.B. Alfred. Kolkata, Zoological Survey of India, 2006.
Asian Elephants: Past, Present and Future by Debabrata Swain. Dehra Dun, International Book Distributors, 2004.
Asiatic Lion on the Brink by Asheem Srivastav and Suvira Srivastav. Dehra Dun, 1999.
Battling for Survival: India's Wilderness Over Two Centuries edited by Valmik Thapar. New Delhi, OUP, 2003.
Bengal Tiger in the Bangladesh Sundarbans by AHM Ali Reza, Md. Anwarul Islam, Md. Mostafa Feeroz and Ainun Nishat. Dhaka, IUCN–The World Conservation Union, 2004.
Bhitarkanika: Myth and Reality by Sanjeev Chadha and Chandra Sekhar Kar. Dehra Dun, 1999.
The Black Panther of Sivanipalli by Kenneth Anderson. New Delhi, Rupa, 2002.
Charger: The Long Living Tiger by Shahbaz Ahmad. Allahabad, Print World, 2001.
Concepts in Wildlife Management by B.B. Hosetti. Second Revised and Enlarged Edition, Delhi, Daya, 2005.
Conservation of Asian Elephants in Bangladesh. Dhaka, IUCN – The world Conservation Union, 2004.
The Cult of the Tiger by Valmik Thapar. New Delhi, OUP, 2002.
The Dance of the Sarus: Essays of a Wandering Naturalist by S. Theodore Baskaran. New Delhi, 1999.
Elephant: The Lady Boss by C.H. Basappanavar. Bangalore, 1998.
Elephas Maximus: A Portrait of the Indian Elephant by Stephen Alter. New Delhi, Penguin Books, 2004.
Eelie and the Big Cats by Arjan Singh. Reprint. New Delhi, OUP, 2001.
Encyclopaedia of Indian Wild Life Sanctuaries and National Parks by S.K. Tiwari. Delhi, 1997.
The End of a Trail: The Cheetah in India by Divya Bhanusinh. Oxford India Paperbacks, 1995.
Eye in the Jungle by M. Krishnan. Compiled by Ashish and Shanthi Chandola with T.N.A. Perumal.

Hyderabad, Universities Press, 2006.
Faunal Diversity in India: A Commemorative Volume in the 50th Year of India's Independence edited by J.R.B. Alfred, A.K. Das and A.K. Sanyal. Calcutta, 1998.
Field Days: A Naturalist's Journey through South and Southeast Asia by AJT. Johnsingh. Hyderabad, Universities Press, 2006.
A Field Guide to Animal Signs by E.A. Jayson and P.S. Easa. Reprint. Peechi, Kerala Forest Research Institute, 2004.
A Field Guide to Indian Mammals by Vivek Menon. Delhi, Dorling Kindersley for Penguin Books, 2003.
Gir Forest and the Saga of the Asiatic Lion by Sudipta Mitra. New Delhi, Indus, 2005.
Gir National Park & Sanctuary: Bibliography by Mahesh Singh, Punil P. Gajjar and Badrish S. Mehra. Dehra Dun, Bishen Singh Mahendra Pal Singh, 2002.
The Great Indian Elephant Book: An Anthology of Writings on Elephants in the Raj edited by Dhriti K. Lahiri-Choudhury. Delhi, 1999.
The Great National Parks of the World edited by Angela S. Ildos and Giorgio G. Bardelli. New Delhi, Om Books, 2001.
The Highlands of Central India: Notes on their Forests and Wild Tribes, Natural History and Sports by Captain J. Forsyth. Reprint. (first published by Chapman and Hall, London in 1919).
Honorary Tiger: The Life of Billy Arjan Singh by Duff Hart-Davis. New Delhi, Roli Books, 2005.
Illustrated Wild Life by E.G. Boulenger. New Delhi, Srishti Book, 2004.
India: Wild & Wonderful by C.P. Oberai. Dehra Dun, Bishen Singh Mahendra Pal Singh, 2001.
Indian National Parks and Sanctuaries: A Living Portrait of Wild India by Anand S. Khati. Reprint. New Delhi, Pelican Creations International, 2004.
Indian Wildlife: Threats and Preservation edited by B.D. Sharma. New Delhi, Anmol, 2002.
India's Wildlife History: An Introduction by Mahesh Rangarajan. Delhi, Permanent Black, 2001.

Jim Corbett: The Hunter-Conservationist by Reeta Dutta Gupta. New Delhi, Rupa, 2006.
Jim Corbett of India (Life and Legend of a Messiah) by Anand S. Khati. Noida, Pelican Creations International, 2003.
Jungle By-ways in India by E.P. Stebbing. Dehra Dun, Natraj, 2001.
The Jungle in Sunlight and Shadow by F.W. Champion. Reprint. 1996.
The Jungle Tide by John Still. Reprint. New Delhi, AES, 1999.
Jungles Long Ago by Kenneth Anderson. New Delhi, Rupa, 2002.
Khairi: The Beloved Tigress by Saroj Raj Choudhury. Dehra Dun, 1999.
The King And I: Travels in Tigerland by Prerna Singh Bindra. New Delhi, Rupa, 2006.
The Last Tiger: Struggling for Survival by Valmik Thapar. New Delhi, OUP, 2006.
Leopards in the Backyard by Rahul Shukla. Delhi, B.R. Publishing, 2002.
Lives in the Wilderness: Three Classic Indian Autobiographies by Jim Corbett, Verrier Elwin and Salim Ali. Delhi, 1999.
Lord of the Grassland by Nirmal Ghosh. New Delhi, Nirmal Ghosh, 1994.
Management of Elephants in Captivity by A.J.W. Milroy. Edited by S.S. Bist. Reprint. Dehradun, Natraj, 2002.
Man-Eaters of Kumaon by Jim Corbett. Reprint. New Delhi, OUP, 2001.
The Man-Eaters of Tsavo by J.H. Patterson. Reprint, Dehra Dun, Natraj, 1999 (first published in 1907).
Man-Eaters and Jungle Killers by Kenneth Anderson. Reprint. New Delhi, Rupa & Co., 2002.
Man-Eating Tigers of Central India by E. Ajaikumar Reddy. New Delhi, Indialog, 2004.
Musings of an Old Shikari: Reflections on Life and Sport in Jungle India by A.I.R. Glasfurd. Dehra Dun, Natraj, 2001.
Nature's Spokesman: M. Krishnan and Indian Wildlife edited by Ramachandra Guha. Delhi, OUP, 2000.
On Jim Corbett's Trail: And Other Tales from Tree-tops by A.J.T.

TRANSPORT

ACCOMMODATION

ACTIVITIES

A–Z

FURTHER READING

ABOVE: painted storks at Bharatpur.

Johnsingh. Delhi, Permanent Black, 2004.
The Oxford Anthology of Indian Wildlife, Volume 2: Watching and Conservation, edited by Mahesh Rangarajan, OUP, 2001. Includes early and contemporary accounts of watching wildlife.
The Oxford India Illustrated Corbett. New Delhi, OUP, 2004.
Prince of Cats by Arjan Singh. Reprint. Delhi, OUP, 2000.
Project Tiger Reserves: Resources Diversity, Sustainability, Ecodevelopment by A.B. Chaudhuri and D.D. Sarkar. Delhi, Daya, 2004.
Ranthambhore Sanctuary: Dilemma of Eco-Development by H.S. Sharma. Delhi, Concept, 2000.
Reminiscences of Indian Wildlife by R.S. Dharmakumarsinhji. 1998.
The Royal Tiger of Bengal: His Life and Death by J. Fayrer. Reprint, 1996 (First published by J & A Churchill, London in 1875).
The Royal Tiger of Bengal by J. Fayrer. Delhi, Asiatic Pub., 2006.
Sariska National Park by Himraj Dang. New Delhi, Indus, 2005.
Saving Wild Tigers, 1900–2000: The Essential Writings edited by Valmik Thapar. Delhi, Permanent Black, 2001.
The Secret Life of Tigers by Valmik Thapar, OUP, 1999.
Shikari Sahib by Peter Byrne. Varanasi, Pilgrims, 2002.
Snow Leopard Manual: Field Study Techniques for the Kingdom of Nepal. Kathmandu, WWF Nepal

Program, 2000.
Snow Leopard in Nepal. Reprint. Kathmandu, WWF Nepal Program, 2003.
Solomon's Saga of a Wildlife Sanctuary: Veerangana Durgavati Abhayaranya by S.K. Tiwari. New Delhi, Sarup & Sons, 2003.
The Sunderbans: A Pictorial Fieldguide by Biswajit Roy Chowdhury and Pradeep Vyas. New Delhi, Rupa and Co., 2005.
Tara: The Cocktail Tigress by Ram Lakhan Singh. Edited by Rahul Karmakar. Allahabad, Print World, 2000.
The Temple Tiger and More Man-Eaters of Kumaon by Jim Corbett. Reprint. New Delhi, OUP, 2000.
Textbook of Wildlife Management by S.K. Singh. Lucknow, International Book Distributing, 2005.
Thirteen Years Among the Wild Beasts of India: Their Haunts and Habits from Personal Observation; With an Account of the Modes of Capturing and Taming Elephants by G.P. Sanderson. Reprint, New Delhi, Asian Educational Services, 2000 (first published 1882).
This is the Jungle by Kenneth Anderson. New Delhi, Rupa, 2005.
Threatened Animals of India by B.K. Tikader. Calcutta, Zoological Survey of India, 1983.
Tiger Haven by Billy Arjan Singh. Edited by John Moorehead. 1998.
The Tiger Hunters by R.G. Burton. New Delhi, Mittal, 2002.
Tiger!: The Story of the Indian Tiger

by Kailash Sankhala. Dehra Dun, Natraj Pub., 2005.
Tiger: The Ultimate Guide by Valmik Thapar. New Delhi, OUP, 2006.
The Tiger in India: A Natural History by J.C. Daniel. Dehra Dun, Natraj Pub., 2001.
Tigers and Tigerwallahs: Saving the Greatest of the Great Cats by Geoffrey C. Ward with Diane Raines Ward; OUP, 2000.
Man-Eaters of Kumaon by Jim Corbett; Repint, OUP India (first published 1946).
The Secret Life of Tigers by Valmik Thapar; Tiger Haven by Billy Arjan Singh. Reprint. New Delhi, OUP, 2006.
Treasures of Indian Wild Life edited by Ashok S. Kothari and Boman F. Chhapgar. Mumbai, Bombay Natural History Society, 2005.
Under the Shadow of Man-eaters: The Life and Legend of Jim Corbett of Kumaon by Jerry A. Jaleel. Reprint, New Delhi, Orient Longman, 2001 (first published in 1997).
Watching India's Wildlife: The Anthology of a Lifetime by Billy Arjan Singh. New Delhi, OUP, 2003.
The Way of the Tiger: Natural History and Conservation of the Endangered Big Cat by K. Ullas Karanth. Hyderabad, Universities Press, 2001.
The Wild Animals of India, Burma, Malaya, and Tibet by R. Lydekker. Reprint. Dehra Dun, Natraj, 2005.
The Wild Beasts of India by G.P. Sanderson. Reprint. New Delhi,

ABOVE: *Dracaena*, Song of India.

Mittal, 2005.
**The Wild Elephant and the Method
of Capturing and Taming It in Ceylon**
by J. Emerson Tennent. Reprint. New
Delhi, AES, 2002.
**Wildlife: Management and
Conservation** by M.M. Ranga.
Jodhpur, Agrobios, 2002.
Wildlife Management in India by
B.B. Hosetti. Jaipur, Pointer, 2003.
**Wildlife Wealth of India: (Resources
& Management)** edited by Trilok
Chandra Majupuria. Thailand,
Tecpress Service, 1990.
Wildlife and Applicable Laws edited
by V.K. Prabhakar. New Delhi, Anmol,
2001.
Wildlife & Disease in India edited by
Budh Dev Sharma. Delhi, Asiatic
Publishing House, 2003.
**Wildlife and Ecotourism: Trends,
Issues and Challenges** edited by R.
Chandra. New Delhi, Akansha, 2005.
**Wildlife and Protected Areas of
Nepal: Resources and Management**
by Trilok Chandra Majupuria and
Rohit Kumar (Majupuria). Saharanpur,
S. Devi, 2006.
Wildlife in India by Gurkamal Basra.
New Delhi, Vishvabharti, 2004.
Wildlife in Nepal by Rishikesh Shaha
and Richard M. Mitchell. New Delhi,
Nirala, 2001.
Wild Tigers of Ranthambhore by
Valmik Thapar. New Delhi, 2000
Wild Tigers of Ranthambhore by
Valmik Thapar. Reprint. New Delhi,
OUP, 2005.
Wild Wonders of Rajasthan by V.D.
Sharma and Rajpal Singh. New Delhi,
1998.

Birds

Birds of Himalaya and Kashmir by
Douglas Dewar. Delhi, Asiatic Pub.,
2006.
Biology of Indian Barbets by H.S.A.
Yahya. New Delhi, Authors Press,
2001.
Birds: Beyond Watching by Abdul
Jamil Urfi. Hyderabad, Universities
Press, 2004.
Birds and Mammals of Ladakh by

Otto Pfister. New Delhi, OUP, 2004.
Birds in Sanskrit Literature by K.N.
Dave. Reprint. Delhi, Motilal
Banarsidass, 2005. With 107 bird
illustrations.
The Birds of Bhutan by Salim Ali,
Biswamoy Biswas and S. Dillon
Ripley. Reprint. Kolkata, Zoological
Survey of India, 2002.
Birds of Delhi by Ranjit Lal. New
Delhi, OUP, 2004.
**Birds of India: Including Nepal, Sri
Lanka, Bhutan, Pakistan and
Bangladesh** by text and photography
by Amano Samarpan. New Delhi,
Wisdom Tree, 2006.
Birds of India by Jagjit Singh. New
Delhi, Books Today, 2001.
**Birds of Nepal: With Reference to
Kashmir and Sikkim** by Robert L.
Fleming, Robert L. Fleming and Lain
Singh Bangdel. Reprint. Delhi, Adarsh
Books, 2000.
Birds of Northern India by Richard
Grimmett and Tim Inskipp. New
Delhi, OUP, 2003.
**Birds of Our Country: Their Eggs,
Nests, Life, Haunts and
Identification** by Frank Finn and E.
Kay Robinson. Reprint (first
published in 1999).
Birds of the Plains by Douglas
Dewar. Delhi, Nidhi, 2004.
**Birds of Western Ghats, Kokan and
Malabar (Including Birds of Goa)** by
Satish Pande, Saleel Tambe, Clement
Francis M. and Niranjan Sant. New
Delhi, OUP, 2003.
A Birdwatchers' Guide to India by
Krys Kazmierczak and Raj Singh.
Reprint, New Delhi, Oxford, 2001.
The Book of Indian Birds by Salim
Ali. Thirteenth revised edition.
Bombay, Bombay Natural History
Society, 2002.
The Common Birds of Bombay by
EHA. Reprint. 1999.
Common Birds of India by Asad R.
Rahmani. New Delhi, Publications
Division, 2005.
**A Field Guide to the Birds of
Southwestern India** by R.J. Ranjit
Daniels. 1997.
Handbook of the Birds of India and

**Pakistan: Together with Those of
Bangladesh, Nepal, Bhutan and Sri
Lanka** by Salim Ali and S. Dillon
Ripley. Reprint. New Delhi, OUP,
2001.
**Handbook on Indian Wetland Birds
and Their Conservation** by Arun
Kumar, J.P. Sati, P.C. Tak and J.R.B.
Alfred. Kolkata, Zoological Survey of
India, 2005.
How to Know the Indian Waders by
F. Finn. Reprint, 1994 (first published
in 1920).
**Important Bird Areas in India:
Priority Sites for Conservation** edited
by M. Zafar-ul Islam and Asad R.
Rahmani. Mumbai, Bombay Natural
History Society, 2004.
Indian Birds by R.K. Gaur. Brijbasi
Printers, 1994
An Introduction to Birds by H.S.
Bhamrah and Kavita Juneja. Edited
by K. Balvinder. Reprint. New Delhi,
Anmol, 2001.
An Introduction to Birds by
Gurdarshan Singh and H. Bhaskar.
New Delhi, Campus Books, 2003
**NC Hills: The Enchanting Land and
the Bird Mystery of Jatinga.**
Photographs and text by Dushyant
Parasher. With an article on Jatinga
by D. Hara Prasad. 1994.
**Pictorial Hand Book: Birds of
Chennai** by G. Thirumalai and S.
Krishnan. Kolkata, Zoological Survey
of India, 2005.
**Pocket Guide to the Birds of the
Indian Subcontinent** by Richard
Grimmett, Carol Inskipp, and Tim
Inskipp. New Delhi, 1999.
Salim Ali's India edited by Ashok S.
Kothari and B.F. Chhapgar.
BNHS/OUP, 1996
Salim Ali: India's Birdman by Reeta
Dutta Gupta. New Delhi, Rupa & Co.,
2003.
**Salim Ali for Schools: A Children's
Biography** by Zai Whitaker. Delhi,
Permanent Black, 2003.
**Shorebirds of Kerala (Including Gulls
and Terns): Pictorial Handbook** by C.
Sashikumar, Muhamed Jafer Palot,
Sathyan Meppayur and C.
Radhakrishnan. Kolkata, Zoological
Survey of India, 2004.
Waterbirds of Northern India by
J.R.B. Alfred, Arun Kumar, P.C. Tak &
J.P. Sati. Kolkata, Zoological Survey
of India, 2001.

Reptiles

The Book of Indian Reptiles by
Daniel, J.C. Bombay: BNHS 1983. An
excellent single volume with useful
plates and drawings.
**Common Indian Snakes: A Field
Guide** by Romulus Whitaker. Reprint.
New Delhi, Macmillan India, 2006,
The Book of Indian Reptiles and

Amphibians by J. C. Daniel. Delhi, Bombay Natural History Society and OUP, 2002.
The Common Snakes of India and Burma and How to Recognize Them by W.H. Cazaly. Reprint, 1984 (first published by The Pioneer Press, Allahabad, India in 1914).
A Field Book of the Lizards of India by T.S.N. Murthy. Vimsat Publishers, Bangalore, 1990.
Hand Book – Indian Amphibians by S.K. Chanda. Kolkata, Zoological Survey of India, 2002.
Handbook: Indian Snakes by R.C. Sharma. Kolkata, Zoological Survey of India, 2003.
Handbook of Indian Snakes by Malcolm A. Smith. New Delhi, Cosmo, 2003.
Herpetofauna of Nepal: A Conservation Companion by Karan Bahadur Shah and Sagendra Tiwari. Kathmandu, IUCN Nepal, 2004.
Indian Poisonous Snakes (An Ecological and Clinical Study) edited by B.D. Sharma. New Delhi, Anmol, 2002.
Indian Snake Poisons their Nature and Effects by A.J. Wall. Delhi, Asiatic Publishing, 2001.
Natural History of Birds, Fishes, Insects and Reptiles by Barr's Buffon. Reprint, 1993 (first published in London in 1808).
Olive Ridley Sea Turtle (Lepidochelys Olivacea) and its Nesting Habitats along the Orissa Coast, India: A Status Survey by Bivash Pandav, B.C. Choudhury and C.S. Kar. Reprint. Dehra Dun, Wildlife Institute of India, 1997.
Snakeman: the story of a naturalist by Whitaker, Zai. New Delhi: India Magazine Books 1989. A fascinating biography of Rom Whitaker.

Insects

The Butterflies of Ceylon by W. Ormiston. Reprint. New Delhi, AES, 2003.
Butterflies of India by Chas. B. Antram. Reprint. New Delhi, Mittal, 2002. A useful introduction to India's insect life from one of its foremost entomologists.
Butterflies of Bangladesh: An Annotated Checklist by Torben B. Larsen. Dhaka, IUCN-The World Conservation Union, 2004.
India–A Lifescape: Butterflies of Peninsular India by Krushnamegh Kunte. Hyderabad, Universities Press, 2000.
Handbook on Common Indian Dragonflies (Insecta: Odonata) by Tridib Ranjan Mitra. Kolkata, Zoological Survey of India, 2006.
Insects of India by Tapan Sengupta.

Kolkata, Tapan Sen Gupta, 2005. Aims at providing a simple and concise account of this extremely diverse and complex insect fauna.
Butterflies of the Indian Region by Wynter-Blyth, M.A. Bombay: BNHS 1957. A detailed and well-illustrated account. 1983 reprint has poor reproduction of plates.

Trees & Flowers

The Book of Indian Trees by K.C. Sahni. 1998. Descriptions of more than 150 species.
Forest Trees of Kerala: A Checklist Including Exotics by N. Sasidharan. Reprint, Peechi, Kerala Forest Research Institute, 2000.
A Handbook of Trees of Nepal: Timber, Fodder, Fruits, Medicinal, Ornamental and Religions by compiled by Baban P. Kayastha. Kathmandu, Savitry Devi Kayastha, 2002.
Sacred Trees and Indian Life by photographs by Susanne Hawkes. Text by Karuna Goswamy. New Delhi, Aryan Books International, 2004.
Some Beautiful Indian Trees, 2nd edition by E. Blatter and Walter S. Millard, 1997.
Trees and Shrubs of Nepal and the Himalayas by Adrian and Jimmie Storrs. Reprint. Kathmandu, Pilgrims Book House, 1990.
Trees in Indian Art, Mythology and Folklore by Bansi Lal Malla. New Delhi, Aryan Books, 2000.
Trees of India by Text by Subhadra Menon. Photography by Pallava Bagla. New Delhi, Timeless, 2000
Field Guide to the Common Trees of India by Bole, P.V. & Yogini Vaghani. Bombay, WWF/OUP 1986.
100 Himalayan Flowers by Photographs: Ashvin Mehta, Text: P.V. Bole. Mapin Publishing, Ahmedabad, 1990.
A Dictionary of the Flowering Plants in India by H. Santapau and A.N. Henry. Reprint (first published in 1973).
Common Indian Wild Flowers by Isaac Kehimkar. Delhi, OUP, 2000
A Field Guide to Bangladeshi Flowers by N.S. Nowroz Jahan. Dhaka, Asiatic Society of Bangladesh, 2005.
Flowers of the Himalaya by Polunin, Oleg & Adam Stainton. Oxford and Delhi: OUP 1984. Detailed descriptions of over 1500 species. Over 690 colour photographs and 315 drawings.
Flowers of the Himalaya; a supplement by Stainton, Adam. New Delhi: OUP 1988. Details 350 species not previously described in Polunin & Stainton's volume.

Bioacoustica

The Sacred Forests of India – Nagarahole, Listening Earth (available from www.wildsong.co.uk). Recordings made at Nagarahole.
British Library Sound Archive – has a selection of Indian wildlife sounds; see www.bl.uk/listentonature

Booksellers in India

Bangalore
Gangarams, 72 M.G. Road
Higginbothams, 68 M.G. Road
Midland Bookshop, Phorum Mall
Premier Bookshop, 46 Church Street, off Brigade Road

Chennai
Bookpoint, 160 Anna Salai
Giggles, Taj Connemara, Binny Road
Higginbothams, 814 Anna Salai
Landmark Books, Spencer Plaza, Anna Salai

Delhi
Bahri Sons, Opp. Main Gate, Khan Market
The Bookshop, Jor Bagh Market, opp. Lodi Gardens
The Bookworm, 29b Connaught Place
Full Circle, Khan Market
Om Book Shop, 45 Basant Lok, Vasant Vihar, also at: 3, Community Centre, Saket
Times Book Gallery, Khan Market

Hyderabad
Akshara, Pavani Estates, Road No.2
Walden, 6-3-871, Green Land Road

Kolkata
Crossword BookStores, 8 Elgin Road
Modern Book Depot, 15a Jawaharlal Nehru Road
Oxford BookStores, Park Street

Mumbai
Crossword Book Stores, M. B. Mansion, Kemps Corner, N.S.P. Marg
Nalanda Book Shop, Taj Mahal Hotel, Apollo Bunder
Oxford Book Store, 3 Dinsha Vaccha Road, Churchgate
Strand Books, P.M. Road, Fort

Pune
Crossword Book Stores, Sohrab Hall, Ist Floor, Junction of RBM, Connaught Road

Thiruvananthapuram
Modern Book Centre, off M.G. Road

On-Line Booksellers
www.bagchee.com
www.firstandsecond.com
www.sapnaonline.com

TRANSPORT

ACCOMMODATION

ACTIVITIES

A–Z

FURTHER READING

ART & PHOTO CREDITS

✸ INSIGHT GUIDE

Indian Wildlife

Cartographic Editor **Zoë Goodwin**
Production **Linton Donaldson**
Art Direction **Klaus Geisler**
Picture Research **Britta Jaschinski, Maria Lord**

INDEX

Numbers in italics refer to photographs